PRIVATISING LONDON'S BUSES

ROGER TORODE

Capital Transport

My thanks to the following who were interviewed for this book:

Douglas Adie	Bryan Gilbert	Nick Newton	Michael Steward
Dave Alexander	Andy Griffiths	Steve Norris	Gordon Tennant
Barry Arnold	Jean Harris	Declan O'Farrell	Simon Thomas
Ian Barlex	Mike Heath	Robin Orbell	John Trayner
Nigel Barrett	Sir Peter Hendy	Julian Peddle	Pat Waterman
Huw Barrington	Clive Hodson	Dai Powell	Dave Weller
Jon Batchelor	David Humphrey	Alan Price	Mike Weston
Peter Batty	Peter Jenner	David Quarmby	Dave Wetzel
David Bayliss	Derek Keeler	Robin Reynolds	Martin Whitley
Ken Blacker	Norman Kemp	John Rigby	John Wilson
Roger Bowker	Tony Kennan	George Roberts	John Wood
Andrew Braddock	Roy Lambe	John Rymer	Owen Woodliffe
Ron Brewer	Peter Larking	David Sayburn	Malcolm Wren
David Brown	Barry Le Jeune	Linda Self	Len Wright
Jeff Chamberlain	Paul London	Ray Stenning	Mark Yexley
Frank Cheroomi	Keith Ludeman		
Mike Clayton	Paul Lynch		
Steve Clayton	Pat Mahon		
Norman Cohen	Phil Margrave		
Bryan Constable	Tom McLachlan		
Leon Daniels	Peter McMahon		
Graham Elliott	Bob Muir		
Steve Fennell	Peter Newman		
Gary Filbey	Robert Newson		

Thanks also to the following for their assistance:

Andrew Boag	David Ruddom
Paul Blackwell	Lionel Shields
Paul Everett	Mike Walton
Susan Gilbert	Caroline Warhurst
Nigel Kavanagh Brown	Professor Peter White
Martin Kingsnorth	Gary Wood
Paul Owens	

© Roger Torode 2015

Published by Capital Transport Publishing Ltd
www.capitaltransport.com

Printed by 1010 Printing International Ltd

Capital Citybus had a bright yellow livery which developed into this attractive red and yellow colour scheme when 80% red liveries were required in the late 1990s. Two of its Volvo double-deckers are seen on route 91, which Capital Citybus took over from London Northern in early 1992. (Colin Stannard)

Foreword

London's bus service today has more passengers since 1959, more scheduled vehicles since 1957, and reliability levels at their best since records began in 1977. This book tells the story of the foundations and the building of this extraordinary revival in the bus service of the world's greatest city, told by many of the people who were involved. History can't be written contemporaneously; events are too near and sometimes emotions too raw. But equally, left too long, memories fade, and sadly some of the actors are no longer with us.

This work is timed brilliantly; sufficient distance for a sober assessment of some difficult events, but still with personal memories able to be faithfully recounted. These were challenging times; as Roger suggests, more change in 15 years than in the previous 30. It made some people's careers, those who grasped the opportunities and had some luck (I count myself as one of them); some were sadly left by the wayside, not always victims of their own misfortune (although some were, too). The staff who drove, who maintained, and who conducted the bus service in this period were not always treated well, and sometimes not with dignity; conversely, given a willingness to change, this industry was and still is one of the very few where jobs are always available and long service always possible, and frequently attained.

All of the above is as much or more to do with politics as with transport operation. For my entire career, many in the industry have said they regret that. But, it's inevitable. Public transport in a major city, properly designed to cope with the peak flows of people to jobs creating wealth, education, healthcare and leisure, consumes public subsidy, and that makes political control inevitable. The challenge is to deliver political objectives and also at the same time to satisfy customers and users – and those two objectives don't always align! Stability is seldom achieved as democracy intervenes, as do macro economic forces.

This book tells the story of a fascinating and extraordinary period very well indeed. Roger rightly cannot quite square all the accounts in here from all of the characters involved because they saw, and still see, things from their own points of view. But it uniquely tells the story through people's own words comprehensively and with rigour. I can't believe there will be another book like it, and there doesn't need to be.

All of us who were and are part of the story owe Roger a debt of gratitude for his painstaking work. And I hope all those who contributed feel a sense of pride in London's bus service of today, which has been built out of the events recounted in this book.

Sir Peter Hendy CBE
Commissioner of Transport
Transport for London
27 December 2014

At Burnt Oak in 1988, an Olympian of BTS overtakes an Olympian of London Country North West. In the first ten years of route tendering, over 25 different company liveries were to be seen on London's buses. (Capital Transport)

Introduction

History is made of personal stories.

When I was asked to write this book, I was attracted by the idea of basing it on the experiences of the people involved, to describe not just 'what happened', but 'what did it feel like at the time?' The best way of approaching this was to go to those people, and to ask them to tell their story in their own words, to capture the flavour of those events in a way that reports alone cannot do. I had lived and worked through this period in London Transport and knew most of the people concerned, and was only a couple of handshakes away from the others. I hope this approach brings alive to the reader this crucial period in the history of London's buses. Allowing everyone to express their own opinions means that there is a range of views, which do not necessarily agree with each other – and may not be those of the author.

The bus service we now have in London results from the momentous events described here. Many people consider these events to have been a necessary series of steps to get to where we are today. London Transport changed from a monolithic state owned bus operator to a tendering authority with competing operators owning buses and employing front-line staff to run a public service. It is a very political story. The early stages were at a time when a radical Conservative government was determined to bring great change. Privatisation became one of their key policies, and what happened in London has been unique, as deregulation of buses in the rest of the country has brought a very different set of experiences.

It is said that history is written by the winners. Every competition has winners and losers and I have included examples of both. At the same time, this cannot be a complete history – it would take several books to mention everyone who was involved and everything that happened. I have interviewed around eighty people at all levels in London's bus system, from drivers to a former Government minister. My thanks to all those I interviewed, and my apologies to another eighty who would also have something to add but who I did not see through lack of time and lack of space. I have aimed for a wide range of people and experiences – two interviews were held less than a mile apart, one in an office on the forecourt of Westminster Abbey, the other in the drivers' mess room above the concourse at Victoria Coach Station.

There is a personal element to this story because I was Commercial Director of London Forest, which unfortunately closed early after a major industrial dispute. The combination of being small and heavily tendered resulted in London Forest being the first to set about introducing major changes throughout the whole company – all the LBL companies did this within a year or so, but we had to face it first. The Trade Union, forewarned by changes at individual garages around London, were on the lookout for this and were determined not to let us proceed, otherwise all the companies would quickly follow. These events are covered in Chapter 6 from several points of view.

In addition to interviews, I have drawn on a range of books, reports and journals to add further background. I give credit to the London Omnibus Traction Society (LOTS) who have produced thorough, comprehensive reports since 1964, which have proved invaluable, and to the website London Bus Routes by Ian Armstrong, which lists the operators of all London's bus routes over an even longer period. My thanks also to the photographers who produced a splendid range of pictures, to Barry Le Jeune and Simon Thomas who read and commented on my drafts, and Norman Cohen and Sir Peter Hendy who read the whole document when it was complete. My wife Anna also read the draft from the viewpoint of an interested observer, as well as providing encouragement, advice and support through the many stages of producing the book.

This has been a long and fascinating project which has revived many friendships and memories. Again, my thanks to all those who have contributed.

London 1 January 2015   Roger Torode

Contents

1 The route to 1983 6

2 Provide or secure (1983-1984) 26

3 The beginning of tendering (1984-1986) 36

4 The area tendering schemes (1987-1988) 66

5 Creating the new companies (1988-1991) 96

6 Major losses, major gains (1990-1993) 126

7 Deregulation – London is different (to 1993) 158

8 The end of public ownership (1994) 174

9 Brave new world (1994-1999) 204

10 Looking back: a view from 2015 236

Appendix 1 Timeline of key events for London's buses, 1970-2000 246

Appendix 2 The sale of the London Buses subsidiaries 248

Appendix 3 Operators with LT contracts, 1992 and 1994 248

Bibliography 249

Index of People 250

General Index 251

Biographies 252

Front cover: Tendering of London's bus services brought a rainbow of colours where there had been only red. Church Street in Enfield always had green country buses as well as the red ones, but in July 1987 has a Leyland Olympian of London Country North East on the 313 to Chingford, followed by Sampson's former London Transport Daimler Fleetline on its way to Upshire, and a Leaside Routemaster setting off for Tottenham Court Road. While this illustrates the challenge that competitive tendering presented to London Buses, both LCNE and Sampson's withdrew from their contracts early following poor performance, while Leaside kept the majority of its network due to competitive pricing and the quality of its operation. (Keith Wood). Smaller images are by John Miller (1) and Peter Horrex (2/3)
Back cover: A Grey-Green Metrobus picking up passengers at Cockfosters Underground station. (Peter Horrex)

1 THE ROUTE TO 1983

A shock to the system

A series of announcements in the early 1980s about tendering, deregulation and privatisation caused shockwaves throughout London Buses, bringing to an end the secure but often frustrating existence of its staff. London Buses caught the reorganisation bug and set about preparing itself for the storms to come.

There had already been one reorganisation, into Bus Operating Districts in 1979, but until then there had been little change to the organisation for more than forty-five years, apart from the abandonment of trams and trolleybuses in 1952 and 1962, and the transfer of Country Buses and Coaches to the National Bus Company in 1970. Chiswick still trained drivers, stripped and rebuilt every bus bit imaginable, Aldenham did the same for bus bodies and the organisation was structured on semi-military lines. Apart from a few havens of enlightenment, most parts of the highly compartmentalised organisation did what they had always done. There were procedures, processes and paperwork for every conceivable task and a hierarchy to match. Staff numbers in the bus organisation stood at 33,400 in 1980. Selection for supervisory and lower management posts was not particularly successful – it was a challenge to find the large number of able managers at all levels needed by such a huge organisation and promotion was often on seniority rather than suitability. While many were skilled and motivated, too many staff in those positions did not have real enthusiasm for the job and were only too glad to have escaped from bus driving or conducting. However, it worked – though at a cost, and with poor reliability – and there were no local comparisons with which to judge efficiency.

Victoria Street in November 1982, when the Routemaster ruled supreme on central London routes. The Red Arrow single-deckers provided short flat-fare services for journeys that were less easy by Underground, here from Victoria and Waterloo stations and points in between. (David Cole)

There had been little change to the organisation for more than forty-five years.

The historical background
London Transport had been a remarkably successful and effective organisation since it was created in 1933, but it was increasingly running into difficulties. It had the largest and oldest underground railway in the world, had had the largest tram and trolleybus systems, and for many years the largest bus fleet in the world. Its standards were high, it was proud of its achievements, and expectations of its performance were also high.

From 1948, everything slowed down. LT became part of the British Transport Commission, a great bureaucracy in which British Railways received priority and LT did not have the money to complete the pre-war programme, while replacement of the remaining trams was simplified by moving straight to motorbuses. Many of the staff came back from war service and returned to peacetime work trained in military ways. The organisation was becoming a little tired, old and self-satisfied – the quality and vision that had existed in the 1930s was now lacking. It still provided an excellent service, but the cracks were beginning to show.

The increasing problems of the 1950s and 1960s focused on getting sufficient staff to maintain the operation, and on the increasing traffic congestion. LT was a very paternalistic employer, providing a secure job and good conditions of service. There were sports clubs, good canteens, playing fields and social events for the staff. This led to almost a family atmosphere in some garages, and there were medical services long before the founding of the National Health Service. However, staff were increasingly being lost to other jobs, as they did not want shift work with unsocial hours and weekend working. As a result, in the 1950s, increasingly women were recruited – as conductors but not yet as drivers – and then there was direct recruitment from the West Indies, Malta and Ireland.

The Trade Unions worked hard to improve the conditions of their members. They considered London bus staff to be the elite of the public transport industry and were determined to maintain this position. They wanted the recruitment problems to be solved by a general increase in wages, and struck to try to achieve this. A major strike in 1958, which saw no buses in service for six weeks, was very damaging and caused a significant loss of passengers that was never recovered. Indeed, a few routes were never restored. Many of these people turned to their own cars, adding to the congestion that delayed the buses. Slower buses caused an increase in costs to be shared amongst fewer passengers. As a result, by the early 1960s, the operations needed more and more to be subsidised.

LT managers did not seem to have a strategy to move things forward. They were smug about the quality of their operation and considered the difficulties to be beyond their control. Engineering developments continued to a high standard with the Routemaster, once the initial significant problems were sorted out, but a good bus could not provide a high quality service if there were insufficient staff or it was stuck in a traffic jam.

What had led to this situation? Peter Hendy joined LT as a graduate trainee in 1975, and recalls that in the late 1970s, the organisation was run by some grand, but very traditional characters. They would manage in the mornings and then go for a good lunch. Morning meetings were often more productive than those in the afternoon. There were some exceptions but a spirit of resigned hopelessness dominated proceedings.

The GLC years
The Transport (London) Act of 1969 created a new London Transport Executive reporting to the Greater London Council (GLC), and including the Central Bus and Underground departments, whilst the Country Bus area passed to the newly formed National Bus Company. The GLC had replaced the London County Council in 1965 and covered all of Greater London, whereas the LCC had only the inner part of the conurbation, the outer areas being part of the adjoining counties. The GLC ran strategic services such as the fire service, emergency planning, waste disposal and flood prevention and shared with the London Boroughs responsibility for roads, housing, city planning and leisure services. It took responsibility for London Transport from 1 January 1970. Political control of the GLC tended to be a reaction against the national government – in all of the six GLC elections the winner was the party currently in opposition in central government.

David Quarmby joined LT in 1970 as Director of Operational Research and rose to become Board Member for Planning and then Managing Director Buses in 1978. "The first 10 years of the relationship with the GLC were fraught, and from my perspective they were fraught because London Transport was a powerful and a strong organisation and, to some extent, a pretty arrogant organisation. It had been taken over by what some of the Board Members in London Transport used to call a 'jumped up local authority', the GLC, and being subject to 'jumped up politicians' like Horace Cutler and Desmond Plummer, was more than some of them could bear. And there was an atmosphere of disdain bordering on contempt for the GLC and what they represented that permeated the senior ranks of London Transport.

"At the same time, the GLC Members felt that this is *our* transport system, we ought to have more say on what the policies are, how things are done, and how services are planned. In the days when it was a nationalised industry, the Ministry of Transport just didn't want to know – they appointed the Board and paid them to get on with it. I think it was entirely understandable that London Transport, reporting to an elected regional authority, should expect to have some scrutiny on how it delivers its services, and what the services are, and what value for money the London ratepayer gets for the money the GLC is putting into it. But that was very strongly resented. The one man who understood this was Ralph Bennett, because of his background in the municipalities, and he was probably the one who was best able to work with the GLC."

Ralph Bennett came to London in 1968 as Board Member for Planning. He had run Manchester's buses and was at Bolton before that. He became Deputy Chairman and Managing Director (Buses) and was appointed Chairman in 1978. David Quarmby was himself invited to Chair LT by Ken Livingstone in 1982 but knew the dangers of such a highly charged post. "I remember saying to Ken, 'Thank you, Ken, I really appreciate this, but I'm 41 and I don't want to be the ex-chair of London Transport when I'm 45, thank you very much, so I won't take it!'"

At first the GLC wrote off the accumulated debt of LT, which was primarily due to the construction of the Victoria Line, and also made a commitment to assist buses by traffic management measures including bus lanes and priority at traffic lights, and introducing a long-term policy to restrain the use of road space. But in practice, the increasing problems of traffic congestion were a hot potato which politicians did not tackle as it would mean constraining the use of the private car and its vocal users. Increasing staff shortages were difficult to solve without raising wages, which would lead to an increase in fares or subsidy. The increasing costs would be against a background of a decline in passenger numbers due to increasing use of the private car, and to social trends such as television which kept people at home in the evenings and so reduced off-peak travel.

The solutions to these problems made the service to passengers worse. To counteract the delays that result from traffic congestion, long routes were cut up into shorter routes with recovery time added to schedules to improve reliability. This led to higher costs per mile and public outrage when long-standing connections were lost. To cut costs while raising wages, more one-person-operated buses were introduced, but increased boarding times slowed the service and increased unreliability, while the loss of the open platform and conductor made the buses even less attractive to passengers.

The increasing subsidy brought greater involvement of politicians, who had to raise the funds through taxation, for which electors would hold them responsible. The politicians wanted an improved public service but at a reduced cost. Conservative councils wanted to cut the cost but were wary of cutting the service too much. Labour councils wanted to protect the service and staff conditions whilst keeping the fares down, but were wary of putting up local taxes. Both parties would try to influence London Transport by putting their own nominees on its Board. Looking back in 1997 Ken Glazier, a London Buses manager and transport historian, wrote that in 1972 "the extent of political control was close to being at its strongest historically". There was direct intervention in day-to-day matters. Pay rises in 1972 increased staffing costs to a degree which could not be covered by a fares increase and so required operational economies, leading to reductions in services, primarily in the evenings and on Sundays.

The LT culture
David Bayliss was Chief Transport Planner at the GLC, and later became LRT Director of Planning. From his time at the GLC he recalls, "We recognised the problems of traffic congestion, and LT's difficult operating environment, which was significantly worse than other places. But we also saw the organisation itself as monolithic and bureaucratic. It was a difficult organisation to deal with. Their view was clearly that 'there is only one outfit that knows about buses in London and we are it!' We had the feeling that the bus service had not been brought up to date in terms of routeings, services and frequencies. Harold Mote, who was Chair of the GLC Transport Committee, tried to get them to change the bus network in a positive way, though with some of his own examples which did seem a little amateurish. He argued that with reorganisation, the bus service could be better at less cost. LT Buses just scoffed at it. They dismissed him as an amateur, and deemed that no change was necessary – but bus passengers didn't think this."

David Quarmby adds that London Transport was organised along rigidly functional lines. "There was the Board and then there were the Chief Officers, you name it and there was a Chief Engineer or Chief Officer in charge of it. There was a Chief Operating Officer for buses and another one for rail and, incredible to think of this, but the Chief Mechanical Engineer was responsible for both buses and railways, so the guy down in the garage reported up through a line that didn't cross to the operating side except at Chief Officer level. Extraordinary!"

Norman Cohen was then Operations Research Manager. "The management structure was akin to a

branch of the armed forces, and all the senior grades were Officers. There were Officers' toilets and even an Officers' Dining Room, and then the very top 10th floor dining room for the Board Members and Chief Officers. It was based on how things were run in the armed forces. All the senior managers in Buses had seen service in the war, and then they came back to work in London Transport. Their idea of how to run an organisation was based on their own experience, and a particular aspect of their experience was that people obeyed orders. Well, people didn't always obey orders in London Transport!"

David Bayliss recalls that, when visiting from the GLC, he would have lunch at 55 Broadway with Board Members in the 10th floor dining room. However, if he visited Officers they went to the Officers' Dining Club on the second floor. It was all very archaic. However, this was not uncommon in transport operators and British industry at the time.

Phil Margrave worked for Charles Greystock, who was in charge of bus rolling stock. "Ken Wakefield from the Department of Transport would come for regular meetings with Charlie. The real purpose was for Charlie to take him to lunch, so we would go into Charlie's office and have a semi-meeting to start with. As soon as this was over, of course, I had to go because I was not allowed in the Officers' Dining Club. Anyway, I got up to go, and Ken said, 'Where are you going?' So I said, 'Oh that's all right, I've got some things to do.' And Charlie's getting embarrassed and says, 'No, he's got some things to do,' and Ken says, 'Well, if you're not going to lunch, then I'm not going to lunch.' So we thought, I'm just going to have to do it. So I walked into the Officers' Dining Club and of course I knew a lot of people who were there, and they are all shaking my hand because they thought I had been promoted! What is worse is that, two or three days before I was made an Officer, they closed the place, so I never went in there legally!"

Outer London in 1975, at Chingford Mount. Any journey on the local route W21 costs 5p. A Routemaster on the 69 offers a trunk service to North Woolwich Free Ferry, while in the background a DMS on the 191 passes through on its way from Chingford to Enfield. At the nearest stop, you can catch a Green Line coach on the 718 from Harlow, through Oxford Circus to Windsor. (John Parkin)

9 "There were Officers' toilets and an Officers' Dining Room, and the 10th floor dining room for Board Members."

The service on the road

Barry Le Jeune spent most of his career in LT's Public Relations, and much of his time there explaining problems to the public. A high proportion of the public letters he dealt with were complaints about the buses. His view at the time was that the service was badly managed. All the problems were well known, but nobody really grasped the nettle to make innovative changes to address them.

Malcolm Wren was in Operational Research where he managed surveys of the bus service, with traffic recording staff at stops along the route tracking the buses. What became clear from this was how unreliable the service was, which was quite a shock to him. "People in London Transport believed that this was due to external factors and that somehow it was 'not our fault'. I had worked with Eastern National and these were all the same problems as other operators faced, but they were not really being solved in London. The view was that London was different and this was true to a degree, but running buses in Romford was no more difficult than in Southend, and Southend was coping, while Romford was not."

Martin Whitley worked in Business Planning and later moved into Bus Operations. He saw that, "London Buses was a very strange organisation where the people you appointed to management and supervisory grades were the people who didn't want to do the basic job. As a result, you didn't get the right sort of supervisors and managers. People were frowned on if they showed initiative."

Pat Mahon joined as a conductor at Wood Green in 1968. They had 70 or 75 buses missing every day. When he became a driver on the 19s, there was little attempt to run the service to the schedule. "The Inspector at Highbury would say, 'Take this down to Sloane Square, back to Tottenham Court Road, Tooting Bec and then straight back here.' There was no time card and no schedule, that's what you had to do that day, and he had it all worked out in his head. So he was completely decimating the service before it started, and then he tried to rebuild it to get it running. Inside the garage, staff were glad to be off the buses themselves – 'The boys outside on the buses are earning more than us, but this is clean and dry and we've got a pension!'"

Steve Clayton joined as a graduate trainee and went into Bus Operations Management. He saw that, prior to the reorganisation into Districts, there were too many disaffected staff, and around a quarter of the fleet didn't run. There were 1,300 NBAs (buses not in service for engineering reasons) across the fleet, and there was little chance of running a full service. At one point thirty fit buses were found parked behind unfit ones at Holloway – they had been there for months and no one knew. When Steve was at Muswell Hill, they discovered five or six new Fleetline B20s double-deckers at Stonebridge Park which had had parts removed to fit to defective buses. The floors inside were completely clean because they had barely been used in service, an expensive way to buy spare parts. There was around 26% staff shortage at Muswell Hill at the time, which had a huge impact on the service.

Despite the staff shortage, Steve still managed to staff 95% of the mileage, with considerable overtime, but the level of service provided fell short of what they expected. "The trade union was more relaxed in some places than others about overtime, particularly where drivers wanted it, but some garages had a history of lower overtime. In others, the supervisors and managers were driving in order to maintain the service. You would start the week and know that you did not have a snowball's chance in hell of running the full service. This all arose through problems with central recruitment, where some garages, mine included, seemed to be destined never to have enough staff, and training buses were given too low a priority. There were too many layers of management, too many departments, and everything was everybody else's fault. Nobody took full responsibility."

There was also an unwillingness to raise the most difficult problems with the Trade Union. The bus schedules could not be operated with the staff available, and they were not reduced to a level that could be operated because the management would not tackle the issue. Norman Cohen, then Operational Research Manager, remembers that, "It was very much a hand-wringing time, with a refusal to face the Union." The Union would not accept a reduction in jobs, even when the staff were not available, requiring instead a wage rise to increase recruitment. There were serious attempts to develop and improve the services, but planning was often driven by schedule efficiency and rigid trade union agreements, leading to unattractive, non-clockface frequencies and many variations to services at weekends.

Industrial relations were often difficult. As Traffic Manager for Area 11 in the early '80s Steve Clayton had to deal with problems at, amongst others, Shepherd's Bush garage. "There had been all sorts of strikes in the area, and nothing had been resolved. Managers were just avoiding trouble, and there was an incident with a Shepherd's Bush driver refusing duty. If the driver was suspended, they would run the buses in (go on strike). I told my local manager to go ahead and suspend the driver. The next morning I was there for the first bus out, and the trade union refused to operate the buses. I said that all drivers, many of whom were in the canteen, should be instructed to take their buses, or leave the premises, 'If they're on the stones, they're on the stones'. This

then escalated throughout the whole of London with 17 bus garages out on strike. The Traffic Manager at Romford North Street rang to ask me what it was all about. He said, 'There are blokes here going on strike and they don't know why!'" There was a widespread feeling that, in the 1970s, the power balance had swung too far from management to the unions, and a lot of the changes in the 1980s and '90s were recovering that balance.

Mark Yexley trained in Bus Operations Management, and recalls that, "Garage performance was appalling in some places, with only 50-60% operated mileage at Holloway, New Cross, Thornton Heath and Peckham. On the other hand, Loughton and Norbiton would regularly deliver 100%." He went to Wood Green as a conductor in 1980 when they had a serious shortage of drivers and less than 80% of the mileage was being run. But he stresses that there were also excellent people who did a good job. Norbiton never lost a mechanical mile, and Brixton was also very good; the manager at Wood Green had a military background and an amazing larger-than-life personality that overawed awkward trade unions and drivers and conductors who wanted to play games. The manager at Leyton would appear first thing in the morning and check staff signing on. If they were not in full uniform, they knew they would be sent home and lose money, even if it led to a loss of service.

George Roberts joined LT in 1975 as a driver at Stamford Hill, before moving to garage engineering. "Interesting times, but they were not maintaining the buses properly. They were ignoring drivers' reports, which annoyed the drivers because they would get the same bus a few days later and see that nothing had been done. There might be a little problem with a cab light flickering. The driver lists the problem on the defect sheet but nothing is done. Then the light is on all the time, and nothing is done, then it doesn't work at all. So a driver is down in Wapping at night and the cab light doesn't work, and he can't do his waybill, so he packs up and takes the bus back to garage and you have no service. The drivers' reports are your eyes and ears – a 'heater blowing hot and cold', or 'lights not working', or 'bus stalls at traffic lights' – if these are ignored, they become bigger problems. Engineers used to just write 'Serviceable' on the sheet and send the bus out again, so the driver was being ignored. The introduction of the Districts began to solve this when there was proper engineering accountability."

Does this count as an apology? A poster displayed on buses in 1974 laboriously explains the difficulties but offers little comfort to the passenger. (Richard Shirley)

"There are blokes going on strike here and they don't know why."

In such a large organisation, it was easy to appear to be doing the job well by providing the reports that were required, rather than reporting what was actually happening. Peter McMahon worked as holiday cover for a Garage Engineering Manager who had a piece of cardboard with holes in it, which he placed on the weekly report form and ticked the sheet through the holes. The next week he turned the cardboard around, the week after he turned the cardboard over, and in the fourth week he turned it around again before ticking through the holes. So his reports changed every week, but were repeated every four weeks. Nobody noticed. George Roberts recalls a garage where not quite all the buses fitted onto the maintenance cycle, so they were left off, and there was no maintenance on those buses unless something went wrong with them.

Those who did a good job went unobserved. When we introduced drop safes at Walthamstow, senior drivers were appointed as invigilators to check the cash counting, acceptable to management and staff. We looked for those with long service and good records. One of the best had very long service, no reports against him, no accidents, lateness, no 'shorts or overs' on his cash, and no public complaints. The Garage Inspectors, his only point of contact with the garage, who allocated his duties and received his cash when he paid in, couldn't remember who he was. They stood around for several minutes – 'Mr Moore? Isn't he that chap who......, you know, he looks like ….' So we invited him in for a cup of tea and to say, 'Thank you', which gave him quite a shock!

Engineering problems and the DMS

Bus engineering was affected by the staff shortage, but it was also exacerbated by the choice of new buses. A contentious decision was the purchase of Daimler Fleetlines in the 1970s, the London DMS, which was originally dubbed 'The Londoner' though the name did not catch on. The Government gave grants for buses suitable for one-person-operation, to help the industry modernise. Of the three buses available, LT chose the Fleetline. The first entered service in January 1971 and 2,646 were delivered between then and 1979.

This bus was popular elsewhere in the country, but was not designed for London's demanding environment, and it did not suit LT's maintenance procedures. Many staff in the organisation took against it. Drivers could not hear the rear-mounted engine. It was unpopular with passengers due to the slow boarding times and the lack of conductor and open platform. The Automatic Fare Collection turnstile was designed to speed boarding but the coin-operated equipment was unreliable with frequent failures and had been abandoned by 1977. Maintenance costs were much higher than for Routemasters.

The Daimler Fleetline one-person-operated double decker was introduced in 1971 and dubbed 'The Londoner', but the bus was unpopular and the name did not catch on. 2,646 were delivered up to 1979, by which time the first buses were being withdrawn. The last example was withdrawn in January 1993. OPO versions operated throughout London, particularly in the suburbs. Walthamstow only operated Fleetlines at one stage and eleven are seen in the garage yard in 1981. (Roger Torode)

A later example, D2576 seen in May 1984, has come across Westminster Bridge and is crossing into the bus-only lane to turn directly into Whitehall avoiding Parliament Square. (David Cole)

David Quarmby recalls, "One of the consequences of the very centralised engineering function, and I think to an extent the arrogance of the engineering function in London Transport, was that they wouldn't rethink from scratch what they needed to do to properly maintain a bus like the Fleetline, compared to what they needed to do to maintain a Routemaster. It is a fundamentally different vehicle, the mechanical parts are different, and it needed a different approach to maintenance and repair. That was not done and there was only one garage that really got its head round how to maintain DMSs and that was Brixton. The garage engineering manager there was an amazing man – he had totally got it. You had to start again from scratch and work out how to maintain these front entrance standardised off-the-shelf buses. And the rest of the fleet just struggled."

Mark Yexley remembers the hankering which people had for a golden era when London Transport was top of the pile, but nostalgia was no cure for the decline in engineering standards as a heavily centralised system geared around simple, standard bus types struggled to adjust to the demands of newer but less robust vehicles. Few places apart from Brixton could maintain a DMS successfully. "All the pressure to get buses out on the road combined with parts shortages and poor diagnostic skills resulted in a general decline in maintenance standards which hit reliability but not safety. One honourable exception was Brixton, where one star person, the engineering manager George Buck, had the nous, engineering brain and sheer strength of character to beat the odds and turn out a star performance."

But Steve Clayton is clear, "The DMS was a bad vehicle. The rear brake pads had to be changed every four weeks. It was an easy bus to unwittingly drive badly. The gearboxes didn't last. It was quicker to drive the bus in semi-automatic, but you could knock the stuffing out of it because you couldn't hear the engine. It was not a good bus for London.

"Then the Metrobuses arrived and the Titans, which were significantly better vehicles, each with its own strengths and weaknesses. Metrobus brake pads lasted nine months because of the built-in retarder in the Voith gearbox which could not be abused; it made its own decisions about changing gears. It was a very good bus, which MCW put together in about nine months. The ideal would have been the MCW chassis and the Titan body. The body let down the MCW – because of poor bonding of steel and aluminium it suffered a lot of rust and corrosion in later years. On the Titan, the chassis let it down. Both vehicles were much better when fitted with air brakes rather than the hydraulic oil systems that were originally specified by LT – who thought they knew better than the manufacturers. Air is free, whereas hydraulic fluid is expensive!"

Phil Margrave had to deal with the Fleetline gearbox failures. "I was on the tools in the Experimental Shop at Chiswick, and it was the advent of the Leyland B20, the quiet Fleetline with the re-designed back. We were having so much trouble with the gearboxes, we were having brand-new chassis delivered from Leyland and we were taking the gearboxes out and sending them out to garages, and then when the bus was built complete from Park Royal, it would be towed into our place. We used to work every weekend putting the gearboxes back in – we didn't have enough gearboxes to put new buses onto the road. The quality was awful."

When the DMSs came due for their seven year recertification, a 50% Government grant for new vehicles made replacement of these unpopular buses a cost-effective option, and withdrawals commenced in 1979 – around the time that the last new ones were delivered. Most were sold to Ensign in Purfleet, who received so many between 1979 and 1983 that their yards became known as the 'DMS graveyards'. However, they proved popular second hand purchases for operators throughout Britain, particularly following bus deregulation.

Peter Newman of Ensign bought them and sold them on. "The DMS was not popular in London. It followed the Routemaster (RM) which itself followed the RT. Engineers in London Buses at that time were more like unit changers rather than engineers. With the RTs and RTLs, if something failed, you replaced it and sent it away – everything was repaired at Chiswick and Aldenham. With the DMS, it was a whole different ballgame, and they were not set up that way."

13 "There was only one garage that really got its head round how to maintain DMSs and that was Brixton."

Peter was in a difficult position. He tendered for all the buses, and his tender was accepted. "Everyone in the trade thought I was mad, but we knew we could make the buses work. The first dilemma was that London Transport was saying the buses were rubbish, but if we were selling them, we would have to say that they were good buses. So the way out of this was to convert them from two door to one door, and then to take off all the London extras so that they became standard Fleetlines. We could then say that, after modification, they were acceptable and reliable, and they were. We sold these far and wide. Hong Kong had 400, and didn't have the problems that London had – Kowloon Motor Bus bought 200 to run for one year while waiting for new buses, and kept them for four or five years."

Bryan Constable was Managing Director of Selkent and bought DMSs back from Peter Newman for his Bexleybus operation. "These had been sold by Ensign to Scotland and had the awful automatic transmission control system removed. So there was direct selection of the gears, and there was absolutely no trouble with them – the gearboxes lasted six times as long. They were not very nice buses to maintain in terms of the wearing parts. On an RM, all the components are very accessible. Some of the components that needed regular replacement on the DMS were less accessible compared with the RM, and these were heavy, inaccessible, unpleasant, dirty jobs. This may have resulted in staff leaving things longer than they should have done so that the buses became down at heel. Other operators would not have had this comparison, so the buses may have been more promptly maintained, and they did not have the automatic transmission system."

In 2013, Peter Newman was awarded the Outstanding Lifetime Achievement Award at the Annual Bus Awards. The citation recorded that he had relieved London Transport of a thousand Fleetlines in the late 1970s, and made a business out of refurbishing and selling them on.

Ensign sold DMSs all over the world. This example was converted to left-hand drive for Chicago Motor Coach. (Roger Torode)

14   "Everyone in the trade thought I was mad, but we knew we could make the buses work."

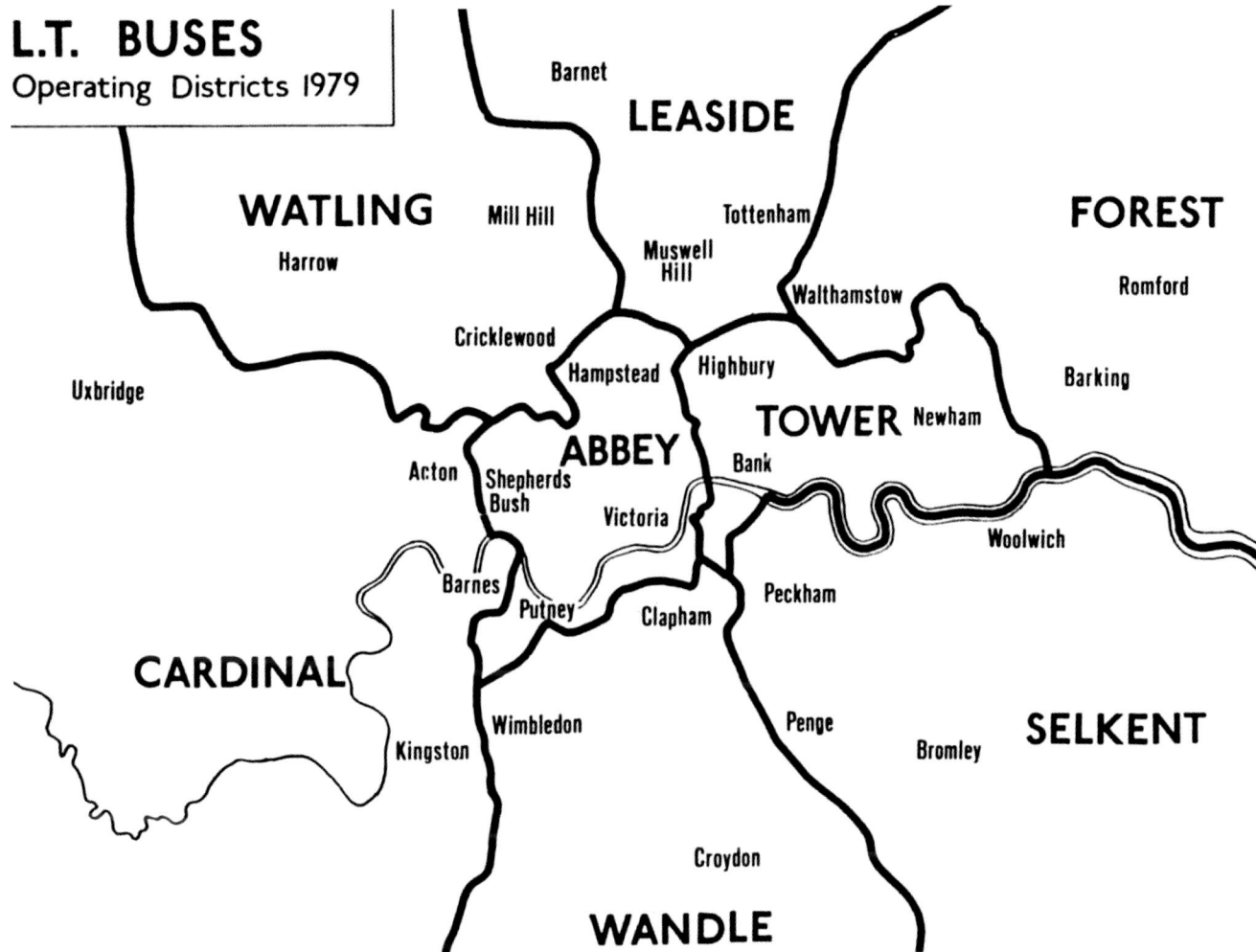

L.T. BUSES Operating Districts 1979

Reorganisation and the eight Districts

In April 1978 Kenneth Robinson retired as Chair of LT, Ralph Bennett became Chairman and David Quarmby became Managing Director Buses. David saw the need for change. "When I took over the Buses in 1978 I insisted that the organisation should be broken up so that all the necessary functions to run the bus business were reported through to me. So then we had a Chief Mechanical Engineer Buses and a Chief Mechanical Engineer Rail and eventually we had our own HR and Finance functions.

"So, my first task was to create the business that we called London Buses, and the Underground followed when Tony Ridley joined in 1980. The next step was to create business units, and we eventually created eight business units that we called Districts, and this is when the embryo of what then enabled London Transport to privatise was first created. It was not part of the thinking at that time, but it was a bit later on.

"It was in 1979 that the decision was made to introduce the District organisation. We had great fun deciding the names of the Districts. There were Abbey and Tower, the two central ones; and Selkent, interestingly the one that still exists; Wandle, which was south London; Cardinal which was west London; Watling; Leaside and Forest. It was when we were developing those names that we realised this truth, that London is a collection of villages, because the places that people know in London are all localities, there are no names that describe sub regions of London. You've got Clapham, Wood Green, Harrow, Ilford, Ealing and so on, but you have no more aggregated way of describing south-east London or east London. So we had to find iconic names that conveyed something, and I guess the one that we failed on was south-east London – that's why we called it Selkent, because we actually couldn't think of a real name. We almost used the name Meridian, which would probably have worked because Greenwich was in the centre of that region, starting at Camberwell and going right over to Bexley and Bexleyheath.

The Eight Districts introduced in 1979 brought a local identity and accountability to bus operations, each managed by a named local Mr Bus. The District insignia were displayed next to the entrance on buses, on bus stops and publicity.

"When I took over the Buses in 1978 I insisted that the organisation should be broken up."

"Our neighbour, a man called Colin Banks, ran a small but very prestigious typographical design company called Banks and Miles, based in Blackheath Village. We set Colin the challenge of doing the logos for the eight Districts. So he designed what I think were lovely logos, the squirrel for Forest, the Swan for Leaside, Wandle was a water wheel, Selkent a sprig of Kentish hops, Cardinal was an outline of a Cardinal. Abbey was an outline of Westminster Abbey, and Tower was an outline of the Tower of London.

"It was those logos that gave expression to the Districts. I remember thinking, this is good, this is sending a clear message that things are changing in the organisation. We actually put the logos on the side of the buses by the door, and we created the District General Manager function, and had District Operations Manager and District Engineering Manager reporting through to the DGMs.

"So we achieved what I was really after, which was to devolve total responsibility for bus operation and delivery of service quality to a District level. Each District had about eight garages, a good size, and it was a big enough job that you could pay a reasonable enough salary to get a good enough person to run it, and we had both operators and engineers promoted to be District General Manager – people like Tony Parsons, the DGM for Cardinal, and Ron Brewer at Forest, and Bryan Constable who was later the DGM for Selkent.

"This District organisation seemed to me at the time to be the right scale and to give the right degree of disaggregation. Eight units for one large business was enough, and each of them ran eight garages. We had 65 garages at the time and it felt about right. We thought that if there was any further fragmentation, the whole business of operational control would get very difficult."

"I remember thinking, 'This is good, this is sending a clear message that things are changing in the organisation.'"

Left The District logos as designed by Colin Banks.

The new organisation took effect on 1 October 1979 and brought operating management much closer to the passenger. Buses, garages and publicity were given the new District insignia and a revised bus map showing the district boundaries was issued. There was additional publicity in Forest and Watling Districts to see if public awareness could be raised.

Norman Cohen became the District General Manager of Abbey District. What did he find when he got there? "The worst thing when I arrived was that Chalk Farm was on strike, because there was huge conflict between the operating and the engineering side. The operating manager and the engineering manager simply didn't get on: communication between them seemed non-existent. The engineering foreman's style was robust – he was a bully par excellence. So all the drivers were out, the union intervened, insisting that they wouldn't take out buses if they had a minor fault, and this had all happened before I got there. They were on strike! I had to deal with it, and I learnt quickly.

"I went and talked to them, and found out what it was all about, and I spoke to the union. The Operating Rep was a Trotskyite, a very intelligent guy. A third of the Chalk Farm buses were unfit anyway, genuinely unfit, and I thought, 'This can't go on.' Moving the foreman to another post was essential as were some other changes.

"I had 10 garages, and it was like a graveyard. The car park down at the side of Holloway bus garage was packed with unfit buses. There were terrible staff shortages. There were routes like the old 239, which used to run from Archway to Waterloo – well, often there was only one bus running on it. And I used to go and talk to the manager about it and he said, 'Well, there aren't the buses and there aren't the staff, what am I supposed to do?' And indeed, what could he do? But the quality of the managers generally speaking was not very high on either side, and all of those things had to be resolved."

Martin Whitley moved to Cardinal District when Joe Fitzpatrick retired. "It was absolutely brilliant. It was exactly where I wanted to be. There were things that needed doing, we could do things our way, and we were taking additional responsibilities from the centre such as finance and the scheduling teams. It therefore became an area business, and quite a big one at that. There were masses of staffing problems, and the staff turnover was horrendous.

"More and more head office functions were being transferred to the districts, making them increasingly autonomous (whoopee!). However all this was under a financial rule of iron and we were expected to be motivated by the comforting thought that if the current year was tough, then just wait for the next one. Conversion of outer London crew routes to OPO continued, and even the busy trunk routes succumbed without much of a problem.

"The whole emphasis was on cost cutting – we were not encouraged to look for new business nor to aggressively fight the cause of the bus. Out of experience and necessity, our planning was all in the direction of widening frequencies and our longer term plans consisted of yet deeper cuts. It was still a bit difficult if you came up with some new project because it was extremely difficult to get approval for it."

Martin recalls the Service Planning Review Meetings where business decisions would be taken which were mostly retrenchment. Sometimes the right things came up and were done, but not always. Martin has no doubt that if you looked at the cost per bus mile, and the cost per passenger mile, that LT was not as efficient as other operators. "There were probably lots of staff doing things that were barely worth doing. LT had good infrastructure, covered garages, a well-oiled machine which had existed for a long time and was running well. But there were lots of things needing to be done to it, and most of those benefits were dismantled as part of the subsequent changes."

The number of Districts was reduced from eight to six from 2 January 1984 'to reflect changing needs and to reduce overheads'. Watling and Tower were absorbed by their neighbours, and additional responsibilities were devolved.

Politics and finance

Horace Cutler had become Leader of the GLC in 1977 and sought to get LT's expenditure under control. He appointed Leslie Chapman as a part-time Board Member for two years from January 1979 to investigate LT's costs – without telling the Chairman, Ralph Bennett, that he was doing so. In May 1979, a Conservative Government was elected and Margaret Thatcher became Prime Minister determined to pursue a radical agenda. In the financial year 1979/80 the overall bus deficit was £53.9 million and, following a significant fare rise during the year, passenger miles dropped by 3%.

1980 was a difficult year. Leslie Chapman received considerable publicity for his accusations of profligate expenditure and excessive waste, and an independent audit of London Transport was commissioned by the GLC. This did not manage to substantiate his claims and concluded that for the size and nature of the organisation, the management of London Transport showed 'moderate competence'.

LT commissioned PA International to analyse and report on their managerial abilities. However, the result of the report, published in June 1980, was that Ralph Bennett, the Chairman, was removed from post by the GLC. The report also said that middle and lower levels of operation throughout London Transport could not be faulted significantly, though this did not receive such media attention. In August, Sir Peter Masefield became chairman initially for a period not to exceed 12 months, until a long-term chairman could be appointed, but in fact he stayed until September 1982.

The Labour GLC and Fares Fair

A new Labour administration was elected to the GLC on 7 May 1981 with a commitment to support and develop public transport and to encourage its use with lower fares. The strict cash limits imposed by the Conservatives were withdrawn, restrictions on overtime and rest day working were lifted and a new target to operate an extra five million bus miles was set. Additional expenditure was approved to encourage recruitment and training. By October, bus miles were over target for the third quarter of the year, despite difficulty with spare parts at Chiswick.

Dave Wetzel was appointed Chair of the GLC Transport Committee. He had been a conductor at Turnham Green from 1962 and then a driver, becoming a garage inspector at Hounslow from 1965. He knew that the service was often awful. He quickly achieved notoriety by signing his letters 'Yours for Socialism' in red ink. "We were immediately able to increase bus mileage. The Horace Cutler regime had had an overtime ban on both buses and Underground, so we released that, which gave an immediate improvement with more buses. I remember doing a TV interview at Catford garage, in which there was a line of buses along the wall, and I stood in front as the drivers got in the buses and drove off!

"So the staffing problem was significantly eased, but this then exposed the fact that the engineers did not have a full complement of buses available. They only had the buses that there were staff for, so when more staff became available, there weren't enough buses. Everything had been very lax; everyone was used to not performing well. I remember the 117 to Staines and Egham regularly had a 40/50 minute gap on a 10 minute service, which was criminal."

David Quarmby recalls that, "Dave Wetzel was, of course, very supportive of retaining the RMs because that meant retaining conductors. So the policy then was to retain the RM for about half the fleet, all the central London routes, because we didn't have a ticketing and fare collection system that would make one-man operation work on the busy routes.

"I think retaining them was the right operational decision at the time. Reliability and the maintainability of buses has improved hugely since the days of the Fleetline. I remember, the Metrobus came along around that time and the Leyland Titan. The Titan was an attempt to apply some RM engineering principles and it was certainly better, but it was a very expensive vehicle I seem to remember."

Labour had pledged to reduce fares by 25%, to be paid for by a supplementary rate. It was introduced as the Fares Fair scheme. Dave Wetzel explained, "We had promised a fares cut of 25% but in fact cut by an average of 32% – never trust a politician to do what he says! It was a larger cut because we didn't want anyone to have a fares increase compared to the previous fare, so with the introduction of zonal fares we had to make sure that no individual was worse off. This led to the 32% reduction overall."

The new fares were introduced on 4 October 1981, dividing London into four zones: Outer, Inner, City and West End. These were 20p for one zone, 30p for two zones and 40p for three or more zones. A short hop fare for journeys of up to about 1 mile was introduced at 10p. The child fare was reduced to 5p while a Sunday maximum fare of 20p applied throughout

London. A new range of passes was also introduced for weekly, monthly and annual periods. The Central Tube Rover was renamed Central London Rover and became available on both buses and Underground, and the Red Bus Rover ticket was reduced to £1.20 adult and 30p child.

Fares Fair was challenged by Bromley Council, who argued that their residents were paying for a fares reduction that they did not benefit from, as the Underground did not reach Bromley. The GLC won the case in the High Court, but Bromley won the Appeal. The case went to the House of Lords, where the Law Lords ruled that the scheme was unlawful.

The result of the ruling was a 'recovery' budget with a 100% increase in fares, a 15% reduction in scheduled bus mileage and a 3% reduction in Tube mileage. 7,000 redundancies were predicted. Fares were generally doubled from 21 March 1982. The three zonal fares became 40p, 60p and 80p with short hop journeys then costing 20p. Child fares became 10p but were no longer available between 9pm and 7am each night because the system was felt to be open to abuse. The service reductions on bus and Underground were expected to save more than £10 million in 1982 and up to £22 million a year in subsequent years.

There were major protests about the judgement. The unions called for a complete one-day stoppage throughout LT on 10 March, when all bus and Underground services ceased for 24 hours. The strike was totally effective – even where some employees reported for work, engineering staff prevented services from operating. The GLC launched their own campaign to 'Keep Fares Fair' and comparisons were made with the levels of subsidy in New York, Milan, Brussels and Paris which were 72%, 71%, 70% and 56% respectively. London, even with Fares Fair, would have been 46% and it was now likely to fall to around 12%. The GLC pointed out that the cost of Fares Fair to London ratepayers was almost doubled as the government imposed penalties by withholding block grant.

Dave Wetzel was active in the 'Can't Pay, Won't Pay' campaign, which had around 2,000 people involved. "I was on a bus coming to Trafalgar Square and gave the conductor a 'Can't Pay, Won't Pay' ticket. When we got to Trafalgar Square, the conductor stopped the bus and refused to continue until I had paid. He called for assistance using the bus radio which I had paid for as Chair of the GLC Transport Committee. As a true democrat I took a show of hands on the lower deck, and people voted for me to stay on the bus. So then I went upstairs, and the people there voted for me to leave the bus, so I did. My wife and I were both prosecuted."

Titan T292 publicises Fares Fair as it unloads at Walthamstow Central in September 1981. (Roger Torode)

21 MARCH

London Transport 100% Increases* from Westminster

Is this fair on London?

KEEP FARES FAIR

ACT NOW! Sign the petitions, write to the press, tell your MP.

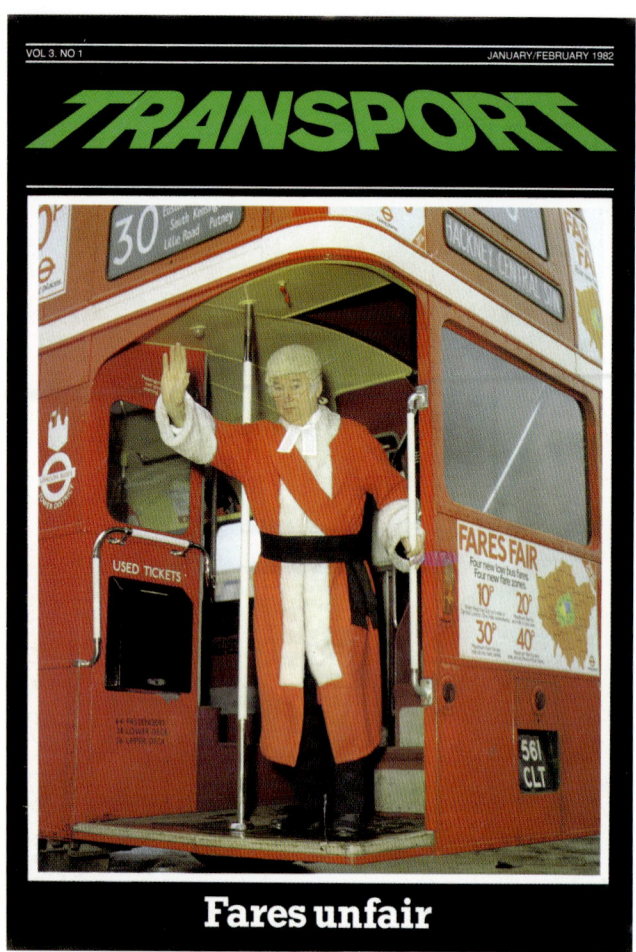

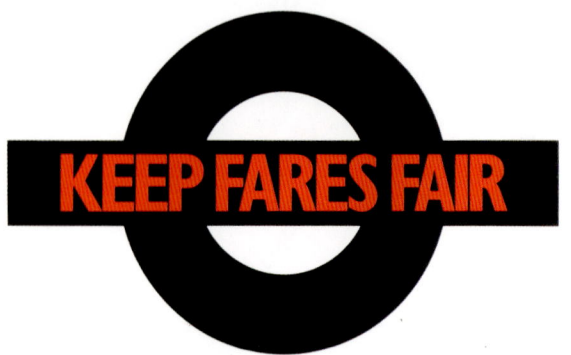

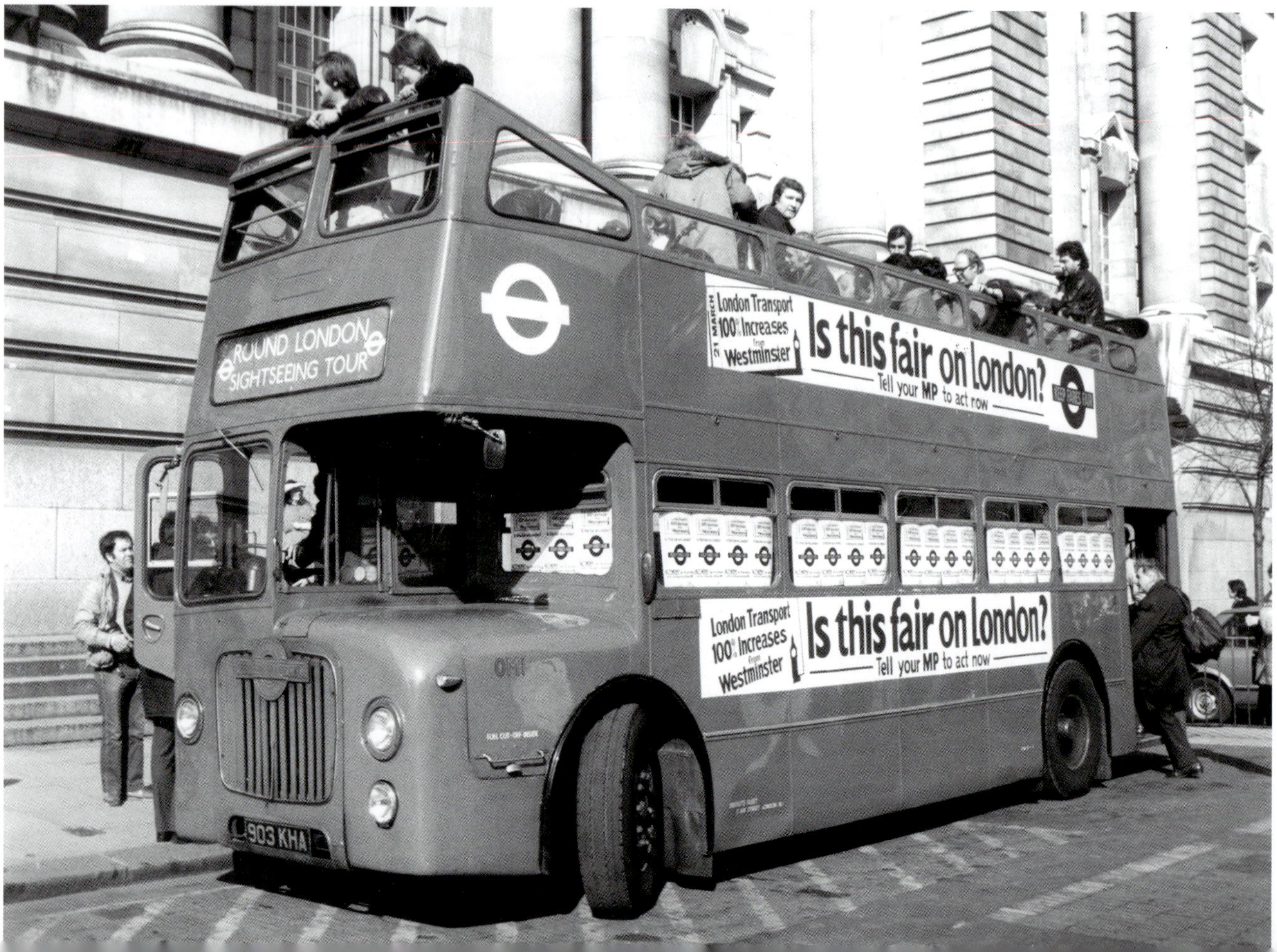

Can't pay... won't pay!

'Alternative tickets' issued by campaign to defend cheap fares

'Fares will treble' — MP

EAST END MPs have added their weight to the campaign by speaking out against the Law Lords' decision.

Nigel Spearing, MP for Newham South said: "What the Law Lords call LT's 'fiduciary duty' and Heseltine's clawback (a £140m block grant penalty imposed on the GLC for overspending) will, unless there is further legislation, require LT and the GLC to put up fares by another 50 per cent in the summer, thus trebling fares." LT officials have confirmed this.

"Economic illiteracy" is how Tottenham MP, Norman Atkinson described the Law Lord's decision.

"Their sheer economic vandalism has made it impossible for a very responsible GLC to provide a good transport system."

Ernie Roberts, Hackney North's MP, described the Law Lords' decision as, "interfering in the democratic right of a democratically elected authority to carry out policies that were put before the electorate, and which are expected to be carried out."

THE WHOLE of the East London underground line is under threat of closure together with sixteen other unnamed stations on the network.

Seven stations, including Shoreditch, the 'top end' of the East London Line, and three branch lines are to be closed down this year, provided ministerial approval being sought is won.

Travellers are being urged to see these cutbacks coupled with the fares rise, due on March 21 as the thin end of the wedge.

According to Dave Wetzel, GLC Transport Chairperson: "It's the start of a long-term run-down in public transport in London."

He is personally backing the fight to defend cheap fares, under the slogan "Can't Pay... Won't Pay".

The traveller-led campaign has advocated the issuing of illegal "Alternative Tickets" handed in with the old fare in lieu of the increase.

The campaign, backed by 13 GLC members, goes beyond official GLC policy — a massive publicity effort aimed at changing the law to bring the GLC/LT grants position back to where everyone thought it was before the Law Lords' decision.

Both campaigns aim to point out the policy's successes:
- increases in service usage of 11 per cent on the buses and 8 per cent on the tube,
- an overall increase in service frequency of 15 per cent. It states that a doubling of fares will lead to:
- a 10 per cent increase in congestion
- a 30 per cent fall off in public transport usage
- more energy waste and pollution
- extra expense on road maintenance

By BILL PARKER

The three main transport unions are launching their own campaign. ASLEF, the NUR and the TGWU have formed a London Transport Trade Union Defence Committee (LTTUDC) and have called a meeting of branch officials at Congress House on February 17 to launch the campaign.

Its aims are to "persuade the Government to introduce legislation clarifying the financial position at LT and its service responsibilities to the general public."

At present, strike action on March 22 is being considered but has not yet been officially endorsed.

The threatened closures together with a half hour loss of service at the start and end of the day and a overall drop in service levels is believed to have placed at least 4,000 jobs at risk.

The transport workers and users group 'Fare Fight' which is co-ordinating 'Can't Pay... Won't Pay' meets every Friday at 7.00 pm at the Central London Poly, New Cavendish St, W1.

"Alternative Tickets" will be distributed on February 19, if a change in legislation has not been forthcoming by then.

The Law Lords' ruling resonated throughout London and the public transport industry. The Journal of the Chartered Institute of Transport illustrated the story with this Journal cover showing a judge on the platform of RM1561, opposite, top left. Ken Livingstone used Obsolete Fleet's OM1 to campaign against the ruling. Examples of Fares Fair campaign literature are shown above and opposite, top right.

Sir Peter Masefield's last LT annual report, for 1981, showed the positive effect of the reduced fares and simplified zonal system of charges, which had reversed a 20-year decline in passengers. Fares Fair had resulted in the largest rise in passenger numbers ever recorded by LT. However, when the fares were subsequently doubled, there was a huge drop. As a result the new Chairman, Keith Bright, suggested an immediate 20% fare cut, which became a 25% cut implemented in 1983. The GLC Conservative opposition supported the zonal fares plans and the introduction of Travelcard included in the package, but were concerned that the scheme could be legally challenged in the way that Fares Fair had been. This did not happen, as the GLC took steps to ensure widespread public consultation on the proposals, but the Government continued to penalise the GLC by withholding rate support grant, resulting in a 14% rise in GLC rates.

In implementing the schedule cuts, services were largely reduced to the level of staff availability. This was a major and historic change – for the first time in 30 years, there should be no cuts due to shortage of staff. In addition, the schedules were increasingly made more robust with additional recovery time. The combined effect was that, whilst there was a reduction in operated miles, the service was more reliable, and LT's Quality of Service Indicators showed that average waiting time went down by 10% even though there was 15% less scheduled service.

Reorganising engineering
London's bus engineering had been under considerable scrutiny, and in 1979 Marcus Smith was appointed as Engineering Manager to sort it out and to get London off the Traffic Commissioner's 'watch list'. He was previously General Manager of the Passenger Vehicle division of Leyland vehicles. In 1981 he became General Manager (Buses) on the retirement of Jack Wooler. It was proposed to transfer total engineering responsibility to the Bus Districts, so there was doubt over the future of Chiswick and Aldenham. In 1981, each Bus District set up a test centre for the new annual Freedom From Defect (FFD) certification system, which replaced the PSV examination from 1 January 1983. The entire fleet of 6,000 buses passed through these new centres over the 18 months leading to the introduction of the new system in order to establish an anniversary date for each vehicle and to spread them evenly throughout the year.

Phil Margrave recalls that, in 1981, the engineering problems were putting the Operator's Licence at risk. "We had had serious numbers of prohibitions and things were really quite bleak at that time for the whole red bus fleet. I went with Marcus Smith for a meeting with the Traffic Commissioner and the Senior Mechanical Engineer of the Department of Transport. The Commissioner said he was going to curtail the licences. It was a five-year licence and he was going to curtail it by 2½ years, which was devastating for London Buses. But we knew how bad it was, and that was the catalyst to try and do something about it. As a result, a task force was set up to go to the worst garages, and we had a couple of supervisors and experts to help all the garages perform better, and to bring the poorer garages round."

Chiswick and Aldenham were also under scrutiny, and in early 1983 the Secretary of State asked the Monopolies and Mergers Commission (MMC) to investigate them. John Trayner had joined as an engineering apprentice in 1975 and spent time in both Chiswick and Aldenham. "It was an interesting place! You had things like 'idle time' you got paid for, when you played snooker or table tennis – there was no real urgency. I was working in the gearbox theatre and building ten gearboxes in a day, and getting told off for doing more than my quota. I was proving what I could do, but it was all time and motion, there was a big department of guys telling you what you could do and what you couldn't do. Once you had done your day's quota they all sat in a big stores area and never seemed to move. At the time you are just a kid and you think, I wonder who needs all this stuff. Eventually it went out to garages, but looking back now it must have cost an absolute fortune and no-one was really focused on whether this was the best way to do it.

"There were a number of reviews going on, a number of things being put out to piloting. Could manufacturers do this? Could garages do it themselves rather than wait for this vast Chiswick or Aldenham Works to overhaul the bus? So it was a period of limbo and eventually it did change."

Robert Newson was a District Financial Adviser. "I remember the DFA for Cardinal District asking, 'Why does it cost £500 to shoot two pigeons?' The answer was that pigeon shoots in bus garages were carried out by the LT Works and Building department, and the cost was re-charged to the Bus District without being subject to any sort of competitive test."

Bryan Constable was District Engineering Manager of Selkent when he was asked to go to manage Aldenham by David Quarmby. However, he saw a limited life for it beyond the RM family as the principal London bus. "My mission was to keep peoples' chins off the ground and output up, while decisions were made about their future. David Quarmby wanted me to explain to people that the prospects were not good. The Aldenham site was so expensive to run, the costs were unsustainable, but it was a superb facility. The whole process of running the Routemasters with Chiswick and Aldenham

Aldenham Works displayed its coach finishing skills with the Aldenham Ambassador, a Leyland Titan, and the Aldenham Aristocrat, Metrobus M57, which is seen here at the Chiswick Gala in July 1983. 'General' fleetnames were applied to celebrate London Transport's 50th Anniversary. (Barry Le Jeune)

fitted together, but a Central Works was no longer appropriate once the heavy overhaul of buses came to an end with the move to annual inspections. But everybody made me extremely welcome. The Aldenham job was the best job I ever had. It was wonderful, and I look back with great affection."

The MMC report concluded that neither Chiswick nor Aldenham was cost-effective due to low volumes of activity, out-dated and restrictive working practices, labour inflexibility, ineffective maintenance accounting, defective bonus schemes and complex industrial relations structures which hindered productivity, although it acknowledged the difficulty of running a large bus undertaking in London when subject to significant political pressure. Their conclusion was that there was no way that Aldenham could be made viable and recommended complete closure in order to achieve an annual saving of £8m. Indeed, the energy, infrastructure maintenance and other fixed costs were so astronomically high that even if the staff worked for nothing, the bus overhaul costs would continue to be way in excess of what emerging operators could ever afford. Bryan Constable showed this graphically on his hand-out given to every member of staff at one particular mass meeting chaired by David Quarmby – who had insisted on by-passing the engineering hierarchy. Chiswick could be viable with a reduction of 300 staff, but there was no such proposal for the 1,100 staff at Aldenham.

Following the report, LT management and the trade unions jointly considered the future of both works, and set up feasibility studies to consider restructuring their activities. Aldenham was re-organised into separate business functions under tight financial targets requiring a reduction in staff of 40%. It was decided to retain a central overhaul works, and so the bus business agreed to contract Aldenham to supply bus garages for an initial five-year period from April 1985, subject to it achieving satisfactory quality and delivery targets.

John Trayner was now working on a project to tool up garages to work on Titans and Metrobuses. "We had a stores in Victoria basement, and our offices were right beside Victoria garage. This project was to build up the ability of garages to handle the annual FFD tests, and also about accountability. Could the work be done at the 'coal face' – the garage? So there were a lot of experimental projects being run, asking questions like, 'Can we overhaul an engine in a garage?' And gradually, once you gave people in garages the tools or the authority to do more things, it was amazing how quickly they developed and were asking 'Why am I sending it somewhere and not getting it back for so long?' People were waking up and thinking it through.

"You look back now and think it can't have been right, but across the network there were 600 NBAs (buses not available for engineering reasons). There was a lot of fat in the process and you just chucked more money at it, it was an endless pot because that was the way it was done. The changes didn't happen overnight, but gradually it was realised that there are different ways of doing things."

Competition and AMOS

London Buses was undoubtedly a high-cost operator. The Strategic Review of May 1982 showed that costs per bus mile were 40% higher than the PTE average, 50% higher than London Country Bus Services (LCBS) and 60% higher in real terms than LB's costs in 1970. The County Councils surrounding London were beginning to prefer supporting LCBS operations rather than London Buses.

David Quarmby was looking for different ways of doing things on the operating side. "In about 1981 or 1982, I was putting together a five-year strategy for London Buses and Ian Phillips (LT Board Member for Finance and Planning) and I really sparked each other off. We were a kind of two-man internal creative and subversive fifth column within London Transport. I think a lot of people knew that, and were tolerant of it because we always had the good of the organisation at heart, but we were always conspiring new ideas to try and move things forward. We came up with the idea of creating a competitive culture within a public organisation, to spur efficiency, customer focus, and all these things that we now take for granted, that the private sector is probably better at than the public sector.

"The first idea we had was to have a bus business still owned by London Transport but in a different part of the organisation, with a contractual relationship with another part of London Transport which specified its strategy and plans. The concept was to create a contractual relationship with each of the districts individually. So that would put them under the pressure of the contract, in terms of clear commitments on revenue and costs, with penalties and bonuses if you did better or worse against your contractual targets. But how do you really bring the spur of competition between Districts to generate some of the pressure on efficiency and on performance that only competition is able to do?

"We didn't get very far down that track but we certainly had the idea that there were probably groups of routes on the borders between the Districts which you could put up for tender, and have both Districts bid for. And it was this idea of creating an arm's-length business under a contractual relationship with a different part of London Transport that was the breakthrough in an otherwise monolithic publicly owned organisation.

"This was after Ralph Bennett had left because he fell out with Horace Cutler, so there was nobody now on the Board with whom Ian and I felt we could have a sympathetic conversation. So it never really got very far, but the seeds were there. What I would say is that the creation of the Districts, and then some of the thoughts about introducing internal competition probably helped create the fertile ground on which the seeds of real privatisation could then be sown and reaped."

Competitive challenges did begin to arise, stimulated by the Conservative government's commitment to competition. Local bus services could at the time only be operated in Greater London by London Transport or by others with its agreement. But Lightgray's application to operate a commercial service between Gloucester Road and Heathrow Airport in 1981 had been refused by London Transport. The promoter then appealed to the Transport Secretary, Norman Fowler, who gave the go-ahead. As a result, subsequent applications by Rickards and Green Line to de-restrict their services between Heathrow and Victoria were granted by LT.

A greater challenge came in 1982 when Associated Minibus Operators Ltd (AMOS) applied to LT to run four services using up to 500 16-seater minibuses. These were long routes crossing the centre of London. The minibuses would pick up and set down anywhere, operating at two-minute intervals in the rush hours and 3-4 minutes at other times. The promoter, Anthony Shephard, had previous experience of such operations from Hong Kong. Keith Bright, the LT Chairman, said that the proposal could offer a new type of public transport service to London, though so many additional vehicles, stopping on a hail and ride basis, could also have profound effects on existing services and London's already choked road system.

Due to the significance of the application LT decided to set up a public hearing under an independent inspector who had experience of road service licensing and other highways and traffic enquiries. There was no statutory provision for such a hearing and LT took this bold decision to avoid being both judge and jury in a matter it had an interest in itself. LT, the GLC, the Transport and General Workers' Union, London Country Bus Services and the United Taxi Trade all agreed to give evidence against the proposals with most London Boroughs, the Trades Unions Congress and the National Union of Railwaymen supplying written evidence.

The hearing opened on 1 March 1983 and lasted eight days. In fact, it was the evidence of AMOS themselves which ensured a refusal. The company proposed to lease out its vehicles to 'associates' who would garage, operate and maintain them. When cross-examined, Anthony Shephard said that they would average 285 miles a day at an average running speed of 12mph. A simple calculation showed that they would therefore be running for just under 24 hours a day! It also became clear that the proposed relationship with the 'associates' meant that each driver would need to have an Operator's Licence.

The report of the independent inspector was clear – routes and terminals had not been clearly defined;

there was no provision for turn-round time at the terminals – not even for staff breaks; the provision for supervision of services and maintenance of vehicles was inadequate; there would be adverse effects on congestion; the stop anywhere principle was neither safe nor practical, except perhaps in the suburbs; the operation would be less safe than existing services because of the pressure on drivers to increase earnings; on AMOS's own estimates, drivers would earn little and might lose money, and indeed the AMOS financial forecasts were described as works of fiction. The conclusion of the Inspector was that, "In my view, the disadvantages and dangers to the public are so overwhelmingly greater than any possible advantage that it would be folly to implement the proposals." LT took this advice and rejected the application, but AMOS appealed to the Secretary of State for Transport and was granted legal assistance to present its case.

Also in March 1983, LT declined to enter into a London Bus Agreement with Vulcancrown Ltd, trading as Shuttlebus, to operate a door-to-door minibus service from anywhere in the Metropolitan Area to and from Heathrow Airport. Vulcancrown also appealed against LT's decision and again the Inspector found in favour of LT's decision. The reasons were similar to those in the AMOS hearing which questioned the viability of the scheme. However, this also went to the Secretary of State for further consideration.

1983 marked the Golden Jubilee of London Transport. But though there was celebration of LT's achievements over 50 years, it was more a year of concern over the future of the organisation, which the politicians were about to decide.

There were few independent bus operators in London, and they could only run bus services with the permission of London Transport. Independent operation of route 98B (Ruislip to North Harrow/Rayners Lane) started in February 1966, following withdrawal of the LT service. The route saw many different operators over the years. Here a Harrington Contender chassisless bus of Elms Coaches, which came second-hand from Maidstone & District, is seen in Ruislip High Street in 1967. (Barry Le Jeune)

London Transport was strangely reluctant to serve the Forestdale Estate adjacent to New Addington. In 1970, North Downs started a minibus service to connect it with East Croydon. This was taken over in 1971 by Orpington and District, using full size buses including this Weymann bodied Leyland Atlantean which started life with Maidstone and District. O&D operation ceased in February 1981, when the route passed to Tillingbourne. (Barry Le Jeune)

25 " The disadvantages and dangers are so overwhelming that it would be folly to implement the AMOS proposals."

2 PROVIDE OR SECURE — 1983-1984

The LRT Act

Secretary of State for Transport is not a sought-after Cabinet position. It tends to be a politician on the way up or on the way back down the 'greasy pole' of a political career, and they don't stay long. It is a useful position for the Prime Minister in placing someone who is to be in the Cabinet but not in one of the Great Offices of State. The contradictions and conflicts of the job led to an episode of 'Yes Minister', entitled 'The Bed of Nails', in which the hapless Minister was persuaded to develop an Integrated Transport Policy – which proved impossible!

Margaret Thatcher's Conservative Government was re-elected in June 1983, and Tom King became Secretary of State for Transport. He replaced David Howell who had held the post for twenty-one months, having replaced Norman Fowler who was there for twenty-eight months. In October, Mrs Thatcher was forced into a reshuffle following the surprise resignation of Cecil Parkinson who had been having an affair with his secretary. So after four months Tom King was replaced by Nicholas Ridley, who held the post for two-and-a-half years until May 1986.

The Government published a White Paper in July 1983 outlining the problems which had been faced by London Transport since the 1960s, and giving the government's solution to these difficulties. Intended as a basis for consultation, it proposed that control of the London Transport Executive should be transferred from the GLC to the Secretary of State for Transport, and then reconstituted on the pattern of a small holding company, with its bus and Underground operations established as separate subsidiaries. The holding body would be renamed London Regional Transport (LRT) and would be responsible for the strategic control of its operating subsidiaries and for securing the cost-effective provision of bus and Underground services from these and other operators.

Buses and politics. The Conservative government re-elected in 1983 took London Transport from Ken Livingstone's GLC in 1984 preparatory to closing down the GLC itself in 1986. The GLC used buses and its County Hall headquarters to argue its case, placing a hoarding on top of County Hall for large posters which faced the Houses of Parliament and Lords across the river. Routemasters 1273 and 1033 cross Westminster Bridge in June 1984. 1033 has front posters reading 'Keep GLC Working for London', while the roof banner on County Hall reads, 'Peers, Listen to Londoners, Don't scrap the GLC elections'. (Roger Torode)

26 LT would be a small holding company, with its bus and Underground operations established as separate subsidiaries.

Grant would come directly from the Secretary of State for Transport, as with British Rail. This would replace the system under which the GLC precepted on the London Boroughs for the ratepayers' contribution to the cost of London Transport. The London Boroughs would be able to enter into agreements to buy specific additional services, and would take back responsibility for concessionary fares for the elderly from the GLC. The proposed separate bus and Underground subsidiaries fitted LT's structure, and LRT would have power to divide their operations into further subsidiaries, which was stated to be particularly relevant to the bus business. LRT would be able to dispose of any of those further subsidiaries subject to the consent of the Secretary of State.

As mentioned in Chapter 1, local bus services could be operated in Greater London only by London Transport or by others with its agreement, and LRT would retain this control. However, bus operators who wished to run services in Greater London without entering into an agreement with LRT would now be able to apply to the Traffic Commissioners. This was intended to permit the licensing of competing bus services in London, as in the rest of Great Britain.

The proposals were prompted by LT's difficulties, by the Government's radical agenda to shake up the public sector, and also by their overwhelming antagonism to the GLC. The odd result of this was that London Transport was, in effect, nationalised by the Conservative government, but only in order to take it away from the GLC!

There was rapid condemnation of the lack of democratic control over subsidy levels and the proposed 'quango', which would be responsible to central Government. Independent Television's London Programme suggested that the proposed cutback in investment from £148m to £132m annually would prevent the investment needed to achieve the proposed staffing economies. The LT Chairman, Dr Keith Bright, was critical that the views of professional transport operators were being obscured by political argument. There was also criticism of the indecent haste of the proposals.

The GLC had achieved an expansion in travel on LT's services of around 16% since the 1983 fares reduction, and the decline in London's public transport had been reversed for the first time in many years. The 1983 Annual Report showed Travelcard results to have been much better than forecast with over 600,000 Travelcards and bus passes issued. There was an 11% increase in bus revenue and 20% on the Underground, giving £23 million more revenue than forecast. Rescheduling the buses to an achievable level of vehicle and staff availability had reduced average waiting times by 10%. The Capitalcard was introduced from 6 January 1985 to add British Rail travel to the existing Travelcard. These were successes by the GLC, and showed a good recovery from the turmoil of Fares Fair and the Law Lords' ruling. But political and policy control was now to pass from the GLC to central Government.

Nicholas Ridley
Nicholas Ridley took over the Transport portfolio on 16 October 1983. He was a controversial man – many considered him difficult but those who knew him well liked his direct and challenging approach. He would listen to his advisers and those who sought to influence him, but then be very clear what his own position was. Ridley was not interested in popularity. As a right-wing Conservative, he was impressed by small-scale, competitive, private enterprise such as the minibuses he had seen in Hong Kong, Buenos Aires and elsewhere. When he visited National Bus Company (NBC) garages he asked, "How many of these buses are owned by their drivers?" The answer of course was, "None!" – they were all owned by the government at that time. It was unfortunate for Ridley that the AMOS proposal was so badly thought out, making it difficult for him to approve.

Steven Norris was MP for Oxford East between 1983 and 1987 and for Epping Forest from 1988 to 1997. He was Parliamentary Private Secretary (PPS) to Nicholas Ridley at the beginning of the latter period. "I'd say that Nick Ridley was very much a Thatcherite before Thatcher. He was an instinctive free marketeer, and above all he was an instinctive free thinker. I was his PPS, but you couldn't get more opposite than him, the younger brother of a significant northern peer and me, a grammar school boy from Liverpool. But we got on terrifically well, not least because I shared a lot of his belief that you should say what you think, and a lot of his beliefs in free markets and liberalisation generally, and government getting off the back of businesses.

"Nick was never prickly and difficult – what he always was was provocative, because he would say exactly how he saw things, and sometimes that would challenge the conventional wisdom. So his officials adored him, because you could have a genuine debate with Nick. He had a clarity and vision that the senior officials really liked – a Secretary of State who genuinely engaged with them. He had a mind of his own and that is, after all, what Ministers are supposed to have. He had always believed that less government was preferable; that wherever government's dead hand existed it tended to restrain rather than to encourage efficient delivery of service.

"When you looked at the position prior to privatisation and deregulation, you had this multiplicity of nationalised and local authority owned and controlled bus services. It's worth saying that at the time, they didn't get a particularly good press. There's this terrible tendency for people to develop this extraordinarily rosy view of the past in almost every issue. It's the same with railways, saying what a wonderful life it was under British Rail. Well, with respect that's not true, and pretty much the same was true with a lot of the bus services. Nick had seen enough of the operation of private bus services in the United States and elsewhere to say, 'What we should really be doing is selling these bus services to the private sector so that we get a capital receipt, and the private sector will invest in new buses and new technology.' He was constantly being told that new buses were actually a very good investment, because you have lower maintenance costs and all the other reasons, but they couldn't be afforded. 'Well that's fine, we'll privatise them and the private sector can invest – that's what the private sector does. It tends to invest more in technology in order to save staff time, and it tends to invest more in good equipment to save maintenance costs and so on.' And so Nick was the prime mover in persuading the government that they should go through with this process, and the general principle was to privatise and to deregulate effectively at the same time.

"Outside London, as we saw later, the bigger fish in the bus industry almost immediately ate the smaller fish, and you can trace the growth of what's now FirstGroup from Badgerline and Grampian, and Stagecoach similarly, back to the very earliest days of privatisation. Deregulation outside London gave rise to the Glasgow bus wars, the Sheffield bus wars and so on. Now if you were a purist like Nick, you would say, 'Well of course that happens, and why is it bad to have too many buses? We kept on being told there weren't enough, now you are telling me there are too many – are you people never happy? And so what if Brian Souter says I'm going to run this service free. That may be deliberately challenging an existing operator but as far as I'm concerned,' he would say, 'every customer seems to be doing rather well out of it. Why on earth should we interfere?' Nick didn't see that the bus wars were anything more than a passing phenomenon which would settle down and in the end would result in a logical rational market, because his argument always was, once these people had run these buses for nothing, queuing behind each other for non-existent passengers, they'll very shortly find that that is a very expensive way of doing business, they'll withdraw, the decent ones with the deepest pockets will stay, and that's what happens in markets.

"Now I suppose if you were marking that strategy, you'd say, 'I'll give you good marks for innovation and good marks for the clarity of your logic, but I'm going to mark you down a couple of points at least because it wasn't just a short-term effect of bus wars. They did have a fairly sustained negative impact on a number of principal cities outside London.'

"Mrs Thatcher did not campaign in 1979 on the basis of wanting to introduce privatisation. It arose almost as an accident, when she was invited to dispose of Amersham International, a government-sponsored laboratory business that was sold in 1982 and raised quite an amount of money for the Treasury. This led the Treasury to wonder how many more businesses we could sell, and if necessary then buy the service back at arm's length. And whilst that was happening, the group of young Turks who had taken over Wandsworth were developing this idea that local services need not be run by directly employed municipal employees but could be run by the private sector, and therefore tendering became commonly used from that point on.

"By the 1983 election, tendering had become a consistent feature of local authority work, hugely resisted by Labour local authorities of course, but with proven benefits in terms of reducing costs. Initially they all said, 'Ah yes, but the service is rubbish,' as if no municipal waste collection authority had ever missed a bin or dropped the contents over the road, or the other dreadful things that people do. So it was a combination of two things: Mrs Thatcher being attracted to the idea of raising money for the Treasury by selling off these industries which would then bring a big capital receipt to the Treasury and better value to taxpayers afterwards; and the growth in local authorities of tendering driven off the Wandsworth experience. The combination of the two fitted very well."

As MP for Oxford East, Steven Norris saw the effect of competition there. "It was City of Oxford Motor Services (COMS) who ran the existing services, and they were absolutely content that they ran a brilliant service, until Harry Blundred came along with his converted bread vans, as they were disparagingly referred to by COMS inspectors. But what Harry did was to bring a service to so many of my outlying communities in Oxford East – I don't mean outlying villages, I mean outlying in the housing estates on the fringe of Oxford on the other side of the ring road. Harry went to those places with his minibuses. He built a business literally providing the capillaries into the arteries of the COMS service, and made himself a huge amount of money. I was very happy for him to make his money because he was also offering my constituents a service they simply didn't have before. It was the quintessence of what Nicholas Ridley's vision was about."

LONDON BUSES

The vital clues to our future

MORE than ever before, the spotlight is focused on how well the Bus Business is performing. Politicians and passengers are looking critically at the service we provide. It is vital everyone in the Bus Business knows how London Buses is being judged, so everyone can make a contribution to its future.

ATTRACTING PASSENGERS

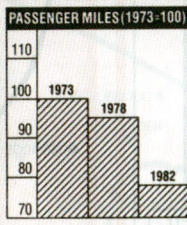

LONDON Buses' future depends very much on the number of passengers we carry. The facts are that passenger mileage has fallen steadily over the last 10 years, at a rate of two per cent each year.

In 1978 we carried our passengers a total of 2,800 million miles. By 1982, the figure was down to 2,300 million miles. The aim is to slow this downward slide. We have to provide a service which is good enough to hold on to our present passengers, and find ways of winning new ones.

STABLE FARES AND COST CONTROL

THE COST of a bus journey is one of the most important factors affecting the number of passengers we carry. But there are others; the quality of the service, the type of services, reliable buses and many other factors can affect the passenger's decision.

Bus fares have risen by one-third, on top of inflation, over the last 10 years.

Stable fares are vital to hold on to and win passengers to bus travel. The zonal fares and travel cards have helped us keep passenger levels steady this year. Before May 1983, travel by bus was 85 per cent more expensive than the same journey by car. Now bus travel is only 35 per cent more expensive.

London Buses aims to keep price levels steady over the next three years. We cannot do this unless we reduce the cost of running the Bus Business. The good news is that the costs of running the Bus Business have levelled off in 1983.

6 DISTRICTS STRONG

On January 2, 1984 London bus operations are reorganised from 8 to 6 Districts. Managing Director David Quarmby outlines the changes.

SINCE 1979 London Buses has given its eight Districts greater freedom and responsibility. Their job is to manage local resources to meet the needs of their own bus passengers.

From January 2, 1984 the six new Districts will have stronger teams to carry on this job with extra resources and skills.

The new District structure will reduce overhead costs and get the Bus Business into shape to meet the challenges of the next few years.

London Buses faces a stiff challenge over the next three years to prove it can provide an efficient cost-effective service to the travelling public in London. The Bus Business has made a start in convincing passengers and politicians alike that it can do the job. Now it has to prove its worth against other forms of travel — cars, motorcycles, bicycles, taxis and other operators, both public and private. London Buses has the strategy to do this and has started to put it into action.

It involves:
- keeping fares stable
- controlling our costs
- attracting passengers
- operating a high quality service
- improving productivity.

But it cannot be done unless staff at all levels within the Bus Business make it work — and are given the opportunity to make it work.

The six Districts will be pushing on with:
- Responding to local needs and competition through an improved traffic organisation
- Improving service quality with strong road control and supervision
- Providing more skills at District level to make the most of decentralisation
- Making use of new technology to speed up administrative tasks
- Controlling their own engineering and operating costs
- Drawing on a reorganised Head Office for specialist help.

BUSES AVAILABLE FOR SERVICE

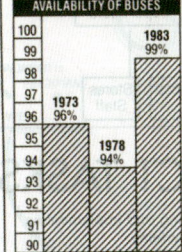

THERE has been a major improvement in engineering performance over the last two years with less than one per cent of buses not available now for service on any one day.

Continuing attention to improving our performance in obtaining Freedom From Defect certificates is needed.

Breakdowns on the road, which have a major impact on customer attitudes to the service, need further reduction.

SCHEDULED MILEAGE

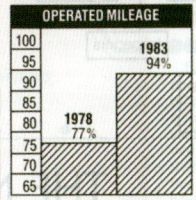

IDEALLY the Bus Business should operate all its published services. Between 1973 and 1982, London Buses never operated more than 77 per cent of its scheduled mileage.

This year has seen a remarkable improvement to 94 per cent of scheduled mileage being operated.

By 1986 this figure must rise to at least 96 per cent.

This is a prime target to help us keep our passengers.

IMPROVING PRODUCTIVITY

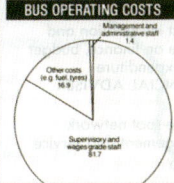

BECAUSE staff costs account for over three-quarters of the total costs of bus operations, better productivity is vital.

More OPO buses have made a significant contribution, but there must be an increased emphasis on more productive working methods in all District activities from both engineering and operations.

RELIABLE SERVICE

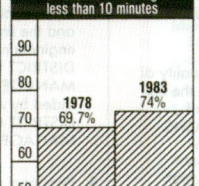

NOT only must we get buses and crews on the road but we have to make sure the quality of the service matches our scheduled timetables.

London conditions make this difficult. Over the last five years, on average a third of our passengers waited more than 10 minutes for a bus.

But 1983 waiting times have shown a move in the right direction, although the need for further improvement remains.

A further reorganisation in January 1984 reduced the number of LBL Districts from eight to six with devolution of more responsibilities from the centre. The challenge being faced, and the need for markedly improved performance, was set out to staff in this 4-page broadsheet.

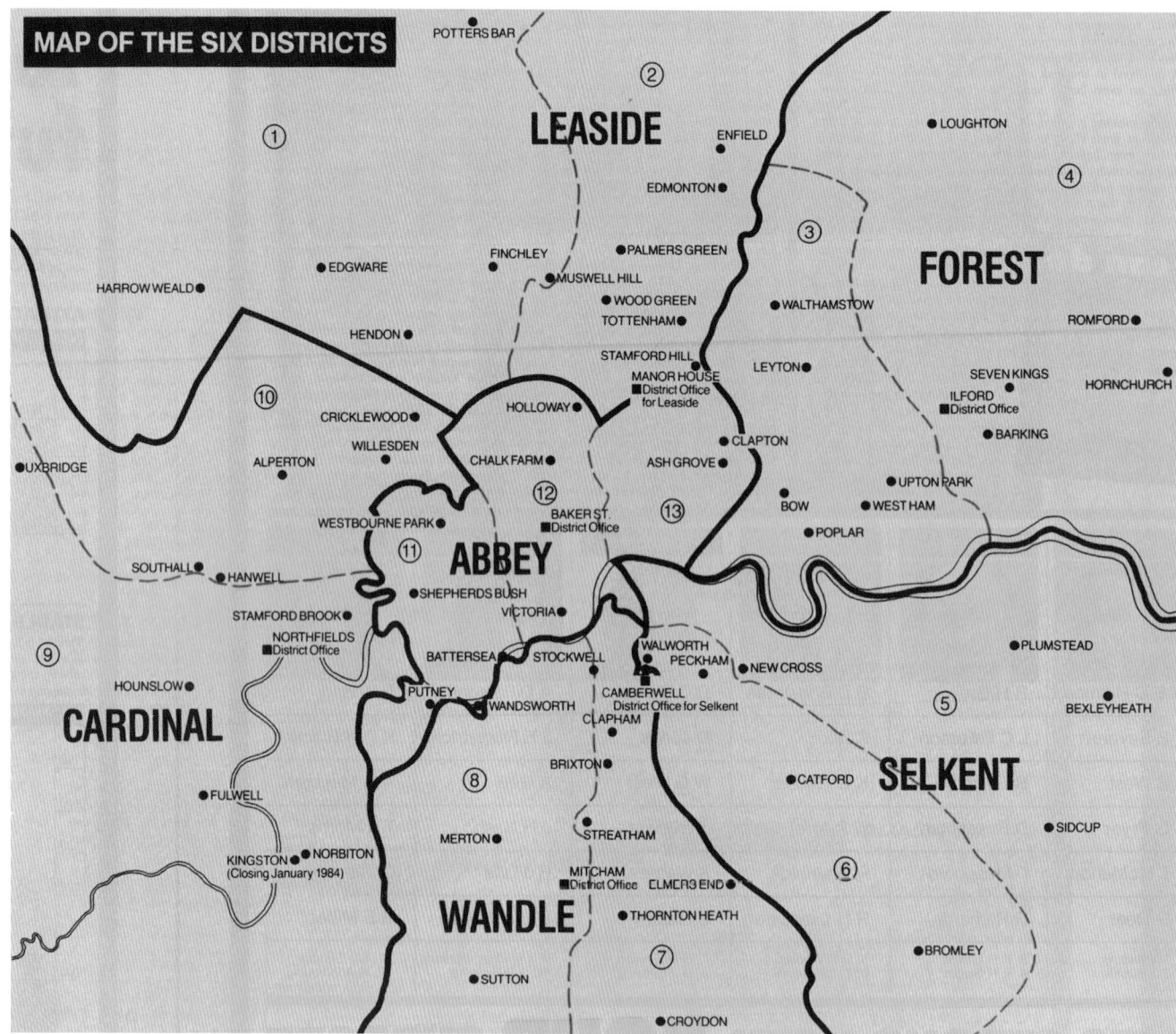

MAP OF THE SIX DISTRICTS

LRT commences

The London Regional Transport Act received Royal assent and LRT was formed on 26 June 1984, taking over from the GLC on 29 June. The four full-time LRT board members were Dr Keith Bright (Chairman), Dr David Quarmby (London Buses), Dr Tony Ridley (Underground) and Ian Phillips (Finance), who continued from the GLC board. The other members were replaced by new part-time Board members appointed by the Government.

LRT's principal duty was to provide or secure bus and tube services which best met the needs of London. It was required to set up subsidiary companies to run the separate parts of the business, which was straightforward in the case of the bus and Underground operations which were now fairly autonomous. These became London Buses Limited (LBL) and London Underground Limited (LUL), which took effect from 1 April 1985. Finance would come from central government funds with a proportion from London ratepayers, and there was a requirement to involve private capital in some parts of the business.

The government was hoping to encourage competition on road operations by enabling Road Service Licences to be obtained from the Traffic Commissioners, as elsewhere in the UK, in addition to the existing arrangements for services to be run under agreement with LRT.

The 1984 reorganisation closed Tower and Watling and reallocated their garages to neighbouring Districts. A new traffic control structure was introduced with 13 traffic areas, two per District except Abbey which had three, each managed by a Uniformed Chief Inspector who was out on the road controlling the quality of services and staff performance.

Nicholas Ridley announced four initial tasks that he had set LRT:
- to improve bus and Underground services for London within the resources available and make the services more attractive to the public;
- to reduce costs and the call on taxpayers' money and generally secure better value;
- to involve the private sector in the provision of services where that is more efficient and to make better use of publicly-owned assets, including the sale of public assets which are no longer required, and
- to promote better management through smaller and more efficient units, with clear goals and measurable objectives.

He also set LRT's prime financial target to reduce the level of revenue support from the ratepayers and taxpayers to £95 million in 1987/88 (compared with £192 million in 1984/85), and he required improved efficiency to make a large contribution to achieving that target. The level of fares was to be maintained at least until the end of 1984 but there would then be a greater than inflation increase designed to alter the balance between travellers and ratepayers, and then to maintain a stable relationship between fares and prices generally.

AMOS

In July 1984 Nicholas Ridley rejected the AMOS appeal on its proposed minibus services. He had little choice, as his own Inspector who heard the Appeal reported that the proposal lacked credibility and that the company was 'not a reliable organisation to whom should be entrusted the introduction of a new private operation which could set an important precedent for the future.' It was surprising that, despite the criticism of their financial estimates presented at the initial application, AMOS provided the same figures to the Appeal hearing, and they had still not discussed their proposals with the Metropolitan Police or the local authorities concerned. Ridley was clearly unhappy to be turning down the proposal, stating his support for 'the introduction of a spirit of individual enterprise into public transport in London,' and noting that 'the proposal contains many innovative and ingenious ideas for the provision of a new kind of public transport service in London'.

However, Ridley did approve the application by Vulcancrown Ltd, trading as Shuttlebus, against the advice of both LRT and his own independent Inspector who had been appointed to hear the Appeal against LRT's refusal of a licence. The Inspector had reported that the company had not established a sound basis for their proposed operation and that their application should therefore be denied.

In LRT, the strong feeling was that unless it acted quickly and radically, these sorts of proposals would return to haunt it.

Devising the tendering system

John Rigby was one of a small team in LRT's Group Planning Office tasked with devising a response to the requirements of the LRT Act. John has provided the following section to describe those events for this book:

No sooner had the new legislative framework for London Transport received Royal Assent in June 1984, than the Secretary of State's objectives for the new London Regional Transport followed quickly afterwards. The Act required LRT to 'provide or secure the provision of public passenger transport services' and obliged LRT to 'invite the submission of tenders for certain activities where it is thought appropriate'. The key tasks set out by the Secretary of State made it clear that the private sector was to be involved. The cost reductions required were seen as a fairly tough target.

The government had declared their intention to deregulate all local bus services in Britain. In London, however, there were two imperatives which produced a different policy. On the one hand, the stand-off between the GLC Leader Ken Livingstone and Prime Minister Margaret Thatcher over the huge success (in Ken Livingstone's view) and wasteful subsidy (in Margaret Thatcher's view) of the 1981 Fares Fair campaign and policy meant that Margaret Thatcher was determined to remove control of London Transport from the Greater London Council. On the other hand, while Nicholas Ridley happily fended off critics who claimed that bus deregulation would be chaotic and wasteful by saying that he was 'blazing a trail', he and the government didn't quite have the determination to blaze this trail right through the heart of a city of seven million people.

Also, at the time of bus deregulation, London Regional Transport and regulated tendering had only just come into force. To introduce a second radical change so soon would have been impractical both organisationally and politically. While the Transport Act 1985, which would deregulate all local bus services outside London, formally had little bearing on transport in London, its key impact was the threat it posed for London, and the Secretary of State indicated that deregulation in London was 'a question of when, not whether'.

Given the statutory obligations of the Act and the clear will of the Secretary of State, LRT needed to respond effectively to the twin challenges of introducing competition and reducing costs. The task of devising a response was given to LRT's Group Planning Office – a team of economists, business planners, mathematicians and other specialists carrying out rigorous appraisal and policy advice work for the LRT Board. Group Planning had access to all of LRT's operational and performance data which it used, backed by (what was then considered) extensive computing power and a commitment to re-assess the operational and investment decisions of LRT using the rigour of transport economics. With the standoff between the Government and the GLC, LRT filled the vacuum with what was then a radical initiative, without being beholden to London Buses management or to Trades Union preferences for the status quo. The Board's expectations were for innovative proposals to be presented speedily for Board consideration, with the necessity that those proposals could demonstrate to government LRT's commitment to achieving radical changes in London's bus services. Group Planning's project team initially comprised Richard Smith (latterly Corporate Planning Director, TfL), Peter Kenway (now Director, New Policy Institute) and John Rigby. Once we had devised a framework to meet the Board's aspirations, a permanent team was established under Nick Newton who led the initial implementation of the pilot phase and the subsequent roll out of tendered services across London.

The project team's initial work focused on two areas: a philosophical debate (with a strong practical edge!) about how best to design a competitive framework for local bus operation, alongside a brief programme of reviewing wider experience in service innovation and tendering/franchising in Britain and further afield. These two apparently distinct areas were in fact closely intermeshed in our thinking. The proponents of open markets, exemplified at the time by the Adam Smith Institute, argued that removing all constraints on market entry was the optimum solution – services would reach a natural equilibrium which would match what customers wanted and at the same time unit costs would fall and fares would be driven down.

The AMOS minibus proposal was an example of this approach and we all knew where the Secretary of State's sympathies lay! Set against this were a number of major concerns raised by transport professionals and led particularly by the Passenger Transport Executive Group who argued strongly for the benefits to passengers of service co-ordination. They argued that an open market would produce: wasteful duplication of service at peak times; service loss at off-peak times; a loss of effective bus/rail co-ordination, and the abandonment of integrated ticketing. Experience of the three 'Trial Areas' established under the Transport Act 1980 justified these fears, though none of them was in a large urban area. Briefly, the experiments demonstrated that peak period services improved, off-peak services declined, co-ordination ceased and County Councils were left to pick up the unprofitable but socially necessary services.

The LRT project team concluded that a system of managed competition would deliver the optimum results. By competing for the right to run services (rather than competing on the road), the public would benefit from lower unit costs of operation whilst retaining the benefits of an integrated network with integrated ticketing. This became the core principle of the LRT tendering system. Its other principal elements were:

- Service levels: LRT would specify the minimum service level, minimum number of departures in each main service period, first and last buses, vehicle capacity, and route.
- Fares and ticketing: fares specified by LRT, all LRT ticket types to be accepted, ticket machines owned by LRT.
- Revenue: level of receipts to be the responsibility of LRT, operators to be responsible for accurately collecting all revenue. Contractors would be paid full agreed costs and the revenue risk lay with LRT.
- Performance measures: cancelled mileage would be deducted at average cost per mile, penalties imposed for running more than two minutes early or more than five minutes late.
- Vehicles: to be agreed with the operator but carrying standard LRT information, minimum hourly capacity specified.
- Contract length: three years with possible annual extensions.

Thus the LRT tendering system was posited on operators competing to run a service whose core elements were specified by LRT, with the operator free to propose their own timetable which more than met the base specification and to propose whichever vehicle type would meet the minimum hourly capacity requirements. Their incentive was to secure the full monthly payment (which they had bid for) by running all the mileage and all operated within the running early/running late parameters set in the contract.

Before launching the first batch of tendered routes for bids, the team were worried by one core problem. Would any operators be interested? Well, of course, NBC operators on the fringes of London would be, especially London Country Bus Services, but if the independent operators failed to bid for and win some tenders, wouldn't the whole project be seen as a failure? More fundamentally, would this be seen as a collective failure by LRT and its insulated transport planners to deliver genuine competition in London, thereby justifying the 'Armageddon' of full deregulation in the Capital? These fears were so important that the team had to make every effort to stimulate the growth of an almost non-existent market – non-existent because LRT was seen as a monolithic monopoly that would squash any rivals, so 'why bother to try and compete in the first place?' The flip side of stimulating a market was endeavouring to ensure that London Buses Ltd (LBL) did not enjoy an 'inside track' on tendering and did not use predatory pricing tactics to scare off the competition. LRT's Board therefore ensured that LBL worked under a number of 'rules of engagement' when bidding for tenders, so that bids were fairly costed (rather than being cross subsidised) and that 'lost' services (those won by other operators) had their costs stripped out of LBL's budget to ensure that LBL's subsidy didn't just rise to compensate for them.

LRT commissioned Martin Higginson of London University to assess the scale of the potential supplier market. He found that although there were 3,500 vehicles owned by independent operators within and adjacent to Greater London, only 100 or so were used on stage carriage services. Few of the companies had the right experience or interest in expanding into stage carriage work – their scepticism was probably a function of 50 years of LT monopoly. Considerable effort was expended in contacting independent operators to convince them that LRT was, indeed, seeking to significantly widen the operator base in London and that it would be fair in handling bids from LBL, against their own submissions.

The Project Team selected a package of 13 routes for tender in the first round. The routes were selected on the basis of being one-person operated (rather than crew operated) and in the top 25% on two or more of the following criteria:
- Low average load per bus
- High cost per bus hour
- Small number of buses required to operate the service.

There was also a focus on routes in outer London and those running cross boundary (into the neighbouring Shire Counties) because of the greater prospect of finding willing independent operators on the fringes of London. The package of thirteen routes comprised 1.2% of total bus mileage. Tenders were advertised on 18 October 1984, with submissions due by February 1985 and services commencing operation in July/August 1985. At least two bids were received for each route and in a number of cases five or more bids were received. Contracts were awarded on twelve routes (the thirteenth was transferred to a later package) with LBL gaining six contracts, NBC subsidiaries four and independent operators two. The first tranche was therefore a clear success in significantly widening operator interest and third party operation of services, but the key beneficiaries were NBC subsidiaries. For London Buses, the experience was somewhat different – other operators could either win or experience 'no change', whereas for LBL it was lose or 'no change'.

The next stage of the roll out proceeded whilst the first tranche was being tendered and comprised:
- A further group of 10 routes (12 Contracts);
- An area review of services in Orpington, and
- A range of service running across the Greater London boundary

The area review was a specific attempt to introduce greater innovation in service provision and thereby avoid 'freezing' the network by an emphasis only on individual routes. The Orpington area was selected because of its wide range of private operators and the potential to introduce high frequency minibus operations. In particular, the private company Metrobus was based in Orpington and ran two commercial bus services into Croydon with LT's agreement. Minibus operation was, at the time, totemic of innovatory intent – AMOS Minibuses may have been several steps too far for London, but a more conventional approach introduced by Harry Blundred in Exeter in February 1984, operating high frequency minibuses, had caught the eye. Indeed, an 'undercover team' was sent to Exeter to see where the 'cutting edge' was and report back on network, reliability, patronage and estimated economics. Why 'undercover'? Simply because at the time, opposing AMOS whilst pursuing LRT's own proposals would have made for good press headlines. Although minibuses were becoming 'all the rage', they were disliked by some passengers for lack of comfort and poor access, and derided by some professionals as 'bread vans'. The advent of the purpose built Citypacer midibus, built by Optare of Leeds, represented a breakthrough in terms of size and comfort – 25 seats instead of 16 seats, and built like a car. Their size transformed the economics of running small buses.

Cross boundary services were selected for tendering because under the 1985 Transport Act, tendering was obligatory for any element of service supported by the Shire Counties. A further factor in selecting cross boundary routes was the issue raised by the then MP for Newham, Tony Banks, who was concerned that GLC subsidy was 'leaking' across the London boundary into the Shire Counties beyond.

The summary position in late 1986 was that 13.5 million miles of service had been tendered – approaching one eighth of LRT's total bus mileage – not a bad start since Nicholas Ridley's starting gun was fired just over two years previously.

In terms of the twin primary aims, the first two years of tendering achieved the aims: cost reductions averaging 20% were delivered and some 205 bids were submitted for 55 tenders. Of these tenders just under half (45%) were won by LBL, 40% by NBC subsidiaries, but only 15% by independents. The success of the NBC subsidiaries meant that operations remained in the public sector and the competitive element was slightly odd in pitting one publicly owned company against another. Apart from the comparatively low level of transfer to the private sector, other indicators were also positive: vehicle mileage was up; reliability improved, in some cases significantly; revenue increased in some cases and in one instance by 35% despite no change in mileage; and no services involved the use of coaches – which had been a significant fear of the Project team, given the difficulties of access for some groups of passengers.

John Rigby concludes with the observation that, in 2015, a fully tendered and privately operated London bus network seems entirely unexceptional. But back in 1984, when LRT decided to proceed with an experimental tranche of tendering, it all seemed very radical, especially as LT had operated largely unchanged for the five decades leading up to 1984.

Setting up the Tendered Bus Unit
Nick Newton was seconded from LT Procurement at Chiswick where he had been buying buses and trains. He had been sent to Ashridge Management College in 1983, after which he was seconded for three months to David Bayliss, then LRT's Director of Planning, to consider bus tendering with John Rigby, Peter Kenway, and Richard Smith. David Connolly, a commercial lawyer, was also in the group. Nick recalls: "The primary issue for the government at that time was closing down the GLC. They set up LRT, and in one line stated their wish to involve the private sector. This was their political policy objective. However, unlike on the railways, they rightly left the practitioners to sort out the best way of doing it.

"The Treasury consider that the private sector makes money from taking risks. I say no, they make money by managing risk. In LRT we got professional people to decide how best to implement the system. The key drivers were revenue and service level. It was decided that LRT would take the revenue risk and the operator would provide the required service level. We got executive approval for this and did not ask the politicians. We commenced the first tranche of tendering in the January of the following year and operations commenced in July. Politicians who had complained about the time it was taking were suddenly surprised when it was introduced so quickly.

"We carried out an analysis of the market. For 60 years private operators had not really been permitted to run front-line bus services in London, so the other operators were NBC companies around London and small coach operators, all in the private sector, whose main business was daily private hire where the margins were high but the revenue risk was also high. They therefore had big credit risks, and some of them spent a considerable amount of time recovering money owed to them. So we decided to design a system that removed the credit risk and our tendered operators became the first suppliers in LT history to be paid by direct debit. As a result, they were willing to bid low margins in order to achieve this regular cash flow. They were paid 75% of their four weekly price halfway through the period by direct debit. As result, if they got the contract, every four weeks they would have this money coming in. This provided the cash flow they needed, and with this, they could get bank loans with which to invest.

"We did not expect wages to be lower, but productivity would be higher with the new operators. We would reject bids where we considered the wages to be too low. Another major difference was that bus garages now did not need cover. Most of them were built in the days of wooden framed buses, which needed to be covered – metal-framed buses only needed a car park.

"Some operators would ask advice on whether they should put in cost-effective or more reliable bids, perhaps with more buses and so more robust schedules, but we told them to put both bids in and we would choose – we could select the best value bid, not necessarily the lowest price, because we were not required to publish the bids." The contract duration was set at three years, with possible contract extensions, in order to maintain continuous competitive pressure, though operators would have preferred five or seven year contracts to provide stability for investment decisions.

Nick created a small Tendered Bus Unit to run the system. One day, John Wood was called in to see his boss in the Commercial Office and told that he was being seconded on two days a week to the newly formed Unit. "It was just three of us doing the initial tendering, Nick, me and an admin guy. Gradually, it increased from two days TBU and three days back, to three days in this job and two days back, and then became full-time. There were still only two of us doing all of the work. In spring 1985 we moved to offices directly above Oxford Circus station. We packed everything we had into three boxes at 5 o'clock on Friday and put it all in a taxi to the new offices, and on Monday morning we went and opened up there."

The TBU started small, but soon got bigger.

David Quarmby leaves, John Telford Beasley arrives
In October 1984, David Quarmby left LT to join Sainsbury's. He published an article in the Guardian as he was leaving, criticising full deregulation and arguing for competitive tendering within a regulated framework: this would eliminate any monopolistic protection of the operator while maintaining an integrated transport network. As a Vice President of the Bus and Coach Council he argued this for the PTEs who were faced with full deregulation. He was strongly critical of any move, now or in the future, to deregulate the London bus network. His last Strategic Review for London Buses, in March 1984, continued with the plans to reduce costs and improve performance while suggesting a 'Suburban Costs Strategy' to defend LB's outer ring of operations which extended into the adjacent counties.

John Telford Beasley arrived as the new Managing Director of LBL in November 1984, appointed by Nicholas Ridley. 'JTB' was an international businessman who had been based in Barcelona in the pharmaceutical industry. He had no experience of public transport but was recruited for his business acumen. He had previously been with Cadburys, where his responsibilities included distribution. Clive Hodson, who was then LBL Finance Director, recalls, "John was very keen that we should have a more commercial outlook. We had various conferences – one or two people in the Districts weren't entirely happy and complained, 'Look, we aren't a sweetshop!'"

The task was to lead London Buses to privatisation, whilst keeping the operation going despite continuing operating and engineering difficulties. In 1984, the Operator's Licence was again granted for two, rather than the expected five years, following a number of vehicles failing Department of Transport (DoT) checks. Clive Hodson continues, "A passing shot had been fired across Marcus Smith's bow by the Traffic Commissioner and we were in danger of losing our Operator's Licence. I remember Marcus coming in to a late meeting we had one evening about the O-Licence, and John said, 'Right Marcus, can we run the buses tomorrow?' 'Yes.' 'Can we run the buses in three months' time?' 'Yes.' 'Right, fine, now we've got to remedy the engineering performance so that we are not threatened.' It would have been an absolute catastrophe if we had lost the licence, and I think it was a good idea then that each company, when they were set up, should have its own Operator's licence – that was very important."

Norman Cohen, then LBL Operations Director, recalls the new impetus of the organisation. "JTB came to work towards privatisation. Nicholas Ridley and Government policy was for privatisation and deregulation, but in which order was not clear. At the time, the government view was that it was deregulation that mattered. This was Conservative dogma, to free up the market, and if the public sector can't cope – exposed to competition – then it will go under.

"What would privatisation mean? Nicholas Ridley had looked at Hong Kong and Istanbul and had seen lots of minibuses, where the driver owned his own bus, and would park his bus at home, and the market would rule. I had to carefully steer JTB and Ridley away from this – this was at the time of the AMOS scheme. We had to show how unworkable this was and Derek Keeler, LBL's Development Director, achieved this. We got to the point where Ridley, I think, accepted that each driver owning his own bus perhaps wasn't realistic, but he then wanted to base privatisation on individual bus garages. We were able to persuade JTB that that was not going to work – there were far too many garages, there was too much interworking between them sharing routes and so on. So it just wasn't going to be practicable, you would have an unholy mess. And this was how we evolved towards creating a number of companies."

Derek Keeler argued the case with the Department of Transport. "We won a really significant battle as they wanted to have total deregulation, and we had the Ministry chap over and said to him, 'This is crazy. What we want, and what London needs, is a structure where the routes are planned and then put out to tender.' And he said, 'Oh, no, no, we want total deregulation.' 'Well,' I said, 'We did have that, and that was why London Transport was formed in 1933! If that's what you insist on, then we will do it. But bear in mind, when it all goes pear shaped, and there are queues of buses around Parliament Square, the politicians are not going to be very happy!' And he backed off really quickly."

But privatisation and deregulation remained Government policy, and it was ten years before this was resolved.

3 THE BEGINNING OF TENDERING 1984-1986

Len Wright got into the lift at 55 Broadway with a group of London coach operators and a quiet man in the corner. As the lift went up, Len joked, "This must be the biggest bunch of cowboys who have ever been allowed into 55 Broadway." When they got to the meeting, he discovered that the quiet man was Ian Harkness, the LRT Director then responsible for the tendering process.

Nick Newton met groups of operators in the 55 Broadway reception and took them up to the meeting rooms. "They were amazed because they had never been allowed in the building before". Leon Daniels was also in the lift. "Going to the upper floors of 55 Broadway we were like schoolchildren let into the staffroom for the first time, looking around at everything in awe, 'Oooh look at this, look at that!'"

LRT had publicised that they would begin to put routes out to competitive tender and private sector operators were invited to 55 Broadway to hear what was proposed. "Nick Newton and others gave presentations, and they talked about paying 75% of 1/13th of the contract every four weeks, and the other 25% being adjusted for mileage and other deductions and paid four weeks after that," recalls Leon.

Tendered operations started on Saturday 13 July 1985 and the first private sector operator was London Buslines, a subsidiary of Len Wright Travel. They used nine former LT Daimler Fleetlines in a brown and yellow livery. The former DM1088 is seen leaving Hounslow Bus Station. The bus did not last long with London Buslines and was sold on in November 1987. (Keith Wood)

36 "This must be the biggest bunch of cowboys who have ever been allowed into 55 Broadway!"

The coach operators were sceptical. They thought it was very onerous, and they didn't believe they would actually win tenders. They saw it as just an attempt to save money and stop deregulation. In Leon's view, the private sector was being used as a battering ram to beat down LT's costs. "We thought they were hoping that some of the staff would go to work for the private operators and then come back saying, 'It's terrible, with 13-hour days and no facilities', and hopefully the rest of the staff would take notice and be more willing to discuss cost savings within London Buses."

Peter Larking of Metrobus was also there. He knew 55 Broadway from meetings about his existing commercial services, and these were all new boys from LRT, "But Nick Newton was a pleasant, approachable guy and you could work with him." Peter felt that coach operators didn't really understand the business and took the easy approach to tendering. They either bid far too cheaply, costing it on a similar basis to a coach and driver for the day, or bid too high thinking it was easy money. He knows of one coach operator who hired a consultant to advise him on his bid but then didn't win the route and refused to pay the consultant. Len Wright saw that not many other operators followed up this new opportunity. "They all went to find out what was being said, but didn't get involved."

Nick Newton organised the meetings to encourage private operators to get involved and to explain the tendering process. "We made it clear at the seminar that we were not London Buses – we separated ourselves from them, and so we got a good response. The LRT contracts led to the development of bus leasing. It was difficult for operators to invest in new buses for 3-year contracts – they would either have to cover the cost over the three years or take a hit at the end. But having 3-year old buses available to lease freed up the market. Some operated old London Fleetlines bought from Ensign. London Buses was annoyed that the independents managed to make these buses work by taking off all the extra features that London had specified!"

Nick was always keen that he, LRT and the bus operators should all be confident with the arrangements. He wanted to work *with* them, a partnership that everyone was comfortable with, though he would take them to task if they didn't do the job properly. The 55 Broadway 'Road Show' was the first stage of this. He rejected the classic view that in tendering you should put the risk onto the bidder, because the bidder will price the risk into the bid, in which case you pay for it. He considered that the risks should be put where they are best managed, and anything that was problematic would be taken by LRT. The contract document was short, so it did not take long to go through it. As a result, all the operators understood the contract and all the bids they made were compliant – he never had a problem with non-compliant bids.

LRT would specify, monitor and audit the quality, safety and maintenance standards of the operator. The services would continue to be marketed as part of the LRT network. The LRT fare scale would apply with all Travelcards, passes, permits and other valid tickets being accepted. Operators would be required to identify their buses as operating a service on behalf of LRT.

The groundwork behind the scheme had concluded that minibuses were not suitable in London, but midibuses might well be. It was decided to start with smaller, outer routes, and to use Gross Cost Contracts (GCCs) where the revenue came to LRT and the contractor was paid for running the service to the required standard, rather than Net Cost Contracts (NCCs) where the operator kept the on-bus revenue. This was primarily because smaller operators were thought to be risk averse – they understood the cost risks, but not the revenue risks. For one tender, both GCCs and NCCs were invited, but it was thought that the operators seriously misread the revenue and this was not considered successful.

Red buses?
What colour should the buses be? The Tendered Bus Unit (TBU) initially thought that by allowing operators to use their own colour scheme they would save money by mixed use of the vehicles, but in practice most operators dedicated the buses to their London contracted services. However, it became clear that both management and staff of the tendered operators were motivated by having buses in their own livery. Peter Larking at Metrobus was proud of running his services his way, and wanted passengers to know it was his bus. Robin Orbell of Eastern National went further saying, "I don't want my buses to be red because the drivers will drive them like red bus drivers."

Nicholas Ridley was initially persuaded by LRT that all the buses should be red, but it is suggested that Margaret Thatcher said "No! One day these people will go on strike, and I want everyone to know who it is." Different coloured buses made a clear statement that LRT was changing and that private operators were now running London bus services. Different colours also helped passengers spot their bus from a distance, and Grey-Green's later operation of the 24 was visibly striking, as were the Kentish Bus Routemasters on the 19. But when some operators ran second hand vehicles in a variety of colour schemes it became messy. It is now considered that the early stages of tendering would not have worked as well if all operators had had the same livery.

The first tranche
The first 13 bus routes chosen for tender were published in October 1984, and were a broad spread of services showing varying requirements. These were the 81, 84A, 146, 152, 193, 215, 228, 258, 313, H2, P4 and W9, together with the 493 operated by London Country Bus Services (LCBS). Operators interested in bidding were required to register by the end of November.

The closing date for bids for the first tranche was in February 1985, and 18 operators showed interest in the contracts. The results were announced on 11 April. Three-year contracts were placed with five bus operators for 12 of the 13 routes. London Buses (LBL) retained six – the 84A, 152, 215, 228, 258 and H2. Two National Bus Company subsidiaries took four of the routes – London Country Bus Services took the 313 and P4 and Eastern National the 193 and W9. Two private sector companies took one route each: Len Wright Travel, trading as London Buslines, was awarded the 81, while Crystal Coaches of Orpington won the 146. A decision on route 493 was deferred pending a detailed review of the local bus network in the Orpington area.

The first routes, 81, 193, 258, 313 and W9, were taken up by their operators on 13 July. The other routes transferred on 3 August except the 146 which was a week later. The contracts were for a three-year period, and all services were to operate with 'Wayfarer' ticket machines and tachographs which would together give data on mileage operated and fares received. The ticketing equipment was supplied by LRT and the services continued the standard LRT fares and conditions.

London Buslines
Len Wright had put the bid in for route 81 and then forgotten about it – he was very busy with coach work at the time. Suddenly one evening he was shocked to get a phone call from Nick Newton telling him that he had won the contract and that they would publicise it tomorrow. Nick was giving him early warning as there was likely to be press interest.

Running buses was completely opposite to Len's existing business but gave an attractive opportunity for a regular income. He had trained with East Kent, where he had begun to specialise in coaches and tourism – this was a growing market at the beginning of the boom in incoming tourism to the UK in the late 1960s. He met John Wilson of Eastern National who then moved to Grey-Green and recruited Len to help. Len later became a driver for National Travel at Samuelson's, and while there he drove Supertramp for their British tour at the end of 1975. They then booked again for their 1976 European tour on condition that Len drove the coach. Nobody else provided what rock bands required – the right coaches and drivers who understood them. The promoters encouraged Len to set up in business himself and paid up front for three tours to get him started. So he formed Len Wright Travel to transport rock bands. Other operators saw his success and tried to compete but he kept the business – he carried virtually all the big bands and it was high-value work. His biggest contracts were for Tina Turner's summer tours in the 1980s, requiring up to six coaches travelling throughout Europe for several months.

13 July 1985 was an interesting day for Len because the route 81 contract started on the same day as the Live Aid concert at Wembley – and he was heavily involved providing transport for the bands. It was made very clear that they would not be paid for this event, but they would have backstage access to the bands and promoters. So Len attended the launch of route 81 at Hounslow bus station, went across to Wembley for networking with rock promoters, returned to Hounslow to check the 81, and returned once again to Wembley!

Len had had to be very aggressive in costing his bid. He had no idea what prices others would offer, and couldn't be sure where to pitch it. He bought second hand Fleetlines from Peter Newman at Ensign which were painted in a yellow and brown livery. These caused cultural issues for his engineers who were used to working on glamorous Volvo coaches up to three years old – suddenly they had to work on old second hand Fleetlines. The buses caused more trouble than he had expected and were not as good as they should have been. He fairly quickly bought new Leyland Lynxes to replace some of them. He did subsequently buy further second hand buses but in combination with new ones. From then on he offered two tender bids, one with old and one with new buses, and LRT increasingly accepted the bids for new buses. He had around half-a-dozen workshop staff, and he realised that he was better off keeping the workshop small and investing in new buses, rather than using older buses with larger workshops and more maintenance staff. The LBL companies already had older buses, with large garages and workshops, and so were at a disadvantage. Len also saw that coach drivers and bus drivers are very different people – you are either one or the other, they don't match.

Len thinks the private sector companies were probably over-optimistic about the on-costs in running bus services, while the LBL companies tended to be bloated with their administration and larger garages. The private companies needed to gradually increase their prices but were still able to show savings over London Buses. This was like a pendulum, where private sector bids would increase, LBL bids would

The Fleetlines caused cultural issues for his engineers who were used to working on glamorous Volvo coaches.

reduce and the pendulum would swing backwards and forwards until achieving equilibrium.

He had enough time to set up the operation as the buses were readily available – he was all ready to go on the first day. As soon as he won the contract he started to get applications from LBL drivers, many of whom did not like the influence of the trade unions and the bureaucracy of working there. "London Buses said we only got their bad drivers, but in fact we got really good ones. They were good people who wanted to work in the independent sector." These staff did not wish to join the trade union and while the TU tried to recruit drivers at London Buslines, the drivers rejected their approaches.

Len started a staff committee which he took seriously and this significantly improved relationships. It would discuss pay, general working arrangements and facilities. They never provided canteen facilities like LBL, but they provided some second hand London taxis for placing journeys and for use as informal restrooms. Drivers got to know cafes nearby and built their own relationship with them. Len felt that London Buses had generous benefits and pensions, sick benefits, and so on – he preferred to offer good competitive rates of pay and it was up to the drivers what they did with it.

Len recalls that the T&G union did stir up opposition leading to a hostile press and bad publicity. "There was a lot of propaganda against us. I had a letter from a lady in Slough who was a cleaner at Heathrow airport and had been told that the private sector bus operators would only run the profitable journeys. She needed to catch the 06.00 bus to Heathrow to get to work. She asked if I would still be running this bus, and what would happen when the driver went on holiday. I sent a suggested reply back to LT confirming that the 06.00 bus would still be running, and I asked her to let me know when she was going on holiday so that I could make sure that our driver took his holidays at the same time. LT didn't appreciate the joke and sent it back with their required changes!"

LBL staff were not helpful but they were not obstructive either. There were no significant problems with them on the road, but there was a problem of access to toilets which Len Wright's staff initially were not allowed to use. The 81 ran into the bus station at Hounslow next to the bus garage. London Buses would not let them use the toilets in the block because it was part of their office building – it also had their canteen, traffic office and conductor's room, so there was a security issue. The cost of these facilities had been included in the LBL bid, which had been lost to London Buslines because they were cheaper.

It was later arranged that contractors would be able to use the toilets, but this became more significant as tendering increased because London bus routes had traditionally been worked around the garages that they ran out of. Most routes went past the garage, or so close that you could go to the toilet, and they had the canteen for meal reliefs. As more and more routes were tendered, they were increasingly being run from places that were nowhere near the routes. Whilst most of these problems were about the use of facilities by private operators, in later years they also arose between London Buses subsidiaries who had won routes from each other.

LBL Supervisors were told not to be involved with the new operators. Steve Fennell became an LBL controller at Hounslow. "It was frustrating because there would be disruption to the service but we couldn't answer passengers' questions. The service was sometimes appalling, but I was nothing to do with it. When passengers asked me about it, I would say, 'We've been told these people can run it far more efficiently than we can.' We had no control over them on the road – this was a cheap operation, so a very 'them and us' situation arose."

John Wood recalls that they had wondered whether there would be any trouble when the first routes went over to private operators. They alerted the local police that there might be problems, but there weren't. John was out of the country when the first routes started. He was flying back into Heathrow when he saw a yellow and brown bus on the 81 and thought, "That's one of ours!"

Eastern National
Eastern National also commenced operation of routes W9 and 193 on 13 July. Malcolm Wren had joined the TBU and had a particular interest in the W9. "Some time before, I had been asked by David Quarmby to produce a list of the 30 best performing and the 30 worst performing routes based on the QSI (Quality of Service Information) data. Right at the bottom of the list was the W9. I went and took a ride on it and it was not good. It was a very unreliable half hourly service with some Bristol LH buses which were pretty unpleasant to travel in. When it was tendered, Eastern National took the route over and I was on the pavement on the first day, hoping that it would work properly – it ran like a dream and revenue increased significantly! It was the day of the Live Aid concert, and I listened to it on the car radio going home." These first routes worked well enough to give confidence that tendering was a good idea.

Robin Orbell was Traffic Manager of Eastern National (EN). He had started his career with the National Bus Company (NBC) and had experience at Bristol Omnibus and West Yorkshire Road Car, including operating services under contract to West

Yorkshire PTE. "We won these two routes in the first tenders. Enfield employed about 11 new drivers and vehicles were parked in the Borough Council yard, working as an outstation of Brentwood. The operation was 100% unionised, and some drivers may have worked for LT, but maybe they were individuals who worked better in a small company. The buses had three steps into the saloon, a mountaineering job, but the bus interiors were more luxurious and the passengers would jokingly ask for 'A single to Clacton'! Drivers fuelled up at the local Esso garage with a company charge card. The garage was giving away glasses with each two gallons of fuel, and the drivers were collecting these to sell at the local car boot sale. The Finance Director was annoyed by this and insisted that the glasses were his. But I took the view that it was a useful perk for the drivers.

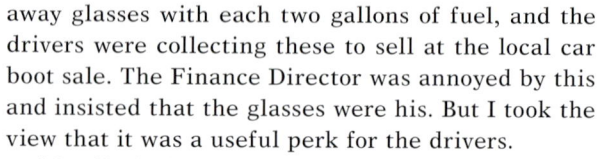

"Geoff Clarkson, the MD, had put in the bids for these services without telling anybody. The first that I knew was when I was told that the routes had been won, and 'Now get it organised!' He was a typical old Tilling MD who worked on the basis that if he didn't tell anybody anything, there wouldn't be any problems."

Above Eastern National provided the W9 with six Wadham-Stringer bodied Bedford single-deckers of eight they had in their fleet. They were in ENOC's striking green and yellow livery with LT roundels. The W9 ran from Muswell Hill to Southgate and Enfield, via Enfield hospital. (Keith Wood)

Opposite top Crystal Coaches of Orpington, the second private sector operator, commenced operation of route 146 on 10 August 1985 using a variety of minibuses. This 29-seat Leyland Cub was used initially with a destination slip board in the windscreen, and is seen at the Downe terminus. (Michael Steward)

Eastern National also took over route 193 between Romford and Hornchurch, using two Bristol VRTs with LT roundels added to their standard livery. They worked from Brentwood garage with dedicated drivers. Detailed destination information was provided at the front and, in the absence of a rear route number blind, a route number was riveted to the rear. 3080 is overtaken by LBL's T36 in Hornchurch High Street. (Colin Fradd)

"The MD had put in the bids for these services without telling anybody. The first that I knew was when I was told that the routes had been won, and 'Now get it organised!'"

Further tenders
While the routes in the first tranche commenced operation, three more tranches were published for tender in the early summer of 1985. The second tranche had 12 routes around London: the 79A, 125, 127, 127A, 145, 145A, 179, 195, 200, 268, 275, 283, chosen on a similar basis to the first tranche.

The third tranche of routes included many of those crossing the Greater London boundary into the counties of Essex, Hertfordshire and Surrey, tendered in association with the County Councils who took responsibility for routes entirely in their areas. On the boundary into Essex, LRT offered for tender the 20, 167, 179A, 206 and 217B, while the County Council invited tenders for the 201, 250 and 251 together with some peak hour and school journeys. Some of these routes were significantly altered for tendering to achieve improvements and economies. On the boundary with Hertfordshire, LRT sought tenders for routes 107, 107A, 142, 259A, 263 and 298. Hertfordshire County Council sought tenders for the 242 and local services in Potters Bar, along with some London Country services. Similar arrangements applied on the boundary with Surrey, with LRT tendering the 116, 116A, 117, 197, 197A, 197B, 203, 293 and 403.

The fourth tranche, published in July 1985, was for a major new network proposed for Orpington with the use of 'exciting smaller buses at improved frequencies on a network of local services based on the High Street.' At first it was proposed to shorten or split the existing long-distance routes through Orpington, but after public consultation these links were retained. The new network was proposed to be introduced from May 1986.

LBL's response
LBL was hit hard by the first tender results and had to respond quickly. At first, bids were put together centrally and could not be marginally costed as this would result in 'grant leakage'. LBL received a 'block grant' from government for running the London bus network, and it would have been inappropriate for the facilities that this paid for to be used for tendered routes without charge, as this would have subsidised those tender bids in competition with private operators who did not receive government funds. So LBL could not bid just the additional cost of a bus and driver for a tendered route, there had also to be a share of the garage costs and overheads. But allocating a proportion of those costs to tender bids made them uncompetitive.

Potters Bar
Leaside faced a serious challenge for its out-county routes into Hertfordshire in the third tranche of tenders. Potters Bar, like Loughton, was located outside the London boundary and could not continue unless it was shown to be covering its full costs. There was also concern about Leaside's engineering performance and Marcus Smith, the General Manager

41   Allocating a proportion of overhead costs to LBL's bids made them uncompetitive.

Buses, took a tough line, changing the Leaside management team overnight. Ken Blacker was brought in as the new District General Manager and Willie Arrol replaced the District Engineering Manager. Ken worked on the Potters Bar proposals with David Sayburn who remained as District Operations Manager.

To reduce operating costs, Ken Blacker had to introduce new, lower, wages and greater flexibility in the schedules. The proposed tender bids were reworked to make them viable. David Sayburn recalls, "When the new terms and conditions were put to the trade union, the T&G refused to do anything about it – it was so different that they washed their hands of it. So the management went ahead and the union then found that it had happened. As a result, there were no industrial relations problems. The staff were very annoyed with the union and felt they had let them down. I remember an open meeting with staff, Ken Blacker and me on the top of an RT bus outside the garage, at which we explained the new contracts and the redundancy on offer. The Leaside trade union representative turned up and the staff bluntly told him to go away because they felt let down by the union. They just wanted to know in detail the pay deal on offer and the redundancy terms. As a result, within a year 90% of them took the LT redundancy payments and left. From that low point, Potters Bar grew and continued and has been a great success. The T&G didn't know how to react to the threat of tendering – whether to accept the worsened terms and conditions, or lose the work. This was the great problem."

The pay deal was still not enough to reduce Potters Bar's costs sufficiently and further economies had to be sought. Ken Blacker takes up the story. "I looked at vehicle depreciation costs which seemed to be higher than the operation could stand, and ascertained that, if good quality second hand vehicles could be obtained at favourable prices, these costs could be considerably reduced. Following deregulation, there was a glut of double deckers on the second hand market at very favourable prices, and the acquisition of some of these seemed to offer a way forward for Potters Bar. My ideal acquisition would have been Metrobuses, which were reliable and were vehicles with which we were thoroughly conversant, but none of these was immediately available, so after talking the matter over with Willie Arrol I decided to investigate the purchase of second hand Volvo Ailsas. To start with, London Buses had three of its own as a result of the Alternative Vehicle Evaluation (AVE) trials, which tested a number of new types of bus in London service. We took these three Volvo Ailsas for operation at Potters Bar in order to gain experience of the type. Two of them were put into service almost immediately but the third, V3, had a dual staircase and rear entrance layout and was unsuitable for one man operation as it stood. Its entry into service had to wait until we could find time and manpower to remove the rear doorway and fill in the step well."

"The two Volvo Ailsas ran well, and being aware that the Ensign dealership had others of this type available for sale, an approach was made to them. At the time we were required to cover any purchase price through the sale of surplus vehicles, so a deal was done to obtain nine Volvo Ailsas formerly with South Yorkshire Transport in exchange for twelve redundant Leyland Nationals. In my view we had done a good deal, especially as Nationals were not a particularly popular vehicle on the second hand market and some dealers would not touch them. The nine Volvos were older than our own ones and had SCG rather than Voith transmissions and older type back axles, but I thought this would be a risk worth taking. Their Irish-built Van Hool McArdle bodies were of an obsolete type, but Ensign's Peter Newman removed panelling from a random vehicle to reveal its method of construction and the satisfactory state of its body framework. With the opportunity of saving £32,650 per annum in Potters Bar's revenue costs the buses were worth having, and when the sale of two more Nationals to Dodds of Troon (Willie Arrol's home town) became possible at a very good price, sufficient funds were released to increase the number of SYT Volvo Ailsas by three to 12. In the end, Ensign could only produce two more but a third was obtained at a bargain basement price direct from South Yorkshire and we got another one to break up at Potters Bar for spares. Overhauled and repainted in our livery by Ensign, V4-15 duly began work at Potters Bar, releasing standard Metrobuses which were urgently needed elsewhere in Leaside to avoid having to use Nationals on double deck services."

Orpington

Changing the conditions of existing staff was extremely difficult and thinking moved to setting up new operations. Norman Cohen, then LBL's Operations Director, discussed the possible responses. "Marcus Smith said, 'We are going to set up some low-cost, wholly owned subsidiaries, to show how costs can really be driven down!'

"The Orpington network presented a suitable challenge and an opportunity. Peter Hendy and Bob Muir, who were based in LBL's Head Office, and Bryan Constable, who was brought back from Aldenham to Selkent, were tasked to put together 'an innovative commercially aggressive bid' for a wholly new operation for the Orpington tenders, and that's how Roundabout came about. Peter and Bob planned the schedules and, with Bryan doing the engineering calculations, put the bid together. When they won the tenders, they set up the Roundabout operation and recruited the staff.

Peter Hendy talked unofficially to the Trade Union Officer, the London Bus Committee member for Selkent, about the proposed wage rates. "We told him what wages we were going to offer and he realised that, though the TU could not accept them, they were ok for the area – he 'turned a blind eye.' I found the two industrial units in St Mary Cray, got planning permissions and leased them."

Norman Cohen and Bryan Gilbert (the Personnel Officer Bus Operations) were keeping an eye on progress. "We were actually tasked to more or less make sure that the job was done. But we were told off in no uncertain terms when we got too involved – we were instructed to keep out, and we did. Fine, it worked, and it carried on working well for a long time."

Initially named 'Rising Star Buses', in the actual bid the proposed fleet of 25 Mercedes 609s would be painted in a livery of 'chocolate and custard' based on the Great Western Railway colour scheme. The team set themselves the task of reducing gross costs per mile by at least 25% and managed 34% with estimates that proved achievable in practice. It was an innovative and commercially aggressive bid for the Orpington midibus network.

Westlink
Westlink was an initiative in Cardinal District. Norman Cohen continues, "Marcus Smith was even more keen on Westlink because Jeff Chamberlain, who was given the job of setting it up and running it, had ideas which suited Marcus down to the ground. They were going to be extremely low-cost, they were going to use premises on an industrial site, there were going to be second hand buses, the wages were going to be more similar to the wage rates in the adjoining counties."

Martin Whitley was Cardinal District Operating Manager and had gone to watch the first of Len Wright's buses go into service on the 81. This brought home to him what was happening and he talked to Tony Parsons, the District General Manager, about the situation. Martin wrote several pages suggesting what their response should be – it was handwritten because he didn't want anybody else to read it, and anyway he couldn't type! For the sake of a name, Martin called it "Wolsey Bus" – the other bit of Cardinal. They took this proposal to Marcus Smith, and Stanwell Buses was set up under the name of Westlink. Both Tony Parsons and Martin Whitley pushed for Jeff Chamberlain to be in charge of the new operation.

Jeff describes a meeting of middle and senior London Buses managers at the Connaught Rooms when Marcus Smith lambasted them. "Marcus was giving people a lot of stick, but I had a lot of confidence in those days and I would 'talk above my grade', so I felt able to put my head above the parapet. He was criticising LBL managers as being inefficient and unable to run buses and so on. But Len Wright and others were winning tenders by pricing them at marginal cost, and then realising that they had the engineering costings wrong. They were running DMSs which suffered far more wear and tear than the coaches they were used to running.

"When Marcus asked if there were any questions, I stood up and said, 'You're wrong to criticise us. We are the finest bus operators in the world. We have London Transport International giving top quality advice worldwide because of the quality of our operations. You've got some great managers, and you shouldn't criticise them. If you give me a level playing field, on an open site, I will win the tenders.' And that's what happened!"

Jeff had previously been seconded to the GLC to work with Dave Wetzel, who he had known from his teens when they had been in the Young Socialists together. He had then come back to LT and been promoted to Area Traffic Manager. He was called up to see Tony Parsons who said, "You must have made an impression at that meeting. I thought you were being suicidal. I've been told to talk to you. I will cover you in your ATM job for three months so that you can come and write up a prospectus for the next round of tenders." Gary Filbey joined Jeff as engineer. He was District Engineering Assistant at Cardinal when Tony Parsons asked him, "Do you want to start a bus company?" And he never looked back.

They were given free rein to put the proposal together. Jeff points out, "The one single big factor in the LBL costings that you had to get away from was the guaranteed and maximum 7 hour 36 minute day. As a driver, you never worked for 7 hours 36 minutes. You could not be scheduled for longer than this and there was no mixing of routes, and so if the route you were on resulted in six hours work, then you were paid the additional time for doing nothing. So every LT bus driver was getting money for nothing." To avoid this, he included in his pay package a requirement for compulsory overtime.

They needed to find a green field site for the new operation. They were bidding for the 116, 117 and 203 and wanted a depot at the Surrey end. He found one in Stanwell Moor Road, which is why the company was called Stanwell Buses. It was cheap and would take 50 buses, but Marcus Smith came to see the site and said, "You're not having that – it's too luxurious!" So they found a site on Green Lane, in Pulborough Way, an area Jeff knew from his childhood. It was midway along the route which led to live changeovers for which he originally had three old cars, but then replaced these with some London taxis which were cheap, reliable and diesel.

Jeff believes that tendering was not about getting London Buses ready for privatisation. "It was the Government's way of trying to slap LT around a bit. Margaret Thatcher had tackled the GLC and had won the conflict with Ken Livingstone, and now they wanted to bring in competition, but they were not then ready to split everything up." He put in the bid, and waited.

Second tranche results
The results of the second round of tenders, announced in December 1985, were even worse for LBL than the first round. Of the eleven routes, three were retained by London Buses, two were taken by London Country, two by Eastern National, and one route each to Len Wright Travel, Ensign, London Cityrama, and Scancoaches.

So while London Buses was winning some routes, overall they could only lose as they had been operating all the routes before tendering – winning some of them was little compensation when they had previously worked them all. London Buses managers talked of "Death by a thousand cuts" and were being forced to respond. But it would take time to adjust the London Buses operation to be able to compete effectively, in particular drastically cutting staff numbers and overhead costs of the traditional operation.

But performance of London Buses' own services continued to decline in 1985 as the organisation worked to reduce costs. Critical comments in the local press became a regular feature and London Buses was forced to admit that rescheduling services to other garages, and staff shortages following significant redundancies, had had an adverse effect. Continuing conversions to driver-only operation were not received well by the travelling public, and rescheduling some services with lower frequencies, in order to achieve economies, was leading to a lack of capacity in some places.

The 1985 Act
The 1985 Transport Act received Royal Assent on 30 October 1985 and gave the Minister powers to deregulate bus services throughout the country, including in London, but Nicholas Ridley stated that "the benefits of deregulation for London were at least two years away." LRT had been temporarily excluded from deregulation since, he said, it needed "a period of convalescence" after the "debilitating effects of GLC stewardship." This "convalescence" required small real fare increases and a major cost-cutting exercise both through economies and by contracting out services, which would also substantially reduce revenue support.

The Act was highly controversial and received considerable criticism, for example from Lord Shepherd, the outgoing NBC chairman, who considered the proposals as "quite inexplicable" and that they would lead to the collapse of rural services. One commentator described it as "Political dogma thinly dressed up in contentious professional logic." (*Surveyor magazine 2/8/84*)

The three new LRT subsidiary companies had taken effect from 1 April 1985 as London Buses Ltd (LBL), London Underground Ltd (LUL) and Bus Engineering Ltd (BEL). London Transport International, the consultancy arm of LT, already existed making four LRT subsidiaries in all. The Tendered Bus Unit (TBU) was within LRT, entirely separate from LBL.

BEL was to provide engineering and overhaul facilities for London Buses, but also for other customers. It took over the Aldenham and Chiswick works but the new arrangements at Aldenham, split into four modular units the previous year, did not last long. London Buses announced on 15 November that from the following year it would perform most overhaul work currently done at Aldenham, requiring an extra 100 maintenance staff at its garages in place of 300 jobs at Aldenham.

Scancoaches took over route 283 from 31 May 1986 using five Scania K92 single-deckers with Jonckheere bodies bought for the operation. These impressive vehicles were well received by passengers though the black on white destination blinds were said to be hard to read. Scancoaches was owned by a Finnish travel agency which had hotels in London and Paris and started a coach operation to transport in-coming Scandinavian tourists. They then tendered for London bus routes to supplement the coaching side of the business. Their operation of route 283 was launched by the Finnish ambassador and the buses advertised Finnish goods and services! (Colin Fradd)

"Tendering was the Government's way of trying to slap LT around a bit."

LBL in 1986

London Buses entered 1986 continuing its economy drive by decentralising further functions to the Districts. Scheduling, service development, recruitment, staff training and premises maintenance were moved, while further administrative offices were closed saving 200 jobs. The driving school at Chiswick works closed and conductor training moved to Abbey District, which had the greatest concentration of conductors. Conversions to one-person operation continued, and four garages, Bexleyheath, Elmers End, Hornchurch and Loughton, were planned for closure.

LBL proposed a new pay agreement for platform staff with termination of the existing agreement. This New Operating Agreement (NOA) abolished many of the unhelpful and costly working practices and gave greater flexibility on the road. It included a proposal to stop paying London weighting at outer London garages, which were at greater risk of competition from operators in the neighbouring counties. This was a defining change in the platform staff agreement and led to strike action during the year. The proposed new wage structure would be based on three zones, increased time at work on the road, a change to 100% driver only operation on Sundays, new conditions for minibus drivers, and the withdrawal of the commitment to provide canteens. Staff had already been warned of reduced severance payments to those displaced by tendering losses. The Transport and General Workers' Union called an all-out indefinite strike but deferred this whilst talks with management continued. They objected strongly to the proposals, but NOA was implemented.

However, strikes took place at some garages due to the introduction of agency staff in the canteens in place of LT catering staff. This culminated in a boycott of canteens and widespread strike action in north-west London. There were also disputes with maintenance staff who worked to rule over modifications to Metrobus and Titan buses being defined as normal, rather than 'unscheduled' work, which as a result would not bring additional payments. However, the real problem was over the annual pay round, and this led to shortages of buses until it was resolved later in the year.

In July, the LRT board decided to close Aldenham Works, and this was completed in November. The level of work required by London Buses had declined more rapidly than had been expected causing a loss of around £5 million per year. BEL stated that consolidating its activities on the single site at Chiswick would enable them 'to provide a complete range of engineering and coachbuilding skills with a minimum of overheads'. The GLC had retained Aldenham in 1973 and 1983 against the advice of LT managements at those times, but the GLC itself had finally closed down in April. £10 million had been allocated to Chiswick Works for investment in engineering activities.

A new Commercial Operations Unit was created by LBL in January 1986 as a separate profit centre for services other than bus routes. It included tours, charters and private hire work which had previously been carried out with other operators, but it was decided to bring the work in-house where possible. The operation took the name London Coaches and was based at the former Battersea bus garage, which had closed in November 1985. Battersea quickly developed a reputation for flexible working, with drivers cleaning out their buses at the end of the day, and engineers carrying out a wide variety of work. The Round London Sightseeing Tour, which had been faced with growing competition from other tour operators, was relaunched in March as the Official London Transport Sightseeing Tour.

A London to Birmingham coach service was also launched in March jointly with the West Midlands Passenger Transport Executive, and then a service to Eastbourne, jointly with Eastbourne Coaches, two months later. However, these were not successful and London Coaches withdrew from them in March 1987. West Midlands Travel continued to operate a reduced version of the Birmingham service but the Eastbourne service ceased.

The relaunched Official London Transport Sightseeing Tour used 50 Routemasters which were refurbished at Aldenham and painted into traditional London Transport livery. Twenty of these were converted to open-top, and RM752 crosses Trafalgar Square. Since 1984, buses on the tour had had side advertisements announcing that 'This is an Official London Sightseeing Bus' but now, after complaints from competitors who considered their tours to be equally official, it was renamed 'The Original London Transport Sightseeing Tour' – which indeed it was! (David Cole)

45 Aldenham works closed in November 1986 with its activities consolidated into Chiswick.

In its Annual Report for 1985/6, LRT reported buoyant passenger business, lower unit costs, and increased Underground services but reduced bus mileage. Financial support for day-to-day operations totalled £97 million compared with a budget of £135 million, so that LRT was close to achieving the target set by the Secretary of State to reduce revenue support to £95 million by 1987/8. LBL had reduced its loss before grants from £185 million in 1984/5 to £140 million. Unit costs per bus fell by 4.6% in real terms while the average passenger load per bus increased by 1.9%. The percentage of scheduled mileage that was operated fell from 94.3% in 1984/5 to 93.7% due to worsening traffic congestion and staff absenteeism, while passenger journeys also declined. By the end of the year driver-only operation had increased to 67% but passenger boarding times had reduced due to the growth of off-bus ticket sales – 60% of bus passengers in the morning peak now had a period ticket.

During 1985/6, 56 bus routes had been put out to tender of which London Buses won 26, NBC companies 22 and private operators eight. The report considered this to be 'one of the most radical changes in the provision of London's bus services for many years'.

LRT's annual Business Plan for 1986/87 aimed to build on these achievements. The key policies were:

1. Total bus mileage to be broadly at the present level with better supervision and more realistic scheduling. There would be further service changes to match demand and driver only operation was expected to rise to 74%. A new experimental bus ticketing system would be introduced with the aim of improving passenger boarding times, given that 55% of bus journeys were then made by pass holders.
2. New buses to include features making them more convenient and attractive to passengers, including clearer internal signs and improved route diagrams.
3. More bus routes to be offered for competitive tender.

In 1986, two new commercial coach services known as the London Liner were launched by London Coaches, between London and Birmingham jointly with the West Midlands Passenger Transport Executive, and between London and Eastbourne jointly with Eastbourne Borough Transport. The Birmingham service was launched in March and ran every two hours, using MCW Metroliner double-decker coaches once these had arrived. One of the Metroliners is seen in Colmore Row, Birmingham, with Paris as destination, and passing a West Midlands Travel Ailsa double-decker which would shortly join the London Buses fleet. (David Cole)

46 In 1985/6, 56 routes were put out to tender, of which LB won 26, NBC companies 22 and private operators eight.

Chiswick training school was opened by the LGOC in 1925 but closed in 1986 as its functions were devolved to the Bus Districts, to which the instructors were moved. The famous skid pan closed with it. It had not been without incidents – Bryan Gilbert remembers "Neville Lobley, the Training School Manager, phoned me up one afternoon and said, 'We've just had the skid bus hit the wall of the toilets.' There were chips in those walls. So this bus had hit the wall and cracked it all the way up. I thought some poor bloke, going for a quiet sit down, when a bus smacks into the wall!" Not for the faint-hearted, RM1740 gives demonstration rides at the Chiswick Open Day in August 1984. (David Cole)

4. Further measures to improve facilities for people with disabilities. LRT was to become responsible for the funding of Dial-a-Ride services.
5. Mileage on the Underground to rise by a further 3% with a continuation of the station modernisation programme.
6. Staff to be reduced by a further 4%.
7. Further reductions in unit costs and revenue support to meet government targets. Substantial reductions in revenue support had already been achieved thereby making it possible to increase capital expenditure by around 20% in 1986/87.

The Chairman said that he was confident that more people would be travelling and they would be giving better value for money to the community at large – fare payers, taxpayers, and ratepayers.

On 21 May 1986 Nicholas Ridley moved from Transport to become Secretary of State for the Environment and John Moore became Secretary of State for Transport.

Cityrama

On 22 March 1986 route 200 was taken over by Cityrama, which was associated with the Limebourne sightseeing business. Huw Barrington joined the company in 1985 when they had decided to bid for LRT contracts. Huw describes this as the cheap and cheerful era of bus tendering. "No one would buy new vehicles for three-year contracts when there was no certainty of those contracts being extended. They would certainly not invest in a new £70,000 bus for such a short period. So we went to Peter Newman at Ensign, and we couldn't believe what he had in a field (DMSs)! However, they were all overhauled and acceptable."

Cityrama had sightseeing work but needed more activity in the winter. "We won route 200 and set up the operation – a tough learning curve for everyone. This was at the beginning of tendering and it was a great time to get in. We had no preconceived ideas. Clearly, LT were picking the problem routes to tender,

Cityrama purchased eleven former LT DM/DMS double deckers from Ensign for route 200 which were repainted blue and operated from their depot in Battersea. The route had previously turned in Brixton garage, and as this was not possible for Cityrama it was extended to Streatham Hill. The frequency of the service was generally increased. No 73, formerly DM 1773, is seen at Mitcham Cricketers on Cityrama's first day, 22 March 1986. (Keith Wood)

"No one would buy new vehicles for three-year contracts when there was no certainty of those contracts being extended."

and the private operators wanted to prove that they were a better proposition running them. Of course, part of the aim was also to bash the union into a bit more reality!"

When they got the contract, relations with TBU were good and there were no problems running the buses at first. They were N-registration DMSs. However, they didn't realise what was going to be involved in the London stage-carriage environment. By the third year the buses were becoming unreliable, and Huw's Managing Director didn't like being dictated to by LT. "Sightseeing is seasonal work and Nick Newton got fed up with playing the numbers game. In the summer, the sightseeing buses got all the attention, and in winter attention went to getting the service buses on the road," says Huw. They worked hard to show commitment when the contract was coming up for renewal and when they bid for another contract. Their second win was the 196 from Brixton to Norwood Junction, which started in February 1987.

At first everything went ok. Their operation of the scheduled service was up, there was no problem in getting staff, and they were reliable staff at the wages they had budgeted. Some drivers came from the red buses, and they also started their own training school for the second contract. Some drivers seem to have followed Huw around from company to company. Cityrama had an associated company, Pegasus Holidays, which ran Caribbean holidays. The 196 ran through Brixton, so they put leaflets on the buses, and painted one of the vehicles in an all-over advertisement – TfL wanted the advertising revenue for this, but there was none because it was a paper financial transfer with an associated company.

Huw is clear: "You can't knock Nick Newton and John Wood – you couldn't have had better support in the early stages, they were very encouraging. Nick Newton managed fairly but firmly – he 'took no prisoners'." However, like Len Wright, they had no idea whether this work was going to continue or whether it was a one-off, just to make London Buses get into shape.

After two to three years their problem was the maintenance of vehicles that really were worn out. They could keep them on the road at first, but it became increasingly difficult. They kept on the right side of the law, which was essential as Huw held the Certificate of Professional Competence (CPC) for the company, but it was costing them more to keep the buses on the road than they were getting for the job.

Route 196 was initially awarded to London Country South East who withdrew due to the closure of their Catford garage, which left them with insufficient capacity. It was then awarded to Cityrama who purchased eleven former South Yorkshire PTE Fleetlines from Ensign. Nine of these had ECW bodies while two were similar to the London DMSs, including No 22 at Norwood Junction with its advert for Pegasus Holidays. (Keith Wood)

"You couldn't have had better support in the early stages. TBU were very encouraging."

Cityrama 82, a former South Yorkshire PTE Fleetline with ECW body, in Norwood High Street with the background colours for its Pegasus Holidays advert already applied. (Keith Wood)

Cityrama suffered severe problems with its Fleetlines and bought two new Leyland Olympians with Optare bodies in 1988 to improve reliability on routes 196 and 200. However, continuing vehicle problems led to them surrendering route 200 in December 1988 and the 196 in October 1989. (Keith Wood)

For the 196, they bought some South Yorkshire Fleetlines from Ensign. These were better than the DMSs and did the trick. But again, as the contract went on, it cost more to maintain them than they were being paid. They then bought two brand-new E-registration Optare double-deckers, which was their commitment to route 196. "Unless you improved your performance, you were unlikely to have the contract renewed – you had to show commitment."

These were a token few new vehicles for Cityrama, but reliability was still not good enough and they were told by TBU that improved performance was needed. Eventually they came to a meeting when Nick Newton said, "You're not doing enough!" They decided that they preferred to give the routes back – they wanted to get out with as little damage as possible, and a few days later they received a letter giving the dates that the routes would be taken off them. The brand new Optare double-deckers were cascaded into sightseeing work.

LBL fights back
The results of the third tranche of LRT routes were announced in February and March 1986. On the boundary with Essex, three services were awarded to Eastern National, one to London Buses, and one to Sampson's. On the Hertfordshire boundary, London Buses, London Country and Eastern National each secured two services. On the boundary with Surrey, London Buses secured four services and London Country five. London Buses also secured two services tendered by Hertfordshire County Council, the 84 and 242 whilst other out County routes were won by West's Coaches, Cullinan Coaches, Sampson's, North Mymms Coaches and Eastern National.

This was the beginning of LBL's fight back. Potters Bar kept the 242 and 263, and won back the 84, so it remained open, starting the new contracts in May and June. Winning the Surrey routes led to the creation of Westlink. These were successes for London Buses, but also for the smaller operators now brought into the system. But Loughton lost almost all its work and was to be closed.

The results for the Orpington network, the fourth tranche, were announced during April with 10 routes being awarded to London Buses, two to London Country and one to Metrobus. London Buses set up the new Roundabout midibus operation. Crystals Coaches, a local operator familiar with small vehicles and already running the 146 for LRT, were not successful in these tenders. Three London Country routes (431, 432 and 471) were withdrawn, the award of the 51 compensating for this loss. Metrobus – who had a good record on the 353/357 – were rewarded

Loughton garage could not compete with the low costs of other Essex operators and lost all but one of its routes on tender. Forest District had converted the garage to a single vehicle type, the Leyland National, in order to reduce costs. The District General Manager, Ron Brewer, achieved fame when he was reported saying that he "had converted Loughton to single-deckers in order to bring down garage overheads", a statement that reached Punch magazine and now appears in dictionaries of quotations. The garage closed after service on 23 May 1986 and the remaining route was transferred to Leyton. LS267 is at Woodford returning from Walthamstow to Loughton earlier in May. (Roger Torode)

Sampson's Coaches of Broxbourne commenced operation of routes 217B, 250 and 251 on 24 May 1986, using Leyland Nationals and former London Transport DMS Fleetlines. These initially looked very smart in an attractive blue and red livery, and one of each is seen in Loughton on their first day. (John Parkin)

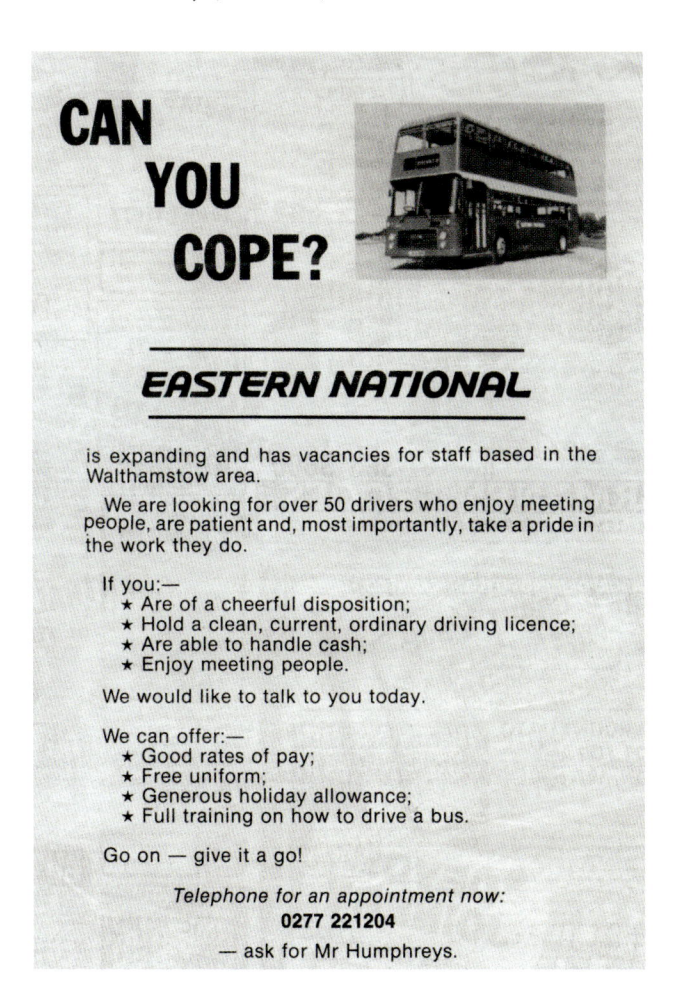

with the contract for the 61. All three operators had other routes in the network which continued without tendering.

The services on the Essex borders from the second and third tranches of tenders changed hands on 24 May 1986. London Buses closed Loughton Garage after 23 May, despite the attempts of the District and operating staff to streamline their operations. LBL retained only the 179 and 179A, which were now operated from Leyton. Route 201, now managed by Essex County Council, was taken over by West's Coaches using second hand Leyland Nationals. Sampson's Coaches took over the 250 and 251 for Essex County Council and the 217B for LRT. Sampson's ran a number of businesses including coaches, an MoT testing centre and a zoo at Broxbourne.

Eastern National at Walthamstow
Eastern National's W9 and 193 operated well and gave them credibility with LRT. As a result, they were encouraged to apply for other routes in north east London. They therefore bid for the 20, 275, 206, 307 and 379. But while they had been given eight months to set up for those first two routes, this time they were called to a meeting with Nick Newton to be told that they had won the contracts and that they had to be in in 13 weeks. This was because the day before, all staff at Loughton garage had been given three months notice as they had lost the contracts.

51 "Unless you improved your performance, you were unlikely to have the contract renewed."

Two depots were now needed, at Walthamstow and Ponders End, together with 15 Leyland Nationals and 40 Bristol VRs. They had to find these buses in a hurry and there was no second hand market for such vehicles at the time. Fortunately United Counties had spare buses, recently carried out service cuts and kept the vehicles ready for deregulation, and so these were taken on a mid-term hire for Walthamstow. Robin Orbell asked Nick Newton for more time with the result that Walthamstow was to be opened in three months as LRT required, because the vehicles were now available, but a later date would be agreed for the two routes at Ponders End; this became January 1987.

Eastern National agreed with the London Borough of Waltham Forest to make use of the council yard in Walthamstow. The Conservative controlled council said that they liked tendering and that EN could use the Council facilities, sharing the undercover maintenance area and canteen, and an office would be made available to them. In May, the council changed to Labour control, and they were then told that they could park in the yard, nothing more. As a result they put two Portakabins in their parking area. The insurance company insisted that the safe should be on solid ground, so they had to make a hole in the floor and build foundations for the night safe.

Walthamstow needed 75 drivers. They were able to recruit around 20 who had been made redundant at Loughton, though these had to finish at Loughton at midnight the night before and be ready for the start of service at 04.00 on the Saturday morning. They also had to train the new recruits, and their training school was dedicated to this task beforehand. There were recruitment difficulties, and they started off with around 45 drivers, 30 short of requirement.

On the first day, they had a perfect run out using the 45 drivers. Robin travelled with one who had been union representative at Loughton on his first journey in a Bristol VR on the 20. The driver sat in the cab and said, "How do I drive this?" He knew route 20, while Robin knew the VR bus, so they worked the journey together. While Loughton drivers were used to fully automatic Leyland Nationals, the EN vehicles were semi automatic. Their licences covered them for these, however, and they soon became familiar with them.

Robin recalls the cramped conditions in the two Portakabins, with a kettle next to the drivers' paying-in line. He set about making tea, queuing with the drivers until he reached the kettle. Drivers asked who he was, wearing a suit, and were surprised to find that he was Traffic Manager, not just for that garage, but for the whole company. They found it hard to believe that he was talking to them and making them tea – not something they were used to.

The local manager at Walthamstow told Robin that the operation was running perfectly, which it had been at the start of the first day. On the Wednesday of the first week he was called into a meeting with Nick Newton at Oxford Circus. The local manager should have travelled on the same train to give him an update on how things were going, but for some reason he got a different one. Robin then discovered that the 45 drivers at Walthamstow included the ex-Loughton drivers, whilst he had understood they were in addition, and that only 50% of the service had run on the Tuesday. He had to eat humble pie with Nick Newton, who wanted a report within a week.

Robin took over Walthamstow himself and the manager left after a few days. Robin had learned from experience that when there are problems it is better to tell people which buses will not run, and a leaflet was produced jointly with LRT showing which were at risk. The leaflet was signed by LRT's Director of Planning, David Bayliss, and Robin as Eastern National's Traffic Manager. This led to significant

Left and above right Routes 20 and 275 were mainly operated by Bristol VRTs with the occasional Leyland National. The 167 and 206 were only operated by Leyland Nationals. All carried the new Citybus livery of dark green and yellow with the slogan 'Citybus – Running in London for London Regional Transport'. The rear route numbers were carried on metal plates. VRT 3116 is seen at Walthamstow Central, while Leyland Nationals on the 20 and 167 are at Loughton station. (Both pictures, Keith Wood)

criticism in the local press as Eastern National had failed to get its act together in time. By prioritising recruitment he was able to take on more drivers – there were plenty available in London. He also brought in staff from other depots, and drivers throughout the company were working six days to cover the work.

Eastern National did not receive much criticism at Walthamstow even though they had taken over routes from Loughton and Potters Bar, which were good London operations. People knew that buses could be unreliable, for example due to blockages on the North Circular Road. EN had been able to solve the problem by bussing drivers in. They used the new Bristol VRs, and found that provincial buses were satisfactory on these suburban London routes. The engineers had to gear up for more intensive operation, but they soon got on top of this.

The operation then worked reasonably well. Robin was not used to variable running times, which were common in London. Nick Newton had said that he could not see anything in the tender for roadside supervisors. Robin replied, "No, the timetable should be robust enough," and suggested that roadside supervisors try to demonstrate their worth by making decisions – by turning buses. He did not want buses turned and so he did not employ supervisors.

Robin liked that TBU told them the times of the first and last buses, and the frequency during different periods of the day. In other words, he was to provide the robust timetable. He did not like being given a timetable that wasn't achievable. From time to time, LRT came to get his advice on making the timetable more robust. The TBU had roadside spotters, so Robin introduced running numbers and had to check to be sure that his Controllers gave the right reason for performance. For example, it might be better to accept that one trip was missing, rather than report that all trips were running late.

Comparing London with elsewhere, Robin says that London is like other places except in the variable running times at different times of day, and that network design is far more complex in London as there are so many local centres. The other difference in London is the number of demonstrations, Royal parades and so on, which disrupt traffic.

After their Walthamstow experience, Eastern National held off seeking new tenders for a time and got Ponders End running in January 1987. This was from a warehouse at Enfield Lock, which operated like a normal bus depot. At first they needed to use some Brentwood drivers, which resulted in a Bristol VR staggering around the M25 to deliver the drivers each day.

Relations with London Buses were awkward. Robin's staff were not allowed to use the facilities at Muswell Hill for the W9, though London Underground allowed them to use their canteen at Leytonstone. There was no brotherly love between drivers at the different companies even though they were all unionised.

For the tender, they had bid their operating costs using their own pay rates with a slight uplift, no supervisors, good vehicle management, plus fuel and cheap premises. Later on, Nick Newton showed him around Hornchurch garage and suggested he might like to lease it, but the canteen was bigger than many of his garages, and he did not want the expense.

Robin felt that LRT wanted to give the red buses a bloody nose. He was rewarded for getting things

53 "The driver sat in the cab and said, 'How do I drive this?' He knew route 20, while I knew the VR bus, so we worked the journey together."

An apology

We're sorry – but please don't blame the driver!

We do apologise for the poor service you may have experienced within the last week or so when using buses on routes 20, 167, 206 or 275.

The problems have been caused by a severe shortage of qualified bus drivers since Eastern National Citybus became responsible on May 24 for operating the routes under contract to London Regional Transport. Despite an extensive recruitment campaign from the start of the year, Eastern National has been unsuccessful in obtaining all the drivers needed to run the full services and consequently random cancellations have occurred, with the result that you may have had a frustratingly long wait for your bus.

As a matter of urgency, Eastern National are pursuing their recruitment efforts and are taking other measures to overcome the problem and we hope that full services will be restored within the next two weeks.

Meanwhile, we shall try to keep disruption to a minimum. Priority for staffing is being given to services timed to run at half-hourly intervals or more and to journeys timed for the convenience of works, hospitals and schools. As a consequence, some journeys are more likely to be cancelled on a regular basis within the next week or two – until we can cover the full timetable again: Details of these are shown on the back of this leaflet.

Again, we are sorry for the inconvenience you may have experienced. We are doing all we can to cover the scheduled services. So please don't blame your driver – and please bear with us just a little longer.

David Bayliss
Director of Planning
London Regional Transport

Robin Orbell
Traffic Manager
EASTERN NATIONAL CityBus

ENOC's apology leaflet for the poor service at Walthamstow until they had built up driver numbers.

We hope to operate the full service on Routes 145A (Goodmayes – Chingford) and 167 (Loughton – Ilford). A full service will also be provided on all routes on Sundays.

The following journeys may NOT operate at present.

Route 20 (Walthamstow – Loughton – Debden)

Mondays to Fridays

From Walthamstow	0855, 0925, 1155, 1240, 1255, 1440, 1455, 1608, 1638, 1723, 1810, 1840, 1855
From Debden Estate	0955, 1025, 1255, 1340, 1355, 1538, 1553, 1710, 1742, 1915, 1945

Saturdays

From Walthamstow	0935*, 1110, 1325, 1425, 1525, 1625, 1740 * time at Woodford Green, Castle
From Debden Estate	1010, 1210, 1425, 1525, 1625, 1725, 1845

Route 206 (Walthamstow – Chigwell)

Mondays to Fridays

From Walthamstow	0946, 1040, 1100, 1140, 1240, 1300, 1340, 1420, 1500, 1540, 1745, 1830, 1900, 1955, 2050, 2220
From Chigwell	1045, 1145, 1205, 1245, 1345, 1405, 1445, 1525, 1605, 1645, 1900, 1928, 1958, 2132, 2302

Saturdays

From Walthamstow	0925, 1005, 1225, 1425
From Chigwell	1025, 1105, 1325, 1525

Route 275 (Walthamstow – Barkingside)

Mondays to Fridays

From Walthamstow	0845, 1035, 1315, 1455, 1535, 1555, 1635, 1715, 1815, 1855, 1915, 1945, 2045, 2215
From Barkingside	0946, 1126, 1406, 1546, 1627, 1707, 1727, 1807, 2000, 2030, 2130, 2300

Saturdays

From Walthamstow	0955, 1155, 1535
From Barkingside	1102, 1302, 1642

The above times should be read in conjunction with the Timetable Leaflets dated 24th May 1986. A full service will be operated as soon as possible.

686/18405/11M (1661A)

The reverse of the leaflet was a timetable of services that were unlikely to run on the 20, 206 and 275!

The problems implementing their new services at Walthamstow led to postponement of Eastern National's operation of route 359 until they were ready in January 1987; London Country North East ran the service for its first three months. The 359 ran between Hammond Street and Manor House, replacing the 259 north of Ponders End and continuing the long-standing practice of making a U-turn in Seven Sisters Road at Manor House. (Colin Fradd)

55

sorted out in 1986. TBU did not publish the tender bids and there was no requirement on them to do so. This did not worry him, he says, because "Life is confidential".

On deregulation outside London in October 1986 Eastern National released some buses and was therefore able to return the hired buses to United Counties. There was no change to the buses used in London. They were re-awarded all the contracts when they expired. Nick Newton called Robin in and said that they had won the lot, based on their performance. Also, their experiences at the beginning of the Walthamstow operation had demonstrated clearly to the politicians that you cannot expect a major transfer of work to take place in only three months.

Buses and bungalows
By the end of June 1986, 8% of LRT's total mileage had been opened up to competitive tender. A further batch of services was announced on 1 July, the tenders to be submitted by 11 August. Nine routes were involved which were generally to be similar to the existing services. However the section of route 153 between Angel, Islington and Tottenham Court Road was withdrawn whilst the Archway to Angel section was to be run by midibuses at a higher frequency up to 19.30 on Mondays to Saturdays. Those tendering for the route were also invited to identify the additional cost of providing an evening and Sunday service so that LRT could decide whether to include this.

Barry Le Jeune's responsibilities included public relations for the implementation of the tendered services, which needed to be separate from London Buses public relations as LBL was one of the competing operators. However, operators dealt with correspondence about their services and received training in dealing with public letters. LRT used the term 'contracted operations' for tendered routes to try and get away from the press and public use of the word 'privatised' when the services were, in fact, still under the control of LRT.

There was very little public concern about the process of tendering itself and the handover of routes to other operators. However, there was considerable concern about the new route networks which usually accompanied tendering and often led to public meetings. When routes were changed there was a lot of comment, whereas who was to operate the route was less controversial. Public reaction to new routeings regularly involved objections from residents to new bus routes passing their homes. This increased as new schemes often involved minibuses penetrating areas that had not previously had a service.

In summer 1986 LRT decided to introduce minibuses to route 193 in Hornchurch. Eastern National would continue to run the route, now using Ford Transits and rerouteing through a residential area. Barry Le Jeune recalls that "Route 193 was re-specified with minibuses diverted to run along Ascot Gardens, near Hornchurch Station, through residential streets. There was strong public feeling, and an irate lady stood up and said, 'Mr Le Jeune, what you don't understand is, we don't need a bus route down our road because we all live in bungalows!'

"This was typical of the sort of person who considered only their own personal environment and because they did not themselves need a bus, they didn't think one should be provided. We took a bus down the disputed roads to show that it was possible, and all the residents parked their cars badly in the road to try and make it difficult. We put a bus in front of Hornchurch Station hoping to show the residents their 'nice-looking cuddly minibus' but no-one was impressed by that!

"At another meeting on the 354, operated by Metrobus, there was a similar reaction until an elderly lady stood up and introduced herself saying, 'I lost my husband recently. Until then, I never wanted a bus because my husband drove me. Since he died, I can't get out of the house.' On this occasion, some of the audience realised that, though they may be fit and healthy now, they might need a service in 10 years time."

Nick Newton would be ready with a swift retort. When a woman at a public meeting said, "You can't put a bus down my road – it's residential," he quickly replied, "I think you'll find that most of our passen-

LBL's conversion of route 193 to minibus operation and its new routeing along residential roads that had not previously had a bus service led to local opposition. An Eastern National Ford Transit minibus is seen in Hornchurch during August 1986 on its way to the bungalows! (Barry Le Jeune)

"What you don't understand is, we don't need a bus route down our road because we all live in bungalows!"

The service was successful and the original Ford Transit minibuses were replaced by larger Mercedes vehicles, one of which is seen in Romford in September 1988. (David Cole)

gers live in houses." New Hail and Ride routes might take time to settle down as elderly people would wait inside their own gates and expect the bus to stop repeatedly. So timetables were put up at certain points and people gathered there, which solved the problem.

One of John Wood's jobs was to go and check the operations at the contractors' garages. At the beginning, they were allocating each depot an Apricot computer with 3½inch floppy discs. They had two discs, one on the left with the programme, and one on the right that they entered the figures onto. "Of course, the garages regularly did them the wrong way around, wiped the programmes and failed to collect the data." They also had the original Wayfarer I ticket machines, which worked by heating up the paper and wouldn't work properly on cold days. They subsequently moved to Wayfarer IIs. Each depot would send the discs back to TBU to be downloaded.

When a new operator won a tendered route, which might be quite a small one, it was necessary to set them up with all the equipment – ticket machines, computer systems, and a radio base station. Graham Elliot was in charge of the LBL Communications Centre. "We insisted they had a Band 3 base station – one or two of them managed to slip the net, but how could we send out information from CentreComm, about an emergency or a bomb in the area, when you can't talk to some of the routes. CentreComm had to ring the base, and get them to use their local radio." Graham insisted that they all have Band 3 radios:

LBL's Bus Districts were encouraged to provide innovative and competitive services. Forest District's contribution was the introduction of route X99 between Harlow and Basildon from 2nd August 1986. The new service was marketed as the "Forester" and ran via Epping, Debden, Buckhurst Hill, Woodford, Ilford, Romford, Harold Hill, Brentwood, Billericay and Laindon. Six Leyland Nationals were converted to single door, fitted with coach seats and given this attractive livery. On the first day free travel was offered, resulting in more passengers than could be carried on some trips at the end of the day. LS 30 is seen at Romford Market. (Keith Wood)

"You can have what system you like, but it must link into CentreComm." On the console at CentreComm they had an extra unit linked into that company, and if they were doing a broadcast to all mobiles, they had to do it again for them.

Westlink
Westlink commenced operation on 9 August 1986 and Roundabout a week later. Westlink led to a reallocation of services in west London and Southall garage was closed, with services being moved to Hounslow, Hanwell and Alperton.

Jeff Chamberlain recruited the Westlink drivers himself. He made a point of employing staff who were not from London Buses. If a driver had a PSV licence and was accepted by Jeff's own instructor, then he was taken on, just like any other private operator. He would schedule up to eight hours including 24 minutes compulsory overtime. This could produce up to two hours additional work for the same pay, compared to London Buses.

Some drivers were surplus at Hounslow, but they would be offered work at other LBL garages. He was willing to take volunteers to transfer if they accepted the new conditions, with no union agreements and no restrictions on their employment, as if to a private company. As long as they worked within the law that was all right – many drivers wanted high earnings and were willing to work long hours. So Jeff paid lower wages than LBL but with higher earning potential. As a member of the Labour Party he believed in working men's rights but didn't believe in restrictive practices.

"It was a bit dramatic getting the service out on the first day. Some buses and some drivers finished at Hounslow the previous night. We had to get the buses over and put vinyls on, and the drivers were needed immediately the next morning."

Pulborough Way was an engineering depot and they kept the buses at North Feltham trading estate. For the first six months, the buses would come to Pulborough Way for fuelling and washing, by hand, and then the managers would drive them over to North Feltham. Four managers were involved – three would drive the buses and the fourth the ferry car, doing repeat trips till all the buses were there, leaving only the last eight at Pulborough Way. In the mornings, a driver ferried the other drivers to North Feltham to fetch the buses, and then became spare driver when all the buses were out. They then leased scrubland next door, which they surfaced, and this solved the problem.

Jeff was now Managing Director of Stanwell Buses. He got on very well with TBU – there were no problems in the relationship. But the pressure on costs remained. "Marcus Smith came to visit one day and I told him something that we needed. He replied, 'This is a one man and his dog operation' and refused. Jeff replied, 'That's fine, but I think my dog has died'."

28 Leyland Nationals were transferred to Westlink for routes 116, 117 and 203. LS317 is at Staines in July 1987. (Roger Torode)

Their bid for further work at Kingston was successful and they took over Kingston garage. "We were going around buying equipment from auctions and from the sale at Aldenham, buying cheap not new. But the VW minibuses with Optare bodies at Orpington were not substantial enough and had lots of engineering problems, so we went for MCW Metroriders. Westlink always completed its mileage and it remained very profitable under subsequent owners including London United."

Westlink was a breath of fresh air in London Buses. When John Telford Beasley came to look around, he said, "This is the most encouraging and positive thing I have seen in London Buses since I came here!"

Jeff built up a small team of staff. Jean Harris was the first female on the LBL Graduate Operations Management Training Scheme, and she completed it quickly to go and help at Westlink when they were setting up. Jean did anything – washing the buses, driving them, interviewing driver recruits, payrolls, route control and so on. They got enough drivers, including some from Hounslow – they were hand-picked as people who would be willing to work the additional hours and the new conditions.

"It was very different from London Buses, because it was less structured. Westlink was a lot of hard work due to the small number of managers involved but it was very jolly, we would have a joke and some fun but we always ran the service. Jeff Chamberlain had a lot of respect from the drivers and engineers because he would get his hands dirty when necessary. I learned a lot about management from Jeff; a different way of doing things and challenging the existing ways. And he was generous when he could be. For example, at Christmas, I remember getting 60 turkeys and 60 Christmas puddings and we gave Christmas hampers to the staff. He took all the Inspectors, their wives and the managers out for a Christmas 'do'."

There were some characters amongst those who were new to bus work. Martin Whitley remembers a particular driver who had been recruited directly. One of the supervisors told him on the radio to stand by. From then on they could not reach him – he was not on the air at all. So one of the supervisors went off in the car to find the bus. When he found it, the driver was literally standing by it!

Roundabout Orpington
Like Westlink, Roundabout was an entirely new operation, started with a clean sheet rather than bringing change to an existing garage. The Orpington scheme commenced on 16 August. Bexleyheath Garage closed, though its forecourt continued to be used as a stand for routes 122 and 160 and the garage remained in use for storage.

The midibuses were in a new maroon and grey

The introduction of new area networks, with revised route patterns and new operators, was usually marked by a launch event for the local press and London Borough representatives. Here buses for the new Orpington network are lined up at Orpington station in August 1986. (Barry Le Jeune)

colour scheme and were marketed as providing "smaller, nippier buses that can get to the parts the double-deckers can't reach", and as "friendly and frequent visitors down your way; so much so that the drivers will soon be established as fully fledged local characters". They were leased from LRT and based at an industrial unit near St Mary Cray station.

25 buses were allocated, being 20 Robin Hood Iveco 21-seaters and five Optare LT55 Citypacer 25-seaters. The Ivecos were given the names of birds whilst the Optares had the names of winds. They penetrated new areas and provided an increase in service together with 'Hail and Ride' operation.

Roundabout R6 ran outside the Greater London area to Knockholt Pound and Sevenoaks. Optare City Pacer OV4, named Chinook, is in a country lane near Chelsfield on the first day of operation. (Colin Fradd)

However, there was significant overcrowding, particularly where they replaced large buses, and the 'Hail and Ride' soon developed into regular, and unmarked, stopping places. The service pattern was successful, other than the overcrowding, whilst shopping trolleys and pushchairs caused difficulty on the midibuses. The service R6 to Sevenoaks, which replaced former route 431, was abandoned in stages due to lack of use. Roundabout also operated some Kent County Council contracts for evening journeys in the Sevenoaks area but this did not last long. Otherwise, the service pattern remained generally similar throughout the life of Roundabout. From October 1994 to January 1995 they also provided buses for the first 'Park and Ride' scheme in Bromley, using buses hired from United Counties.

The Roundabout services were popular and the vehicles gradually got larger. From January 1988 new longer MRL Metroriders took over routes R1 and R11, and these were replaced by new Dennis Darts in 1990. Additional Optare CityPacers came in 1989/90 when they were no longer needed in central London, and in 1990 the original Optares were replaced by larger Mercedes 33-seaters, providing increased capacity for route R3. The original Ivecos were replaced with new ones in 1993 named after the signs of the Zodiac. Only the Iveco RH1s continued from the beginning to the end of Roundabout operation.

Above Changing the face of bus services in Orpington: three Roundabout midibuses in the High Street on the first day. RH2 was an Iveco Daily bodied by Robin Hood and named 'Robin'. (Keith Wood)

Exchanging first-day experiences, the drivers of Optare OV3 'Tornado' and Iveco RH24 'Seagull' meet on the forecourt of the Rose and Crown at Green Street Green. (John Parkin)

Metrobus

Metrobus was a local bus company with a good reputation running commercial routes 353 and 357 by agreement with LT. They had bid unsuccessfully for the 146 in the first tranche of tendering. They then won the 61 in the Orpington tenders and ran it from 16 August 1986, followed by the 261 when some routes were retendered in 1987. Peter Larking considered this to be 'gravy train stuff'. He made a lot of money from it because their costs were around £1 per mile compared with a London Buses average of around £4 per mile, a figure that included crew routes. "It was easy to bid on a fully-costed basis with a big margin and win. We could have won anything we wanted on price!"

Running the 261 into Lewisham made them think they had become a London bus operator. They did not put in further bids after that, letting other opportunities like the 208 go because they thought it would be too much to take on.

Staff recruitment was straightforward because LBL's Elmers End garage was closing and he recruited quite a few staff from there. There were also some from Sidcup, so in 1986 there was no problem recruiting. There were drivers disillusioned with working for 'the big bus company', who felt it was run by the trade union. He was a non-union operator where you knew the governor, there were flexible working conditions on both sides, and as manager his door was always open. If a driver wanted a day off that would be arranged, but this was two-way flexibility and he might want the driver to come in on a day when he needed more staff. He guaranteed a 40-hour week with no restrictions. This could mean 12 hours on one day with a 14-hour spreadover, and another day with a five-hour shift.

Some of his staff had a bad reputation from LT, but his company was small enough to turn them round. He paid a performance bonus of £8 a day, £40 per week, which depended on the driver being punctual, running on schedule, being smart in full uniform, safe driving and no uncollected fares. The bonus might be docked on a daily or weekly basis depending on the error – not wearing a tie might result in losing the bonus for one day, whilst a blameworthy accident would lose it for the week. The loss of a week's bonus counted as a formal warning. He was clear when recruiting drivers – he would say, "We want good drivers. If you don't intend to work well, go somewhere else!" With the bonus, his pay rates were comparable to London Buses and he kept his staff.

Peter felt that problems in other companies were created by the union. His staff took pride in being out there and different, wearing their blue and yellow striped tie, in a blue and yellow bus, so they were obviously different from other companies. When it was later suggested that all buses should be red, he felt it lost all the advantages of being a private operator and doing the job well. He could see why they wanted to do this, to portray a network. But in the early days, LRT made a thing of the different colours, for example showing in the publicity that there would be 'Blue and yellow buses for Route 61 from 16 August,' and this was crucial to the tendering process.

Running into Lewisham was different from the suburbs, and they decided they would have to fit assault screens. They had avoided these in Orpington and the drivers had not wanted them, thinking that they would cause trouble rather than resolve it. From then on, Metrobus looked warily at running into London, realising that this was going to be a different type of bus operation with busier services and heavy traffic.

Did he think that competition with London buses was fair? No, it wasn't, though it became fairer as the years went by. "London Buses managers thought that the country and private operators were not in it for the long term, and when they had sorted themselves out they'd get it all back again." He crossed swords with Bryan Constable at Selkent over publicity at bus stops. Selkent looked after bus stops but Peter's commercial routes used them, so he wanted to put his timetables in spare panels in the stops. Selkent refused, so he went to Bryan Constable who still said no. So he went round and put the timetables in himself, and Selkent took them out! Then he sat down with Bryan Constable and, in the end, won the argument, but it took a long time.

Another issue was Staff Passes. London Buses employees had passes so that they and their partner could use both the bus and Underground free of charge. Employees of the private operators did not enjoy this privilege, even though they worked on the same bus network. Peter Larking found this to be a clear example of an uneven playing field and he pursued the matter through the Bus Operators' Forum. "It took several years, but eventually the argument was won and an agreement for the issue of staff passes to all London bus staff, to use on all London buses, still exists today." There were very rarely issues on the road with red bus drivers, perhaps more in the early days, but as many of his staff came from local London Buses garages and knew the other drivers, this was not generally a problem.

Metrobus ran DMSs purchased from Ensign who had prepared many for second-life London service. "Ensign knew what needed to be done in terms of mechanical and electrical modifications, changing the destination boxes, up-seating by replacing a single seat upstairs with a double and replacing the AFC equipment with a sideways-facing seat. The modifications were simple, readily accepted for certification and when painted the buses looked as good as new."

Peter considered TBU monitoring to be fair and reasonable, and most of the staff doing that work were old boys who were on side. In some cases, his drivers knew them. He did cross swords with some Revenue Inspectors. "I was travelling on one of my buses one day when a Revenue Inspector got on in jeans, looking scruffy and unshaven. I told him that I required my staff to have a collar and tie, and to be shaved. I understood that Inspectors might be in plain clothes but I did not consider that they should be scruffy. This was my bus and I was not having it, and I told the inspector to get off!

"There was another incident with a Revenue Inspector who got on a bus and went to sit upstairs. He then pressed the bell for every stop but did not get off. Eventually the driver, a large man, went up and asked him what he was doing. He said he was a Revenue Inspector and could do what he liked. The driver said that he was the driver of the bus and he could also do what he liked, and if the Inspector carried on ringing the bell he would push him through the windscreen. I then had to get involved because the driver was now at fault, so I contacted Revenue Control to calm the situation. They agreed to take the Inspector off the area."

Bryan Constable thinks that Metrobus got away with murder in the early days! They were ruthless employers with their drivers and had to change. He suggests that the bonus system was punitive and could lead to serious loss of earnings. A lot of their drivers were awful employees who had been sacked by Bryan, so they had to work for Metrobus conditions in order to keep a job. They only got their full salary if they didn't involve the firm in any expense. But he acknowledges that some of them did turn around on their performance.

When tendering started and Metrobus took its first routes, Bryan made it his business to get along with the new people. There were Brian Hurst and Norman Kemp at Kentish Bus, Alan Price at Maidstone Boro'line, and Peter Larking and Gary Wood from Metrobus. On Bryan's initiative, they agreed to meet once a month and they would take it in turns to host lunch at the Bromley Court hotel, "Just to stay civilised and keep talking."

Metrobus's former LT DMSs look smart in their attractive blue and yellow livery, at Bromley North Station on their first day, as does the driver of the first bus in his white shirt and tie. (Keith Wood)

"TBU monitoring was fair and reasonable, and most of the staff doing that work were old boys who were on side."

Central London Minibuses

25 October 1986 saw the introduction of high-frequency minibuses to three routes in Central London. The C1 operated during Monday to Saturday shopping hours between Kensington and Westminster via the narrow streets of Belgravia, some of which had never had a bus service. In the evening, the minibuses switched to two new routes numbered C20 and C21 linking the West End theatres with Victoria and Waterloo stations. Unfortunately, parked cars in the narrow streets around Covent Garden prevented operation there and they had to be diverted via the Strand. The new services were run by London Buses under contract to LRT from a new unit, Central London Minibuses, located in the basement at Victoria Garage. The buses were on contract maintenance.

LRT wanted to introduce these routes quickly and so awarded them directly to London Buses. Nick Newton had been pressed to introduce minibuses in central London similar to those Harry Blundred had in Exeter. They chose Optares for the C1 as these were on VW chassis and had automatic transmission – but they were sluggish. Nick had heard that on the H2 service, the Ford Transits had manual gearboxes so the drivers just drove in third gear and repeatedly wore out the clutches!

The next new route, the C2, started on 24 March 1987 and took over the northern end of route 53 between Parliament Hill Fields and Oxford Circus, running every four minutes for most of the day on Mondays to Saturdays, with an enhanced service at peak times. LRT provided the buses and the operation was won by London Country North West on tender. They also took over route 153, converted to midibuses, from 4 March.

John Rymer was a bus driver at Battersea and saw moving to CLM as a good opportunity, even though he would have a pay cut driving minibuses. He became a Controller a few months later. "It was a lot of fun. It did feel special – we were trying to run a service in a customer-led, non-bureaucratic way. Adverts for staff were posted throughout London and the drivers were hand-picked, the best they could find. Everyone in the Unit had a PSV licence: all the controllers and some of the engineers would drive when necessary. All the staff were very co-operative – the drivers and the controllers were cleaning out the minibuses. It was four months before there was a single complaint – quite unlike the big buses. The

Two Optare CityPacers of Central London Minibuses lay over at the Embankment on route C1. (Keith Wood)

63 "It was a lot of fun. It did feel special – we were trying to run a service in a customer-led, non-bureaucratic way."

routes were controlled by radio, and we put buses in position to match the demand and give even headways despite traffic problems.

"The routes were all new, running through residential areas of Knightsbridge. When there was traffic congestion we would find another route to get back on time – we made it work! There was tremendous spirit and it was great fun. On the big buses, everything had been done for our own convenience – the inspectors, the drivers and the engineers, and it was hugely inefficient!"

The Optare minibuses were a striking design and very attractive, but as the passenger numbers grew they were too small and suffered from overloading. John remembers the day one was hit by a car driven by the wife of the Chancellor of the Exchequer in Victoria Street, watched over by New Scotland Yard. She gave her address as No. 11 Downing Street. John was the Controller on duty at the time, and within half-an-hour the newspapers were calling in for details. "We had to protect the driver and sent him home, but next day the press were out in force riding on the buses, asking for information and trying to find the driver."

Paul London was a London Buses manager who gained his PCV licence and became a CLM driver to gain experience. "The training on customers and how to use the ticket machine was by a 'buddy' accompanying you for the first half shift. But my bus failed and I didn't complete that half shift, so I didn't receive the training!

"They had lots of drivers for the launch. They were young, some from outside the industry, very transitory people, most smart though some were scruffy. CLM were very strict on passing the test within two tries – two failures and you were out. Route learning was done properly, usually sending out a group of new drivers to ride the route on service buses.

"Some of the Optare VWs were powerful and reliable, but some wouldn't pull the skin off a rice pudding! To top up the radiator, you had to remove the parcel rack from the front, then remove some of the fascia! However they were still better than the Ivecos, which were 'provincial minibuses' – they had a major design fault in that when the brake shoes wore down, the adjusters would overcompensate, so the brakes bound on.

Minibus routes C2 and 153 were initially run by London Country North West, but their operation was not satisfactory and, following problems with their operating base in Muswell Hill, LCNW asked to be relieved of the two routes. LRT transferred the vehicles and operation to Central London Minibuses at Victoria Garage basement from June 1988 until they could be retendered, and CLM then won long term contracts for them in November 1988. An LCNW Iveco midibus is seen at Archway bus stand on route 153 in June 1988. (Keith Wood).

64 "Some of the Optare VWs were powerful and reliable, but some wouldn't pull the skin off a rice pudding!"

"There were very lumpy running times on these minibus services, with increased time given in the peaks, so that on some journeys just before the peak you could not avoid running late, and then suddenly there was a lot more time, and Inspectors were booking people for running early! The 153 had badly insufficient running time, you would regularly lose half a round-trip in each spell of duty. Boarding on these buses was normally ok, but you noticed the difference on Fridays when people were going home for the weekend and would board, with their luggage, during the rush hour. This really took longer."

Deregulation outside London
Bus services outside London were deregulated from Sunday 26 October 1986 and, as a result, London Buses services that operated on a commercial basis and crossed the boundary had to be registered. LBL initially registered three new routes, the 303, 306 and 310A, which were in direct competition with London Country. The 306 was operated by Cardinal District between Kingston and Epsom, running alongside London Country 406 during the daytime on Mondays to Saturdays. However, it was deregistered after three months.

In taking over Leaside, Ken Blacker reconsidered the planned 303 and 310A. "The 303 did not look viable – in my view there was insufficient business to be had north of Barnet so I cancelled the registration. The 310A was very different. It served a string of developing commuter belt towns beyond Waltham Cross – Cheshunt, Broxbourne, Hoddesdon and Ware – which showed good passenger potential. Also the 310A was registered to operate via Ponders End and Enfield Highway instead of via the sparsely populated Great Cambridge Road served by London Country North East's 310, offering a new round-the-corner link at Ponders End and a cross-town facility at Waltham Cross from the densely populated Hertford Road. The operation performed well from the first day, helped – it must be admitted – by the poor performance of LCNE, which was having problems of its own at the time. Although an instruction subsequently came from 'on high' to cease out-county competitive operations, I decided to keep the 310A going on the grounds of its profitability – although I 'covered my back' by examining the 310A receipts daily to make sure it stayed that way. Fortunately an agreement with Hertfordshire County Council over payment for school children's travel helped to boost finances, and when a Saturdays-only 310B was introduced to serve Harlow this quickly became very lucrative."

Alongside deregulation, the privatisation of the National Bus Company was gathering pace and Eastern National was sold to its managers on 23 December 1986. Robin Orbell remarks, "It was the only one of the larger NBC companies that was not split into smaller companies, because we argued that we could not support the London tendered operations if we were split. The buyout was led by the four directors with seven senior managers as shareholders. The bank which lent the money saw it as a sound business and were impressed by our Finance Director – we paid the bank back within a year!"

While London had been 'temporarily excluded' from deregulation, it remained Government policy to extend it to London. David Mitchell MP, Minister of State at the Department of Transport said, "Looking ahead to the 1990s, I would expect to see bus users in the capital enjoying the same benefits of deregulation as those outside. London Buses will soon be ready to face the full force of competition. Deregulation will stimulate local initiative in the provision and marketing of services and the crucial element that is currently missing from the bus scene in London – real competition."

However, tendering was gathering pace and achieving significant results. By late 1986, almost one eighth of LRT's total bus mileage had been opened to competition, 13.5 million miles of service. 205 bids had been received for 55 tenders. Of these, 45% were won by London Buses, 40% by NBC subsidiaries and 15% by independents. Cost reductions averaging 20% had been achieved on these operations, while mileage operated, reliability and revenue had all increased. London Buses was now successfully defending itself where it was able to open new operations or achieve substantial changes in existing garages.

4 THE AREA TENDERING SCHEMES 1987-1988

Following the success of Orpington, LRT began to tender more local area networks. Schemes for Kingston, Harrow and Bexley were all introduced in 1987. This led LBL to set up 'ring fenced' operations based on the affected garages – LBL's bids were then based on the full costs of running those garages, but with tougher conditions for all grades of staff and higher productivity than at standard LBL garages. If the work was lost, the garage was closed and savings were achieved. Leon Daniels, who was bidding for routes at Ensign with Peter Newman, recalls that, "This was because London Buses could not achieve savings in their overheads when they lost individual routes – the garage still existed, but the costs were spread over fewer routes. So the idea of area schemes was to allow entire garages to be closed – otherwise, tendering was effectively making LBL's costs worse."

London Buses was also being challenged on 'grant leakage'. In early 1987 six routes which had been won by London Buses in previous tendering rounds were re-tendered because it had been found that their costings broke these rules, and the operation of those contracts was deemed to be subsidised by the block grant operations. The routes retendered were the 79A, 84A, 125, 179, 179A and 261 – five of these went to other operators and one was retained by LBL.

By spring 1987, Chiswick had undergone a major reorganisation costing around £6 million in order to take over the work previously performed at Aldenham. LRT's subsidiary BEL said that Chiswick now offered a comprehensive range of bus engineering facilities,

The change in London's suburban scene as a result of tendering is clear in this view in Bromley in May 1988, where three blue and yellow double deckers of Metrobus provide the bus service. Deregulation in the rest of the UK outside London resulted in a thinning of bus fleets elsewhere and a supply of good quality second-hand vehicles. The low-height ECW bodied Olympian on route 61 came from West Riding, while the full-height Roe bodied bus on route 261 originated with West Yorkshire PTE. (Graham Sanders, courtesy Gary Wood)

66 "London Buses could not achieve savings in their overheads when they lost individual routes."

The Kingston area scheme was implemented in June 1987 although there were considerable industrial relations difficulties. London Buses was awarded all but one of the routes, based on a new subsidiary, Kingston Buses Ltd, while the remaining route went to London Country South West. Kingston Buses used elderly DMSs, some of which had been driver trainers but were refurbished with a local fleetname added. DMS 1862, heavily loaded in Kingston on 16 May 1988, has a general air of neglect, with a fleetname which appears to have been applied over graffiti! Route 213 had previously operated from Norbiton and Sutton but was now operated solely by Norbiton. (David Cole)

but was also able to handle repairs to commercial vehicles. It was still expected that LBL would continue to be BEL's biggest customer but the amount of work from them had declined and there was a need to obtain work from elsewhere. BEL was already recognised as a service dealer for a number of companies and their customer numbers reached 155 during 1986. BEL's managers were hopeful that their company would become established as a major engineering supplier throughout the PSV industry. But it was still making a loss and later in 1987 LRT announced that it was seeking offers for the company. In January 1988 it was sold to Frontsource, a group of companies which included eight of the engineering companies formed from National Bus Company subsidiaries when they were split up and privatised.

A number of tendered services were now being criticised for poor performance. An example was route 81 where London Buslines was proving unreliable due to the high failure rate of its Daimler Fleetlines. This led to the company hiring buses from Portsmouth and Ensign. A new precedent was then set as the company was given a three-year extension on the contract for route 81 in order to justify the purchase of six brand-new Leyland Lynx single-deckers. It also won route 79 which would use second hand former Manchester vehicles.

Ensignbus
Peter Newman and Leon Daniels worked together to bid for routes 145 and 145A. The bid for the 145A was not successful, but the 145 was won and started in January 1986. They worked as Ensign Bus Services, running the route together with London Pride Sightseeing. Leon recalls, "We won the 62 as well, from January 1987, but it was a period of short three-year contracts which were terrible. Then tendering began to move to area schemes." LRT tendered the work of Hornchurch garage and Ensign got all of it except the 248 and 252, which went to Frontrunner, owned by East Midland, and which was later sold to Stagecoach. This led to the closure of Hornchurch garage in September 1988.

Peter Newman saw the London tendering as a genuine attempt to get new people into London bus work and they became involved in the early stages. They also did railway replacement work, and when deregulation came they ran express services into London. Peter considered that operating tendered routes was just the same as other bus routes. However, Ensignbus had high standards. They were very keen on presentation, with a good livery and smart buses. The DMSs all had wheel nut rings, the blinds were white on blue, the drivers wore ties and were the first on tendered services to have epaulettes.

He is sure there was no favouritism for London Buses – he was confident that Nick Newton was absolutely fair. He had no problem with monitoring by TBU – the service was so much better than it had been. However, when they won their first route, the local paper ran a headline saying, "Scrap dealer wins bus route" – which he says came courtesy of the T&GWU.

Ensignbus made an immediate impact with its smart blue and silver buses. Former LT DMS B2166 and Metrobus 299, originally with South Yorkshire PTE, are seen in Romford. (Michael Steward)

"It was a period of short three-year contracts, which were terrible."

Changes to your local buses

From 28th February
Orange and brown buses for Route 173

Route 173 will be operated by Eastenderbus for London Regional Transport using orange, brown and white pay-as-you-enter double-deck buses. Eastenderbus is part of the Cowie Group.

No change to the frequency
Buses will continue to run on Mondays to Saturdays between Stratford and Becontree Heath via Plaistow, Victoria & Albert Docks, East Beckton, Newham Way, Rippleside and Dagenham at 20 minute intervals during the day, and half-hourly during evenings.
There will be some useful later journeys from Stratford to Dagenham, and the last bus will depart at 12.35 am. As now, there will be no Sunday service.

Fares and Passes to remain the same
There will be no change to the fares on Bus 173 – just 30p for adults and 15p for under 16s until 10 pm (35p and 20p respectively before 9.30 am on Mondays to Fridays. Bus Passes, Travelcards, Capitalcards, Elderly and Handicapped Persons' Permits and all similar tickets valid on London Buses will continue to be accepted.

A LONDON REGIONAL TRANSPORT SERVICE

Grey-Green commenced tendered bus operations on 28 February 1987 trading as Eastenderbus and operating from the premises of the former Dix coach company in Dagenham. This Fleetline with MCW body was very similar to the London DMS, but came from South Yorkshire PTE. (Owen Woodliffe)

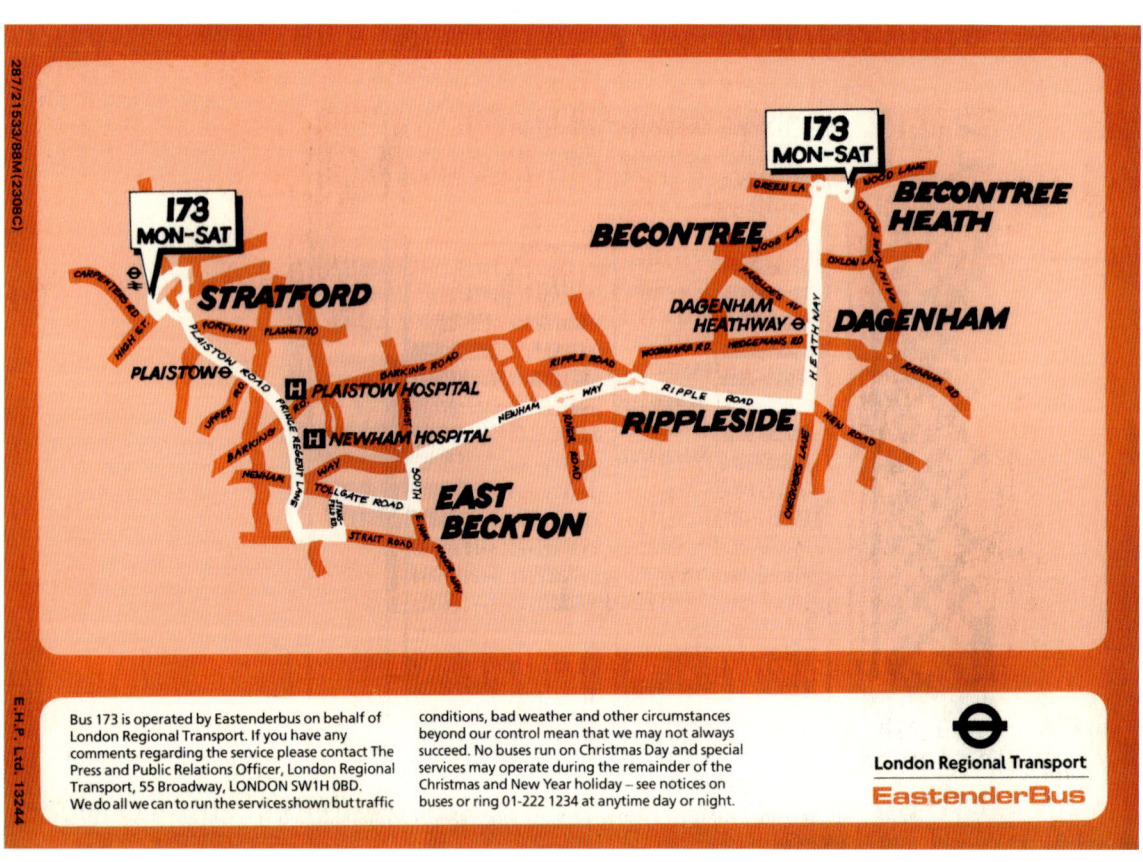

Bus 173 is operated by Eastenderbus on behalf of London Regional Transport. If you have any comments regarding the service please contact The Press and Public Relations Officer, London Regional Transport, 55 Broadway, LONDON SW1H 0BD. We do all we can to run the services shown but traffic conditions, bad weather and other circumstances beyond our control mean that we may not always succeed. No buses run on Christmas Day and special services may operate during the remainder of the Christmas and New Year holiday – see notices on buses or ring 01-222 1234 at anytime day or night.

London Regional Transport
EastenderBus

68

Kingston and Norbiton

Throughout 1987, LBL staff could see themselves being faced with more arduous duties, worse pay for extended hours on the road, and less secure working conditions. Norbiton became a flash point. LBL won six of the seven routes in the Kingston network, based on ring-fencing Norbiton garage which would be run on substantially reduced overheads. Only route 131 went to London Country South West.

LBL managers went into the Trade Union discussions saying that "This is a non-negotiable deal." When it became clear that Norbiton staff would face harsher working conditions there were a number of strikes. Similar strikes took place elsewhere in London where major tendering schemes were proposed. It was a difficult dilemma for staff having to accept worse pay and longer hours or no job. Those at Norbiton received notice terminating their present employment whilst being offered new conditions on a three-year contract. By the deadline of 28 April, a minimal number of them had taken up the offer, many feeling so betrayed that they left the industry altogether.

There was concern that LBL would have to revoke the Kingston contracts, but in the event there were sufficient staff to launch the service on 27 June. However, the Transport & General Workers' Union suggested there were errors in the process, which led them to seek an injunction against LRT in the High Court on 10 June. While this went through the legal process, an out-of-court agreement resulted in the services being operated for the first six months directly by LBL, with the staff remaining LBL employees.

The High Court judge ruled in favour of London Buses, determining that it had the right to change the terms and conditions of employment of staff to be transferred to its subsidiary company, Kingston Buses Ltd. Although the new contracts involved longer hours for less pay, existing staff were to receive compensatory payments over the next three years. LBL's actions in issuing notices of termination to staff conditions of contract were held to be lawful and, as they were not surplus to requirements, severance pay was not applicable. He therefore rejected the application, ordering the Union to pay costs. A factor which had counted against the Trade Union was that Peter Hendy had sent a letter to them on the proposals in the previous December, and they had never replied. Counsel for the T&GWU in the case was Peter Hendy's brother, John Hendy QC, and Peter was expecting to appear as a witness for London Buses and be cross-examined, but in the event he was not called!

The High Court judgement led to a further strike at Norbiton on 16 July, supported by other garages, particularly those, like Harrow, which were facing a similar change. Union meetings and strikes were held across London during August, Norbiton itself being out for six days and, in response, LBL issued dismissal notices to the striking staff. In early September the re-tendering of all Norbiton's routes was threatened, causing another strike. A further offer was made to the staff following talks at the Arbitration and Conciliation Service (ACAS) but this offer was also rejected by the staff. The next day, LBL announced that Norbiton garage would be closed and asked LRT to make alternative arrangements for the Kingston network. However this resulted in hurried negotiations over the following weekend and agreement of a deal with the union for the resumption of normal working. The deal allowed existing staff to be paid at LBL rates for the first six months before transferring onto the new conditions. After many months of meetings and strikes, the Trade Union officer remarked that, "This is the longest set of non-negotiable negotiations I have ever been involved in!"

David Brown was one of the small team setting up the new garage management with Brian Jefferies. "Brian would pick me up in Harrow before 7 o'clock in the morning. Brian lived near me and he was also an early starter. On the journey to Norbiton we would be wondering whether we were operating a service or not, or whether we were in dispute – there were no mobile phones then. It was always a relief when we saw a 65 bus. We'd start to see buses and we'd say, 'That's it, we're at work!' The disputes were regular at the time, but it was about breaking the mould and doing things differently.

"After the agreement, staff gradually slipped onto the new conditions, and we transferred people out to other garages as fast as possible. We were doing our own recruitment, so that as staff were going out of one door, we were recruiting new people in through the other door, on the new terms and conditions.

"We hand-picked a lot of people to run the garage. We set out to create a self-sustaining operation – it was almost self-sufficient, and it was quite exciting times. But we had real staff angst."

Steve Fennell was a driver at Norbiton. He was a crew driver from 1978, and went OPO in March 1979. He worked on DMSs, SMSs and Leyland Nationals. "Norbiton was a nice garage, a good crowd and easy-going. It was at the leading edge of all these changes, which was appalling. I think they picked on Norbiton as a soft touch, as there was not much militancy there."

Steve received two letters on the same day. The first told him of his new contract, 'From a certain date you will be employed by Kingston Buses, a subsidiary of London Buses, your wages will be such, and your working hours will be such.' The second letter said 'You have been successful in your application to become an Area Inspector in Cardinal District.' He accepted the second letter.

"The Norbiton guys didn't deserve what happened to them. They were given tatty old training buses, and appalling duties, and they did away with the roadside Inspectors on all the routes – not a single Inspector got a job at Norbiton."

Norbiton subsequently became part of London United when the Units were created, by which time many garages had different staff conditions. It was closed in September 1991 following tender losses.

Harrow
With the Harrow tendering on the horizon, Leaside needed more second hand buses. Their tender avoided the Potters Bar downfall of wage cuts, although flexible working conditions were necessary and, in some instances, longer hours. The group of staff most severely put out were skilled engineers in various specialist categories classed officially as 'craftsmen' who would be required to work at week-ends for the first time. It was also possible to introduce a high proportion of new buses – 27 Metrobuses on contract hire and 30 Metrorider midibuses which were purchased, but the double deck balance of 26 needed to comprise second hand vehicles to keep the tender competitive. Ken Blacker was aware that West Midlands Travel possessed 50 Volvo Ailsas with Alexander aluminium framed bodies which had become non-standard in its fleet since plans to purchase further vehicles of the type had been vetoed by WMT's political masters, as they were not built in the West Midlands. If the 50 vehicles could be obtained, they would meet Harrow's needs (26) and almost complete the conversion to second hand double deckers at Potters Bar (24). Willie Arrol was asked to sound out WMT on their willingness to sell the vehicles, and on 5 June 1987 a meeting was held at their Tyburn Road works to examine a sample vehicle and to thrash out a deal. Ken recalls, "We found that they had semi-automatic transmissions unlike our own Volvo Ailsas which were all automatic, but I didn't see this as any great problem. A very good price was negotiated on the strict understanding that we would purchase all 50, but we were asked to keep quiet about the transaction for a while as WMT hadn't yet informed its unions that they were thinking of disposing of these vehicles." After purchase most of V16-65 were driven the short distance across Birmingham to MCW's premises where they were repainted and prepared for service although one, V20, was dealt with by Scottish Bus Engineering and another, V45, by United Counties. Both needed repairs to their wiring circuits which had suffered fires.

The Harrow bid was won and Gordon Tennant was appointed General Manager. He set up the operation with a new team based at Harrow Weald garage and an outstation for midibus operations on the GEC

Westlink won three minibus routes in the Kingston network and ran them from the former Kingston garage. The new routes were marketed as "Kingston Hoppa" and once again they introduced bus services to previously unserved areas. One of the Metroriders leaves on the K2 to Hook. Route 216 was a commercial operation by London Buses and in September it was transferred to Westlink who could operate it more cheaply. (Keith Wood)

70 "We were losing 4 or 5 big bus drivers at Harrow Weald every week."

Estate in North Wembley. A new image was selected for the operation which was named Harrow Buses, and Ken Blacker chose a red and pale cream colour scheme based on the cheerful livery formerly used by the old Southport Corporation but embellished with a black skirt in common with the rest of the Leaside fleet, although Gordon subsequently favoured a larger area of red on the upper deck, arranging for some of the Volvo Ailsas and all the new Metrobuses to be painted in this way.

The start date was 14 November 1987. Although MCW delivered the Metroriders on time, the new Metrobuses were late and old Greater Manchester Fleetlines had to be used in the short term. Gordon comments, "It got off to a bad start. We had the staff in place and recruited around 50 midibus drivers at North Wembley, but we were losing 4 or 5 big bus drivers at Harrow Weald every week, causing major problems. Those who stayed were finding it worse than previously with longer shifts. The TBU had changed some of the routes and while most of the changes were good, the 201 ran around a loop and would serve Harrow twice in each direction. In addition, the recovery times had been pared down and so were unsustainable. It was never as good as it could have been. The old Manchester Fleetlines limped on but started to die on us, and we were not allowed to have fleet Metrobuses as it would be a breach of the separation of the operation from the block grant network. Eventually we were allowed three."

The Metroriders proved disappointingly unreliable at first, due almost entirely to deficiencies in their braking system, and it became necessary for each vehicle to be checked weekly by MCW staff until a programme of installing electric retarders could be introduced which largely solved the problem. The Volvo Ailsas also proved troublesome. Their maintenance under WMT had not been anywhere near as good as anticipated, with engines a particular problem until many of the vehicles had been sent to a variety of outside contractors to be put right. Eventually two more new Metrobuses were supplied by MCW at short notice, who diverted them from a batch then being built for East Kent, with the latter's permission, of course.

The local Harrow Observer newspaper made great play of these early difficulties. The operation did settle down once the new Metrobuses arrived in their red and cream colour scheme and the staff situation stabilised.

Leaside bought an entire batch of 50 Volvo Ailsa double deckers from West Midlands Travel in 1987. New in 1976, 26 of these went to Harrow and 24 to Potters Bar for the tendered services there. V30 and V23 are seen at Potters Bar. (Keith Wood)

71 West Midlands Travel had 50 Volvo Ailsas which had become non-standard in its fleet.

Potters Bar postscript

Leaside's purchase of second hand double deckers was not yet quite over. In March 1987 some single door Metrobuses came on the market as a result of a second round of post-deregulation service cuts by some of the former PTE operators, and nine were purchased for service at Potters Bar. Five had formerly operated for Greater Manchester (M1443-1447) and four for West Yorkshire (M1448-1451). The previous requirement that the capital cost of acquiring second hand buses needed to be covered by receipts from selling other vehicles had been dropped, which simplified negotiations. The former Greater Manchester buses were prepared and painted at the premises of Kirkby Bus & Coach and the ex-West Yorkshire ones at Ensign's prior to starting work at Potters Bar in June 1987, releasing more Metrobuses.

At the end of 1987 five Metrobuses in very good condition were bought from Busways Travel Services at a price well below that paid for other Metrobuses, and they were driven direct from Newcastle to Scottish Bus Engineering in Edinburgh for repainting. They started service at Potters Bar as M1479-1483 between February and April 1988, initially to partly cover for Volvo Ailsas whose entry into service had been unavoidably delayed, and to operate an additional Hertfordshire County Council contract. Later, when things settled down, they effectively replaced ex-Greater Manchester M1443-1447 which were more costly to run due to having hydraulic rather than air braking and were transferred for service elsewhere. By now the security of Potters Bar garage had been achieved, at least in the short term – in an era of tendering no-one could predict what the future might bring. Although a separate company, P B Buses Ltd, was registered in case it might be needed, it remained dormant and was later dissolved. Potters Bar's saviour had largely come about through the use of good second hand double deckers, and when the garage was finally handed over from Leaside District to the new London Northern all but four of its double deckers (V1-3 and M1277) were second hand.

72 *"The security of Potters Bar garage had been achieved, at least in the short term."*

Above left Harrow Weald bus garage on the first day of the new operation, 14 November 1987. A Greater Manchester Fleetline stands in the entrance while a former West Midlands Travel Volvo Ailsa waits inside.

Left Two of the new Metroriders stand at Pinner.

Above Ken Blacker chose a red and pale cream colour scheme for Harrow, seen here on Volvo Ailsa V29, near Harrow Weald garage with two Metrobuses from Alperton garage on the 182.

Right Harrow began to receive its new 27 new Mark II Metrobuses in November. These were single-door buses in the red and cream Harrow Buses livery. M1453 is seen Golders Green on 28 November. (all Keith Wood)

Bexleybus

London Buses retained the majority of routes in the Bexley scheme, which were to be operated by another low-cost unit named 'Bexleybus' with vehicles in a blue and cream livery. Four routes were won by Maidstone Boro'line. Norman Cohen recalls, "Bexleybus was set up by Selkent as a low-cost operation. It was Bryan Constable's answer to what Marcus was challenging all of the companies, to set up low cost companies, and if you didn't, what would happen is what happened to Loughton."

Mike Clayton had put the bid together. "Bexleybus did not go so well. It was a higher risk operation. We tried to run Bexleybus as a self-contained operation with low overheads, and we tried to be like Ensign. We consciously said to ourselves, if we were Ensign, how would we do it? And we did it that way. So we used second hand buses, and we basically said to TBU, "If you want cheap prices and crappy buses, here's our bid with cheap prices and crappy buses." The problem was that there was a reluctance to pay more for better quality – if we wanted the work, we had to put in those sort of prices. The engineering staff were not up to that sort of structure, with second or third hand DMSs. They were used to working with newer buses and with a reasonable amount of resources and support."

Mike recalls a meeting with staff. "The first four rows of the audience were full of the wives of all the drivers who were going at it hammer and tongs, complaining that we were cutting the wages of their husbands. We said that we had to in order to win the work." It would always be a very competitive part of London. The network was mostly won by London Buses with 17 of the 20 routes on the basis of a new operating base in the reopened Bexleyheath garage. The remaining three routes were won by Maidstone Boro'line. The scheme involved new midibus routes. However, the reopening of Bexleyheath garage led to the closure of Sidcup which was not convenient for the network.

The new operation had a blue and cream livery and the vehicles were renumbered into a new series. 28 new Northern Counties-bodied Leyland Olympians

Bexleybus received 28 new Leyland Olympians with Northern Counties bodies taken from an order cancelled by Greater Manchester and leased from Kirkby Central. Number 23 is at Bexleyheath Broadway on 16 January, the first day of operation of the new network. The experimental Autocheck ticketing system in the Bexley and Plumstead area used cardreaders linked to the Wayfarer driver's ticket machine to check London Underground-style magnetic tickets, but the precision cardreaders did not cope well with intensive bus operation. (Keith Wood)

74 "The first four rows of the audience were full of the wives of all the drivers, complaining that we were cutting the wages of their husbands."

14 DMSs were reacquired from Clydeside Scottish in exchange for Routemasters. Clydeside repainted the buses into Bexleybus livery and Ensignbus checked their mechanical condition. They retained their Scottish modifications including the single door and destination screens, making them different from other DMSs in the Bexleybus fleet. (David Cole)

Below Two former London Buses DMSs return to London bus work and are seen at Lewisham Bus Station in July 1988. DMS1671 went to Scotland and came back for Bexleybus, while DMS1922 was sold by Ensign to Metrobus in 1986. (Keith Wood)

were leased – these were part of a cancelled Greater Manchester order and were to their specification with single doors. There were 12 new Metroriders, and 24 Leyland Nationals which were surplus within LBL and were repainted by Eastbourne Buses. 17 DMS Fleetlines were taken from the AEC site in Southall where they had lain derelict for some years – they were overhauled and refurbished by Ensign. Another 14 former DMSs were re-acquired from Clydeside Scottish in exchange for Routemasters and were repainted into Bexleybus livery by Clydeside. Mechanical attention was carried out by Ensign, but they retained their Clydeside destination blind boxes. The rear destination blind boxes had been painted over and there were other minor modifications including removal of the engine shrouds at the rear. Peter Newman was amused by this – he was selling back to LBL buses he had bought from them, sold to Western SMT who didn't want them any longer, and he bought them back and passed them on to Bexleybus.

75 "If you want cheap prices and crappy buses, here's our bid with cheap prices and crappy buses."

The new operation was introduced on 16 January 1988. Following the difficulties at Kingston and Harrow, LBL gave assurances about implementation. But there were still problems with staff shortages, tight scheduling and vehicle deployment. Bob Muir recalls that they were let down by drivers from Kentish Bus who said they were going to turn up and didn't, so there was a major staff shortage from day one. There was a lot of joint compilation and it imploded – the service was dreadful. Mothers complained about their kids being left at bus stops when the bus didn't turn up.

The demoralised drivers faced reduced wages, longer shifts and rotas incorporating difficult headways together with public hostility because of the poor service, and many resigned in the first few days. They struck at the beginning of February, which caused even more public hostility. Complaints of buses bunching and overcrowding grew worse when single-deckers appeared on double-decker workings. Posters appeared inside buses saying to passengers "Don't blame the driver". A further strike in March was due to the lack of staff facilities. Whilst the vehicles were ready on time, some of them had been standing idle for some years and were unreliable as a result.

Some re-scheduling of services took effect from 14 May, but the problems remained. Peter Hendy was called in by Bryan Constable to run an enquiry into the situation. He saw that the local managers were far too aggressive in the handling of their staff, adding to the demoralisation of the workforce, and suggested a replacement manager, Alan Mecham, to try to resolve the difficulties. "Things then improved – he was a nicer and more reasonable manager with considerable experience." In November, Bexleybus gave up operation of the 422 and 492 in order to concentrate resources on the other routes. Nick Newton said at the time, "Sadly, reliability of the new Bexleyheath area route network has been adversely affected by these persistent staff shortages experienced by Bexleybus. LRT has therefore renegotiated its contract with Bexleybus in a way which matches that undertaking's commitment more closely to its resources". Alan Mecham said that, "This part of London has a very competitive labour market". Of the 212 drivers required by Bexleybus, only 195 were available in October and 135 had joined and left during the first nine months of the operation. An increase in pay was made, together with improvements to the facilities at Bexleyheath garage, but the target of 212 drivers was never achieved.

Bexleyheath garage with two DMSs and an Iveco minibus. Both DMSs had been stored at the former AEC works at Southall and were recertified by Ensign. The minibus was one of 12 Ivecos which came from Roundabout in exchange for new, larger, Metroriders. (Keith Wood)

76 The target of 212 drivers at Bexleybus was never achieved.

Boro'line London

Boro'line Maidstone commenced LRT contracted services on 16 January 1988 from a compound within the London Borough of Bexley depot at Crayford using the name Boro'line London. Bus enthusiasts were warned that visitors were not welcome there. They operated the 132, 233, 228 and 328. The four routes had a peak vehicle requirement of 13 buses, and because the 14 new Leyland Olympian double deckers were late in arriving, the Leyland distributors arranged to supply 1973 and 1982 Roe-bodied Leyland Atlanteans from Hull as well as a Greater Manchester Olympian in orange GM Buses livery. The new Olympians began to arrive from 4 February.

Maidstone Borough Council had operated a co-ordination agreement with Maidstone & District and East Kent, the two local NBC companies, but this was outlawed under deregulation in 1986. Both NBC companies were privatised, and Maidstone had to fight their own corner instead of having friends alongside. Alan Price, the MD, was shrewd and realised that they were only 30 minutes from the nearest part of London, so they took an interest in LRT work. "We were looking for an alternative income stream to prepare for the inevitable bus wars in Maidstone," said Alan, "and Bexley was the only profitable bus area in Kent." They had bid for the Orpington routes in 1985 when still part of Maidstone Borough Council. They became an arms length company in October 1986. They also moved into coaching in a big way.

Norman Kemp was Operations Manager for Boro'line. He had joined Maidstone Borough Council in 1983 and was with them till mid-1988. "We initially had a small operation from January 1988. We had to hire buses at first as Optare couldn't deliver. Then we had new buses, motivated staff and it was a cracking little operation which made money. The operation was set up at a time of huge change in the bus industry in south east London and there was no problem in recruiting local staff of a high calibre – many had been displaced from London Country just a mile along the road at Dartford – the garage here had borne the brunt of the tendering upheaval with the loss of nearly all local work."

With the Boro'line operation going well, Norman left in mid-1988 to go to Kentish Bus. That November, Boro'line took over two Bexley services, 422 and 492, due to poor performance by Bexleybus. This had been under discussion for some months and was then carried out at short notice as Bexleybus could not fulfil the contract. Suddenly what had been a small profitable operation had become a big operation, and they had problems through growing very quickly. Good staff were now harder to find. They also added the 188 that month, for which Norman Kemp had prepared the bid, a high profile central London route.

Maidstone Boro'line provided a rainbow of colours all on its own! Atlanteans from Kingston upon Hull and Greater Manchester wait at Eltham Station in 1988 alongside Boro'line's own blue and yellow Olympian. The livery, and the logo which is on all three vehicles, were by Best Impressions. Ray Stenning advised calling the operation Boro'line London but this was not adopted. Eltham Station was then fairly new having replaced the original Eltham Park and Eltham Well Hall stations to allow construction of the Rochester Way Relief Road. (Colin Fradd)

"We had new buses, motivated staff and it was a cracking little operation which made money."

78

Maidstone Boro'line used a variety of hired vehicles until new buses arrived.

Above left Ipswich Number 1, on hire to Maidstone, working as a London bus at Surrey Quays in November 1988. (Keith Wood)

Left Nottingham 200 is at Euston in March 1989. (David Cole)

Above Boro'line received 14 new Volvo Citybuses with Alexander bodies in 1989, their bright blue and yellow livery contrasting with the traditional red of London Buses – except when it was dirty! No. 928 is at Greenwich in November 1990. (Keith Wood)

Developments in London Buses
In autumn 1987, the six Bus Districts were reduced to five and renamed as Regions to reflect their changed responsibilities and greater autonomy intended for the garages. Abbey District closed. The Central Traffic Division (CTD) was created to plan, schedule and supervise services that came into the centre, to provide infrastructure and to liaise with the Local Authorities there. The first individual Garage General Managers were appointed, responsible for specific services, budget preparation and financial and operational monitoring. The number of Bus Directors was reduced to five, together with 500 administrative and support jobs to save £30 million annually.

John Telford Beasley told LRT News, "The whole aim of the restructuring is to meet competition and to prepare for the possibility of deregulation of bus services in London. But whatever the future, we have a duty to run the services efficiently. This programme is the basis of future growth for London Buses, and it should put us in a strong position over the next couple of years – and into the future".

David Sayburn was in charge of CTD with an Operating Manager, a Planning Manager and 250 Inspectors. "LRT gradually took over service planning which led to continuing conflict over whether service changes should be based on operating experience or computer models. The 1984 Act had given them this power and so they gradually took over, leading to many longer routes being shortened. The 73, for example, was cut back to Victoria in 1988." David monitored the performance of Block Grant routes in central London, argued the case for traffic management and bus priorities with the central London boroughs, and would call the LBL operators to account for any poor performance on their services. Supervision became increasingly by radio rather than roadside inspectors and over the following years CTD's remaining roles were gradually devolved to the Districts and, finally, the LBL companies.

The combination of a declining fleet through tender losses and government spending restrictions led to a complete ban on LBL buying new buses unless they were for a specific new purpose, and the routine

The new LBL corporate livery was introduced from November 1987 and quickly appeared throughout the fleet. The grey skirt and white band above the lower deck windows looked attractive, particularly as a major programme led to a third of the fleet being repainted during 1988. D2532 enters Trafalgar Square. (David Cole)

replacement of the fleet came to a halt. From 1988 to 1991, only 69 new double-deckers and 17 full-size single-deckers joined the fleet. This encouraged the development of minibus schemes, for which money was available, and in those same years 980 new mini and midibuses did arrive – 90% of the new vehicle deliveries. Refurbishment programmes helped keep the fleet presentable, but it was not until 1992 that larger numbers of new vehicles were received.

LBL continued to modernise its operating systems throughout the 1980s. Service control by radio was developed; major computer systems were introduced for garage operating and engineering administration to improve efficiency and replace the costly Garage Inspectors; and electronic ticket machines replaced the mechanical machines on OPO buses with an immediate payback in reduced driver signing on and off times, together with increased information on passenger numbers. The Autocheck system in Thamesmead experimented with magnetic card readers to check Underground-style magnetic tickets in a second boarding stream on OPO buses, though the card readers proved too sensitive to provide sufficient reliability when used in buses.

LBL announced further garage closures during 1987 at Clapton, Hendon and Wandsworth, with others throughout London under consideration. Closing Clapton and Wandsworth was part of a larger reorganisation which resulted in a new open–air operating base for the Red Arrow services on the former bus stand at Waterloo. This was delayed while waiting for planning consent and Walworth garage was used as a temporary base until October 1990.

LRT and LBL both adopted new logos to emphasise their respective functions and to promote a better understanding of the structure of public transport in London. The new London Buses logo was a variant of the roundel consisting of a red circle with a yellow bar showing the words 'London Buses' in red, and went with a new corporate livery. The new symbol was gradually applied to LBL owned vehicles. London Underground continued using its existing roundel, a red circle with a blue bar. LBL introduced new fleet liveries which began to appear on buses from November 1987. The effect on Routemasters was minimal but more significant on the double decker OPO vehicles.

As LRT were responsible for planning and organising transport, rather than the day-to-day operation of services, the roundel was not used and a new emblem was devised comprising the letters LRT in white on a blue background with the words "Organising Transport for London" underneath. The plain red roundel was to continue in cases where both bus and Underground activities took place such as Travel Information Centres, the LT Museum, LT Advertising and the Lost Property Office.

LBL's General Manager Buses, Marcus Smith, retired during 1987. It was also announced during 1987 that LRT was seeking offers for Bus Engineering Ltd. It was suggested that a private buyer, with access to wider markets, would be able to make the business viable and preserve jobs.

A tragedy for London and an event which deeply wounded LRT was the King's Cross Underground Station fire on 18 November 1987, in which 31 people died. This was found to result from the decline of traditional maintenance arrangements and had a profound effect on the whole of London Transport.

Contracts terminated and the growth of BTS
At the beginning of 1988, LRT terminated the London Country North East (LCNE) contracts for routes 292, 298 and 313, after a damaging strike. These routes had suffered significant unreliability ever since they were tendered in 1987.

Malcolm Wren recalled, "It was inevitable that we would have to take this action, and it demonstrated to other contractors that we would respond to inadequate performance. On the day we called in London Country North East to remove them from their contract, there was another operator who came in for a review due to their poor performance. They got wind of what was going on and the manager went back to the garage and insisted there should be a full service tomorrow. His staff replied, 'But Governor, we never run a full service' but he responded, 'You

From 1988 to 1991, 980 new mini and midibuses arrived, 90% of new vehicle deliveries.

will start tomorrow!' Some of this makes you shudder, but it was stimulating as you really felt that we were making progress."

Borehamwood Travel Services (BTS) worked the 292 and Grey-Green worked the 298 and 313 on emergency contracts during the February strike, and then took over on 6-month contracts from 22 February. LCNE's contracts were terminated.

Nick Newton stresses that operators trusted TBU to be honest and straightforward. "The LCNE service on the 292 service was awful – I gave 36 hours notice, and had already arranged for BTS to take over. When there was a problem operators helped out straight away and were willing to agree the price later – they knew it would be ok with us."

Dave Alexander joined BTS in the early 1980s. He had bought a car MoT station when he was 19 and ran it for a couple of years. Then he sold it and needed a job, so he went to the coach company next door. "I didn't set out to do it – it was fate! When LCNE had their strike on the 292, LT were looking to cover part of it. We had our depot at Borehamwood, and so we ran the route for them with Leyland Leopard coaches. The drivers used Gibson ticket machines which used to fly across the front window as they went down the A1! There was a novelty factor for the BTS staff. I suppose they were excited about doing it – it was something different. Nowadays we would see it as competing but in those days it was a sort of fighting spirit. We were a small private company so you could really rally the troops. But it was really good, and I did some of the driving myself.

"That was the start of BTS becoming a bus company because we began to see that we could probably do quite well with buses as opposed to coaches. So then we mixed buses and coaches and we started tendering for Hertfordshire routes. When the 292 came up for retender we won the route, much to our surprise. That was a big thing for us and I remember going and buying six brand-new Scania 113 buses. And that was the turning point because then we tendered for the 114 in 1991 and won that. That added another 14 buses to the six that we already had and all of a sudden we had 20 buses in a company that was running 20 coaches, and you could really see the change. This was the reason that we ditched the coaches and carried on as a bus company.

"It was quite simple bidding for routes. At first, you did a timetable, you worked out your duties and

From the beginning of tendering, LRT was concerned that coach operators might use high-floor vehicles on local bus services, but at times this was unavoidable. When London Country North East lost three services in early 1988 following a strike, Grey-Green took over the 298 and 313 and worked them with coaches until permanent contracts were won and suitable vehicles were acquired. Their Leyland Leopard coach is shown on the 313 in Enfield during March 1988. (Keith Wood)

81 The drivers used Gibson ticket machines which used to fly across the front window as they went down the A1!

Above Grey-Green were later able to allocate double-deckers to the 298 and 313. Volvo Citybus 158 passes through Enfield on the 313. Grey-Green was now building up a portfolio of tendered services in north London where the Eastenderbus fleetname was not appropriate, so Grey-Green was used. (Colin Fradd)

Below A BTS Park Royal bodied Leyland Atlantean is seen in Elstree in August 1986, shortly after the company took over the contract for the route. (Barry Le Jeune)

your costs, you filled in a sheet; it was a three year contract so you had three columns, one for each year – it was as simple as that. I guess it got more and more bureaucratic, but it was a good system and was easily understood. It certainly didn't create any sort of barrier to us submitting bids, and we did bid for a number of routes but we were only ever successful for the 292, the 13 and the 114. We did look at expanding and we did look at other depots, but you needed a critical mass of work. We weren't going to take on a 150 bus depot and put a 10 bus route into it and try and make it work.

"As time went on and the company got bigger, we introduced more and more infrastructure. By the time you finish running in at 1 o'clock in the morning and the next day's buses are going out at 3.30 or 4 o'clock, you get to the stage where you realise that you may as well not shut. You end up moving from a 12 hour a day operation to 24 hours day, seven days a week."

Kentish Bus

London Country Bus Services was split into four companies by the National Bus Company (NBC) in September 1986. London Country South East renamed itself Kentish Bus in April 1987 and worked towards privatisation. There was a management bid for the company but it was sold to the Proudmutual Group on 15 March 1988.

Tony Kennan was Commercial Director of Proudmutual. He and his fellow Directors of the Northumbria subsidiary of the National Bus Company had bid to buy their company on privatisation. All NBC companies were provided with advisers to assist them in putting together their bids. The adviser appointed to them told him that, "I love coming here. You are so clearly a management team. I can't put a fag paper between you. You are very credible as a team. You have a good business plan and you clearly agree with each other. However, I believe there is a question that you haven't asked yourselves. If Brian Souter bids more than the 5% differential over your bid, I will have to say, 'Sorry guys, you put in all of that effort but you haven't got the company.' What will you say to me? Do I tell Brian Souter that he has a company with a management team, or that he has to find himself a new management team? Will you be willing to work for somebody else?

"We went off and had lunch, and a few pints, and some more pints, and an evening meal, and after a lot of heart searching decided that we would not stay and work for somebody else." Their adviser then told them that, within his portfolio, there was another company he didn't feel were a convincing team. Every time he saw them, one of them asked to see him privately afterwards. He did not believe their business plan. He suggested that the Northumbria team should bid for this other company as an insurance policy in case they didn't get their own company."

The company was Kentish Bus, and they did bid for it, setting up a holding company called Proudmutual. When they looked at the company's Business Plan they thought, 'Is it worth it?' "We felt the plan was full of entrenchment, retreating into a corner. But I could see possibilities from Bluewater, which was about to open, from the Channel Tunnel, and one big opportunity in the London tendering. I knew that those who are there first are the ones who will make money – they will be rewarded with more contracts."

They were successful in buying Northumbria and got on with running their new company. A couple of months later, the adviser called them again and said, "You know that insurance policy – it's just cashed in!" They bought Kentish Bus in March 1988. They then had the task of managing the company from Northumberland. Their decision was, with hindsight, their biggest mistake – they said to the Kentish Bus Management team, "There is your business plan – you make it work! Your role is to prove to us that you can make this company profitable, over a period of time. You've got to work it out." In fact, they didn't believe the Business Plan and sure enough, it started to fail. The management team at Kentish Bus were clearly not succeeding. So they decided at a Board Meeting to spend more time down in Kent. Tony remembers arriving at the Kentish Bus head office at 08.40 one morning. "I couldn't get into the building until it was opened at 09.20, and the senior management turned up at around 10 o'clock. So we had to make some tough decisions and decided we needed a new team." Tony recalls staff reaction being very supportive of the directors and they set about getting a new management team, needing a personality at the top who would stamp his mark on the company. They knew Brian Hurst and recruited him as Managing Director in 1989, from Alder Valley. They wanted a personality who would work his socks off and achieve a change in attitudes, some of which still came from London Transport days. "No one would make a decision, and there was a feeling that the trade union was stronger than anyone else." Tony started looking at London tendering.

Norman Kemp moved from Maidstone Boro'line to become Commercial Manager at Kentish Bus just after Proudmutual took over. "Proudmutual had to sort out Kentish Bus, and I came as part of the sorting out process". He was with them from 1988 until 1993.

Kentish Bus closely monitored the deteriorating Boro'line Maidstone situation and was ready to jump in, and eventually took over Boro'line's London operations in February 1992. They were good contracts

---

83 "I couldn't get into the building until it was opened at 09.20, and the senior management turned up at around 10 o'clock."

Above left An early tender win by Kentish Bus was the P14 from Surrey Docks Station to the Isle of Dogs. Their Metrorider is seen at Surrey Quays. (Keith Wood)

Above Pan Atlas took over route 112 in July 1988 and their Leyland Lynx loads at Brent Cross on its way to Finchley. (Keith Wood)

and it was profitable to take them over. When he left, Kentish Bus was the biggest private sector provider of contracted services to LRT, just ahead of Capital Citybus. Kentish Bus had been transformed into a far bigger player in London than just in Metropolitan Kent, though Brian Hurst's long-held ambition for Kentish Bus to serve Kentish Town was never fulfilled.

Changes in East London

The network of routes in the Romford and Hornchurch area was also tendered in 1988. The scheme included small bus operation but retained larger buses to counter criticism of overcrowding at busy times. Frontrunner (East Midlands) won two routes and Ensign four. The two minibus routes were awarded to London Buses and joined the 193 as Hornchurch Hoppas, but these results decimated the red buses in the area and Hornchurch garage closed on 24 September.

Leon Daniels remembers that night well. "Ensign were running route N99 between Chadwell Heath and Upminster. This route was interworked with the 62, and it went past Hornchurch garage. We didn't think of this beforehand, but the staff were outside the garage marking its closure, a little worse for wear, as our Leyland National on the N99 went past. Their reaction was vicious, with stuff being thrown at the bus." Nick Newton referred to that point as being "the moment when the staff realised that they didn't have a God-given right to run these routes for ever."

Frontrunner South East

Frontrunner South East was a new operator for LRT and won the 248 and 252 from September 1988. It was a subsidiary of East Midland Motor Services, which was a combination of the former East Midland and Mansfield and District companies. They already had some Essex County Council contracts and had registered a coach service to bring staff to Essex to work the routes.

Peter Jenner was Commercial Manager and one of the team who bought the company on privatisation. Why had they bid for work in Essex and London? "Hunger", said Peter. As a result of deregulation, they considered what was their commercial network, which was clearly going to be less than what they had at the time. They had to consider what to do about the new situation. Network support from the local authority was about to disappear. There clearly was a commercial network, and some services would be tendered, but if local independents acted opportunistically, then they wouldn't enjoy the same volume of business. Reducing the scale of their operation would have a significant cost. They were therefore looking for opportunities.

They considered the possibilities on the edges of principal cities – it would be difficult to set up in those cities, but a fringe position would be possible. A bid for some tenders in Essex came up, so they punted for some Essex services to Blackmore and Ongar. Of all the tenders they had submitted at the beginning of deregulation, Essex was the first answer they got, and this led to the X90 service to Chipping Ongar. This was originally from Worksop and subsequently cut back to Mansfield, operating on Fridays and Sundays in the evenings through Cambridge to Chipping Ongar. The X90 was the supply line for the three buses then operating out of Brentwood. They were in service in order to earn fuel tax rebate and this was fully costed within the tender bid.

Peter turned up at Chipping Ongar at 5 o'clock one day and saw the X90 with half a load on it. He asked

84 "That was the moment when the staff realised that they didn't have a God-given right to run these routes for ever."

the driver where all these passengers were going, and was told that this was fairly normal, that the majority were going to Mansfield. A few ferry drivers used the service, which returned buses in service to and from their main operation.

The Brentwood operation had three buses and around 10 drivers who were in digs in Brentwood. There was a supervising inspector and he had an arrangement with local people for mechanical support. The vehicles were parked at Wyatt's Green outside Brentwood, basically in someone's back garden where he had planning permission.

They then decided to have a punt for some LT routes in the area. Bidding for LT work was like writing a book – they had to provide lots of documentation, explaining who they were, and what and how they were going to do it. He went for a grilling at TBU, and then won the 248 and 252. To carry out this contract they acquired depot premises in Rainham with management and drivers recruited locally. They needed to develop into more of a mainstream bus operation – they had previously managed it from the north but now they had to establish a local organisation. They also took over a disused cafe at Roneo Corner which became their control centre where the inspectors were based, and which was a focal point for both routes. This also provided a driver tea room and relief point – it was ideally located and worked extremely well.

The driver recruitment and training was done locally. They wanted to establish a new ethos which was not necessarily the London Transport ethos, so they recruited and trained most of the new recruits themselves. They had their own trainer/examiner but their man, who was authorised by the North West and the North East Traffic Areas to examine and pass out drivers, needed permission to examine in the Metropolitan area, which was achieved. They built up a team of very good people who looked after their customers properly – the operation was well executed.

At the beginning of the 252 they had help from Grey-Green, who were building up a supply of trained drivers for the 24 and were lent to Frontrunner to get the 252 running – it was not a problem recruiting staff. All went smoothly – they had issues but these were similar to those back at home. Bussing drivers from Chesterfield and Mansfield was initially for the Essex routes, and they recruited locally for the LT tenders. But some of the original drivers stayed on in Rainham – they clubbed together to buy a caravan. There was great spirit, enthusiasm and pride that these drivers brought to Essex and took back to Chesterfield and Mansfield. This raised the spirits of everybody back home. The drivers were there for some time but would regularly bounce back for some R&R at home.

One day, Peter Jenner was at Brentwood "at one of those moments when there was a bus and no driver," so he took it over until a replacement driver was found. He went into Romford, and the first person in the queue was Malcolm Wren of the TBU. They chatted on the platform for a few moments and then he checked his running board to see when he was due out. Malcolm replied, "Seven and a half minutes after the bus in front!" This made them think through the whole concept of what they were operating compared to what LT had bought.

They were not used to variable running times, or routes running on a frequency basis, until they came to London. The travel patterns were also very different. "On the 248, you lurched from Underground station to Underground station. On a morning peak journey, 95 people would get off the bus at Upminster. You then carried on and another 95 would get off at the next Underground station. In the Derby and Nottinghamshire areas it was much quieter with not the same local town centre focus. One driver commented that he always got a full load on the 248 going to church at 8 o'clock on a Sunday morning. Normally in Mansfield, he said, the full load going to 'church' is at opening time, around 12 noon!"

Frontrunner had another operation on the fringes of Manchester, based in Glossop, operating into and around the Greater Manchester area. They also operated in the Dearne Valley near Doncaster. Peter still recalls the tremendous spirit of the drivers. They gave every driver the opportunity to go to London, and no one had their arm twisted. And many asked to go!

A variety of colour schemes in Romford with Frontrunner, Ensign and LBL buses at work soon after the introduction of the new network. (Michael Steward)

"There was great spirit, enthusiasm and pride that these drivers brought to Essex and took back to Chesterfield and Mansfield."

In April 1989, Stagecoach bought the East Midland Motor Services Group, including the Essex operation. This introduced Stagecoach to London tendered operations and soon, buses from other Stagecoach companies arrived to improve availability. At the end of June, Stagecoach sold these operations to Ensign, who immediately resold the Essex routes to County Bus and Coach without having worked them. The remaining services were moved to Ensign's Purfleet depot and operated from 1 July 1989.

Grey-Green and the 24

In April 1988 it was announced that route 24 would be tendered, the first central London route, running from Hampstead Heath to Pimlico via Trafalgar Square, Westminster and Victoria. This was a confident move by LRT, bringing tendered operations into the heart of London and past the Houses of Parliament. It was chosen because costs were high and the service performance from Chalk Farm garage was poor. On 5 November 1988 the route passed to Grey-Green, who bought a new fleet of Volvo buses in a smart grey, green and orange livery operated from their Stamford Hill depot. They could accommodate double deckers there as it had been built to accommodate their removal vans. This was also the first route transfer to be given national press coverage – suburban routes didn't get press launches, but the 24 did.

Grey-Green was a long-standing coach operator with roots back to the horse carriage business set up by George Ewer in 1885. Their traditional business of taking north and east Londoners to the seaside in Kent and East Anglia was declining as Londoners moved out and bought cars. They were now owned by Cowie, and Andrew Cowie was leading them away from car dealerships, developing the bus business based on the experience built up by Grey-Green in north and east London. This had initially used the name Eastenderbus and operated from the former Dix depot in Dagenham, but as their operations became more widespread the name returned to Grey-Green.

Grey-Green's takeover of route 24 brought national press coverage. Their Volvo Citybus 120 enters Cambridge Circus from Shaftesbury Avenue. (Keith Wood)

The 24 was the first route transfer to be given national press coverage.

Walthamstow and Sutton

A further area scheme was introduced in Walthamstow on 19 November 1988. The new network once again resulted from an extensive survey and consultation, and affected 17 existing bus routes and introduced seven new midibus routes. The contract was negotiated between the TBU and LBL's Forest District – the routes were not competitively tendered. This achieved comparable economies and was intended to speed up the transition to tendered operations, as the scheme was ready to be implemented and there was already a heavy tendering programme. Ron Brewer, who was General Manager of Forest District, suggests that it was also intended to see what economies could be achieved with an individual garage operation by negotiation with the Trade Union.

The big bus routes and some of the midibus routes went to the new LBL Walthamstow operation, and other midibus routes to Eastern National. Forest District and the T&GWU agreed some relaxation of scheduling conditions, and new midibus drivers were recruited at lower rates of pay. I, Roger Torode, was Operating Manager at Walthamstow and was now appointed Garage General Manager. We introduced the scheme without disruption at Walthamstow, though the staff resented the changes to their conditions which were not happening at neighbouring garages such as Leyton. There was no special branding. The new network included services in Leaside district and at West Ham garage, and due to industrial relations issues at West Ham, and other schedule changes in Leaside, the scheme was phased in over several weeks. One of the shortest-lived routes ever was Route 102A which ran between Chingford and Edmonton from 5 to 19 November 1988 to fill a gap between the Leaside and Walthamstow changes.

The scheme was completed on 4 March 1989 when new 'Walthamstow Hoppa' minibus routes W13 and W14, operated by Eastern National, and W16 operated by LBL were introduced in place of existing services, together with a number of other service changes.

Another scheme was introduced at Sutton on 26 November, again involving the whole garage. The start was delayed from 22 October due to industrial action over the pay and conditions package on which the routes had been won. A new fleet name logo was applied together with the telephone number. Dave Weller had joined LT in 1976 as a conductor at Norwood, transferred to Sutton, and became a driver there in 1980. "The first we were affected by tendering was when LT bullied us into signing new contracts, saying that Sutton was now a separate operation and we had to sign. Sixteen of us held out and refused to sign. All the staff were transferred to SuttonBus – one day we worked for LT, the next day we were working for SuttonBus."

Walthamstow Central Bus Station in 1991, with large and small red and green buses, and an Eastern National taxi used for crew transfers. (Roger Torode)

87 The Walthamstow contract was intended to see what economies could be achieved by negotiation with the Trade Union.

"There were a couple of strikes at the time, but it took effect anyway. The pay changed dramatically, and the hours of working changed. They were desperate times then and people wanted to keep their jobs. They were told that, 'If you don't come in, you haven't got a job!'" Dave never signed the contract but he had to go over to the new conditions.

"Anyway, we had a wage and kept our jobs. We worked longer hours for the same money, but new people were brought in on lower rates. The existing staff didn't lose money, but lost certain benefits like London Weighting and Stabilisation Pay. The buses were the same, they simply had a brown line around the bottom and said SuttonBus on the front. They were not around for long, around five years, because in 1994 we became part of London General on privatisation and the SuttonBus conditions changed to the London General ones."

Above SuttonBus was introduced on 26 November 1988 based on a low-cost operation from Sutton garage using both big bus and minibus services. This Metrorider at Sutton Station is working route 522 to Gatwick Airport, a Sunday service supported by Surrey County Council. (Keith Wood)

SuttonBus D2624 rounds the corner at Carshalton Ponds (Colin Fradd)

88 "They were desperate times then and people wanted to keep their jobs."

Cityrama and Sampson's

On 3 December 1988, Cityrama were replaced on route 200 following service reliability problems. Kingston Bus took over the service from Norbiton garage. Cityrama then continued to work route 196 only. Malcolm Wren considers this one of the bad moments of tendered services. He received a public complaint that Cityrama were asking passengers on the 196 in South Norwood to get off the bus at the bottom of the hill and walk up, because the bus didn't have enough power to get up with passengers on. When they were called in to explain themselves, Cityrama asked, "Is there a way we can get out of this contract?" and Malcolm said, "Yes, there certainly is." Their first route had run well but they couldn't keep it up. The TBU moved quickly to replace Cityrama, giving London United a short term contract to run the 200 from Kingston while it was retendered. London and Country similarly took over the 196 on a short term contract from October 1989 and this was also retendered.

John Wood went up to see Sampson's about all the problems with their operation. "Peter Sampson, owner of Sampson's Coaches, was a very nice man but, like several of the companies initially involved in tendered routes, he was less competent at operating buses than running coaches. They were running route 317 with old DMSs. His depot at Waltham Cross was also a zoo, and one of the drivers said that you would drive back into the depot late at night to park up and there would be lions roaring in the dark! Coaches are very different from buses – it is a different sort of operation. I had to say, 'Either you surrender the contract, or we take it off you', so they surrendered it."

Sampson's gave up the 317 from 2 July 1988 and it returned to LBL's Enfield garage until fresh tenders could be awarded. The Sampson family sold their coach and bus operation and their MoT Testing Centre and garage in 1990 to concentrate on their Zoo and Wildlife Park.

Uxbridge

After Norbiton, David Brown was given the task by Tony Parsons, Cardinal DGM, of setting up Uxbridge Buses, which commenced on 18 February 1989. Uxbridge was seen as having a suitable route network for midibus operation, and a young age profile in the Borough suggesting a more dynamic market for bus traffic. The existing five big bus routes were replaced in part by five midibus routes which also extended coverage to new areas. Thirty-seven stretched midibuses would replace 19 Leyland Nationals. A report in 1990 showed a growth in passenger revenue of 15% whilst revenue costs had risen by less than 5%. This was the first LBL initiative in designing and implementing a new midibus network without LRT sponsorship or tendering.

David had a scheduler to help him and he set up a network of minibuses, often seeking the advice of Peter Hendy. He also had to create the business case and get it approved. Tony Parsons then said, "You've got approval, now go and deliver it!" So David became GM Uxbridge. There were tremendous changes going on in LBL at the time, and he would never have been given that amount of responsibility a few years before.

David had to recruit 75 midibus staff on new pay and conditions. He had done the calculations very carefully, but the accountants had gone through the sums and found an error, so he had to reduce the drivers rate by 50p an hour. "I pitched the wages at what I thought was the right wages to get new staff in, and this really messed up my plan." Of the 170 big bus drivers, 117 then at Uxbridge would remain on big bus work, while the rest were offered transfers or work on midibuses at protected pay rates until big bus vacancies became available.

"We did a big transition and we didn't get IR problems because we brought new staff in on the new terms and conditions – we didn't try to convert the old staff. But I remember, I was worried about whether I had got the frequencies right on all the new routes, and I can remember standing up on the corner near the hospital on what was the 204 route but had become the U4, thinking, 'Have we got this right?'"

"On the morning of the first day, we were in very early and everyone was signing on in Uxbridge garage. One of the terminals for the OPAL computer signing-on system went down, and because I thought I knew how to do this, I tried to get it going, and the other one went down as well! So we had some drivers signing on, and then nobody could sign on, so I took the unilateral decision of saying, 'It's all free fares then, free promotional offer on the first day of the service.' So they went out for several hours, and nobody was any the wiser that I'd made the decision of free fares. Then the system was up and running, and the only complaint we got was someone saying, 'Well, it was free fares this morning, why isn't it free fares this afternoon?'

"It was quite an interesting breed of new midibus drivers because what they wanted was to get promoted from midibus to double-deck, and then they got more money. There was a high attrition rate because they weren't paid enough, and they weren't the best in the world. Plus we were asking them to drive vehicles that were not the best. The 811's gearboxes were a bit clunky, although perhaps the vehicle was better than the Renaults subsequently used on the Greenford network. But we did have a picture of Lady Di boarding MA104! The Uxbridge network, which was called the U-Line, was successful and received larger and larger vehicles, but the network stayed the same and it is only recently that it has changed."

David recollects that there was 'a bit of an esprit de corps' amongst the midibus drivers to start with, so it was sustainable for quite a while, a new operation with new people. They were all youngsters, so there was a lot of 'socialising' going on. They went out a lot together, but there was a high rate of turnover and later on he realised that only two of the original drivers had survived for any length of time. Very few stayed on for a long-term career, though some of them were good and got promoted.

Conversely, there was a hard core of engineering people who stayed for ever. Phil Margrave says that, "The Union rep was as hard as nails but did really well – there was a lot of respect for him. He was difficult in some respects, but he had very high principles. Engineers are a bit more loyal to the business. They quite like the engineering job as a group and they hardly ever caused any difficulty. The way to improve the engineering performance was to reduce the staff numbers, and to pay the ones who were good more money for being more flexible and getting the job done. You could get away with that with the engineers in a way that you couldn't with drivers."

David went back to Uxbridge in 2007 with Ken Livingstone to launch a Safer Transport Police Team and was in his element because all the engineers were still there, just older and greyer, and all pleased to see him. He remarks on how he had a huge amount of autonomy, compared to what had happened before at London Buses. "There was very little oversight – no one was allowed that sort of freedom a few years before. I think there were so many bigger issues being tackled at the time such as privatisation, new structures, and people applying for their own jobs that I was allowed to 'just get on with it'."

Revenue Protection

Graham Elliott was in charge of LBL's Revenue Protection. "At the beginning of tendering, TBU was thinking of setting up their own Revenue Protection. They came to me and wanted to know all about it, but I was concerned that it would be wasteful, with their Inspectors ending up in their 'dead areas' and our Inspectors likewise, so I spoke to Nick Newton and said we could do it for him on a contract basis, which is what then happened. Building up a new organisation from the beginning would have been very difficult.

"At first there was some concern about revenue officials from London Buses working on other companies' buses, being totally impartial and maintaining standards of integrity. It all worked out well,

The Uxbridge scheme commenced on 18 February 1989, replacing five big bus routes with midibuses named 'U-Line'. Mercedes/Alexander 28 seat midibuses were used, here in Kingston Lane Uxbridge on service U4 to Hayes. (Keith Wood)

and we used to charge TBU an agreed sum for doing a fixed level of checking on tendered services. In revenue checking you are intelligence led, you hit the routes that have the highest level of irregularities. It also reflects the fare structure – if you have a route with only one fare on it, you are not looking for overriding, and as long as everybody has paid at least something when they get on the bus, then the level of irregularities will be quite small. You are just looking for out-of-date Travelcards and passes. We provided TBU with that Revenue Protection Service for a long time, including handling all their investigations and cases for prosecution.

"Some of the operators weren't used to having Revenue Inspectors on their buses and thought it was a bit weird, but obviously Nick Newton had to have some way of measuring their performance in terms of collecting the revenue, because the contracts were purely cost contracts. It wasn't the bus operator's money, and if there was no check on the quality of their fare collection, then the staff were going to sit there and basically do nothing.

"There was a system of fines, a multiple of what the irregularity was. There were quite a lot of penalties, but we were checking private operators and London Buses, who also could be fined. So it did put the revenue people in an odd position, fining their own organisation, while the private operators were being fined by an organisation which was their competitor. But we seemed to get through it all right."

Len Wright faced these penalties as an operator. "There was a problem with the checks by Revenue Inspectors because, if a passenger was found with an incorrect fare, the proportion of uncollected fares would be factored up for the whole operation. We didn't think this was fair but it was changed after a time."

LBL's Area Inspectors were not involved with other operators' services, but passengers did not understand this. Steve Fennell, an Inspector at Hounslow, was told not to touch Westlink's services. On one occasion he moved one of their buses which was parked and causing disruption, and he was told not to touch them again under any circumstances, by both Westlink and his own management. On another occasion, when Harrow Buses had been set up, he was on duty at Heathrow and there were no 140s coming through. Because these were red buses, the passengers thought that he had responsibility for them. He rang Harrow Weald, and was told that it was "Nothing to do with you". He said, "I need a service down here." Then four buses arrived together going through to Heathrow Terminal 4. So he pulled three of them out, letting one bus go through to T4. He turned the other three and marked their cards in order to provide a service back, and to get them back on time.

"I was told off for that too. I did it for self protection – I was trying to provide a service. It was horrible in the early stages."

The first years of tendering

After some initial problems, the bus tendering system was by 1988 working more effectively. By the end of March, around 18% (106 routes) of LRT's total bus mileage was operating under contract and this was expected to increase to 25% by the end of March 1989. A further 63 bus routes had been offered for tender in 1987/8 with LBL winning 63% of them. Both bus and Underground had increased passenger levels by 8% in the year, and there was a 1% increase in service levels on the buses.

There was a small improvement in LBL's operated mileage despite continuing staff shortages, industrial disputes and traffic congestion. Unit costs fell by 4.7% while the operating loss before grants was reduced from £114 million to £96 million. There had been a significant improvement in engineering performance and a 92% FFD first-time pass rate was recorded in the first half of 1988, rising to 96% in the second half of the year.

Malcolm Wren observes, "It was necessary to demonstrate that if you went about things the right way you could produce a decent bus service, even in London. Of the operators we asked to run the services, not all got it right, but those who made the effort and got the basics right could run a reasonable and presentable bus service. A good example of this was the 24, which attracted the attention, but there were also others. Some parts of London Buses also enhanced their service, for example Roundabout and Westlink. Indeed, most London Buses managers took the process seriously and learnt from their competitors. They behaved very professionally despite it probably not being very easy for them to see routes which they had regarded as theirs put out to tender and operated by someone else." But there were some difficult moments. "There were some operators who couldn't get it right. Some started ok but couldn't keep it up, and other operators started and maintained it. Some never got it right."

Most operators found that the relationship with TBU worked well. Tony Kennan found it a pleasure working with Nick Newton and Mike Weston. "Nick Newton was very pragmatic. If you were open with him, and never tried to hoodwink him, then everything would go well, and the open relationship worked."

The London private sector operators created a committee called the London Independent Bus Operators, or LIBO, to represent their interests with Len Wright as chairman and Tom McLachlan of Grey-Green as Secretary – they did not feel they were being represented by the Bus and Coach Council. London Buses was a principal funder of the B&CC and did not like this development. However, Nick Newton was very happy to deal with the group which Len feels gained some useful achievements and brought the London independent operators working together.

Len feels that most private operators did not fully understand all the costs involved in bus operations, for example the pressure on labour costs and the higher costs for fuel, maintenance, and wear and tear on buses in London bus operation. TBU realised that it was in their interests not to have failures amongst the contractors and were realistic about recruitment costs. TBU had to get the system working well.

Len considered the tendering process to have been well-managed, particularly as there was no precedent. "Nick Newton achieved a good balance of LT's interests and the operators' interests and was flexible in allowing the market to develop for people to come into it." He thinks that it would be very different now, due to the greater demand for transparency and a greater likelihood of legal challenge if people are not happy with process. Overall, Len agrees that tendering has been very beneficial. He thinks LBL companies should have tackled their expensive depots and administrative staff rather than driver wages. He thinks bus drivers wages are appropriate nowadays, and it is the tube drivers who cost too much.

In the early days the tenders were judged for best overall value, but the tenders were not published. There were no objections to this, but it led to differing views on how the choice was made. It was widely agreed that contracts should not be let solely on price but also on the quality of the operator. Some felt that routes were often awarded in order to get new contractors in – TBU might consider it valid to spend a little more if it brought more operators in, and so it might not always be the cheapest bid that won.

But a common view in London Buses was that the TBU were simply looking for low costs. Malcolm Wren insists that "This was not us. The private operators such as Ensign who had lower costs did deliver; you knew the bus would turn up. Those who did not deliver were removed from the contract. The problem with some of the LBL contracts was that they seemed to be buying volume in anticipation of deregulation and took on too much. If they had done less, but done it well, it would have been much better.

"Some smaller operators would also bid for a lot, not knowing what the competition was or which they would win. So they would bid for everything and see what they got. Some would indicate how much they thought they could take on but leave us to decide the content. We would have to make a judgement on what they could manage. In addition, it is no good putting in a cheap price that you can't fulfil, you have to be able to live with it. TBU would have to consider whether to give them, say, several routes or just one or two for now until they proved their worth."

Norman Kemp suggests that the LBL companies were not doing as well as possible with the money they received – but they always saw the private operators as the problem! Peter Larking had watched the contract documents getting bigger and bigger over time. He thinks that at the beginning there was a lot of naiveté on both sides. The first contract document was 10 or 12 typewritten pages, without enough safeguards, though there was much concern about checking up on operators, for example by requiring tachograph discs. As time went on, more and more clauses went in to counter problems that became apparent. Looking back, he considers it was all so quaint at the beginning! It has moved on a long way now.

There was considerable criticism in the early stages of the tendered operations from the London Regional Passengers Committee (LRPC), while Capital, the Campaign to Protect and Improve Transport in London, and the Lambeth Passenger Transport Campaign provided detailed analyses of problems. Articles appeared in the Design Journal noting the declining standards applying to both LBL and London Underground, particularly the move away from the classic Johnston typeface for blinds and sign writing. This visual link, they said, had given the corporate style of London Transport and was getting lost, losing the visual cohesion and civic pride in London's transport system.

The tendered operations gradually improved. Nick Newton explains, "We were now delivering much greater reliability and adding quality to the scheduled operation. Before tendering, LBL were providing around 90% of the scheduled operation, and around one in 10 buses did not operate. After four or five years, only one in 200 of TBU services didn't operate." Nick said at the time that he had been told off by the LRT Board for overspending, when what he had done had been to deliver more service than budgeted!

Dave Alexander at BTS took the changes on board. "When we first started, it was all about running the mileage, and that was your measure. And then the mileage you ran was added to by the punctuality of the mileage, and then as time went on it became about the customer experience and customer satisfaction. So it changed from 'Just get the bus from A to B and we'll send you a cheque' to a situation where you had to run the mileage but you had to run it very well."

LBL's 'heads we win, tails you lose' relationship with its workforce was very difficult when such major changes were being tackled. Independent operators did not seem to have a problem with driver recruitment. Len Wright had a steady stream of refugees from London buses, and his area around Southall "had a big population with a strong work ethic who were keen to get their money and go home, and were very flexible in their working practices."

Relationships between operators and between the drivers of the various companies gradually improved. Huw Barrington, then at Cityrama, recalls that, "The problems with red bus operators at the beginning of tendering were minor issues like use of the toilets and some 'verbals' to the drivers, accusing them of having sold their souls. This broke down over time and people became more co-operative. For example, route 260 passed Willesden garage, where it had been taken from, but after a couple of years relations were all right, even to the extent of being able to stop there to get water for an overheating bus. This would never have happened in the first couple of years. We are all busmen, and once they saw that we were here to stay they accepted the situation. At first they felt threatened but then they came to accept it."

A further issue was that private operators used ferry cars and buses to take staff from their garage. Where there was a busy bus station and one or two of the routes went over to a private operator, they might start to use these vehicles for staff changeovers, which would get in the way. This led to arguments about whether London Buses was being helpful enough, or just making life difficult for the new operators.

Attracting new operators to bid for contracts was a challenge from the beginning. Huw Barrington thinks that property was a major part for all those who started on the fringes of London. "Kentish Bus was the first in the central area and they were able to find premises. Also, the predominance of the red buses worried the independents. They were not sure what they would get out of it in the long term. A number of small operators tried, like Sampson's, and the stronger ones became established. It is difficult to set up a new operation. You need premises and experience, and a 'Get out of jail' card. It is a big cost to set up a contract without knowing what will happen at the end of it. TfL rode over that and got rid of some of the underperformers, so it is more stable now."

The independent sector in London was quite a modest size when tendering began. There was not a large established private operator bus sector other than Grey-Green and Metrobus. Grey-Green were bold and decisive with a budget big enough to enter this new area of work. Also, London Country seized the initiative of tendering and in effect shielded many other operators, excepting Eastern National.

While Ensignbus was seen by some as a low cost operator, they had high standards and gave a reliable service. Metrobus 297 came from South Yorkshire and is seen at Havering Park in February 1989. (Keith Wood)

93 "The problems with red bus operators were minor issues like use of the toilets and some 'verbals' to the drivers, accusing them of having sold their souls."

A further study by Martin Higginson of the University of London researched the views of independent bus and coach operators in mid-1986. He found that, since the award of eight routes to independent operators, they were now confident that a genuine tendering scheme was taking place which would not simply favour LRT's subsidiaries. Operators who had bid in the past intended to bid again, and cautious operators who had not bid were, in some cases, now considering doing so. These operators had taken note of the difficulties experienced by Eastern National at Walthamstow and were wary of expanding too quickly. Few of them would be able to bid for large routes, but tendering of routes in inner London would be accessible to more operators. They preferred the gross cost contract, which left the revenue risk with LRT, and while they preferred a longer contract than three years, this was not critical. They wanted to be able to lease newer vehicles for the duration of the contract, aware of the poor impression given by older vehicles on tendered routes. They had a comprehensive dislike for full deregulation and preferred an expansion of the London route tendering system to revitalise bus services.

Some operators were naive about the challenge. Peter Newman comments, "Bus services *look* simple, you just have to run a bus from A to B. Some operators also think it is the same as school runs. They think, 'What's the difference in running a bus service?' The answer is, 'A lot!' They have to maintain the buses, they have to keep driver availability and suitability, they have to deal with fare collection, the cash and the ticket machines. They have to keep the buses clean, and they have to deal with the early and late services. Coaches and buses – never the twain shall meet." Peter supplied many operators with buses at the beginning of tendering. He even supplied Grey-Green at first, and they had come to him saying, "How should we do it?" He had worked for Grey-Green before Cowie took over, when it was George Ewer. He also supplied Limebourne, Sampson's and Len Wright with buses. All of these found it far more difficult to run bus services than running coaches and school services.

Leon Daniels agrees that many second hand vehicle purchasers obviously thought they could buy old DMSs, put fuel in them and expect them to keep going. They got the driver costs down, but lost quality. But Len Wright had to use coaches on the 81 when his double-deckers were not available. Cityrama achieved cost savings but the quality was awful. Sampson's and several others fell by the wayside. They were attracted by the market and worked well for a while, but couldn't keep it up – they were not able to do a really good job day in and day out for months and years. Were the TBU promoting new entrants faster than they were checking on their credentials?

Malcolm Wren agrees that, "Some independents were inexperienced but they seemed to feel that, 'It must be possible because LT has asked us to do it. So let's find a way, let's work it out.' They may not have been sophisticated, but they had a naive determination. It worked for some but not for others, and they were better in some ways – Grey-Green didn't stand any nonsense from the staff!

"There is nothing fundamentally difficult about running buses but you do need flexibility and a commitment to reliability – the traditional LT ethic did not provide flexibility. A lot of the ideas that operators came up with had not been tried before. For example, when there was disruption, rather than the traditional curtailment, they would break up a bunch by sending one bus out of service as quickly as possible to the end of the route, so that people get a bus to bring them back rather than leave them stranded. They would use the motorway if it was quicker. Nick Newton, similarly, would answer a question about challenges by saying, 'I don't know but I'll find a way. I'll come up with an answer.' Operators also felt that confidence."

Malcolm adds, "Tendering needs a good supply base. You don't want only two bidders, and you have to open it up. We generally got around six bids for a route, sometimes more. We sometimes went out to respond to interest shown by other operators. For example, we visited a couple of East Anglian operators, Ipswich Buses and Hedingham Omnibuses, to talk it through with them in response to their

London Buslines needed help with vehicles in March 1987, when a Starrider coach is seen at Southall Town Hall on route 195. (John Parkin)

"Many second hand bus purchasers obviously thought they could buy old DMSs, put fuel in them and expect them to keep going."

interest. However neither did come in and they were probably right not to. Operation in London was not everybody's cup of tea."

Len Wright is clear that the important issue to independent operators was the regular cash flow where a known sum of money would arrive regularly on a known date. He did not consider that there was any prestige in operating LT contracts. He preferred single route contracts to networks so that he could build up a portfolio of routes. He could afford to lose any one of these, though he would prefer not to, and still carry on – so he purposely sought a mix of routes with different expiry dates. Networks were not so interesting to private operators and did tend to favour the big operators. They would need huge premises and significant set up costs, and could all expire on the contract end date.

Peter Larking agrees on the risks to smaller operators. "Tendering is wonderful when you're winning, and terrible when you're losing. If I was to lose work for 10 buses, that would be 25 staff, and how do you pay for the infrastructure you have built up." His old company had a winning streak, and then the tables turned and they had a losing streak – route 261 was lost after 26 years. The larger company can manage this but to a small company it is frightful to lose that much work.

Three-year contracts were not good for investment in new vehicles. Len Wright was able to negotiate a longer contract which enabled him to buy new Leyland Lynxes. He had bought Alexander Olympians to provincial specification so that that there would be a market for them at the end of the contract. Now, vehicles are more tightly specified in the contract documents to provide a generic specification which allows contractors to buy the vehicles they choose from a range of manufacturers who can provide vehicles to the London specification.

Dave Alexander was happy that the tendering system worked for them as a small company coming into the London market. "Whether it worked for the larger companies that were already in it, and having to evolve from public to private, I don't know, but it worked for us because it was an opportunity for us as opposed to a threat."

John Wood mentions one small but significant change to the contracts. At first, in the early tenders, they did not include Boxing Day and as a result they were awarding separate tenders for Boxing Day, and the NBC companies didn't want to run these. TBU therefore had a separate group of operators and contracts just for Boxing Day, until this became incorporated into the main tenders.

Overall, Malcolm Wren concludes, "People did understand the system – both sides understood how it worked. In the end, you need two sides who understand each other." What was the high point of the early years of tendering? He suggests that route 24 was Nick's best move. "It was a confidant action bringing an alternative and high quality operation into the heart of London."

LBL reorganises
London Buses continued to reorganise, change and develop throughout 1987 and 1988. Staff negotiations continued to be difficult, and they were not over yet.

LBL's strategy of "ring-fencing" operations at garages running local networks was successful in allowing LBL to win local networks based on Orpington, Hounslow, Potters Bar, Norbiton, Harrow, Bexleyheath, Sutton and Walthamstow, all of which were in outer London. But Trade Union opposition was fierce, particularly at Norbiton, where the legality of LBL's position was vindicated in a court case brought by the union. But the problems arising at these large schemes led to LRT tendering individual routes, even when part of a large area scheme. Whilst setting up new low-cost operations had worked elsewhere in the country, a difference in London was that there were plenty of alternative jobs for busmen to go to.

LBL had improved performance with 93.8% of scheduled bus journeys being operated, whilst operating costs had fallen again by 3.3%, so that since 1983/4 there had been an overall 20% reduction. LBL was winning more tenders, now around 50%, whilst at March 1989 the Tendered Bus Unit of LRT was securing the provision of 25% of all services.

John Telford Beasley was stamping his mark on LBL. He was an inspiring leader preparing the organisation for privatisation and deregulation. Clive Hodson recalls, "It was his whole attitude to things like ethics, because he had worked in the Pharmaceutical industry and for Cadburys before that. The whole business of accountability was so important to him. 'Well, if so and so is not doing the job, you try and encourage them, train them and help and if at the end of the day it is not working then they have to go.'

To David Brown, "JTB was forward thinking and very impressive. He knew that he needed to change the culture of the business. He carried out a thorough organisation review and also arranged leadership training for all managers, guiding them in managing people at all levels, depending on their abilities and your confidence in them, which may change as people's responsibilities change. This was leadership training unlike anything before and I look back now with the eyes of a CEO and realise how good it was."

In 1988 LBL was reorganising once again, now into Units which would become the companies ready for privatisation.

5 CREATING THE NEW COMPANIES 1988-1991

Norman Cohen was asked to divide up London!

"It was clear that LBL's organisation of five divisions was unsuited to future privatisation, and John Telford Beasley gave me the job of designing a number of separate, independent bus companies which would make sense in terms of geography, markets, and availability of labour. It was a government insistence that they didn't want any company to be able to have bus garages at opposite ends of London – there had got to be competition across London. I remember the example was that you don't want one owner to have a garage like Croydon and also Enfield – that would be wrong. So we designed it to avoid that, but of course it is precisely what happened when Arriva bought Leaside and South London!"

There was considerable discussion about the best size and geographic arrangement of the new units, and a number of proposals before the final scheme. One idea was for pairs of garages in different parts of London, perhaps Holloway and Bow, so that they did not have their own patch but would compete for work everywhere, or groups of three garages.

An internal paper by Norman Cohen in October 1987 considered the optimum size and number of companies to promote competition, and to be commercially and geographically sensible. This required a larger number of small companies so that they neither dominated competition nor inhibited new operators entering the market. They needed to be large enough to have a reasonable prospect of trading profitably, and have a clear geographical area as their base operating territory.

Whilst a new company could in principle be one garage, it would not be big enough to compete with the newly privatised ex-NBC companies surrounding London, the smallest of which – Kentish Bus – had 222 vehicles and the largest, Eastern National, had 500 vehicles and 13 garages. Other competitors such

CentreWest's conversion of Routemaster services 28 and 31 to minibuses was controversial and successful. Named Gold Arrow, the service initially ran with Mercedes minibuses but the good loadings achieved meant that these soon had to be replaced by larger vehicles. (Barry Le Jeune)

96 *The government insisted that they didn't want any company to be able to have bus garages at opposite ends of London – there had got to be competition across London.*

as Grey-Green and Ensign had small bus fleets but considerable resources in their other activities, and large bus groups were beginning to form from the ex-NBC privatisation. Though Roundabout and Westlink were operating as single-garage companies, they had some backup from LBL and also benefited from 3-year cost contracts for their services, which would not be the case after deregulation.

It was therefore suggested that the new companies should be between 250 and 500 buses in size so that key supporting services, such as accounting and vehicle maintenance, would become viable in-house rather than buying-in. Fourteen Units were proposed, each with three, four or five garages and between 218 and 455 buses.

As Operations Planning Manager, Jean Harris was one of a working group led by Norman Cohen with the task of creating the business units. "We tried various ways of grouping the garages, to try and get each of the companies to be of broadly equal value. This depended on the actual garages and the routes they operated. Some of the central garages were worth so much that this was very difficult. So, for example, we were experimenting with moving route 11 from Victoria elsewhere. We were asked to consider everything, including concentric circles around London at one stage – the circles would be divided into quadrants in the outer regions. Consultants were appointed to help and they were surprised to find that the central sites were worth so much."

John Telford Beasley and Derek Keeler had had meetings with the Department of Transport. Derek recalls, "The Ministry thought it would be a good idea to have concentric circles. It was absolutely ludicrous. So we fought them on that and said, 'No, the way we will do it is related to the structure that we've got at the moment.' There was talk at one stage of each garage becoming a separate company. They had no idea about joint compilation of services, routes running from two or even three garages. The way

The crudely-drawn plan for 14 Units, some in inner London and some more suburban. This was replaced by an alternative scheme with 11 Units mostly segments or 'slices of a cake'.

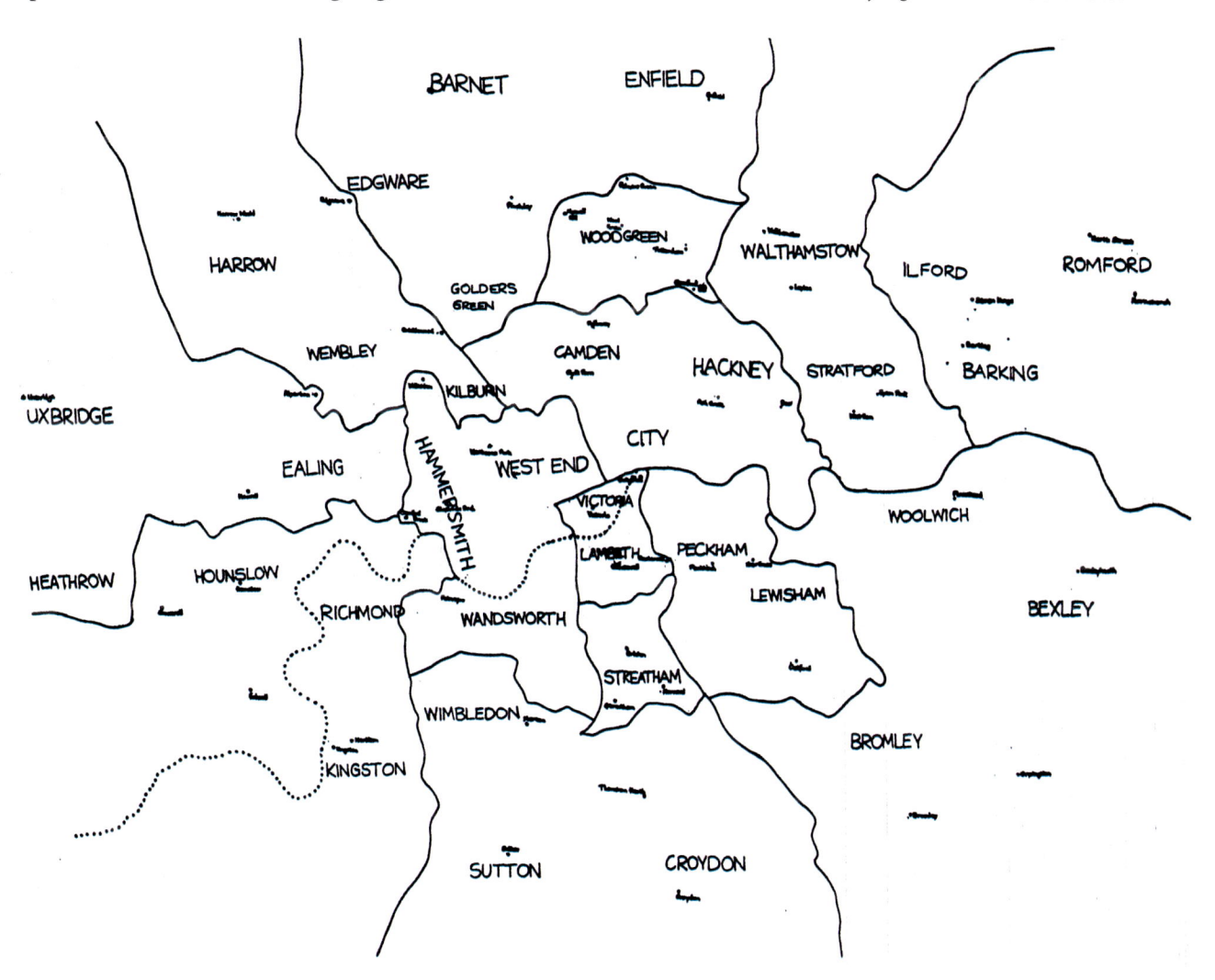

97 It was suggested that the new companies should be between 250 and 500 buses in size.

Unlike other parts of London, Selkent was divided into inner and outer sections, the inner named London Central. Selkent became a very suburban operation, and its Leyland Titan is seen in Addiscombe Road, Croydon, where Croydon trams now run. (Colin Fradd)

that it was eventually done, like slices of a cake, meant that you had routes coming in and out of London in the area that the company controlled."

A bulletin of January 1988 referred to 14 Units, but by May 1988 a review of their likely commercial networks and the possible level of tendered work led to a preference for 11 Units. The Units became 'slices of the cake' in order to get over the high value of central properties, but the companies were not the same size as each other.

Norman Cohen recalls, "We came up with the idea that we should have these segments all the way round London. This was not particularly scientific, it's what made sense in terms of the geography of London. The one exception to these radial segments was due to Bryan Constable, the DGM of Selkent District, who said couldn't he just have the outer parts of Selkent. I was going to make a radial unit that would have had Southwark, Lewisham down to Bromley and then another one that would have hugged the river more, with Woolwich, Greenwich and Bexley. So I redesigned it to create London Central and Selkent. I thought it was crazy, because now I had created London Central with three very large garages at Camberwell, New Cross, and Peckham, and I was concerned about how they could recruit staff with no outer region, but in fact, it was an area that was pretty good for recruitment. And so that's how those companies were formed. Nobody ever asked me why we had an outer Selkent and an inner one, London Central, and I never explained it to anyone!"

So in December 1988, the five bus Districts were replaced by eleven Units. From 1 April 1989, these became subsidiary companies each with their own four-man board of directors, which would become the companies to be privatised. Many of the Managing Directors were recruited from outside London; the companies were chaired by a member of the parent LBL Board, and each had its own 'home' territory and local identity.

Within the Units, each garage would have a Garage General Manager and further managers based on the needs of that garage. Each Unit had around 350 to 500 buses. They would operate as smaller commercial companies to gain experience up to deregulation, which was expected in 1990 or 1991. The Central Traffic Division continued its function of overseeing bus operations in inner London. Units 1 and 2 took effect from 7 November 1988, followed by the rest on 5 December and the new identities and logos began to appear on buses at that time.

The perpetual reorganisation and changes to the plan had been very unsettling in the Districts, where managers were preparing themselves for the new organisation. Martin Whitley, progressing from Cardinal District to the new London United company, recalls the problem. "The plans from the centre for the Unit boundaries were always changing, and the geographic areas changed in the process. Seeing how things were being organised, I had tried to move people I wanted where I wanted them to be in the new organisation. Then they changed the boundaries, so I got caught out and lost some people I wanted and gained others I didn't want! Everyone had schemes at that time, and some of the schemes didn't work as well as others."

Changes in garage organisation led to the creation of Operating Managers (OM) and Assistant Operating Managers (AOM), with a recruitment process to select them. David Brown saw this at first hand in Cardinal District. "Martin Whitley tried to arrange a very objective way of allocating people with scores. Each GM was only allowed one person with the top score, and the attempt was to be very fair, but it became more of a bun fight when all the OMs tried to get the best AOMs for their garage." But David managed to get the people he wanted and deliberately chose a smaller team, also he knew one of the people with a top score better than the others so "grabbed" him first!

Some OMs overdid it – that at Hanwell wanted 15 AOMs. "They would be herding kittens", says David. He only wanted five and he chose wisely – he still regards his team then as one of the best. "We made massive progress, and one of them still works for me." John Trayner recalls that Camberwell had 13 AOMs, which didn't last long. "You soon realise that they're getting in the way of each other, but you had to go through that process because there were too many people who needed jobs – you look back and wonder how did it ever work?"

98 In December 1988, the five bus Districts were replaced by eleven Units.

Implementing the Companies

The LRT Business Plan for 1988/9 set out the process of reorganising London Buses into the autonomous companies. The aim was for them to have established themselves and to have gained operating experience before deregulation was introduced, which was expected to be 1 April 1991 at the earliest. But lack of Parliamentary time was delaying the passage of legislation so that it might not take effect until 1993. The Business Plan also set out reasons why LRT should retain its planning role into the future. Around 45 million annual bus miles were planned to be operating under contract by the end of 1988/89.

The Business Plan intended to cut LRT's costs by a further 20% by reducing the numbers of staff employed by around 2,000 and an increase in bus OPO to 90% of operations. It acknowledged that OPO was not yet realistic in central London, and LRT also stated that a 'positive crew network' would be retained, and that no further routes beyond those already announced would be converted – there was even a suggestion of converting some services back from OPO. LBL also made clear that Routemasters were preferred to OPO vehicles in central London. The cost of additional vehicles and their staff to compensate for slower running times, the effect on traffic congestion, and the additional fuel and engineering costs, made further conversions prohibitive.

The LRT Statement of Strategy continued this theme. LRT was to work closely with the Department of Transport on preparations for a smooth transition to deregulation in London. Once the new bus units were privatised, LRT's responsibilities would include the registration of commercial bus routes and procurer of socially desirable services; the ownership of passenger related facilities such as bus stops and stands and the freehold of bus garages; the provision of a Central Travel Information Service and the administration of concessionary bus schemes and facilities for the disabled.

Once deregulation was introduced, LRT would not be empowered to impose integrated fares and ticketing but it would 'seek to encourage and facilitate multi-operator ticketing arrangements'. The document stated that it was government policy that passengers themselves should generally pay for the benefits they enjoy. External support was to be 'focused on achieving identified benefits, such as the relief of road traffic congestion'.

Clive Hodson saw the benefits of the introduction of the Companies. "Setting up the limited liability companies was saying to Managers in LBL, 'You are responsible for these companies as Directors,' which is extremely important. Directors have a lot of responsibility to the principal shareholders, and that set the tone better than the Districts had done in accountability. So I think that was a sound move although not everybody was happy with it at the time. It was also good that you then got smaller outfits, of a size like London Country, with your own Operator's Licence, which was very important, so you had to maintain your engineering standards. John (Telford Beasley) brought the expertise of marketing and sales, a more commercial outlook which people in LT didn't have."

A new Chairman

In November 1988, following the report into the King's Cross Underground disaster, LRT Chairman Sir Keith Bright and London Underground Chairman Dr Tony Ridley both resigned. The new chairman of LRT was Sir Neil Shields. John Telford Beasley (JTB), Chairman and Managing Director of London Buses Ltd, was also appointed Chief Executive of London Regional Transport.

Appointing the Unit General Managers

Derek Keeler ran the process of selecting the Unit Management Teams. "Once the Board had decided how many subsidiaries were wanted, it was then a question of setting up a structure that would manage them. We started to advertise for Directors, both internally and externally, and we had a selection process. When we decided that somebody had potential, we put them through an Assessment Centre – those were quite good actually." The Management Assessment Centres were designed to identify the best candidates. All senior managers were assessed by April 1986 and the process would then move to middle and lower levels. Norman Cohen adds, "We wanted a mixture of people from within LBL and certainly lots of external ones. And we had a very good field internally."

Keith Ludeman was reading the paper in bed one Sunday morning and saw the advertisement in the Sunday Times. He had started his career in a Passenger Transport Executive and then with a northern municipal operation. Some of the people he had worked with in the past had become multi-millionaires through privatisation, so he was keen to be involved! This was the first time that London Transport had ever advertised externally for such an extensive group of people to manage such change. For him, he would return home to London where he was born. He had gone to Newcastle University and been out of London for twenty years. He had seen deregulation, managed the transition, and had dealt with the trade unions at Burnley and Pendle – which had had the worst industrial relations in the municipal sector, and now he could be coming home.

Keith recalls the selection process at LT's training centre at Flagstaff House. "It was a good bonding process but also part of the selection – some of the people there did not reappear. I was asked what Unit I wanted, I lived in Wimbledon and I decided that the biggest company would be the best. Unit 4 met both those criteria and had routes into central London." Bryan Gilbert interviewed the candidates with Derek Keeler. He recalls Keith Ludeman coming in with balloons and freebies from his marketing exercises. "He said he had a fleet of Routemasters in Burnley. When we said, 'How many is it actually?' he said, 'Three!'"

Bryan Constable was an internal candidate. "This selection process with its Assessment Centre was appropriate, but new to London Transport. Keith Ludeman said to me, 'It's a good job this process wasn't in place to select the Board Members, as none of them would have got the job.'" But everybody did go through it, including the Board Members. Derek Keeler remembers it well. "John Beasley said that all the Directors had got to do it, so we did. We all got our own personal reports, and I took this home and showed it to my wife and she said, 'They've summed you up well, haven't they!'"

Derek continues, "The theory of all this was all very well, but you had still got to have the personalities that could work with other people. It's no good having the ideal people if they won't get on with one another. So we also assessed the type of people they were, and the idea was to have representatives of each of these sorts of people on each of the Boards. So our initial recommendation was taking that into account, and then that had to be modified with the Unit Chairman saying, 'I don't want that person, I want this one.' And so it all then got slightly modified." Were they looking for a balance of people from within LT and from outside? "No, we were looking for the best. We wanted the best, and we really weren't bothered where they came from as long as they came up to scratch." Bryan Gilbert adds, "I think what it did show was the value of our graduate training scheme, because our guys who'd been through our scheme were very good."

The Assessment Centres became part of the interview process and successfully weeded out some people who might come over well at interview. The final interview was by the Board. Eleven people were then chosen, and each had a personal interview with JTB who took a close interest in the appointments. David Humphrey recalls a friendly, informal, personal chat, "It was very clever as it lulled you into a false sense of security." Keith Ludeman was coming down from Manchester by train for his meeting with JTB when the train broke down. This was before mobile phones were common, but he managed to borrow one from someone on the train, and phoned to say that he was dreadfully sorry but the train had broken down and he would be about two hours late. JTB said that was all right, and he would wait. Keith learned later that they did check whether the story of the broken down train was true."

Roger Bowker was General Manager of Eastbourne Buses, and a call came out of the blue from a firm of head-hunters. They wanted him to apply for a General Manager job in London. He said "Thank you, but no thank you!" He really liked it in Eastbourne – he was doing well, it was high profile, a very pleasant, happy job. Eastbourne was the first Municipal operator to form an arm's-length company. They had a Board, which was not a committee of the Council, with Roger as MD – it was an experiment prior to deregulation and privatisation. The politicians wanted to make changes to a municipality prior to the countrywide changes, and the Conservative Council was keen to do this. Nicholas Ridley was impressed; it was successful and it gave them a 'heads up' before privatisation. Roger had good staff who worked well together; the marketing and the quality were good, he was very happy there. He had heard of strikes and all the problems in London. He was not really interested and said, "No, I'm really happy where I am."

But the head-hunters kept in touch and asked him to come and show an interest, saying that they were seeing other people as well, so in the end Roger went to take a look. He knew they had made an appointment to East London but the man did not pass the 'JTB test'. So East London became the last post to be filled, and there were 30 people in the first round for that one last job. Roger saw JTB in his office at 55 Broadway. "He was very amicable and courteous. I enjoyed the meeting; we had a great deal in common, particularly the importance of quality and efficiency. I really enjoyed meeting him." Bryan Constable had known Roger Bowker at Eastbourne Buses and had suggested that he should be considered. Linda Self, one of the recruitment team, remembers, "Roger Bowker didn't want anyone at Eastbourne to know he was being considered. We had to smuggle him in for his interview, almost under a paper bag, and interviewed him in a bedroom so no one noticed!"

Roger accepted the job. "So I went to East London and it was exactly the opposite of what I thought it would be. I thought there would be a lot of industrial unrest, but the staff were superb. The union were tough though very straight and drove a hard bargain. I was helped by a superb management team and hit it off very well with Barry Arnold, the Commercial Director." Barry Arnold concurs. "Roger arrived and was a very friendly guy. He was good with people and very straightforward. He offered the trade union the choice of a quick negotiation where everyone was clear and open, or the traditional long-winded approach. The trade union had not expected someone to be straight with them."

While the recruitment procedure generally worked well, too little research may have been done on some recruits. There were cases of people appointed who did not have the qualifications they claimed, and one case where a poor reputation was not picked up. But overall it worked well and Derek Keeler remembers, "Actually, I really enjoyed those last two years. We played God! We worked out what should happen and said 'This is what we suggest', and everyone went along with it!"

The Units

The first two Units went live from 7 November 1988, followed by the rest on 5 December.

The Units were to become separate LBL subsidiaries from 1 April 1989 with their own Operating licences, at which point the Unit Managers became Company Directors. Pay and conditions would be negotiated locally from 1990 onwards, and smaller scale, lower-cost companies were intended to counteract the loss of economies of scale which had previously been claimed. There were, however, cases where neighbouring units needed to co-operate with each other, for example arrangements between London Central and Selkent over chassis cleaning, vehicle testing, driver training, vehicle recovery and engineering stores. Whilst London Coaches and Westlink remained as separate entities after this reorganisation, Bexleybus, Harrow Buses, Kingston Bus and Roundabout became garages within the new units.

From December 1988, local identities of the new Units began to appear on vehicles. The headquarters of LBL was moved from 55 Broadway to offices alongside Victoria Coach Station, known as 172 Buckingham Palace Road. This was intended to bring all LBL headquarters staff together from a number of locations and so improve efficiency and communications.

The design standards for the bus liveries and communications of the new subsidiaries were set out in the London Buses' Local Subsidiary Companies' Design Manual of August 1989.

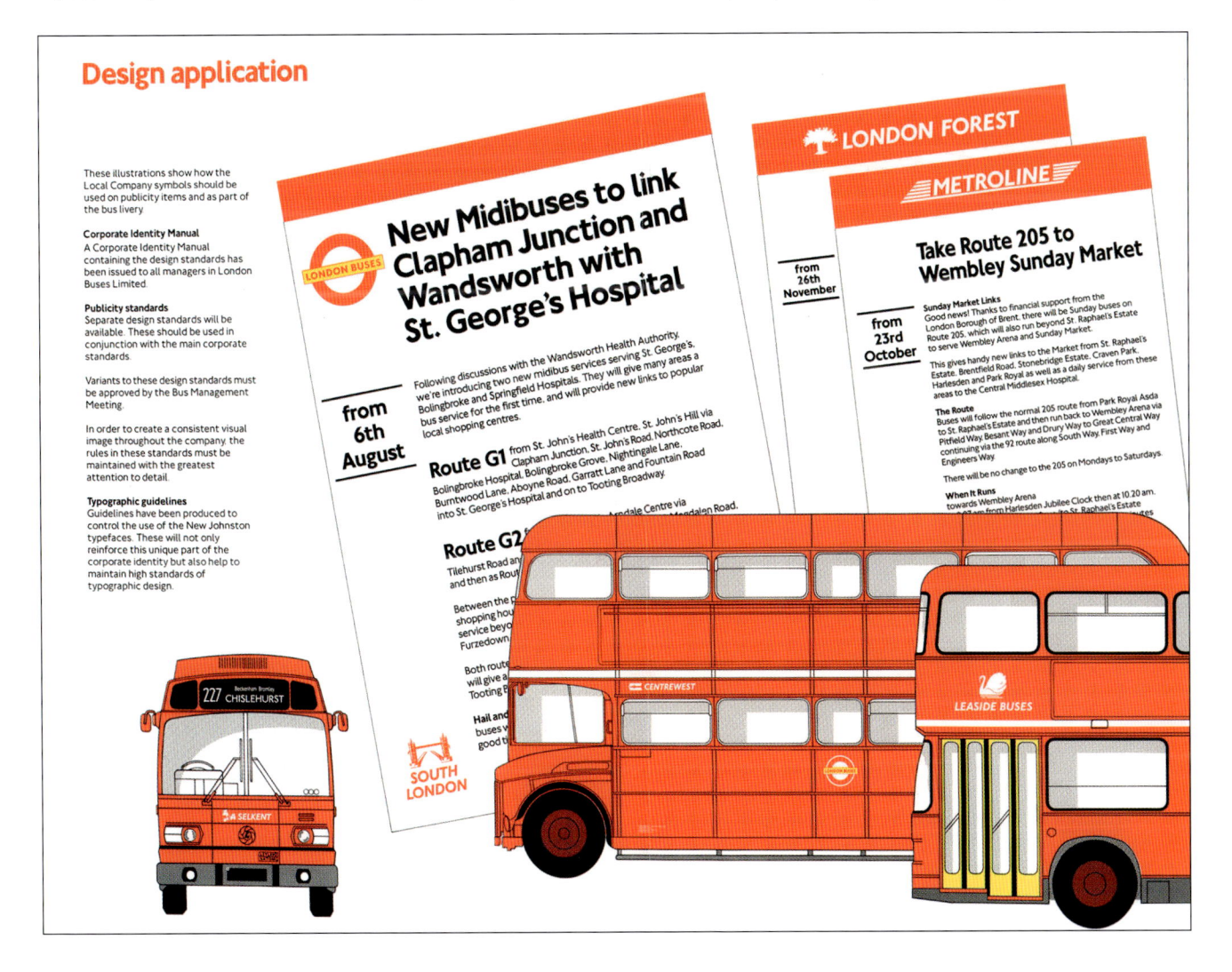

101 The first Units went live in November 1988, followed by the rest in December, when their identities began to appear on vehicles. They were to become separate subsidiaries from 1 April 1989, at which point the Unit Managers became Company Directors.

At your service.

London Buses want to give you a better local service.

So they have set up eleven subsidiary bus companies that can respond quickly and efficiently to local needs.

From April 1st these eleven local bus companies will be responsible for all their bus services in London.

Using their local knowledge and experience they will meet passenger needs by improving routes, introducing new bus services and speeding up services. They will be listening to what you the passenger wants from your local bus company.

Prove it for yourself. The new local bus companies are listed and they can provide full details of routes and services. Don't forget all our local bus companies accept Bus Passes, Travelcards and all concessionary passes and permits. They are at your service.

LONDON BUSES

LONDON CENTRAL
1 4th Floor
Riverdale Office Centre
68 Molesworth Street
Lewisham
London SE13 7EU
Tel: 01-463 0553

SELKENT
2 5th Floor
Riverdale Offices
68 Molesworth Street
Lewisham
London SE13 7EU
Tel: 01-318 7421

SOUTH LONDON
3 Sycamore House
799 London Road
Thornton Heath
Surrey CR4 6AW
Tel: 01-683 1211

LONDON GENERAL
4 Keith Ludeman
London General House
25 Raleigh Gardens
Mitcham
Surrey CR4 3NS
Tel: 01-646 1747

LONDON UNITED
5 Wellington Road
Twickenham TW2 5NX

CENTREWEST
6 12th Floor
Telstar House
Eastbourne Terrace
Paddington
London W2 6LG
Tel: 01-706 0877

METROLINE
7 118-122 College Road
Harrow
Middlesex HA1 1DB

LONDON NORTHERN
8 INFOCENTRE
2nd Floor
Hobson House
155 Gower Street
London WC1E 6LB
Tel: 01-380 1314

LEASIDE BUSES
9 Manor House Offices
279 Seven Sisters Road
London N4 1QG
Tel: 01-227 5828

LONDON FOREST
10 London Forest Travel Ltd
The Old Tramways Office
Chingford Road
Walthamstow
London E17 4PN
Tel: 01-527 9690

EAST LONDON
11 16-20 Clements Road
Ilford
Essex IG1 1BA
Tel: 01-553 3420

CentreWest

The new company managements began to innovate and develop their operations. CentreWest implemented the Uxbridge midibus scheme in February 1989 replacing big bus services with more frequent minibuses named 'U-Line'. Peter Hendy, then CentreWest's General Manager, was quoted saying that, "We can't wait for the whole of our business to be driven by LRT tendering" and, concerning Uxbridge, he added "I don't know what LRT intentions are for the area but I am assuming that we will be able to get our network in ourselves."

A much more ambitious move was the conversion of trunk Routemaster services 28 and 31 to minibuses named Gold Arrow. Peter Hendy had worked on this scheme before the implementation of the Units. The routes were busy and skirted, but did not enter, the central area, and the change took place in March and April 1989. The routes operated from open parking at Westbourne Park garage, a garage which LBL recruitment had found difficult to find staff for. Over 170 new drivers were recruited locally for the two routes, and they were given thorough training in customer relations as well as bus driving. The buses were controlled by an automatic vehicle location system through Band-3 radio connected to the LBL control centre at Baker Street – the first use of Band 3 on London's buses. The service claimed a 60% increase in scheduled service at some times of day and, like the Uxbridge "U-line" network, it was commercially successful.

This was a bold and unusual move to convert major trunk routes to minibuses, bringing considerable comment and, at first, passenger hostility. Some passengers considered the minibuses to be less safe because of their greater acceleration and braking power, and also due to the driving techniques of small buses. The Capital Transport Campaign made comments about bunching and gaps in service, but praised the effort and initiative displayed by CentreWest in introducing the service.

CentreWest countered criticism by showing a 10% increase in ridership and insisted that the minibuses were safer than the previous open platform Routemasters. Their design had been based on research and comments from the London Regional Passengers' Committee, the Transport and Road Research Laboratory and LRT's Unit for Disabled Passengers.

CentreWest introduced route 607 in July 1990 to provide a limited stop service on the long 207 route between Shepherd's Bush and Uxbridge. 60,000 passengers were using the 207 each day and CentreWest identified significant end-to-end traffic. Initially Metrobuses were used, one of which is passing through Acton in October 1991. These were replaced in November 1991 with Leyland National II and Lynx single-deckers. (Colin Fradd)

"We can't wait for the whole of our business to be driven by LRT tendering!"

Gold Arrow operated from a base adjacent to Westbourne Park Garage. The staff were generally recruited from outside London Buses, although some did transfer from the existing operations.

The 28 and 31 conversion was intended to compare the commercial results of a more frequent minibus service to those of conventional OPO. The scheme had been designed to have the same resource costs as a double deck service and hoped to increase passenger numbers and income through the increased frequency and quality of service. The emphasis was to be on friendly and helpful staff, and national press advertising had been used to attract recruits through a local agency.

Peter Hendy admitted at the time that there was initial passenger hostility to Gold Arrow and to the removal of Routemasters. He had travelled on the last Routemaster, which was full of transport enthusiasts, and commented. "Had they known who we were, I don't think that a lynching would have been out of the question." Once the new operation had settled in, he was certain that the right decision had been made as many more passengers were using the routes. He added that it was always going to be the right move financially, and had put them at least 18 months ahead of other operators in the run-up to privatisation.

Peter Hendy says he was driving the revenue and improving service quality so there was no need for LRT to tender his routes. Nick Newton made similar comment – many TBU schemes introduced new services with minibuses, but Peter Hendy went ahead and did it himself!

Overall, Peter Hendy stresses that in the Units, managers were able to get to grips with the problems and sort them out. They no longer had to rely on central departments who did not deliver, such as corporate recruitment, which had failed them in the past, nor were they relying on the Central Works who would say, "There are no gearboxes, so you can't have gearboxes."

London General

Keith Ludeman came from Burnley with a reputation. He looked at the situation in London and was shaken to see scruffy buses and crews in jeans and T-shirts – far less smart than his Routemasters in Burnley.

His Unit was formed out of Wandle District, but all the staff wanted to go to South London. Keith said to Norman Cohen that this was giving John Withey at South London an unfair advantage. Norman said, "Who do you want?" and he asked for Phil Margrave as Engineering Director. Phil was unhappy at first, but soon came round and agreed that this was for the best. Martin Elms, with a background in service planning, was appointed Operations Manager, which became Commercial Director. The trade union respected Martin, and Keith knew that scheduling is the most important issue – "If you get that right, you get everything else right. With Phil and Martin I had two guys who knew their way around LT." Roger Davies came from London Country Buses South as Finance Director.

Keith was then building the team up. "My people were up to the hard new world we were going into! We had the biggest fleet of DMSs in London, some of the worst garages at central London sites in difficult locations with bad industrial relations, bad lost mileage, staff shortages and the whole range of staff problems. Some of those challenges remain to this day."

Keith was trying to smarten things up, to get staff to wear the uniform including the tie and eventually got an agreement signed with the trade union. Even if there were problems and they wanted to get the service out on the road, he would still have staff sent home if they had no tie. "Staff in London General are still very smart compared to the others.

"London was then very difficult. The terms and conditions were unaffordable. The degree of tendering in London General was high – 70% of our routes were already tendered. Major changes had to be made."

Keith Ludeman wanted to use the name "London General", but not LGOC, and his choice of London General Transport Services was influenced by Blackpool Transport Services. He chose the B-type bus as the logo which was displayed on his buses, as shown by DMS 2564 at the Norwood Junction terminus of the 196. When Cityrama gave up this route in October 1989 it was run by London Country while it was re-tendered. London General won the tender and ran it from April 1990. (Keith Wood)

104 "London was then very difficult. The terms and conditions were unaffordable."

In October 1990 the Red Arrow operation was moved to a new open-air base at Waterloo, on the site of the Cornwall Road bus stand. This had been delayed for several years while planning consent was obtained, and opened under London General's management. Walworth garage had been used in the meantime. The new base was set up as a low-cost operation with a simplified management structure. Leyland National 2 LS499 is seen on the 510 at Victoria Station in March 1990 with London General logos. (David Cole)

With Wandle District divided between South London and London General, Phil Margrave thinks that South London got the better group of garages, which is why at first he wanted to go there. But he was pleased to be in at the start of all the changes, with the Unit General Managers arriving with fresh ideas. "It changed almost overnight in terms of what you were expected to do, and nobody had expected that – it was a bit of a shock to a lot of people. I think, being in London General, we had an advantage, because almost 70% of what we operated had been tendered by the time privatisation came. So I think we managed to get the message over about what was needed when it became clear that privatisation was going to happen."

The Trade Union had been checking up on the new managers, and Keith Ludeman had had industrial relations issues in Burnley. "I gave a paper at a conference on how I had turned Burnley and Pendle around – largely through another large change in Terms and Conditions, and I got a reputation as a result. The TGWU were aware of this and Ollie Jackson, who was in charge of the London Region, sent Pat Mahon, who was their District Officer in north London, to man mark me! Lesson learned forever about giving conference papers.......!"

So Pat Mahon then worked with London General, London Central and Metroline. He had a reputation as a tough negotiator who kept his word, and he did his homework on Keith Ludeman. "He was the biggest bastard coming into London and I was the biggest bastard waiting for him. He was probably one of the shrewdest boys that came into London, and one of the toughest – well, he had a tough exterior, but underneath all that he wasn't. He later wrote in the newspaper about our first meeting, and described us as two bulls in a field when we first met. And we had this Clash Clash Clash because he was the man that had vision, and he wanted to get there, but he wanted to get there soon. He didn't like weak people and when he met someone that was just as strong as him, they had to come to some level of understanding, and so we did." Ludeman and Mahon sparked off each other at first, but gradually gained a great respect for each other.

London United
Shortly after the new Managing Directors were appointed in 1988, the LBL Public Relations department swung into action and invited all the London MPs to meet their new local bus company managers at an informal evening at the House of Commons.

David Humphrey, MD of London United, has provided the story. "Only four MPs turned up, but one who did was Jeremy Hanley, then the Conservative MP for Richmond upon Thames. His constituency was firmly in my patch, so we were introduced. Within the first half-sentence, Jeremy proceeded to impress upon me the importance of a place called Lonsdale Road and its immediate environs in Barnes, allegedly long-neglected by all previous bus planners. It is a difficult road that does not lead anywhere useful, and not providing a bus service produced some of those Londoners who do not live within 400 yards of a bus stop.

"There was clearly some sort of issue here, so the next day I went into the schedules and planning office in Cardinal District to ask for some history. 'Oh, that', one of them said. 'Yes, JTB has been going on about that for ages, he's been nobbled by Jeremy Hanley to get a bus service down there. But there's no point, there's plenty of capacity on the 9s.' I made two mental notes: one, some influential people think Lonsdale Road needs a bus service, and two, don't appoint such a negative person to the schedules team at London United.

"This remained on our agenda. The area was a little corner, not far from some high frequency bus services, but with long walking routes to get to the bus stops. Once we had developed a midi-bus scheme, trying out an off-peak service through the Lonsdale Road area was quite a low-cost means of testing levels of demand, and the London Borough of Richmond upon Thames undertook to help out with some money.

105 "He was the biggest bastard coming into London and I was the biggest bastard waiting for him!"

The launch of London United's R69 midibus on 7 April 1990 with, from the left, John Telford Beasley, the Mayor of Richmond, Jeremy Hanley MP cutting the ribbon, and David Humphrey, with a Dixieland Jazz Band in attendance.

"The poor old ladies can't get to the shops," was the clarion cry, so an off peak service linking Lonsdale Road to Hammersmith Broadway and Richmond would soon tease out any latent demand.

"On 7 April 1990, amidst great fanfare and a formal launch at Richmond Council's fine old converted mansion attended by Jeremy Hanley and John Telford Beasley, route R69 was born. To begin with, just five off-peak round trips were operated. Demand was moderately encouraging, but a subsequent little difficulty with Hammersmith Bridge helped in justifying a service level every half hour, still to this day offered by the renumbered route 419.

"Bus services in southwest London had for many years been subject to aggressive paring down, partly due to shortages of operating staff, but also due to the changing nature of economic activity. Traditional industry along the "Golden Mile" of the Great West Road had almost completely closed down by the late 1980s, as had virtually all of it in the rest of Brentford and Chiswick. Large areas were economically moribund. Twenty years later and the area has been transformed, with extensive modern housing and office accommodation. Areas such as Kingston and Teddington were undergoing similar changes, though to a lesser extent.

"The effect was that, when London United was formed, bus service frequencies were low by London standards. Experience earlier in the decade with mini-bus conversions in National Bus Company subsidiaries had shown the value of converting to high frequencies. London United therefore embarked on a strategy of increasing its service frequencies.

"Coincidentally, Dennis Vehicles of Guildford had just announced their new 'Dart' midibus, a real improvement on the light van conversions that had been used for minibus conversions. Dennis showed its first prototype to the London Buses Board and the MDs of the subsidiary companies. All were very impressed, but pointed out that they had made it half a metre too long. Pardon? The definition of a 'small bus' in the London Buses agreement for wages and conditions was the then Class 3 PSV licence, which applied to vehicles less than 27 feet long (8.5 metres), a former maximum length for buses. Dennis had made their Dart 9 metres long. After a commendably quick re-design the Dennis Dart was ready.

"The next hurdle was to convince the London Buses Board that the higher capital cost of a Dart was better value than the cheaper van conversions. The Board was divided on the matter – some members were initially utterly unconvinced of the justification for paying a higher price for a Dennis Dart than that of the 'bread van' conversions which had been the norm until then. Passengers on the routes with van conversions would have had no doubts at all! Capital

London United had fun with local launch ceremonies. In April 1990, midibus operation of the new routes H21, H22 and H23 was celebrated by David Humphrey (left), the Mayor and Mayoress of Hounslow and a pipe band at Hounslow bus station. (David Humphrey)

106

expenditure was eventually authorised after some considerable debate and lobbying. However, having secured the Board's blessing, and then having obtained approval for the acquisition of 91 vehicles, it was a bit galling to have some of that order diverted to another LBL company which had by then "caught up" and realised the vehicles were actually quite useful!

"So the new R70 was launched with the R69 on 7 April 1990, replacing the 270, Richmond to Hampton (Nurserylands Estate). Its daytime frequency was every twenty minutes, except during the peak period when it was every twenty-five minutes – because it took longer for the vehicles to get round in busy traffic.

"In April 1990, we increased the frequency to every ten minutes. The results were quite astonishing. The route became so busy that we had to increase the frequency to every seven/eight minutes, then again to every six minutes, then we even had to schedule double-deck duplication at peaks and on last buses at night. Passenger numbers increased four-fold over a period of about two years, and with no discernible reduction in loadings on other routes over common sections. We were on to a winner! Numerous other routes followed over the next couple of years with similar results, though none as striking as those of the R70. The local prefix letter to the route number made it more "local", and Hounslow area routes were prefixed "H" upon conversion to midibus – the plan was to drop the letters upon deregulation in order to have a simpler numbering format for the company.

"The change is generally regarded as a 'midibus' revolution; in fact it was a 'frequency revolution' – passengers are attracted to high frequency bus services. Gosh!"

Riverside Bus
In the meantime, London United also commenced their new 'Riverside Bus' operation at Stamford Brook on 6 January 1990. This operated route 237, won on tender, and route 283 which had been retained on retender, together with the Airbus services.

Stamford Brook operated the Riverside Bus network as well as London United's Airbus services. A press launch was held for the new unit at Heathrow alongside a Concorde plane with all 23 Olympians purchased for the 237. This was arranged because Heathrow was firmly in London United's patch, but London United also had good contacts with senior Heathrow personnel. (Martin Whitley)

"In April 1990, we increased the frequency of the R70 to every ten minutes. The results were quite astonishing."

Other London United services were reallocated to other garages, but this caused significant dead mileage. Staff at Stamford Brook had been offered the opportunity to transfer to adjacent garages or opt to remain at Stamford Brook under the different working conditions. Martin Whitley, the LU Commercial Director, had a bad conscience about this. "I had serious qualms about what we were having to do. We were holding the Sword of Damocles over the staff, in effect telling them to agree or you lose your job. We were forcibly changing Terms and Conditions which had been agreed over the years, and here we were ripping them all up. It gave me a very bad feeling. The Airbus negotiations were going up to the wire, but we got there, and I remained on good terms with the Trade Union."

Martin had been Operations Manager at Cardinal District before becoming LU's Commercial Director. "Those early days, before a significant amount of tendering, were just what planning and running bus services should have been. We had initiatives of minibus routes around Richmond, and it was quite clear that they were striking a chord with the passengers. We were putting more staff in, and it was appreciated. If you're out on the buses, you get a good appreciation of what is good and what is bad and what is needed. Planners might say, 'You need the right data,' but data doesn't speak to you in the same way. If the staff see you out there, it is noticed and you can get a good idea – and they can't get away with any tall stories. I spent some time looking at deregulation in Manchester and to be honest I found it really exciting. There was new blood running new services and the passenger was king.

"However the true ownership of the London network remained in the hands of the central planners. Even when local management showed what remarkable results could be achieved, such as with our R70, the success was not ours to savour – at least only until the route was tendered out to someone else. However good some of the individuals at the centre were, there was still the inevitable gulf between a 9-5 five-day-a-week planner in a central London office and the 24/7 world of the real market we were serving."

Westlink

While London United wanted independence from LRT, Jeff Chamberlain at Westlink wanted independence from London United! With the introduction of the 11 new units, Westlink was to be included in LU. Jeff fought to keep his own identity and independence as a separate operator, and he won that argument having persuaded the LBL Board members. "London United was always trying to find ways of absorbing us, but I resisted." The other ring-fenced garage units were absorbed into the new companies.

Jeff had won out-County work on tender, and ran an early kneeling bus in service. "DAF modified one of our Leyland Nationals to become more easily accessible. I wanted to run wheelchair accessible buses and suggested adding one into the schedule, but this was thought to be impractical. Then we introduced the first wheelchair accessible bus service in the country, the H20 between Ivy Bridge and Hounslow Civic Centre, in conjunction with Hounslow Council – the leader at the time was Dave Wetzel."

He also put monitors and video recorders on Leyland National buses and sold space to local businesses who provided their own advertising video clips. It was done locally and the advertising was route specific. He got the idea from a visit to Las Vegas where a similar system operated in taxis – no one had yet done it on buses. "We would have developed this further if we had not been privatised the next year, but it would have made more money

Opposite top Westlink ran route H20 for Hounslow Council between Ivy Bridge and Hounslow Civic Centre from 18 March 1989 using three Omni wheelchair-accessible buses owned by the Council – the first wheelchair accessible bus service in the country. These were based on a Land Rover with body by City Vehicle Engineering, and one is shown at the Hounslow Civic Centre terminus. (Barry Le Jeune)

In April 1990, Westlink received seven new DAF SB220 kneeling buses with Optare flat floor bodies for route 110. DA3 is seen at Twickenham Station in March 1991. (David Cole)

"I had serious qualms about what we were having to do. We were holding the Sword of Damocles over the staff."

than the tender and would have supported the tender bid. We pioneered innovation because we had freedom. We didn't have to get approval from some stodgy person in the centre!"

Metroline

Gordon Tennant was General Manager at Harrow Buses. He applied for a Commercial Manager job and was interviewed by several of the fledgling companies. He already knew Declan O'Farrell, who was appointed General Manager for Unit 7, so joined him as Commercial Manager when offered the post there. "Unit 7 was made up of parts of two Districts (Cardinal and Leaside) so we had two different District cultures. In addition, Cricklewood Garage had another culture all of its own, and was a real challenge. We did not have an existing District to take a share of staff from, but we were able to recruit some good people that we wanted.

"Unit 7 then became Metroline and we became Company Directors. We seemed to suffer death by a thousand cuts with losses of routes in the tendering process! The tendering had to be seen to be fair, but LBL companies' bids had to be vetted centrally to ensure that they had been properly costed with no grant leakage. It was particularly frustrating as we were making changes to reduce costs, but would then be told, 'You can't do that,' and then, 'You've lost the route.'" There were a lot of very active small companies in the area including BTS, R&I and Atlas Bus, and Metroline lost a lot of routes. Gordon also believes that the TBU had a mandate to stimulate competition and that in doing so was encouraging the independents. But some of the new operators misunderstood the intensity of use of the vehicles, the cost of accidents and insurance, and the need to manage effectively the full costs of the operation.

Declan O'Farrell was clear on his business strategy through all this. He wanted to keep the base secure and maintain the footprint of the company and its resources, because the situation had to change. Declan's view was that when they suffered a loss, they would cut back on the overheads, and as and when they won routes they would build up again only as they needed. They worked hard to get the cost base under control, through pay bargaining over the years, and by getting lower overheads compared to LBL days. As a result, Metroline began to win back routes.

Leaside

Steve Clayton was appointed UGM and then Managing Director for Unit 9, Leaside. He had joined London Transport in 1975, and had been a Garage Manager and an Area Traffic Manager. He was joined by Ted

Milburn, Engineering Director; Mark Yexley, Commercial Director and Robert Newson, Finance Director. At first Units 7, 8 and 9 were all in the Manor House offices on different floors.

Steve immediately saw the benefit of the new organisation. "The progressive devolution to Units made many things a lot better. Even buying fuel became cheaper in the subsidiaries than centrally – there comes a point when the volume of fuel is less important, unless you are an airline for example. Everybody worked hard to make the company successful." Minibuses were not really appropriate in Leaside where the routes were more suited to conventional double-deckers. The actual route structure did not change much because it was already well designed, although they had OPO conversions.

On the engineering side, they had a vehicle repair shop at Enfield, which was carrying out major rebuilding of Metrobuses and some Routemasters. The inherited fleet was not in a good state of repair and required substantial investment and management focus to restore to a better condition to survive after privatisation. A key objective was to improve the condition of the fleet, which would otherwise have impacted on service reliability and future costs. They wanted to spend money sooner, rather than later, by investing in their assets, as well as taking costs out.

Leaside was lucky in not having large parts of its route network put out for tender, but this was also because they were performing well on their routes. LRT selected routes to tender in order to improve their operational and financial performance. Robert Newson points out, "In Leaside we often managed to achieve the highest percentage of mileage operated in the fleet, and many of our routes were fundamentally profitable, with heavy traffic flows down the Green Lanes and Hertford Road corridors. This is still prime territory for buses. So when LRT were deciding which routes to tender, much of Leaside's operation would not stick out as needing improvement."

Steve Clayton was philosophical about the tendering system. "The truth was that the LBL companies were loaded with so much overhead that Grey-Green, when tendering for route 24 for example, didn't have to do much to win it. They paid well, made the drivers work slightly longer hours, didn't have the pension scheme, and this was enough for them to win the work with significantly better margins.

"There was some competition between LBL subsidiaries. But you would not put too many sticks in a hornets' nest. If they were doing a bad job you might bid for a route, or if they were doing a good job and you felt you had a commercial advantage you might bid against a fellow subsidiary. But you did not want to encourage everyone else to have a pop at you, you didn't want too many enemies.

"Then London Buses changed the accounting rules but still required a minimum 5% on our tender operations." The new rules meant that Steve was not making 5% and he was told that he couldn't tender for any more work. A catch 22. "All this left me to do was to manage decline. This was a major difference between the private and public sectors – private sector companies would never let accounting rules get in the way of good management practice, but London Buses would and did."

The change in rules resulted from a KPMG report on the operation of the tendering system. Clive Hodson recalls, "KPMG came up with a report suggesting that to make it a level playing field with the private sector, we should include a profit margin of, say, 5%. The Board insisted we make a 5% profit on our bids. Now that wasn't in the original tenders. Of course that upset us, though we still won some on that basis."

London Northern
Colin Clubb was appointed to lead London Northern. He was Managing Director of London Country South West and was interviewed in great secrecy using the back door and cars with darkened windows to avoid his application becoming public knowledge! Gordon Tennant was invited to become Commercial Director but refused, seeing a very 'old school' management style. Colin Clubb then asked for Bill Gunning, who had until recently been MD of Kentish Bus, to take the position. Willie Arrol, the Engineering Manager, came from LBL's Leaside District.

Andy Griffiths was Operating Manager at Finchley and was appointed Garage General Manager at Holloway. His fleet was looking run down – he had 150 buses needing a repaint, so he set up a programme of painting one each week. He dealt with a third of the buses in the first year, and after two years his fleet was looking very good. "Then Willie Arrol wanted to improve the whole fleet and introduced the concept of a 'bottom half repaint', but my repaint programme was nearly complete so I carried on with it.

"Colin Clubb was 'Presidential' in style," says Andy. For the first 12 months, the GGMs in effect ran the company as we were all from LBL and knew how things worked, whereas Colin and Bill were from NBC. They then realised that they were not in fact running the company and the GGMs were all moved to other posts, the garages being run by Operating and Engineering Managers." As a result Andy became Marketing Manager in 1990.

Norman Cohen was Chairman of London Northern

and was concerned at the company's prospects. "I was concerned about London Northern and it did seem to me that it, and Metroline, were actually too small to be viable, and I tried to persuade Clive Hodson that we should merge them before we got much further, but he was clear that we couldn't do that because we'd already got blessing from the Department of Transport for the plan as it was. Well, guess what happened! They combined again, after a period of London Northern being owned by the Liverpudlians."

Andy Griffiths continues, "London Northern was always struggling. It had a high cost base, very high overheads for a small number of garages. It had been set up with full staffing by Leaside but it was all too costly. There were 25 Inspectors at Holloway for 100 buses. There were two Inspector points at the Nags Head to cover reliefs, one in each direction due to the one-way system, and two points at Finsbury Park, due to the two bus stations. There were also officials at the other garages."

Muswell Hill garage was the first to go. Colin Clubb asked Andy's advice and he suggested Muswell Hill as it was in a residential area and could not be expanded. The next to close was Chalk Farm whose remaining work was moved into Holloway. They then closed Finchley and so were only left with Holloway and Potters Bar, which was cheaper to run with out-county wages and loyal staff. Holloway was a community in itself. Some of the staff would take their families to the canteen for their Sunday lunch."

Above London Northern's ageing fleet is exemplified by Titan T449 on the W7, turning from Stroud Green Road into Lennox Road to reach Finsbury Park station. (Colin Fradd)

Left London Northern retained route 263 from Potters Bar when it was retendered in 1989, using new Scania double-deckers with Alexander bodies. S2 is seen at Holloway in April 1991. (David Cole)

"London Northern was always struggling. It had very high overheads for a small number of garages."

Selkent

Bryan Constable wanted to become MD of Selkent because he had lived all his youth in south-east London, from trolleybus days, the STLs and the RTs. He knew the area, its geography and the people, all of which are important in bus operations. He took Selkent from District to Unit and to Company. The change was seamless in their case because the organisation was virtually the same. He was at Aldenham when it was decided to make changes in London Buses and came back to run Selkent.

Selkent included Roundabout, a great success. The maroon and grey livery was replaced by standard London Buses corporate red in 1990, though one minibus, RH1, remained in maroon and grey. But Bexleybus had been a problem for Selkent, and in 1990 it was tendered – and the great shock was that London Central put in a competitive tender and won it! London Central was the inner-London neighbour of Selkent, originally formed as Bryan Constable had wanted Selkent to be a suburban company!

Some companies complained of the way LBL would vet tender bids, making sure there was a 5% return and no grant leakage. Mike Clayton, then Finance Director at Selkent, didn't have problems with this.

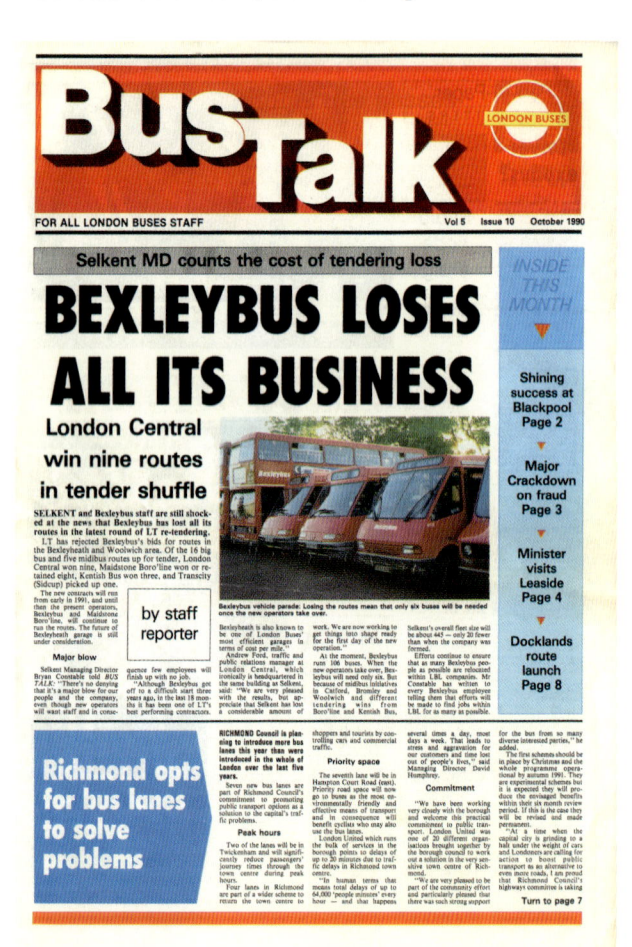

The very first bids for tendered routes had been put together centrally, not in Districts, and he had done many of them at the time. He had no issues with the way the centre did it, and no knowledge of what anyone else was bidding. He found the tendering system clear and above board – fair within the limitations of what they were doing. The problem was the quality of what they were buying, because there was a reluctance to pay more for better quality. That was why Bexleybus was such a cheap operation – if they wanted the work, they had to put in those sorts of prices.

London Central

On its formation, London Central ran 34 services in south east and central London from New Cross, Camberwell and Peckham garages. Thirty of these were block grant and three were contracted for TBU. Its operating area had limited London Underground services and a high level of bus usage.

The Managing Director was Douglas Adie, who had been a Divisional Director with the National Bus Company, and had then run the United Transport minibuses in Manchester following deregulation. Living in Oxford, and being asked if he had a preference amongst the London companies, he suggested one in the west or north – and was given south east London! "But it was a pleasure to go there and there was terrific spirit within the company." However, Douglas could not understand why the old Selkent had been divided into inner and outer companies, rather than segments like the others, but he was very happy to have the money-spinning inner company rather than the suburban and less profitable Selkent. "The 36s and the 12s made so much money!"

Robin Young, the Commercial Director, had been Operating Manager at Victoria and Planning Manager at the CTD where he had organised the Busplan 88 central London reshaping plan. He had previously been a GLC Councillor and a member of Ken Livingstone's administration. Robin developed private hire, excursion and contract services, as well as commercial services to Lakeside and night services. The 'Bus for Night Hawks' – the NX1 'Medway Night Express' ran from Trafalgar Square to Gillingham from October 1990 to provide a bus home 'for those who like an evening out in the West End without the worry of having to dash for the last train'. "Robin was very keen on service quality and he was the king of night services," says Douglas Adie.

Robin Reynolds, the Engineering Director, had joined LT at Chiswick Works as an apprentice in 1959 and had acted as an engineering trouble-shooter under Marcus Smith. Robin recalls a great eight years in London Central. "We were a good team, the four directors. It was tremendous running our own

Asked if he had a preference amongst the London companies, he suggested one in the west or north – and was given south east London!

company and we did a good job. Everyone was working for the best and we were all going through a big learning curve. The problem in London Buses had been that people just accepted things when they were wrong, but Robin Young and I would not accept it – we insisted on doing things properly."

London Central won and lost a number of services through competitive tendering, but had a major boost in 1990 when it won the contracts for nine services previously operated by Bexleybus which were re-tendered. They had bid for the routes, and for combinations of the routes, and for the whole network. "To our amazement," recalls Douglas Adie, "we got almost the whole network!" They had a new garage lined up in Belvedere, but as Selkent only had one route left in Bexleyheath they were asked to take over the garage, staff and vehicles, together with the remaining route which Selkent had won. Bexleyheath garage became a London Central 'island' in the Selkent area. While Maidstone Boro'line, Kentish Bus and Transcity of Sidcup also won routes, London Central were the big winners.

South London
South London had five garages at Brixton, Croydon, Norwood, Streatham and Thornton Heath. It initially operated 35 services, all of which were part of the block grant arrangements. It was the predominant operator of services along the A23 corridor linking Purley, Croydon, Streatham and Brixton with Central London, and provided local bus services in south and central London with an intensive network of local services to Croydon, the largest suburban centre of employment in Greater London and a major shopping and leisure centre.

The Managing Director John Withey and Commercial Director David Jones had been DGM and DOM of Wandle District. The Finance Director, Mick Dobson, had joined LT in 1987 having been Financial Controller of Tyne and Wear PTE. Chris Healey, the Engineering Director, had worked for LT since 1965. However, South London was less than half of Wandle District, the larger share going to London General with some of Abbey District. So it was a small company, and it was attackable on all sides – it had a mixed experience of winning and losing tendered services with other LBL subsidiaries, and with London & Country.

The 109 was a tram-replacement route from Purley which divided at Kennington Oval, half the service crossing Westminster Bridge and returning via Blackfriars, the other half travelling around that loop in the other direction. When it was converted to one-person-operation in 1987 it was simplified to terminate in Trafalgar Square. From 1992 it was worked by Olympians from Croydon and Titans from Thornton Heath, and one of each is seen in Trafalgar Square with a Leaside Metrobus on the 29 which also terminated there from November 1991. (Colin Fradd)

113 South London was the predominant operator along the A23 corridor linking Purley, Croydon, Streatham and Brixton with central London.

South London was well placed for excursions and private hires, being only an hour from the south coast and with good pickup routes throughout its area. It also had a large proportion of the 259 Leyland Olympian double-deckers delivered up to 1987, some of which had coach seats and high-speed rear axles for the X68 service, and so were ideal for excursions and private hires. The company marked its inauguration on 1 April 1989 with a commemorative service on the 159 to Godstone, using RML 2305 which was then at Brixton garage but had been loaned to Godstone garage when new in 1965 until the arrival of new green RMLs. It was also innovative with commercial services, including the 853 which commenced in spring 1990 and ran from Croydon to Sevenoaks on Sundays and Bank Holidays, well into Kentish Bus territory. It also undertook private hire and excursion work, and rail replacement work for British Rail and London Underground.

London Forest
London Forest was one of the smallest LBL companies. On formation it had 357 vehicles, 100 million passengers per annum and a turnover of £30m. There were three garages, at Ash Grove, Leyton and Walthamstow, which increased to four when Clapton Garage was reopened as Hackney Midibus Base. It covered the Lea Bridge Road corridor, from Walthamstow and Leyton into Hackney and central London, together with a suburban network from Walthamstow and central London routes from Ash Grove. It had been intended to have a mixture of company sizes, and the location of Unit 10 kept both Leaside and East London down to a better size. Norman Cohen recalls, "It was certainly smaller than some of the other companies, but that was not necessarily a bad thing and you could envisage a scenario where a small company might have been more successful than the larger ones."

Tom Young, the Managing Director, was Commercial Manager of South Yorkshire Transport and had a background with the NBC. He wanted a small-scale, low cost operation and was keen to operate his Head Office from a garage, so moved to the old Tramways Offices at Walthamstow. The small building would help constrain the number of staff. He was a dour and independent man, determined not to become part of the existing London organisation and eager to 'break the mould' of London Buses operation. He kept himself to himself with most of the other General Managers and with LBL generally. He did not seek popularity and he did not enjoy meetings with the Trade Union, and this was apparent to them. Peter McMahon, the Engineering Director, had a background in LT Bus Engineering while I, Roger Torode, was GGM at Walthamstow and became Commercial Director, and the Finance Director, Tony Oliva, came from outside LT.

The company had a heavy proportion of tendered and LRT-defined routes. Road conditions in Hackney and across the Lea Valley were difficult, and there were problems of performance at Ash Grove, so that the Hackney routes had already been selected for tender before London Forest took over. There was little block grant work under the company's own control, and so little scope for service development. Walthamstow was already a fully tendered operation which had brought changes to pay and conditions, and whilst we had achieved a smooth transition to the new arrangements, there was a lingering resentment amongst the staff that they were being treated differently. The midibus scheme introduced as part of the Walthamstow changes led to the reopening of Clapton garage as a midibus base. This had closed in 1987 and was in use as an indoor go-kart race track and, for a time, the go-karts and minibuses worked alongside each other.

Ash Grove was a large modern garage with considerable difficulties. It had opened in 1981 to replace Dalston and Hackney garages, merging the two groups of staff. David Sayburn, who was District Operating Manager at Tower District at the time, recalls that, "The detailed design of the garage was poor and the management had to spend considerable time troubleshooting structural defects rather than running the bus service." In London Forest, George Roberts went to Ash Grove to sort out the engineering performance. "Ash Grove was a nightmare garage, the volume of service was low, NBAs and availability were awful." George did sort it out, but saw that, "At

May 1990 at Chingford Mount terminus. Walthamstow's repainted Titan on the 158 has full London Forest markings, while Leyton's Titan on the 257 and a long Metrorider on the W16 wait behind. The bus stop identifies itself as a pick up point for Leyton's coach tours. (Roger Torode)

Following the Hackney network changes, route 100 was introduced by London Forest connecting the City with Wapping, replacing part of route 22A. Branded the Wapping Citylink, the route was operated by Metroriders from the Hackney midibus base in Clapton garage. (Barry Le Jeune)

Ash Grove, there had been no structure, no-one cared, there was no ownership of the problems." Nevertheless the performance of the garage had caused difficulties with its services which contributed to the decision to tender them.

The immediate tendering challenge for London Forest was the Hackney network in 1989. This was largely work at Ash Grove garage and the results brought bad news for London Forest, who won only two of the nine routes, while East London won four and Kentish Bus three. Kentish Bus was to operate new Leyland Olympians while London Forest and East London used existing vehicles.

The Hackney scheme involved shortening routes 38 and 55, which had previously continued east of Clapton along the Lea Bridge Road to Leyton, providing a direct link to the West End. This led to a major and continuing public campaign to "Save Our Buses" and restore the through link, but LRT were adamant that fewer than 5% of existing passengers would be affected, and they felt it better to concentrate on providing an enhanced service between Hackney and central London. Links between Leyton and the City were maintained by route 48 and the new route 56, which ran between Whipps Cross, the Angel, Islington and Smithfield.

LRT insisted that a Hackney operating base should be used for the 38 and required London Forest to move the route, and a considerable number of long-

Below In 1989, East London Buses agreed with the London Docklands Development Corporation to provide an express Monday to Friday service D1 between Waterloo and Blackwall via London Bridge. However, LRT decided that, as outside money was being contributed, the service should be tendered to arrange the most efficient and cost-effective operation. LRT invited bids to operate the service and the contract was awarded to London Forest, who arranged with LDDC to provide a special livery for the Ash Grove Titans, adding white panels with the LDDC logo between decks and the route number D1 either side of the front destination box. The Monday to Friday service commenced on 28 August 1990. Buses ran in service from Waterloo during the morning peak and towards Waterloo during the evening peak, operating out of service against the peak flow. A standard two-way service operated during the midday period and this was extended to the peak hours from November. The service took some time to build up custom through Docklands, which was developing from what had been an empty wasteland. Two London Forest Titans are seen at the terminus in Harbour Exchange Square, T827 in the full colour scheme, and T545 in a partial scheme for its role as a reserve vehicle. (Roger Torode)

standing staff, from Leyton to Clapton garage where the go-karts were removed and replaced by Routemasters. The new arrangements commenced in February 1990.

Leyton garage built up a coaching operation, while another small win was the special service for the Department of Health linking its London headquarters buildings. London Forest won the D1 Docklands Express on tender, which operated from Ash Grove, while Walthamstow won two small Essex County Council routes at Waltham Abbey.

Paul Lynch, who was GGM for Leyton and Clapton, recalls, "The coaching developments in Leyton showed that Tom Young had come to London with a plan. He knew how he would build his business up, though he didn't necessarily reveal it to other people. We were developing the idea of a commercial coaching unit at Leyton and had bought an old Leyland Tiger coach. We then developed a business plan for a second old coach, but Tom could be hard to please and we came to the London Forest Board Meeting with our presentation expecting to be scornfully rejected. We were therefore surprised when he not only supported us completely but told us we should get four much newer coaches, then after two years another four, until it built up to around 20 vehicles! The coaching development was stimulating and a morale boost for Leyton garage. It did not proceed entirely smoothly but we built up a good business." Tom also had ideas about competing in the Cambridge area once the company became independent. London Forest also took a lead in taking over catering in garages and direct purchase of uniforms.

East London
At East London, Roger Bowker quickly found that it was *not* different running buses in London. All he had been told of the great differences in London was 'a load of rubbish.' And Bryan Constable, who he had become friends with when he was in Eastbourne, was a lot of help at General Managers' and business meetings. Norman Cohen was a superb chairman to East London and very supportive. He had a great team around him. The Units then became subsidiary companies so that he became Managing Director with Commercial, Engineering and Finance Directors.

East London did well with the Hackney tenders but were hit hard in Hornchurch, where the loss

116 "It was not different running buses in London. All I had been told of the great differences in London was a load of rubbish."

of routes decimated red bus services in the area resulting in the closure of Hornchurch garage. Ensign and Frontrunner took most of the services with London Buses only keeping a toehold in Hornchurch itself with the minibus route 256 and 346. Hornchurch garage closed on 23 September 1988.

A new route network was introduced to Docklands by East London from 4 March 1989, following a joint LRT/LDDC study into the area's transport needs. Nigel Barrett was manager of East London's West Ham garage, responsible for developing the Docklands services. "We were building up a network of routes in anticipation of the demand when Docklands was fully developed. The routes carried very few passengers at first, but this was as expected until loadings built up over time."

Docklands Transit
In November 1988 Harry Blundred, who was well known for introducing minibuses in Exeter and Oxford, announced plans to run 100 minibuses in Docklands in competition with London Buses. The proposal required approval by LRT, who did not grant a London Bus Agreement but allowed the new service to operate once it had licences from the Metropolitan Traffic Commissioner. LRT did not allow use of its Travelcards and passes on the new service, as it was a commercial venture by a firm that LRT had no control over, and there was no guarantee of continuity of operation. As a result passengers would have to pay a cash fare to use the new service. Transit Holdings objected to this and called for immediate deregulation of London's bus services!

Three London Boroughs objected to Blundred's proposal and the Traffic Commissioners only granted experimental 18-month licences to two of the services, compared with five years for the others. The services were planned to be 'hail and ride', but restrictions were placed on stopping in bus lanes and some other areas where existing bus stops were to be used.

The immediate success of East London's new services was the X15 Express between Beckton and Aldwych, which ran non-stop between Canning Town and Tower Hill using comfortable, refurbished Routemaster coaches in a red and gold livery. The conductors worked successfully to provide a luxury service, including selling newspapers and coffee to passengers in the morning peak. It was soon extended to Oxford Circus, and shoppers' journeys were added in the midday and on Saturdays. The service quickly achieved far greater passenger numbers than the 200 each day that had been predicted. It was intended to run until the opening of the Beckton extension of the Docklands Light Railway. Five RMC training buses were refurbished and the success of the route led to two more soon being added together with a front-entrance RMA.

Opposite RMC1490, named King Edward VII, rests outside Canada House in Trafalgar Square with RMC1496 behind, before returning to East Beckton. (Colin Fradd)

Above RMA8 was a Staff Bus at Bus Engineering Ltd (BEL) when it was rescued and refurbished for East London Coaches and also used on the X15. (Keith Wood)

117 Harry Blundred announced plans to run 100 minibuses in Docklands in competition with London Buses.

Docklands Transit launched the first two of its new services on 30 March 1989, the D11 from Tower Gateway to Wapping, extended to the Isle of Dogs on Saturdays, and the D13 from Mile End to the Isle of Dogs. OAP permit holders travelled at half fare after 09.30. Fares were otherwise similar to LRT, using the LRT zonal system. Weekly, monthly and annual passes were offered, and a transfer ticket giving two hours travel on its services for £1.20. Further services were introduced as more staff were recruited and trained, mostly north of the River Thames but also one to the south. Seven routes were proposed in total in the Stepney, Stratford, Barking and Lewisham areas.

This was the first example of a competitive London bus service since LT was created in 1933. It came six years after the proposed AMOS minibus scheme had been proposed and rejected. Roger Bowker, MD of East London, responded by saying that, "I don't think Mr Blundred would expect me to sit idly by and do nothing!" Ilford councillors were unhappy that the new route would simply take their residents out of their Borough to shop in Barking.

Frank Cheroomi joined Docklands Transit as a minibus driver when the service started, earning £3.75 an hour. He had done all sorts of work before that, handyman, cars, building, painting and decorating. His wife had been pestering him to get a proper job and made him an appointment without telling him. Now she keeps reminding him that it was all her idea.

They were driving 16 seat Transits and competing with LT bus routes. The first year of operation was difficult because they could not accept Travelcard or OAP passes. A year later they thought they would be able to accept OAP passes, but this was cancelled at the last minute. They were selling their own Travelcards and working on a Hail and Ride basis.

They had a depot in Silvertown and the operating base at Asda, and ran routes from Asda to Bethnal Green, Island Gardens, Barking Road and Tobacco Dock. They did well by watching the queues building up for red buses and then going and picking up the passengers – the passengers had to get to work and would pay the Docklands fare even though they already had a Travelcard or Bus Pass. So Docklands employed someone to watch the LT buses and let them know the best time to go to the stop. One driver regularly didn't take much money, and Frank made a point of doing that job one day competing with the 100 and took more money than anybody ever had done. They also secured a private contract with Reuters.

The black cabs did not like them and tried to baulk them when they could, following them down the

Docklands Transit used 16-seat Ford Transits in a blue livery, running at 5-10 minute frequencies, and two are seen at the Isle of Dogs terminus of route D13. Newspapers in Torbay complained that their new vehicles had been taken to London and replaced by older buses! (Barry Le Jeune)

118   The black cabs did not like them and tried to baulk them when they could.

roads. They would also sometimes be boxed in by red buses, front and back. They had their own radio system but the frequency was not brilliant.

Harry Blundred had sent managers from Exeter to run the London operations and all went back because they could not handle it. They did not realise that London people are different – they tried to be nice to them and were walked all over. So Blundred asked Frank if he would run it. Frank says that he didn't run it, he handled the people. He was firm but fair and did not let them cross over the line, and so there was mutual respect.

In the early days Docklands Transit made money but not enough. Harry Blundred also lost money on the site which he bought at the height of the property boom and sold during the crunch. The original 16-seater buses had manual transmission so they could not take LT drivers, who were licensed for automatic transmission, and at first they had to train every driver. Frank could not understand why black and Asian drivers were not passing through the training until one Sunday the News of the World reported on the centre pages that their driving instructor was a member of the Ku Klux Klan. Frank got rid of him.

Nigel Barrett at West Ham naturally found Harry Blundred's 'bread vans' were a nuisance, nipping around and pinching passengers from his services. They were not beyond making a U-turn in order to pick up passengers they saw at a bus stop. This was particularly annoying at a time when some of the routes were on net cost contracts, so Nigel's operation was losing money.

There were complaints that the Docklands Minibus services were not being run in accordance with the terms of their licences. At the time, Transit Holdings was expecting to receive serious competition to its biggest operation, Devon General, from City of Oxford Motor Services in reprisal for Thames Transit's operations in Oxford. This would have made it more difficult for Transit Holdings to subsidise losses in Docklands. However, the operation continued and Harry Blundred denied that it was in financial trouble. He expected it to turn into profit within the calendar year – his previous operations in Oxford had taken nearly 2 years to get into profit.

Docklands Transit did complain to the Office of Fair Trading (OFT) about LRT's refusal to allow use of Travelcard. The OFT reported quickly, deciding that there were no grounds for action because the Docklands Minibus routes 'did not add sufficiently to the network of services provided by other operators for compensation for the recognition of Travelcards to be worthwhile.' Following this, the operation ended on 16 November. Harry Blundred also blamed the recession at the time, and competition with their other operations. The company was wound up on 17 November after nearly 20 months' operation. The Reuters contract was retained and Frank Cheroomi was left in charge of it.

Boro'line London
Boro'line had been suffering from shortage of staff and this became worse during 1989 with unreliable services leading to emergency timetables on routes 132, 228, 328 and 422. They had taken over the 422 because Bexleybus had had staff shortages. Boro'line advertised for staff in newspapers all over the country and hired in drivers from as far away as Blackburn. But the new staff were paid less than those who had been with the company for some time, and were therefore not staying long.

Boro'line had been awarded the contract for route 108 in spring 1989, but due to their recruitment problems East London continued to operate the route on a temporary contract. Boro'line also suffered from the late delivery of new Leyland Lynx buses and from difficulty in finding an operating base in a suitable location. This was solved when they obtained a site near the southern entrance of the Blackwall Tunnel, which opened in November for the 108 and 188. However, the new site attracted criticism. Graham Elliott was responsible for safety in LRT's bus operations and says, "It was absolutely awful, a disused gas works. To get to it, you were going down this unmade road, made of spoil from the gas works, with no street lighting – a dreadful place, and even worse in a bus with the width and overhangs. We were so concerned

The double deckers bought new by Maidstone Boro'line were 11 Leyland Olympians, two Scanias and one Volvo Citybus. An Olympian and a Scania are seen at Bexleyheath Market Place in November 1991. (Colin Fradd)

"The guy who scheduled the 108 did the crew reliefs at the wrong end of the Blackwall Tunnel."

that I sent down some PCOs (Plain-Clothed Officials) to take a video all the way in and out of the garage. I felt that it wasn't good for our reputation. It had a couple of little old brick buildings used as an office."

Norman Kemp, who had moved on from Boro'line to Kentish Bus in mid-1988, recalls, "This was not a nice story after I left." He had held together the commercial and operating functions and, afterwards, problems developed. "The guy who scheduled the 108 did the crew reliefs at the wrong end of the Blackwall Tunnel. You can't get away with that, a silly mistake by someone who didn't know. You need to know the details of services and really the Blackwall peninsula base was too far from Maidstone where maintenance was carried out."

In November 1990 Boro'line took on the 272 in exchange for the 188. Alan Price, who was the Managing Director, acknowledges that they may have been too ambitious with the second London operation. Norman adds, "The coaching operation also ran into difficulties because of lack of work outside the summer months, and Boro'line came a cropper. They had too much on their hands, in particular the coaching."

By October 1991, Maidstone Borough Council decided to sell the company. The council regretted this decision and had criticised provisions in the 1985 Transport Act which prevented it from supporting Boro'line without government permission. Whilst a management buyout initially looked likely, a Council meeting in January 1992 resulted in Proudmutual becoming preferred bidder. However, having investigated the operation, Proudmutual did not proceed with the purchase but did take over the London operations which passed to Kentish Bus on 17 February 1992. Two days later, Boro'line was placed into administration. Their operation, which had started well, had grown too quickly. As Mike Weston recalls, "They were perfect at first, but then took on too much."

Kentish Bus

Whilst taking over the 19 with Routemasters in 1993 caused a bigger splash, Norman Kemp thinks that winning the Hackney routes, 22A, 22B and 55 in 1989 was a bigger achievement, requiring a new operation to be set up at some distance. In the period between tender submission and award, it was generally the case that senior TBU managers would meet bidders in confidence; these 'post-tender negotiations' allowed LRT to clarify any matters of detail in the bid as well

Kentish Bus took over their Hackney routes in February 1990 using Leyland Olympians in a maroon and cream livery. Two are seen in Mare Street close to Clapton garage. (Keith Wood)

120 The double-decker buses were passing the bank's headquarters in the City, so they put Kentish Bus on the roofs so the bank staff would notice them.

as to satisfy themselves that bidders knew the enormity of the task that they might be entrusted to. Malcolm Wren came and saw Norman to go over their bids and asked, "What can you cope with?" Norman said, around 40 buses – "Maybe if I had said 70 we would have got more work!" Malcolm would go over the bids in detail, where they would be run from, details of the scheduling and so on. This casual question was very significant.

Norman's first route at Kentish Bus had been the P14, from November 1988, using Metroriders and operating through the Rotherhithe Tunnel. The P14 was based at a converted former rail depot always described as Leyton by Kentish Bus. BRS had inherited this from National Carriers, at Temple Mills on the borders of Leyton and Hackney – the site is now part of the Olympic Park. BRS then decided to rebuild the site and encouraged them to use it for their buses. So when they won the Hackney work in 1989 they had a ready-made depot. Given the catchment area, recruiting driving staff was easy. An excellent group of depot supervisors came from the ranks of experienced Northfleet drivers – on a good day, only a 30-minute drive up the A2 and through the Blackwall Tunnel.

The 22A, 22B and 55 started on 24 February 1990, settled down and ran well, but then not a great deal more happened into early 1990. Proudmutual got finance for the three Hackney routes through the Standard Chartered Bank. They then realised that their double-decker buses were passing the bank's headquarters in the City, so they put their name Kentish Bus on the roof of the buses, thinking that staff in the company would begin to notice them. This worked a treat – when they went to the company again seeking further funding they were told that the bank staff were all aware of the buses because of the names on the roofs.

Proudmutual brought some staff down from the north-east to help run the services, bringing them for a week at a time and putting them up in digs, but as they now had a management team in Kentish Bus all recruitment was handled locally.

Armchair

After Cityrama had ceased tendered operations, Huw Barrington met Simon Newman, MD of Armchair, at an LT meeting. Armchair had been interested in LT tenders since 1986 and were bidding for them but had not won any yet, probably pitching too high. They were also busy with coach work. Huw joined them in January 1990 as Assistant General Manager, responsible for the buses, and they then won route 260, starting from 23 June 1990, from North Finchley to Shepherd's Bush, followed by the 65 in January 1991 from Kingston to Ealing. The 260 had a peak vehicle requirement (PVR) of 12, and the 65 had 18, giving a total PVR of 30 buses.

Huw set up the operation from scratch, as he had done at Cityrama. He poached some staff from Cityrama including his business manager. They used new orange Leyland Olympian double-deckers for the basic requirement, but the backups were three two-door South Yorkshire Roe-bodied Atlantean double-deckers. These were outer suburban routes and the new buses were one-door double-deckers. The secondhand buses were quickly reregistered with Irish registrations that would not show their age!

They operated from a base in Brentford and Huw did the schedules. The only major difference from Cityrama was that they couldn't get double-deckers into the Armchair depot because of the low roof, so they contracted out the maintenance to London Buslines. This was evidence of "the private sector boys keeping together", and it was useful for him to be able to show LRT that the maintenance problem he had had at Cityrama had been resolved in his new company by contracting it out – it was still their responsibility and their O-licence, but someone else was doing it. Once again, there was no difficulty in getting drivers – Hanwell garage had just closed, and Norbiton closed with the loss of route 65 to Armchair.

Armchair won the 65 in 1990 and commenced operation on 26 January 1991 with a fleet of 17 Leyland Olympians with ECW bodies, one of which is seen at Ealing Broadway two days later. (David Cole)

"Armchair had been bidding for LRT tenders but had not won any, probably pitching too high."

There was a surplus of disgruntled drivers who felt let down by the trade union.

Simon Thomas, LT's Contracts Tendering Manager, remembers a visit to Armchair to discuss tender bids the company had submitted. The owner had friendly pet dogs that roamed freely in the meeting room. Biscuits were brought in and put on a low table, and while tea was being made the dogs came in and licked the biscuits. When the tea arrived the biscuits were offered round – and everybody refused!

Huw recalls that Armchair's two routes were quickly knocked into shape and were making money at first. Armchair did not have any union representation – the T&G tried, and ballots were held, but the staff didn't want to. Armchair kept going for some years – their performance was all right, and the 65 and the 260 contracts were renewed.

Armchair's sightseeing work was low due to the Gulf War, which reduced tourism. As a result, a year-round bus operation was attractive – the 65 was one of the top performing high-frequency routes. The radio system they used was their own, and they had to have special agreement from LBL to operate! They were 'A for Armchair' on the network. Marconi offered them a trial of a bus tracking system, which was fitted along the route and permitted them to extend it to the second route. Marconi used Armchair as their shop window, and it became a good system that worked well. The system did not require the driver to input any details, though this meant that it could not tell you the destination of the bus, and it didn't integrate with LT's Countdown location system.

It was at this time that Huw spent a lot of time tendering for routes to no avail. They were a quality coach operation and they wanted quality on their bus operations as well, and it may be that the resulting higher prices made them uncompetitive – they were delivering quality at a price but bid for 20 or more tenders and were getting nothing out of it. "When we went for feedback we were told to drop our prices, but we didn't wish to because we wanted to maintain quality. Everyone likes to have the work, but not at any price, and our prices were around 5% out!"

The management team who had bought Eastern National on privatisation sold the company on to Badgerline in April 1990, the group becoming Firstgroup in 1995. In May 1990 it was announced that the company would be split into Eastern National, the northern part, and Thamesway, the southern part. Robin Orbell declined the opportunity to become MD of Thamesway and went to Eastern National, but in June 1996 it was decided that he should manage both companies. Thamesway adopted this maroon and yellow colour scheme – largely because every other colour had already been used by another operator in the area! (Colin Fradd)

122 Armchair's sightseeing work was low due to the Gulf War, which reduced tourism.

LBL in 1989

In 1989 LBL had improved performance with 93.8% of scheduled bus journeys being operated, whilst operating costs had fallen again by 3.3%, so that since 1983/4 there had been an overall 20% reduction in costs. By March 1989, 25% of London bus services were under contract from the Tendered Bus Unit and LBL was winning around 50% of the contracts.

But industrial relations were fraught and the trade union was keen to secure a good pay award in this last year of central pay negotiations, before they were devolved to the new subsidiary companies. Following some individual strikes, general dissatisfaction eventually caused a series of all-out strikes over wages. The union argued that the high turnover of staff and resulting shortages made a substantial wage increase necessary, whilst management responded that LBL would become uncompetitive with such high wage levels, resulting in job losses through tendering losses.

With no progress on their claim, the union called an all-out strike from 15 May, on alternate Mondays until agreement was reached. This was supported throughout London except in garages with separately negotiated pay scales. There was also a tube strike on that first day together with an overtime ban on parts of the British Rail network, which led to considerable criticism of transport workers. A further stoppage on 21 June was again simultaneous with an Underground strike and, this time, an all-out strike on British Rail, leading to the greatest loss of public transport in London since the General Strike of 1926. Having all three transport undertakings on strike detracted from the issues involved in each of them, while the arrival of the new LRT Chairman, Wilfrid Newton, from Hong Kong (discussed below) led to suggestions that he was seeking to impose Hong Kong wages and conditions in London.

The LBL platform staff eventually settled for a 9% increase but engineering staff remained in dispute. They argued that their special skills deserved greater recognition, particularly as there were some significant shortages. Their stoppage on 5 July resulted in hardly any vehicles running and there were further stoppages later in the month. The engineers eventually settled with an 8% increase in basic pay plus other improvements. From 1990, the LBL subsidiary companies settled their own wage rates.

Logos, colours and new buses

Later in 1989 LRT began to define its roles more clearly. The red roundel was adopted once again as the corporate symbol and the New Johnston typeface restored as the LT house style. From then on LRT traded as 'London Transport' – though the full legal name remained London Regional Transport, this was not used publicly. The LT Design Director said that whilst the separate LRT corporate identity had served its purpose, giving operating subsidiary companies time to establish themselves, "we believe the time has now come when LRT must associate itself visually more closely with its subsidiaries, if only to reassure the public that the commercially operated companies are the ultimate responsibility of the corporate supervisory body". The Tendered Bus Unit was renamed Tendered Bus Division (TBD).

LBL decided at the beginning of 1990 to restore the corporate image to all of its buses, even those which had individual local liveries. In practice little repainting was needed because most of the small operations, Kingston Bus (within London United), Harrow Buses (in Metroline) and Bexleybus (in Selkent), lost much of their work in the 1990 retendering, and leased vehicles were returned to their owners. Only at Roundabout was a major repainting programme necessary. Westlink continued with its own identity. This did not affect other contractors, and Nick Newton said, "at present there is no policy to require contractors to have red vehicles. In some

The LRT logo shown here was replaced by the red roundel in 1989. This late use of it announced the expansion of the tendering programme from late 1989.

LRT
ORGANISING TRANSPORT FOR LONDON

THE TENDERING PROGRAMME EXPANDS

London Regional Transport started competitive tendering of London's bus services in 1985. From these modest beginnings the process has grown to the current position where broadly 25% of all the Capital's bus services now operate under contract. The 40 million miles involved utilise some 1,500 buses and are operated by a number of contractors.

The success of the system has resulted in a decision to accelerate the programme so that in 1990/91 an additional 18 million miles (10% of the network) will be tendered. This level of service will require approaching 500 buses and the nature of the routes involved will offer additional business opportunities to all operators.

The schedule overleaf gives details of next year's new tendered services, in addition to which there will be frequent retendering of existing contracts.

If you would like more information on the opportunities that London bus service tendering provides, please feel free to contact me.

Nick Newton
Tendered Bus Unit Manager
London Regional Transport
55 Broadway
London
SW1H 0BD
Telephone 01-227 3468

The trade union was keen to secure a good pay award in this last year of central pay negotiations.

Left LBL's decision to restore its corporate image to all it buses resulted in the loss of Roundabout's maroon and grey colour scheme. This Dennis Dart at Orpington in May 1991 shows its ownership by Selkent, but still has prominent Roundabout fleetnames. (David Cole)

Below left R&I Coaches were new to London tendering and won three contracts in their first year. They took over route 268 from London Country North West in June 1989 using new Iveco minibuses, one of which is seen arriving in Golders Green on the 268 shortly after the takeover. (Barry Le Jeune).

Below PanAtlas, trading as AtlasBus, won the tender for route 107 in 1989 using nine new Leyland Olympians with Northern Counties bodies, one of which is seen at Edgware Station on its way to New Barnet. (David Cole)

circumstances we might seek to advise on colour schemes, but ultimately it is a decision for the contractor".

In 1989 the TBD were increasingly requiring the use of new buses as a condition of new contracts. This led to new double-deckers for Kentish Bus, London and Country, London Country North West, BTS, Boro'line, Ensign, London Buslines, Metrobus and Pan Atlas, with new single-deckers to Boro'line and midibuses to Eastern National Citybus and R&I Tours. R&I were the only newcomer to LRT work during the year.

Left Delay in the delivery of new buses to London & Country for routes 78 and 176 in November 1990 led to the hire of 24 Atlanteans from South Yorkshire Transport. SYT 1706 carries two South Yorkshire fleetnames together with London and Country and LRT identification. It is at the Elephant and Castle in November 1990. (John Parkin)

124 The TBD were increasingly requiring the use of new buses as a condition of new contracts.

A new Chairman

In March 1989 Wilfrid Newton CBE arrived for a five-year appointment as the new Chairman of LT. John Telford Beasley remained Chairman of London Buses and Clive Hodson was appointed Managing Director. Also in March, Cecil Parkinson was appointed Secretary of State for Transport.

Wilfrid Newton had been Chairman of the Hong Kong Mass Transit Railway Corporation since 1983. His priority was to take forward the recommendations of the Fennell Report on the King's Cross fire, to continue the restructuring of LBL, and to improve its performance ahead of deregulation. The Secretary of State also asked him for proposals on a management, investment and financial strategy to give London safe and reliable services but transferring costs, wherever possible, from the taxpayer to the passenger and other beneficiaries.

Wilfrid Newton was highly regarded within and outside LT. Steven Norris wrote that he was "an inspired choice as Chairman." His career had primarily been as an accountant in the oil industry before moving into transport. "Tall and imposing, he had suffered badly in a car accident, losing a leg and the sight of one eye. He had lost none of his sharpness however, and remained a director of Hong Kong and Shanghai Bank where he was Chairman of the audit committee. He was tough, competent and experienced and he brought a much-needed discipline to the whole organisation."

It was Wilfrid Newton who now continued the drive towards deregulation and privatisation.

London and Country's new Volvo Citybuses with East Lancs bodies arrived in late 1990 and early 1991. 676 works its way through a congested Trafalgar Square on its way to Oxford Circus in April 1991, with a Grey-Green Volvo on the 24 and a Routemaster on the 9. (John Parkin)

125 "Wilfrid Newton was an inspired choice as Chairman."

6 MAJOR LOSSES, MAJOR GAINS 1990-1993

Declan O'Farrell recalls the shock of Metroline losing the Harrow routes in 1990. "In 1987, we won the lot. When it was re-tendered in 1990, we lost virtually everything. The only reason we kept routes was because others couldn't take any more of them. That was the year the Harrow network was broken up. We all thought it was a quasi-political decision, because LT – and the government behind them – were trying to introduce a bit more local competition. They wanted the markets to be seen to be a bit more vibrant than they had been up to that point.

"When we inherited Metroline it included Edgware Garage which was new and very expensive, with very light usage – the costs were huge. And we had our dearly beloved Cricklewood and Willesden garages. At the time there were something like 55 bus garages left in London, and these two were in the bottom five on performance. The only shining light that we had was Harrow Weald, which had won the original Harrow tender and was now decimated. And so we had to decide what to do and I was very very reluctant to close Harrow.

"But at the time we were facing two other challenges. One was that there was a bit of a recession in the early 1990s and secondly, it was starting to become embarrassing that London Buses was paying out huge amounts in redundancy to drivers who were walking out of the door and starting on Monday morning with the private operators. Clive Hodson was very sensitive about that, so I went to him and said, 'Look, we can't turn back the clock, but I think Harrow Weald is the most efficient on the system – not only is it operationally excellent, but it is also one of the cheapest sheds in London, and a great role model for what we are hoping to do in the future. And here they are about to destroy it! I would like to keep Harrow and empty Cricklewood. I'll keep a couple of routes there, so that it is operational, but I want to

Lower Regent Street in May 1992 still provides a sea of red buses, most of which are Routemasters. Selkent's Olympian L98 is working its way through the congestion to Oxford Circus, but RML2363 on the 94 seems to have failed. (Roger Torode collection)

> 126 "It was starting to become embarrassing that London Buses was paying out huge amounts in redundancy to drivers who were walking out of the door and starting on Monday morning with the private operators."

take work from the rest of Metroline so that Harrow does not have any redundancies, and it will allow me to significantly reduce Cricklewood's capacity.'

"I wanted to reduce Cricklewood because it was very old and expensive to run, and basically too full. And secondly, it had lots and lots of operational difficulties. The plus side of this was that, rather than make over 100 people redundant, I would expect maybe 30 people to be going, so it would save a lot of money and save embarrassment as well. It would also create problems for the private sector because they would have to go out and recruit their own staff. So the plan was to retain the staff at Harrow and to let people go at Cricklewood and, rather than have redundancies centred on one place, have redundancies at all the garages, because we were moving the work around.

"Now the big weakness in my plan was that it didn't take into account expectations. When the Harrow announcement was made the staff thought, 'Well, that's it, our number is up, there'll be loads of redundancies, it will be done on seniority, I'll buy that cottage in Ireland or book my ticket back to the West Indies. People were already salivating over having big redundancy cheques. So when we announced that we weren't closing Harrow there was uproar. It culminated in mass demonstrations outside our head office, because they wanted redundancy. There was a march up from Cricklewood, I think they drove up to the outskirts of Harrow and marched, and there they met the staff from Harrow Weald and they marched up to our headquarters protesting. And basically the protest was, 'Where's our redundancy?' And I was saying, 'Look, these are hard times. We're trying to keep redundancies to the minimum and guarantee work for you all. But they weren't interested. And the union were between a rock and a hard place, because they wanted to defend jobs, but they were being absolutely pilloried by their members because they were not getting their redundancy cheques. It would have been so much easier to just close Harrow and disappear into the shadows!'

"So we decided to do what we had planned, we took work out of Edgware and Cricklewood and Willesden, and we kept North Wembley minibus base, but we'd negotiated additional capacity just down the road with a coach company. When we didn't win any of the work they had a ready set agreement to give to Sovereign, who moved in down the road and so we had them on our doorstep, and that was John Wilson with his Harrow midibuses."

Nick Newton observed this too. "Trade Union members liked tendering, they liked redundancy from LT, particularly the long service guys who got good redundancy money. The unions could not mount a formal protest when members liked it."

Sovereign
John Wilson was running Sovereign buses based in Stevenage when they were awarded some of the Harrow routes from 1 December 1990. They had garages in St Albans, Hertford and Stevenage. They offered existing drivers work at Harrow but there were no recruitment problems and indeed, they offered a lower rate of pay to new entrants. He used some St Albans staff at Harrow at the beginning to get the new operation going as he wanted to be confident of a good start. They had taken on a variety of staff who were new to PSV work, and they also recruited three former LT supervisors who were doing a great job – they used them to lead the new recruits, though they only wanted to work the basic 40 hours. They had their LT pensions and didn't need the money, but their wives wanted them out of the house! They were the kingpins of the driving staff and schooled the others into their new job. They were based in Pinner Road, the old Venture garage, which Transdev still use.

They commenced in December 1990 with just two routes – they had tendered for a number of routes both double and single deck, putting in realistic prices, and had not got them, and then Nick Newton phoned to say, "You've got four contracts in Harrow." The company was owned by AJS Holdings at the time, but by the time the operation started, AJS had been sold to Blazefield Holdings. All the Harrow routes had been retendered. BTS, Luton and District, and Sovereign between them got the lion's share of the routes, and Metroline kept only a few.

John had been in the coaching industry and knew that the Venture garage was far too big. Venture had

Sovereign's blue Mercedes minibus is at Harrow with green London Country North West and red Metroline buses. (David Cole)

"The union were between a rock and a hard place, because they wanted to defend jobs, but they were being pilloried by their members because they were not getting their redundancy cheques."

been part of Valiant and was running 20 coaches from a site with a capacity of 60, so they would be able to lease the covered garage while Venture used the open parking. They installed two Portakabins inside the covered garage for offices and facilities, and maintenance was on contract with Mercedes, carried out at night by a local Mercedes dealer. They collected the vehicles in the evening and generally got them back for the morning, and John had no engineers himself.

John remarks that this was the finest garage he has ever run – there were fewer headaches, everything worked and they could plan everything properly. He had a new driver agreement and did not inherit any 'Spanish customs'! John himself did most of the scheduling "the old busman's way" as he had done at Eastern National, rather than the 'London Country' way which had been common at Sovereign. The duties were of different lengths, and they did what was needed.

John found the TBD could be helpful when they were needed but they did not bother him otherwise. He realised that he had little contact from Nick Newton, and when he asked why, Nick's response was that he had no need to contact John because things were going well.

Harrow also ran two buses in St Albans on Sundays as the Sovereign operation there had moved into the local Council depot which did not open on Sundays – so they could not get the buses out. So the Sunday work, for Hertfordshire County Council, was given to Harrow drivers to give them a change from the work around Harrow.

Green Line
In 1991 the Green Line services were reviewed by LT in order to reduce or eliminate the subsidy paid to Green Line for charging fares at LT levels. Unfortunately, this resulted in all the remaining Green Line routes in London being considered uneconomic. As a result, LT announced that it would withdraw from some of these agreements from 29 June. Some of the routes that were commercially registered continued to operate, generally those that provided services to popular destinations such as Windsor, Gatwick and Stansted.

The withdrawal of Green Line routes caused a public outcry. The loudest campaign concerned route 726, which ran between Dartford and Heathrow Airport, through Bexleyheath, Bromley, Croydon, Sutton and Kingston, but which suffered from traffic congestion throughout the route. The strength of public feeling led LT to reconsider, and a six-month contract from 29 June 1991 was given to Kentish Bus and Luton and District, who were the existing operators from Dartford and Slough. The route was subsequently fully tendered and awarded to London Coaches, who took over in February 1992 using ten new DAF Ikarus coaches marketed as the 726 Expresslink, one of which is seen in Kingston. Most of the remaining Green Line routes were replaced by new or revised bus routes. The route was later retendered in a revised form which was no longer viable for London Coaches. (Keith Wood)

"He had little contact from Nick Newton, and when he asked why, Nick's response was that he had no need for contact because things were going well."

The Wandsworth network was a huge win for London General and was thought to be the largest single amount of work ever won from LT by a single contractor, requiring 120 vehicles. Keith Ludemann described it as, "A wonderful early Christmas present. Not only have we kept our current routes but the extra work has prevented job losses and the closure of one garage – which would have been a near certainty". The new midibuses were named Streetline, and a Dennis Dart is seen at Clapham Junction on the first day, 25 May 1991. (David Cole)

Below In August 1991, London General's route 413 was converted to midibus operation branded as Hoppa, and extended to Lower Morden. Optare Metrorider MRL 135 is in Carshalton on its way to Belmont Station. (Colin Fradd)

London General

For London General, a defining moment was in 1991 when the Wandsworth network came up for tender. This was a major challenge, with 102 buses and around 400 drivers at Stockwell. Keith Ludeman had heard that LCBS had brought in a new manager specifically to win the Wandsworth network, and they already had a garage in Wandsworth to run it.

With this threat, he had to negotiate different terms and conditions with the TU Officer Pat Mahon. They had built up a firm but close working relationship. "You'd never get one over on him and you would sit down and discuss the issues with him." They negotiated a drivers' pay and conditions package for the Wandsworth tender. Some staff had to transfer from block grant to the new terms and conditions in order to achieve a competitive package. The cost rates for double deckers were too high, so he bid using 1980 Metrobuses, and got a fleet of old vehicles from CentreWest and other Units.

Keith had a lot of sleepless nights over this tender. Then he was called to see Nick Newton who said, "You haven't got the work till you've got the work." Nick questioned him at length and then said, "Do you realise this is the lowest pence per mile for double-decker operation in London? Do you think you can

129 "Do you realise this is the lowest pence per mile for double-decker operation in London? Do you think you can achieve it?"

BUS NEWS

HOPPING AROUND BY BUS HAS NEVER BEEN EASIER

We've looked long and hard at your local buses, listened to what you've had to say about them, and improved the network to make it easier to get to all the places you want to go.

Streetline comes to 156, 170 & 265

More frequent Streetline minibuses bring improved reliability to these routes. You'll like their smart looks and friendly service.

London Transport Service

Wandsworth
Clapham
Putney including Roehampton
Tooting

BIG IMPROVEMENTS TO LOCAL BUS SERVICES

- new routes
- better timekeeping
- improved frequencies

Your detailed guide to changes for the better in South West and West London — Wandsworth, Clapham, Putney and Roehampton, Fulham, Hammersmith, Wimbledon, Tooting and Mitcham areas. Where they go, what's new and how often they run.

FULL DETAILS INSIDE

from Saturday 25 May 1991

achieve it?" Keith said, yes, he could. Nick then picked up the phone and a splendid lunch came in on a trolley. Wandsworth set London General up very well for privatisation, because they had already done most of the cost cutting.

London Forest
My description of other companies has been based on interviews with those involved, but as I was Commercial Director of London Forest I am at this point, in a sense, interviewing myself along with others who were involved. Tom Young was invited to contribute but did not respond.

Following the Hackney tenders in 1989, London Forest's four garages were largely dedicated to tender work on three year contracts, and it was the most reliant on this type of work within the LBL subsidiaries, excepting Westlink. This was a continuous challenge but could be an advantage if it forced the pace of change in the company and put it onto a more commercial footing.

But London Forest was a small company with little scope to spread its overheads. This was quite unlike most other LBL companies, who had substantial block grant work that guaranteed their existence for many years to come. London Forest also had several credible low cost competitors nearby – County Bus and Coach, Capital Citybus, Eastern National/Thamesway and Grey-Green, who were able to set up new low-cost operations, paying out-of-London wage rates. The neighbouring LBL companies were also eager to compete. The Walthamstow negotiated tenders had resulted in separate conditions for the garage but resentment from the staff at being singled out, while Nick Newton considered that they "had not gone

Larger numbers of new vehicles were bought in 1992 and 1993, including full-size single-deckers and some double-deckers. London General received 13 Volvo single-deckers for route 88 and branded them The Clapham Omnibus with a livery by Best Impressions. Keith Ludeman pre-booked KLL personalised registrations for them, but soon realised it was a step too far. "Luckily, my stock was high and I got away with it – otherwise, I might have been shown the door!" (Colin Stannard)

through the pains" of competitive tendering as had staff at the other contracted operations. So at London Forest we needed major changes to quickly make the company more competitive. This would require a new, more commercial, pay and conditions package and a new style of operation as had happened elsewhere in London, but the pressure from the LBL Board was for change throughout London Forest.

We were all working to bring change, and Tom Young had been recruited to lead this. He was clear sighted and knew where he wanted to get to, but he could be difficult with people. You could not repeatedly try and constrain him, or you would be seen as a typical London backwoodsman preventing him doing what was necessary. Tom was making himself stand out and keeping his distance from all things LBL in the hope that London Forest would be privatised first.

Whilst some of the other subsidiary Managing Directors found Tom Young distant, Declan O'Farrell at Metroline got on well with him. "We were the MDs of the two smallest companies, with similar problems of scale. It was mandatory for companies to include their overheads in tender bids, and the larger companies like East London had half the pence per

London Forest had several credible low cost competitors nearby, who were able to set up new low-cost operations, paying out-of-London wage rates.

mile of overheads compared to the smaller companies. So there was an inbuilt injustice – Metroline and London Forest were under considerable pressure, and we had to look more at the labour side of costs."

But Graham Elliott remembers, "Tom got up everybody's nose; he didn't get on with us to be honest, because he saw us as dyed in the wool London Buses people. He was very anti-LBL, he basically showed open contempt." Paul Lynch adds that, "Yes, Tom was dour and often awkward, and even hard and rude at times, but he was strong and experienced in the ways of the commercial world, and I regarded him at the time as someone I was happy to work for – I felt he was helpful to me as a young manager." Peter McMahon, the Engineering Director, did not get on with Tom and they disagreed on a question of engineering standards. Peter left to join London Underground, and was replaced by Peter Duff from Newcastle who brought a down-to-earth style to his responsibilities, which he liked to call 'Duff Engineering'!

The management team met at Down Hall in Hertfordshire to plan the company's strategy. The atmosphere was bullish – the feeling was that there was a tough job to be done; we were the people who had to do it; we had to start doing it now; it would be difficult but it was the only way for the company to survive. The staff would have to face changed conditions within the next few years, either with us, or with another company if we closed down. So the best we could do would be to implement change ourselves in a considerate fashion, giving as much continuity and compensation as we could. George Roberts was then General Manager at Walthamstow. He remembers the energy that went into the plan. "Everybody was 'up for it'. The general feeling was, 'It's time this got sorted out.' There was a sense of freedom, proper freedom, to do what needed doing."

The retendering of the Walthamstow routes in 1991 became the focus for change, but with tenders arising regularly at all the company's garages the new agreement was needed for the whole company. The plan was to offer all staff the choice of a new contract at market rates with a compensation payment; the traditional London Transport voluntary severance arrangement, which was attractive to long-service staff; or transfer to another garage in LBL where possible. This was comparable to what had happened at other LBL garages in response to tendering, but it was the first time an entire company was tackled. Duties would be scheduled up to the legal maximum where necessary, and there would also be redundancies among managers, supervisors, administrative staff and unskilled engineers. There would clearly be a major loss of platform staff, but there was significant unemployment at the time, which would reduce the numbers who left and also make recruitment of replacement staff relatively easy.

The calm before the storm. A midday scene in Walthamstow garage. (Roger Torode)

The feeling was that there was a tough job to be done; we were the people who had to do it; we had to start doing it now; it would be difficult but it was the only way for the company to survive.

At a late stage, LBL insisted on withdrawing the option of voluntary severance, because it would be too expensive and was not legally necessary following the Norbiton ruling. So a major attraction to long-service staff was removed, and an element of compulsion was introduced to the negotiation. LT's lawyers also tightened up the new contract with various additions that they had long wanted to include. This set the scene for the difficulties to come. Tom Young invited Sir John Harvey Jones's 'Troubleshooter' television programme to come and monitor the events. A researcher visited but they did not take it further.

Winning the London Forest tender
Our tender for the Walthamstow network was based on the restructuring of the company and the intended pay and conditions package. There was a series of bids for individual routes and combinations of them, with a final discount if the company was awarded all the routes. We felt it was a good bid, truly competitive with the other operators who would be bidding. Indeed six other operators bid for the Walthamstow services.

Malcolm Wren at TBD remembers his shock on opening the London Forest tender. "We wanted bids that would work, and we were prepared to pay more for it. This bid was below market rates and we questioned whether it was workable. If London Forest had tendered a bit higher they would still have retained most of the network, while other operators may have taken a few routes – instead, in the end they got all of it. The TBD didn't want bargain basement bus services despite what some people thought!"

Nick Newton met with Tom Young and said he did not believe that Tom could achieve the wage rates he proposed. Nick agreed with the TBD Board to approve a second-place bidder, and he then set Tom a deadline to deliver the staff agreement by a fixed date. Nick knew that Tom may not want the Unions to know about the deadline so he did not announce it publicly – but Tom immediately told the union. A public announcement was made that the London Forest network, based on Walthamstow Garage, was wholly retained by the operator following retendering and that contracts for three years were awarded to run from November 1991.

The London Forest strike
The new pay and conditions package, and compensation arrangements, were put to the Trade Unions, who reacted angrily. It was a radical change from the existing conditions of service, and the first time that an LBL company had tried to apply such changes to all their operations, rather than just the routes affected by tendering – though all the LBL companies did this shortly afterwards. The Trade Union saw this as the first domino in London Buses and strongly resisted, with support throughout London.

In a newsletter to staff, Tom Young wrote that, "Two or three years ago it was believed by many in LT that the newcomers to running buses in London would fail to provide a good level of service and that their costs would have to increase to around the level of ours. We all have to admit that this has not happened. They are now established, making money out of their contracts and generally well-regarded on quality of service by LT".

But it became increasingly difficult for us to communicate the need for change and the proposals to the staff themselves. A one day strike at Walthamstow on 4 July was followed by another on 10 July which spread to the other London Forest garages. The following day it was decided to hold an indefinite strike. Continued negotiations and an improved offer were rejected and the strike continued. The whole company was now on strike, and it became the longest running London bus strike since 1958.

After an awkward TV interview, and the difficult relationship between Tom Young and the Trade Unions becoming apparent, Clive Hodson, the company Chairman, instructed that I should take over the negotiations with the drivers' union and all media contact. Paul Lynch remembers the atmosphere well. "Part of the problem at London Forest was the personality clash between Tom Young and Ken Fuller, the full-time TU officer. Ken was a strong personality who could get on well with people, but he was also a very stubborn individual, just like Tom Young. This was an important point, because he met an immovable object in Tom. So it may not have been such a difficult dispute if these two had not hated each other so much. Neither would give in, and the same strike anywhere else would not have gone like that. There was a point at which it could have been solved but these two wouldn't. Ken could be very unpleasant, and Roger was caught in the middle of all this."

One Friday evening in July, with no buses running, I went to Walthamstow garage to be interviewed by Radio London from their radio car, with Ken Fuller representing the Union. While we were waiting for them to set up, Ken and I were talking on the forecourt. After a few minutes, the interviewer came over looking puzzled and said, 'I can't understand this. You two are on opposite sides of a major strike, but you are standing here chatting quite normally with each other.' Ken turned to him and said, 'It would be different if it was the Managing Director!'"

Paul Lynch remembers that the atmosphere was good at Leyton during the strike, even though the staff there were solid in supporting it. However, they

133 At a late stage, LBL insisted on withdrawing the option of voluntary severance, because it would be too expensive and was not legally necessary following the Norbiton ruling.

Rumours
LONDON BUSES
NEWS FOR EVERYONE AT LONDON FOREST TRAVEL

Special Issue 27

CHAMPION!

Today, 31 May, we have learned that London Forest has been awarded the contract by London Transport to continue to run all eleven of the Walthamstow Area tendered services. This is really welcome news for everyone who has anxiously awaited the result of the Walthamstow retenders which - at 90 buses, 300 jobs and a complete garage - have a major impact on the whole of the London Forest company.

WALTHAMSTOW TENDERS SPECIAL 31 MAY 1991

"EXCELLENT OUTCOME"

London Forest's Managing Director, Tom Young said "This is an excellent outcome to five months of hard work in putting our tenders together, a splendid performance on the road by everyone at Walthamstow in recent weeks and an anxious waiting period for the result - which took a month longer to come than we expected. We can be rightly proud that we are the first LBL Company to be re-awarded the full contract for such a major area network upon retendering".

Eleven Routes

The Walthamstow network comprises six big-bus routes, four existing midibus routes and one route - the 144 - which is to be converted to midibus operation and receive a fleet of new Dennis Darts. The routes cover 3,500,000 miles each year and are:-

Titan Operation

97	Leyton-Chingford
97A	Walthamstow-Chingford
123	Ilford-Wood Green
158	Chingford Mount-Stratford
212	Walthamstow-Chingford
215	Walthamstow-Chingford

Midibuses

W11	Walthamstow local
W12	Walthamstow-Wanstead
W15	Walthamstow-Hackney
W16	Leytonstone-Chingford
144	Chingford-Edmonton

Jobs Safeguarded

All of the Walthamstow drivers and engineers will continue to have jobs with the new tenders which are due to take over from the existing contract for the routes in mid-November this year. But MD Tom Young tempered the good news of the contract award - "It comes as no surprise that the bidding for these routes by non-LBL companies was fierce and we believe that our price is only slightly lower than our nearest competitors. We will now have to take stringent action to cut costs and concentrate our workload - and we shall have to act quickly to demonstrate to LT that the service and price they demand can be delivered by us. This process will affect all of London Forest".

Meetings Next Week

A Consultative Meeting with the Trade Unions representing London Forest employees will be held on Wednesday, 5 June, which will also see the start of negotiations on the restructuring of the Company to reflect the impact of competitive tendering.

Another "Rumours Special" will be published shortly, outlining the detailed changes being discussed with your representatives.

LONDON FOREST

"Rumours" is the Company Newspaper of London Forest Travel Limited, The Old Tramways Office, Chingford Road, Walthamstow, London E17 4PN.

The London Forest staff bulletin on 31 May announced the Walthamstow results but also the need for negotiations over the restructuring of the company.

On 15 July a march to the London Forest offices at Walthamstow garage and picket of the site took place by busmen and their families. Pickets had collecting buckets at London Forest garages but elsewhere in LBL collections were also made in support. At London United, the T&GWU representative decided to make a 'compulsory collection' of £5 for every member. It was reported that £960 was raised at Shepherd's Bush garage on 19 July. Walthamstow drivers erected a 'For Sale' sign outside the garage and issued a leaflet to passengers entitled 'Why your bus is not running' to explain their position. (Roger Torode)

never stopped being chatty. "On both sides, the drivers and the supervisors were doing what they were bloody well told, maintaining the line."

Attempts were made to resolve the strike. We moved to limit the changes to Walthamstow but the Union refused to back off from the full strike saying, "We started this together and we'll finish it together!" A group of drivers asked to meet George Roberts, then GGM at Walthamstow, and they met for coffee at the nearby William Morris Gallery. George recalls, "They said, 'We can't go on like this.' They wanted to get back to work, and asked for phone numbers of drivers so they could phone them and get them to come in. The people on the picket line were the hard-core union members – most of the drivers were at home. But LT's HR department refused to give over the phone numbers!"

Just as the trade union realised that if London Forest succeeded all the other companies would follow suit, so did the LBL Board know that if LFT succeeded then everyone else would follow on. To Paul Lynch, it was clear that the LBL Board was saying, "You go for it and we will be right behind you! Then, when the strike went wrong, they disappeared, about two weeks in. This still sticks in my mind, over twenty years later. This was my first experience of a major strike and we were bound up in it – you believe in it. We had put a lot of effort into what we were trying to achieve, and when LBL pulled the rug from under us I felt betrayed. Maybe that's a bit strong, but I felt very let down. You do it to the full at a time like that. It is very important."

Special services during the strike
The TBD was worried by the effect of a continuous strike throughout the London Forest area. After the 1958 bus strike, which was London-wide, many of the passengers never came back. They did not want that to happen in Walthamstow, so some special services were arranged, particularly where there was no alternative bus or parallel rail service. Three special services began on the morning of Friday 12 July with a fourth later in the day. County Bus ran a 10 minute service between Walthamstow and Chingford on route 505, which normally ran hourly from Walthamstow to Waltham Abbey. When asked, County Bus drivers had said, "When we had problems, London Bus drivers wouldn't support us." But they would not take on a London bus route, so it was run as the 505 and, instead of one minibus per hour, they ran one big bus every 10 minutes replacing route 97. Essex County Council were told that their minibus service was being greatly augmented!

Kentish Bus ran on route 56 to provide a service along the Lea Bridge Road which otherwise had no service during the strike. Spare Atlanteans were found from Dunton Green for the duration and provided a shuttle service between Whipps Cross and Clapton Pond. Norman Kemp explains, "Kentish Bus was a little organisation trying to keep on the right side of a big organisation. You had to say yes because you wanted more work from them. There were not many examples of strikebreaking. The Trade Union was not happy, but we had plenty of volunteers, and we needed from time to time to remind them who ran the company! But above all, we were providing a service for passengers."

Thamesway worked extra buses on route 251 between Walthamstow and Gants Hill to cover the 123 between 12 and 18 July. In the following week, TBD arranged another service on the 123 between Tottenham High Road and Gants Hill, every 20 minutes operated by London Buslines and Grey-Green.

Nick Newton was determined that the D1 (Docklands Express) would continue running. Ensign Citybus was willing to help, and was not bothered about the implications. Then Tom Young was mischievous, and suggested that they should use LFT's branded vehicles from Ash Grove garage. Nick Newton rang Leon Daniels at Citybus to ask him his view of this, but Leon said that he was not willing to cross Ash Grove picket lines and he ran the D1 with his own vehicles.

London Forest's private hire operations at Leyton continued unaffected by the strike, driven by inspectors or managers. Paul Lynch, the Leyton GGM, drove an excursion to Chessington World of Adventures and one of his striking drivers was on the trip with his

County Bus ran an enhanced service on their 505 between Chingford and Walthamstow, and their Leyland Lynx is at Walthamstow Central with a handwritten destination board. (Owen Woodliffe)

136 Just as the trade union realised that if London Forest succeeded all the other companies would follow suit, so did the LBL Board know that if LFT succeeded then everyone else would follow on.

family – and gave Paul a tip at the end! The DHSS contract in central London also continued to operate from Clapton, and the Essex County Council services 211/213 continued to run from Walthamstow. Some buses ran on route 212 from 15th July, driven by the handful of drivers who did not take part in the strike, but the service was infrequent and few passengers were aware of them.

Above Kentish Bus provided buses on the 56 between Clapton and Whipps Cross along the Lea Bridge Road, which would not otherwise have had a service. (Roger Torode)

Right A London Buslines Olympian at Tottenham Hale. (Andrew Mead)

Below Grey-Green and London Buslines provided buses for the 123 between Tottenham and Gants Hill. A Grey-Green double-deck coach pauses at Gants Hill. (Roger Torode)

137 Paul Lynch, the Leyton GGM, drove an excursion to Chessington World of Adventures and one of his striking drivers was on the trip with his family – and gave Paul a tip at the end!

End of strike and closure

The TBD contracts for the Walthamstow network had been awarded on condition that sufficient of the staff accepted the pay and conditions package by the deadline which Nick Newton had set Tom Young. By that date, only a quarter of the drivers had accepted and the London Forest drivers were on indefinite strike. Tom rang Nick asking for an extension for 24 hours, but Nick heard nothing more from him.

As the TBD could not now be confident that London Forest could take up the contracts reliably, they re-awarded them to the other companies who had been kept in reserve. On 24 July, they announced that all 11 Walthamstow routes would be awarded to other operators: County Bus taking routes 144, W15 and W16; Thamesway gaining minibus routes W11 and W12; and Citybus taking over 50 buses-worth of big bus work on routes 97, 97A, 123, 158, 212 and 215. Walthamstow garage was thus to lose all its work, but some needed to be handed over earlier as staff left. The trade union called off the strike and London Forest services resumed on Monday 29 July.

Ken Fuller maintained that he had won the strike, because he had in effect decided who would (or more particularly who would not) win the contracts for the routes. He had arranged for all the Walthamstow staff to be interviewed by Ensign Citybus for continued employment on the local routes, and the union would retain negotiating rights with Ensign which had, until then, been a non-union company. Ken said, "This is a victory. Ensign will pay more than London Forest was offering and the union will have full negotiating rights. London Forest has agreed a formula for dealing with future tenders involving prior discussion with the aim of safeguarding wages and hours. This too is a victory." But Leon Daniels only agreed TU recognition for Northumberland Park, which took over the Walthamstow routes, and the drivers who came to him were so angry with the T&GWU that they ripped up their membership cards.

Tom Young commented at the time that, "The Union seem to think the loss of 300 jobs is some kind of victory. I would be surprised if more than 100 get jobs with the winning contractors. We still have 250 buses and three garages. There is no reason why the company should not have a future either in the current or a deregulated situation."

The handover of routes was gradual. The first phase was to take over the 97A and 215, a further mischievous move by Tom. In the aftermath of the strike, he deliberately chose two routes that passed Walthamstow garage to hand over first, so that the Ensign Citybuses passing the garage would bring home to the staff what was happening.

However, on 20th August Tom Young left London Buses. His replacement as Acting Managing Director was Graham Elliott, formerly London Buses Network Services Manager. Graham remembers, "I was approached very close to the time, probably the previous day, and asked if I would go out to run London Forest because the MD was leaving the next day, though he didn't know it yet!"

Those of us remaining in the management team put a forward plan together, but LBL announced that London Forest was no longer viable and would be closed. It ceased operating on 23 November when Ash Grove and Walthamstow garages were closed. Leyton garage was taken into East London and Clapton into Leaside. Graham Elliot presided over the closure, while Paul Lynch and a team interviewed staff throughout the company and sought new positions for them. Some drivers transferred to other LBL garages, some took severance and went to Ensign Citybus, County and other operators.

There were many opportunities for the engineers, managers and administrative staff who were generally successful in getting new positions. It was the Inspectors and Driving Instructors who came off badly, with declining opportunities throughout London. Many went back to driving for one of the other companies. Paul Lynch and Peter Duff moved to East London. Graham Elliot returned to LBL headquarters, and I was asked to look at a new technology

The forest is felled. Peter Duff points out a modification made to the tree symbol on some buses, once closure of the company was announced. (Roger Torode)

The 97A and 215 were the first routes to pass to Capital Citybus on 14 September. Their 97A is seen with a London Forest 97 at Chingford Station on 24 September. (John Parkin)

Thamesway took over the W11 from 23 November (David Cole)

using contactless smartcards to see if they might be useful in bus ticketing!

A year or so later, Mike Weston at the TBD looked back at the London Forest proposals and saw that they were broadly similar to what the other LBL companies were by then paying.

Review of London Forest

Unfortunately, in the creation of the companies, London Forest drew not one, but several short straws. It was a particularly small company, and had a far smaller operation over which to spread its overheads. It already had a high proportion of tendered work, and more routes already planned for tender because of unreliability caused by traffic difficulties in Hackney and the East End, and historic difficulties at Ash Grove garage. As a result, major parts of its operation were being tendered each year on three-year contracts. Other companies had little or no tendered work right up to privatisation, and sufficient 'block grant' work to withstand far greater knocks. And there were several credible, low cost

139 A year or so later, Mike Weston at the TBD looked back at the London Forest proposals and saw that they were broadly similar to what the other LBL companies were by then paying.

competitors on London Forest's doorstep, four of whom bid for the Walthamstow routes, together with two neighbouring LBL subsidiaries.

Other contributors to this book have said that, in Tom Young's view, there was always going to be a casualty amongst the LBL companies and it just happened to be him. Paul Lynch felt betrayed by LBL, "A strong word but that's how it felt at the time. London Forest was not like any of the other companies – it was much smaller. If exactly the same experience had happened to any of the other companies, they would have lost a depot but the rest of the company would have carried on. We knew that in London Forest, if we failed, we would lose the company and it could happen at any time. So we were pushed into an impossible situation."

Leon Daniels sees London Forest as an astonishing example of how the trade union, supposedly supporting public ownership, in fact acted to transfer work from the public sector to the private sector, and then claim it as a victory. He compares London Forest's brief history with others who later failed on basic engineering standards – there was no performance failure in London Forest, this was industrial relations. George Roberts remembers the energy trying to make the company work. "Most the drivers who went on strike ended up working on the same routes with worse conditions."

London Forest sent shock waves through London Buses. Tom Young's fellow MDs had mixed feelings, some suggesting that he had had 'a bad steer' from those above him, others that he was doing what everybody did later – he just did it too soon. A typical comment is that "Many of these things did change elsewhere just a year later."

All of the LBL companies had industrial disputes, lost tenders and garage closures, but they had the size to accommodate them and survive. All the LBL companies tackled wages and conditions, but London Forest became the first full-scale battleground with both sides determined to prove themselves. There was no desire to unnecessarily worsen the rewards of the staff, but there was a need to improve cost effectiveness and performance, and to compete effectively with other operators or else lose the work to them, in which case their pay and conditions would prevail. The combination of a Managing Director determined to be first to make his mark, and a strong TU officer on the lookout and probably incensed that anyone should try this with him, neither of them willing to give in and not much respect between them, produced an impossible situation.

Clive Hodson comments, "I suppose others benefited from this. Leaside and East London were gaining work and even Metroline got a route! We got the MDs together and said, 'Look, come on, what's the best way of dividing this up. None of that was public." Graham Elliott went in with Roger Bowker and Steve Clayton to sort it all out with the Trade Unions. Steve recalls, "As on other occasions, the people in London Buses Head Office just wanted the problem to go away. There was huge reorganisation to effect the changes and some long nights and tough negotiations. We had to shift large numbers of Titans from Ash Grove to Stamford Hill, and as always in the bus business, we just got on with it and did it. When there is a crisis we just get on with it and deal with it."

Moving to East London
With the closure of London Forest, Paul Lynch was offered a job by Barry Arnold at East London. "I remember thinking, 'I'm not going to East London. You must be joking, that's the last thing I'm going to do.' Fortunately, Barry did ask again."

Paul's view was that London Forest was lean, mean and quick on its feet, whilst East London was large, fat, expensive and corporate. He compared the East London coaching unit with his operation at Leyton. After a time in East London, he perhaps took a different view – was London Forest efficient and lean, or cheapskate and not doing it right? Was East London bureaucratic, or was it professional, measured and doing things properly? The truth was probably somewhere in between.

When Paul joined East London, changes were taking place which would reduce the number of garage managers, while he was being brought in from outside – an awkward situation. "But once Leyton garage was in East London, it became apparent that we were in fact doing better on all the performance measures than the other East London garages – it was East London's best depot! So fairly soon people were asking, 'Why is Leyton better?' and Leyton became the garage that people in East London were coming to and asking, 'How do you do this, and how do you do that?'"

By early 1992, East London reached a pay agreement for Leyton staff taken over from London Forest. The package was designed to ensure that routes 48 and 56, due for retender in 1993, would be retained. Staff had the choice of transferring to another East London garage, or accepting the new deal with a £500 lump sum payment.

East London
East London were working to reduce costs into the early 1990s, and they got the company into shape. They closed Seven Kings and (the original) West Ham – a very expensive garage which cost a fortune just to light – and opened the low-cost base at Stratford, Waterden Road, with minibuses. They also converted

the 8 and the 15 to OPO. So they got into good financial shape ready for privatisation.

Roger Bowker had pushed for the closure of the London Forest Central Stores, which he considered to be an unnecessary overhead. There was a deep depression in the early 1990s. If manufacturers wanted to supply a big company like East London, they should be prepared to supply direct to the garages and he would have a small buying department at Head Office. Everybody told him that it couldn't be done, but he pushed them away and the closure of London Forest gave him the opportunity. His purchasing manager did very well working directly with the suppliers. He knew you could save a lot of money by not double-handling all this stock, and he was proved right.

Capital Citybus
Whilst Leaside and East London gained garages from London Forest, Metroline and London Central gained additional work. But the big winner from the London Forest closure was Capital Citybus.

Capital Citybus grew out of the Ensign contracted bus operations. Peter Newman explains. "We thought the writing was on the wall for tendered operations. At first, it was an open market, no one knew the right price nor how it would work – prices were based on a finger in the air. And the resulting rates were very good. They were a lot cheaper than London Transport costs, so everybody was happy. But when the tenders were coming up for renewal, there was more competition, the rates were going down and tender prices were a lot less. We asked ourselves, 'Do we want to be there any more?' We therefore decided to sell the bus operations."

Peter had contacts with China Motor Bus in Hong Kong, and with Citybus Hong Kong, through his sales of DMSs. In 1990, the Ensign contracted bus operations were sold to CNT of Hong Kong, the parent company of Citybus. Ensign Citybus was the new name under the Chinese and they had the rights to the Ensign name and blue/silver livery for an agreed period. During that period, the Walthamstow work was won and operated under the name Capital Citybus, using yellow and red liveried vehicles and an 'O' Licence in the name of Walthamstow Citybus Ltd. In due course, the rights to the Ensign name expired, all operations were under the name Capital Citybus and the vehicles were progressively repainted. Ensignbus was no longer involved in London bus operations and they then stayed out of it and were not going to go back in. They are still involved with tendering for London Underground emergency and rail replacement services – TfL wants them to be involved, and they are the fifth emergency service!

Leon Daniels went with the Ensign Citybus operation and oversaw the expansion and transition into Capital Citybus. The Walthamstow events came in the very early days of ownership by Hong Kong. They had never lost any work before, but they had just lost route 145. In a Chinese sense this was a loss of face and he was under pressure. At the time, LT had built up a logjam of route tenders coming up for decision. He was bidding away normally for the London Forest routes and others such as the 153. Nick Newton rang him and said that they were going to give the whole Walthamstow network to London Forest. However, they believed that the London Forest bid was on the basis of terms and conditions for the entire operation that had not yet been agreed with the staff. He said there could easily be some developments and his best advice would be to not complain very loudly that this was unfair. There were hurdles left for London Forest to jump!

On the day that the London Forest dispute became indefinite, Leon was out with Mike Weston and Malcolm Wren testing a three axle Hong Kong double-decker on the 29, checking the turning points at Wood Green. Suddenly Mike and Malcolm had to go back to their office to deal with the London Forest situation. There was a particular problem with the D1 which was financially supported by the LDDC. They needed to keep it going because, if it did not run, it would not take long for the LDDC to realise that there was little passenger impact – in other words it was not achieving any significant benefit, and so they might remove their funding. LT did not want to lose the route, so they needed Capital Citybus to take it over quickly and keep a service running. The next

Capital Citybus ran the D1 during the London Forest strike, and used its own vehicles rather than the specially-liveried buses at Ash Grove. Dennis Dominator 273 is seen at Marsh Wall. (Mike Harris)

"They had never lost any work before, but they had just lost route 145. In a Chinese sense this was a loss of face and he was under pressure."

problem was to swing this with the T&GWU. So Leon took Ken Fuller for a pint, told him of the risk to the D1 and the possible risk of some of the bus drivers losing their jobs. Ken Fuller acknowledged the point and said that this would require a donation to the Union's distress fund!

Once the TBD Board decided to re-award the Walthamstow routes, Nick Newton rang Leon and said that, as it appeared that London Forest were incapable of operating the routes, he was re-awarding them to Capital Citybus! Leon remembers that, "This was the only time in my life that I needed a stiff drink! At the time, our tenders were worth £3-£4 million a year to run. This contract doubled it overnight!" He had to buy property, lease vehicles, recruit staff and set up an entire operation.

Nick Newton then rang again and said, "The private sector has acquitted itself well, and we only need one more favour from you." He was concerned that London Forest staff would start leaving very rapidly, and he therefore wanted Leon to take over the routes early. However, Leon had a tremendous job in setting up the new operation and the starting date was very important to him: they eventually agreed that he would take the routes over in phases. As he did not yet have a depot arranged, the routes were initially run from Dagenham where he took on additional land next to the existing depot, with a hole in the fence in between. So he set up a 'virtual Northumberland Park' at Dagenham.

Recognising the trade union was the price that Leon would have to pay for getting this new work. So Leon agreed to recognise the trade union at Northumberland Park only, not at Dagenham. He reasoned that the large number of drivers joining him from London Forest were already members of the Union, though they were coming from a bad industrial relations situation there. "It turned out that they felt they had been sold down the river by the Union. They wanted to work at Walthamstow and here they were now at Northumberland Park, with tougher working conditions and vastly inferior facilities. When they saw Ken Fuller, some of them told him, 'How can you believe in a publicly owned bus service when your own actions lead to us being taken over by this lot.' They were so disgusted that they were collecting their cards, ripping them up and setting fire to them. Ken Fuller left saying, 'We don't feel that the depot is an appropriate location for recruitment.'"

Finance from Hong Kong

In order to finance the new operation Leon needed £2m of funding from Hong Kong. The fleet of vehicles was to be financed from within the UK and they did this with a mix of new Olympians from Leyland and second hand Metrobuses from South Yorkshire. He was able to do a favour for his old friend Ian Murray, who was Managing Director of Northern Counties, which was in administration, and they had a stock of Olympians that they could not sell. Leon could have as many Olympians as he needed from the Leyland/Volvo factory at Workington, but he insisted that the Northern Counties buses be included, and he managed to get them all financed through Volvo Credit.

Leon had to go to Hong Kong to get the money to buy the Northumberland Park site. Board meetings in Hong Kong were of around 50 people who would be

YOUR NEW TIMETABLE

97A CHINGFORD STATION - WALTHAMSTOW CENTRAL STATION

Blue and silver buses for Route 97A

London Transport Service

Operated by Ensign Citybus

From Saturday 14th September 1991

"They were so disgusted that they were collecting their union cards, ripping them up and setting fire to them."

speaking in Cantonese. "They would be talking very quickly, and every now and then they would look in my direction and the name Leon would be mentioned, and I would try to assess whether the inflection in their voices was favourable or not. The Chairman was TT Tsui, who had the biggest collection of Chinese antiques known to man. I produced a video to show them the bus depot that I wanted to buy, with vehicles moving around. I needed the £2 million to be sorted quickly or we would have nowhere to run the new operation from – it needed sorting out. There was much discussion about whether the money should simply be invested in Hong Kong where the rates are better."

Leon continues, "At this point there was a crash and the swing doors of the room opened. A little Chinese lad came in with a carrier bag with the neck of a vase sticking out and brought it up to the Chairman, who pulled out this old Chinese vase. He was over the moon, he was jubilant! He stood up and shouted 'We must have a celebration lunch', but Leon called out 'Oi, one moment, we must decide about this property. What about the property?' 'Ah yes,' said the Chairman, 'everything is ok, that is all agreed!' So it is important to note that the whole cornerstone of the new Capital Citybus operation hinged on the acquisition of some old Chinese vase." And Leon flew back

Life imitating art! Walthamstow Citybus was planned to have yellow buses from the start, but the LT Publicity Department produced leaflets announcing that blue and silver buses would be taking over on routes 97A and 215. As a result, the yellow buses were put on route 252, and blue and silver buses were transferred to the 97A and 215. (John Parkin)

Capital Citybus received 29 new Leyland Olympians, together with second-hand purchases, for the Walthamstow routes. The new yellow livery included bilingual fleetnames and some had the registration number 888, a lucky number in China, on which the following three letters represented the initials of one of the company's directors. 135, with Northern Counties body, worked on the 252 before moving to Walthamstow. (John Parkin)

143 "The whole cornerstone of the new Capital Citybus operation hinged on the acquisition of some old Chinese vase."

to London the next day. The premises are now owned by Go-Ahead.

Walthamstow put Capital Citybus on the map. Until then any single contract loss was a catastrophe for them, but now they had 12 or 13 contracts so that gave them some stability – they could bear the loss of one or two without it being catastrophic. However, the Walthamstow routes were 2+1 year contracts, so they came up for renewal fairly quickly, and Capital Citybus did lose some tendered work in the autumn when route 62 returned to East London buses.

Tendering policy
Speaking in September 1991 to the London Omnibus Traction Society (LOTS), Nick Newton described a number of aspects of tendering. The choice of routes to put out to tender was made by LT's Group Planning department, following assessment of individual operating costs supplied by LBL. Until recently, the TBD had had a policy that if a contractor had been performing successfully, negotiations could be made to extend the original tender for a further two or three-year period. However this would only be done

Above Walthamstow schoolkids quickly discovered that the seat cushions on these former Portsmouth Dennis double deckers fitted through the upper deck sliding windows. A driver on the 158 was stopped by a following motorist to be told that most of his upper deck seat cushions were spread out along the road. An adjustment was quickly made to reduce the window opening. (Roger Torode)

Winning the Walthamstow routes provided the Great Leap Forward for Chinese-owned Capital Citybus, and Chingford changed from red to yellow. A convoy of buses on the 215, 97 and 158 set off from Chingford Mount in February 1995. The picture is taken from the same spot as the picture on page 9, 20 years later. (Roger Torode)

144 Until then any single contract loss was a catastrophe, but now they had 12 or 13 contracts so that gave them some stability.

once. The route would then be fully re-tendered. A recent example of this was the 146. Crystals had performed well during their period of operation and he was sad that they should lose the work. But on re-tendering, Metrobus had put in the better bid. However, this policy had been changed and, provided performance was up to the standard of 97% of operated mileage, tenders could be extended indefinitely. This reflected the investment in new vehicles which many operators were making, and provided a degree of stability for them and their staff. The bad side, for competitors, was that once a route was lost it was likely to remain lost.

On the question of whether all tendered buses should have a standard livery, Nick stated that, whilst there had been enthusiasm for this within his department, it had cooled when deregulation was looking more of a certainty. He also mentioned that the requirement for vehicles used on tendered services to be less than seven years old had ended, as it had placed some restriction on tenderers. This had not been publicly announced but was apparent from some of the recent tender awards.

Nick Newton stressed that, as has been said before, tenders were not necessarily awarded to the cheapest bidder. A number of factors were taken into consideration, including price, past performance, likely future performance, and type of vehicle proposed. The tenderer chosen was the one deemed likely to provide the best value for money. This could be a little subjective, of course, and occasionally errors were made, in which case steps were always taken to put matters right as soon as possible should things appear to be going wrong – Boro'line Maidstone was an example of this. In the company's early days on LT work, TBD identified ineffective management at the Crayford depot as the reason behind poor performance. Pressure was placed on the company to correct this, which was done and service quality was then acceptable. Some other operators were considered to be poor performers and he said that steps were being taken to put these right. Clearly BTS and Metrobus were seen to be working well as he noted that – if all operators were as good as them – many of his monitoring staff could be out of a job! Asked whether London Buses companies had an advantage over other operators in tendering, or vice versa, Nick pointed out that opinions varied depending on which side people were on. "All you can hope for is that, if both sides are complaining, you've an equality of imbalance."

In late 1991, the Lambeth Public Transport Group issued a highly critical report on the performance of routes 77 and 77A since tendering, claiming that the service had become a shambles and that the withdrawal of on-street inspectors, and wage cuts imposed on driving staff causing low morale, were the causes of the problems. Nick Newton admitted that there were problems with the services and placed the blame on the lack of roadside control. He said that, since tendering, bus volumes had been good but reliability might still be a problem. He noted that the routes were not very reliable before, which was why they had been part of a network area study leading to tendering. He said that the latest figures showed a remarkable improvement.

London United
London United's move to minibuses, and minibus staff conditions, was helped by the closure of Hammersmith Bridge which prevented route 9 buses from crossing it. The 105-year old bridge had had a ban since 1984 on all vehicles weighing more than 3 tonnes except for buses and emergency vehicles.

David Humphrey writes, "The Borough Engineer of Hammersmith and Fulham Council was also the 'bridgemaster' of Hammersmith Bridge, a splendid suspension bridge across the Thames, a west London landmark with iconic status. During the winter of 1991/2, he approached London United with the news that the bridge had developed some serious structural defects. The longitudinal stays holding the suspended slabs together were showing signs of deterioration. Should one of them fail in tension, the bridge would, in his words, 'unzip' into the Thames.

"The bridge was shut whilst everyone pondered what to do about it. It was subsequently decided to carry out some remedial work, and then re-open the bridge but with a strict weight limit. Double-deck buses were well in excess of this limit, which was a pity because several very busy double deck routes operated across it. The bridge is a natural "funnel" for travel from a wide area south of the river to Hammersmith Broadway, just north of the bridge. However, after some hand-wringing, it was decided that Dennis Dart midi-buses, one at a time, could be allowed across the bridge.

"A major conversion scheme was launched and on 18 July 1992, the crew operated Routemaster service 9 from Mortlake to Liverpool Street or Aldgate was truncated at Hammersmith, and its western end converted to high-frequency midibus operation, route 9A. Similarly, routes 33, Fulwell to Hammersmith, every 15 minutes at the Hammersmith end, was doubled in frequency, as was route 72, Roehampton – East Acton, from every 20 to every ten minutes. The 283, from Hammersmith to East Acton, was extended across the bridge to Barnes, running every ten minutes, and the R69 became a half-hourly service, though still mostly off-peak.

"The pressure on capacity was considerable, and

"Hammersmith bridge had developed serious structural defects. Should one of the stays fail in tension, the bridge would 'unzip' into the Thames."

London United continued to build up its midibus operations. The R70 was extended at the Richmond end from November 1990, and a Carlyle-bodied Dart is seen in Twickenham in March 1991. (David Cole)

several 'tweaks' had to be implemented to try to get the right number of buses in the right places for the peaks of the peak periods. At one point, service 9A had the highest frequency of all bus routes in London, 28 buses per hour providing a midibus every two minutes – it was more frequent even than the 38! London United could therefore look forward to deregulation with a combined frequency of just under 50 buses per hour running up Castelnau and across the bridge. We needed to provide good frequency to defend the patch against intrusion, and this was pretty good market coverage! We set up an outstation at Wood Lane with 40 buses for these services."

South London

South London had considerable pressure on tender prices, being hit by Selkent and Kentish Bus on one side, in addition to London & Country, who took over the 196 from Cityrama and ran it from Chelsham whilst also opening a new garage in Beddington in 1990 specifically to compete in Croydon – Roger Freeman, the Transport Minister, opened the depot. In 1991/2, after the loss of the 166, 194 and 198 to Selkent, Streatham garage was closed and its remaining services allocated to other garages.

Peter Batty, the Traffic Manager, became South London's Commercial Development Manager, preparing the company for deregulation. One of the biggest tendered networks was Croydon, where the 50, 60, 250, 264, 312 and 412 were all tendered together – a large bundle of routes. "We had kept these routes in 1988 but were struggling to give the mileage. We needed to achieve 99%, and we made a huge effort to achieve this. Then it was retendered in 1992 for a 1993 start."

In 1990 the 612 service was introduced between Battersea and Brighton, running every Saturday through Croydon and Crawley. This was a shopping service connecting the main shopping centres along the route. The company adopted the "Connexions" identity for a number of its midibus services.

In 1994 South London introduced an attractive red and cream livery for the Routemasters on route 159, together with a route diagram on the side panels. Buses in new and standard colour schemes pass Hamley's in Regent Street. (Colin Fradd)

146 At one point, service 9A had the highest frequency of all bus routes in London, 28 buses per hour providing a midibus every two minutes.

Docklands Transit

In late 1992 Docklands Transit successfully bid for three LT routes, the 287, 366 and 368, which they started operating in March 1993. Frank Cheroomi had to recruit drivers, mechanics and administration staff at Barking job centre. A lot of East London drivers had been made redundant at Barking and he took 90% of his drivers from them. He was just in time to stop a major mistake when Harry Blundred ordered 22 Iveco buses with manual gearboxes, which most London bus drivers would not have been able to drive, and so these were sent to Oxford and he received older Mercedes automatics with 29 seats. These were generally ok but they had problems with the gearboxes, all of which were changed from Mercedes to Allison. Frank had been able to lease a site in Silvertown from Tate & Lyle sugar, only one minute down the road from Harry Blundred's original base in Thames Road. On the first day there were worries about whether the drivers would turn up, but they all did.

Leaside

After the 1992 election Leaside were preparing for privatisation and developing their management buyout plan. Ted Milburn, the Engineering Director, and Mark Yexley, the Operations Director, were reducing the numbers of garage staff. Ted took a lot of people out leaving those left behind to work smarter and harder. Mark took out garage staff, the Inspector numbers dropped significantly, and a lot of non-essential jobs were removed. They also changed the cash counting to drop safes and did away with the

---

SOUTH LONDON

BIGGIN HILL INTERNATIONAL AIR FAIR

Special Bus Service
From West & East Croydon
Saturday 19 June & Sunday 20 June 1993

From West Croydon Bus Station	From East Croydon Station
0830 0900 0930	0835 0905 0935
1000 1030 1100	1005 1035 1105
1130 1200 1230	1135 1205 1235

BUSES RUN NON-STOP FROM EAST CROYDON

Buses return from Biggin Hill
at 1530 1600 1630 1700
1730 1800 1830 1900

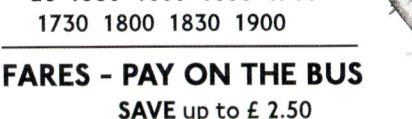

FARES - PAY ON THE BUS
SAVE up to £ 2.50
with Special Discounted Biggin Hill Admission Tickets available from the driver.

Adult
Return £3.00   Single £2.00
Return (inc. discounted admission) £9.50
Single (inc. discounted admission) £8.50

Child
Return £1.50   Single £1.00
Single (inc. discounted admission) £3.50
Return (inc. discounted admission) £4.00

For further information,
please call

South London Transport
on 081 688 3221.

In early 1990 route 29 was converted to one-person-operation running from Victoria to Enfield, worked by Leaside from Wood Green and Palmers Green garages, together with London Northern from Chalk Farm. Leaside worked hard at the route but felt that Chalk Farm were being difficult, "especially finding their way to the foreign country called Enfield Town!" In 1991 the route was terminated at Trafalgar Square and then tendered to run from there to Palmers Green, as part of a number of changes around Wood Green. Leaside won the contract, commencing in February 1992. The Leaside Metrobus here is clearly going to be first away from the traffic lights at Manor House, with London Northern behind as all three buses turn right towards Finsbury Park, in the days when the 29 still ran to Victoria. (Colin Fradd)

147 Chalk Farm drivers seemed to have difficulty finding their way up the 29 road to Enfield!

night garage staff, with one central cash counting operation at Enfield and their own security van to carry cash from each of the garages. Robert Newson, the Finance Director, was not taking costs out before privatisation but he had economies ready to make after privatisation. Some of the companies were saving money by deferring payment to suppliers, but he took the view that he may need their goodwill after privatisation.

Steve Clayton was clear that he did not want to make radical changes to the company for privatisation. He didn't want to be paying people off just for the sake of it, and he didn't want to worsen the staff conditions following the 1991 reduction in drivers' pay and conditions. He did make 50 or 60 people redundant at the higher end of the pay scale. He felt the operation was pretty much right. "Our operating area was not suited to minibuses, we had double-decker buses that were very full. We did have staff on different conditions but in general I didn't want to change the pay and conditions again; they and we had been through enough in 1991. It was my call and I wasn't going to do it!" Leaside grew through work from elsewhere, including Clapton garage and the 38 when London Forest closed. They then had two Routemaster services, the 38 and 73, which were not picked for tendering at this stage.

In 1993, Leaside moved its head office from Manor House to Wood Green. The Manor House office was a big inefficient office building, with vast rooms and much bigger than they needed, and they gained approval to build a new Head Office at the back of Wood Green garage. It was system built, a modular building, so went up very quickly in 1993 – and then they handed back Manor House, which became a block of flats.

Leaside built up a successful coaching and private hire business. In May 1993, they provided their open-top DMS to parade the Arsenal football team following the FA Cup final played against Sheffield Wednesday the previous day. The game had been a draw, but Arsenal won the replay on May 20th. DMS2291 had been driven under a low bridge when working as a driver trainer and was converted to open top. It was also used for the Lea Valley Leisure service 333 each summer. The second bus carries the Arsenal ladies team who had also won the Ladies' FA Cup that year. (Arriva London)

148 "Our operating area was not suited to minibuses, we had double-decker buses that were very full."

New and changed operators

Westlink suffered the loss of 80% of the work of its Hounslow base with the 1992 announcement of the tender awards for routes 116, 117 and 203. This left them with only the 110, H20 and a number of Surrey County Council contracts. Two new companies, Javelin Coaches and F E Thorpe, secured tender contracts during the year.

Grey-Green's route 24 was declared in the House of Lords to be 'the best run bus service in London'. Michael Foot, the veteran MP and former Leader of the Labour Party, was a regular passenger from his home in Hampstead to the House of Commons. Grey-Green now had 13 routes using 128 buses, running five million miles and carrying around 12 million passengers each year.

1993 was a difficult year for the LBL companies, who lost around 15 routes to private operators and only regained one, though other existing routes were retained.

Kentish Bus and Route 19

In 1993 the Routemaster fleet was being refurbished, and so it was decided for the first time to tender a crew-operated route, and the 19 (Finsbury Park to Battersea) was chosen. Route 13 was also tendered later in the year.

Tony Kennan was sitting in the window of Pizza Express in Shaftesbury Avenue watching the buses go by with a Director colleague, John Fickling. Thinking about the tender for route 19, Tony suggested that it couldn't be any different from the 22s and 55, so they finished their pizzas and decided to bid for it!

Tony was keen that the conductors should be called Customer Assistants, and be trained in customer care before anything else. Their way of running the service should be to make sure that people are comfortable on the bus, knowing what is happening. He was also keen that drivers should do a duty on the back from time to time, so that they knew what it was like there.

Norman Kemp knew they had to do a better job on the 19 than the previous operator, which was, he says, not a hard act to follow! When studying the route as part of the tender bid preparations he had spent many an hour waiting at Finsbury Park for 19s that had been curtailed under the old operation. Grey-

A new operator in 1993 was London Suburban Buses, a subsidiary of Gemsam Holdings, which ran around 50 vehicles in the Liverpool area. They took over routes 4 and 271 from MTL London Northern in September 1993, using new Volvo Olympians and former London Leyland Titans, but their performance soon deteriorated. They were taken over by MTL in April 1995, who were themselves bought out by Metroline in 1998. London Suburban Titan 1508 has an exposed radiator and no front number plate at Aldwych in October 1993. (Kevin Cooper)

149 Grey-Green's route 24 was declared in the House of Lords to be 'the best run bus service in London'.

Green had won route 24 in 1988, running through the heart of London, and it was seen as the flagship for tendered operations. Route 19 served areas in the West End, Knightsbridge and Chelsea which had never before been served by non-red buses under the tender regime. Kentish Bus had received awards from the Passengers Committee for their performance on other tendered routes and had a reputation to maintain. They were also aware that operating on the streets of central London helped the profile of Proudmutual for when the time came to sell the group; their advisers had said that, "the exit is more important than the purchase." They had buses going through the City with fleetnames on the roof, and they wanted a strong West End presence too.

Kentish Bus won the contract and took over the 19 on 24 April 1993. The emphasis on customer care worked well and they won an *Evening Standard* award. Tony Kennan was aware of the different social areas that the route went through, and wanted a service which pleased people in Sloane Square, and Chelsea, and Finsbury Park. "If we can please all those people," he said, " then we're onto a winner!" They added "Welcome Aboard" on the platform of the Routemasters, had "Team 19" for the crews, and handed out passenger wallets for passes. Their performance was far better than London General. They did not take on existing conductors because they were looking for a fresh start with people with sales experience rather than bus experience.

The tender bid was based on operation from the south end of the route and enquiries were made to use the former LBL Battersea garage – a spiritual home of the 19 which had been modernised and, later, mothballed. This was not possible, and a potential depot site was identified at a disused flour mill just along the river bank from Battersea garage. Here planning permission was refused due to residents' opposition and, at a late stage, the 19 had to run from New Covent Garden. At first, the office accommodation was a hospitality bus converted from a Bristol VR and loaned from Ensignbus.

Norman points out that, "Most of London's night and day traffic hot spots seemed to be on the line of route 19, making it difficult to run, but our operation of the route was well received from Day One. The very fact of going up and down the Kings Road with buses that weren't red alerted people to the fact that something was different. The newly-refurbished RMLs wore a Ray Stenning livery which really was a head turner. Kentish Bus delivered a very different customer experience, and if the passengers are appreciative of the staff, it helps the staff to do a better job – when Kentish Bus started a new route, it was generally better than the week before."

Route 19 was the first Routemaster service to be tendered and was operated by Kentish Bus from April 1993. RML 2410, in the stylish livery introduced for the service, leads red Routemasters at Hyde Park Corner in July 1994. (Colin Fradd)

"The very fact of going up and down the Kings Road with buses that weren't red alerted people to the fact that something was different."

Tony Kennan stresses that you had to crack the issue of staff terms and conditions. "For bus work in a difficult environment like London, you need staff to clock on when they do, but at the end keep working until the supervisor says you can go." His staff who came from the north-east to London didn't want to go home because they were just sitting in their digs. But the local staff didn't like this way of working. Tony adds, "I needed people of a mindset to be flexible, people who would help regulate the service by hanging back for five minutes when asked, who would understand how the contract worked, which was to require a regular service running every seven or eight minutes. We explained to the people doing the job how we as a company were rewarded, which got most of them onside. Some didn't like it, but they didn't last long.

"Basic bus operation had got lost somewhere in the history of London Transport. What was needed was a regular headway and reliable service. Nick Newton and his colleagues had been very clear, saying 'We want to get back to a situation where, if it should be every 10 minutes, you give us a bus every 10 minutes.' Nick was pragmatic and you could sit with him and talk through the issues. When you had problems he would understand, but he had a philosophy of 'Let's get back to reliable bus operation.' And you were rewarded very handsomely if you did it, in the early days. We had a guy in an old phone box in Kentish Bus colours at the junction of Oxford Street and Tottenham Court Road. The two supervisors who worked there were brilliant in spreading out the service interval. We used to call this phone box 'World Headquarters'!"

Kentish Bus acquired the vehicles and services of Transcity in October 1993. About 60 staff and 23 vehicles were involved to operate LT routes 286 and B15 together with some services in Kent. In May 1994 they began use of the closed Ash Grove garage for some of their tendered services, calling it Cambridge Heath.

CentreWest

After implementing Uxbridge, David Brown was moved to Hanwell as Garage General Manager. The garage was not performing well and there were huge industrial relations issues. "I remember the first day I arrived, I walked into the garage and there were 15 NSBs (buses cut from the service because no vehicle was available for engineering reasons). The engineers put the running plates of the missing buses up against the inspectors box, so all the drivers knew there were no spare buses and started 'playing around' a bit more, claiming there were mechanical faults with their buses and asking for a replacement, knowing there were no buses to replace them with. So one of the first things I did was to take the plates down so that nobody would know. We also had a Running Shift office around one side, and an Inspector's box at the front, and they never spoke to each other. The first thing I did each morning was to walk between them to communicate and find out who thinks what is going on. And that was good bus operation!"

CentreWest recognised that Hanwell would always have industrial relations difficulties. Strikes were a regular occurrence and, eventually, closing the garage was seen as the only solution. This produced the biggest minibus scheme of all, needing around 90 buses. Michael Steward came to CentreWest from London Buses where he was Assistant Development Manager and had been the link person between the central planners and the Bus Districts. He was the one person in LBL who understood how the Group Planning appraisal system worked, and he tried to build bridges where there was antagonism. Cardinal District had begun to develop ideas for minibuses and CentreWest made the strategic decision to develop and implement the scheme. Planning started in mid 1989 and the first phase was implemented in late 1990, taking the core of routes in Ealing and Greenford and converting them to midibus.

The first step was to reopen Acton Tram Depot for the E3. It was considered crucial to open a separate base for the midibuses to flourish, starting with a clean sheet and without any hangover from previous arrangements. Peter Hendy arranged with Ealing Council to use spare space at their Greenford depot. David Brown set up the new base. "It was a wholly new operation, a 'game changer'. Many people had said, 'You can't do that,' but Peter Hendy said, 'Yes, we can,' and he was prepared to take the risk. It was

The Ealing scheme started in July 1990, using Renault 75 minibuses with Wright bodies. These were registered by Wright's in Northern Ireland, and RW71 (HDZ5471) is at Ealing on the E9 to Smith's Farm. Larger Dennis Darts replaced these buses from May 1997. (David Cole)

151 "We want to get back to a situation where, if it should be every 10 minutes, you give us a bus every 10 minutes."

In 1990 CentreWest won the 297 on tender from Metroline, and took over the route in December, converting it to midibuses. The first deliveries of Dennis Darts with Wright's Handybus bodies were used and JDZ2314 is seen at Ealing on 29 December. These had sloping windscreens to reduce reflections, reminiscent of London Transport's RF single-deckers of the 1950s. (David Cole)

a good team at CentreWest, the four Directors were very close and so were the seven General Managers." In 1990 CentreWest also won the 282, which LT had tendered as a big bus route, beating the competition with a midibus bid variant. The 297 was also won with conversion to midibuses.

When Greenford opened in March 1993 there was a major shuffle round of services. The E3 midibuses moved to Greenford, and the 207 moved to Acton, which became a double-deck garage. Hanwell garage closed, and some of the most militant staff took the redundancy payment and went to work quite happily at London Buslines at worse pay and conditions and with no trade union!

This was a dense network of services which were all operated by Renault minibuses with Wright bodies – these began to arrive in 1990 and were the first in London. Recruitment was based on the experience with Gold Arrow. A large number of drivers were needed for the increased frequencies and they recruited people with customer service experience rather than those with driving experience. This brought a greater number of women and young people, helping to break the old and unco-operative ways of working.

As with the Gold Arrow services, the short headways generated passengers and the midibuses were soon too small, leading to unacceptable levels of overcrowding. Later in the 1990s the minibuses were replaced by low-floor Wright-bodied Dennis Dart single-deckers, then with dual-door buses, and then most became double-deck – but keeping the better minibus frequencies. Route E2, which had been a 20-minute frequency double-decker service before the minibuses were introduced, was now running double-deckers at 7/8 minute intervals!

The scheme was designed and implemented by CentreWest, but service planning was the responsibility of the central planners. With his liaison background, Michael Steward was well placed to handle this. "You had to persuade them that you had a good plan. CentreWest's schemes headed off Group Planning and the Tendered Bus Division. This was before privatisation, and we aimed to build strong identifiable networks so that if the Government went for area franchising, our big networks would be franchised as a whole and CentreWest would be in a good position to run them. It was all about doing a great job quickly, in order to convince everyone that 'these people are doing a good job, let's let them run it'.

"Within a few years, CentreWest had very few double-deck routes left and we successfully fended off tendering. By the time of privatisation in 1994, hardly any CentreWest routes had been tendered. Performance on the routes also improved rapidly. Peter Hendy had details of the daily run out on his wall. One day he came out saying, 'Look, 100% service!' He and his engineering team worked miracles to get the engineering side in order. John Whitworth came from South Wales and was a very 'hands on' sort of person who worked on the entrenched engineering management attitudes. It was a unique situation – a period when everyone realised that the Units were going to have to defend their businesses against the independents."

"Some of the most militant staff took the redundancy payment and went to work quite happily at London Buslines at worse pay and conditions and with no trade union."

London Central

London Central grew from commercial developments and tender wins. By December 1993, it was operating 47 LT services, 15 of which had been competitively tendered, together with mobility bus services for LT's Unit for Disabled Passengers, private hire, excursion, contract and rail replacement work. Five services extended out of London into Kent and one, a shopping service to Lakeside, into Essex. The company was operating in a competitive area with Kentish Bus and London & Country both active. Kentish Bus had increased its strength when it acquired the contracts of Maidstone Boro'line, while London & Country had won several TBD tenders and then occupied the former Walworth garage, opposite London Central's Camberwell garage.

London Central had 500 buses but it was an ageing fleet and over 80% of its double-deckers were Routemasters and Titans over twelve years old. In 1992, when restrictions on new buses were eased a little, London Central received 24 new Optare Spectra double-deckers for the OPO conversion of route 3. The company had a generally good industrial relations record though there was some industrial action over the new pay and conditions package in 1993.

London Northern

Colin Clubb had expected to take London Northern into privatisation but when this was delayed he retired. Norman Kemp was at Kentish Bus when adverts for London Northern Managing Director appeared in the weekly trade press. Industry colleagues encouraged him to apply, and the interview was held in central London – on a day when there were no red buses running due to a strike. Norman vividly recalls wondering what he could be letting himself in for! He joined in May 1993, leaving Kentish Bus just as they started operation of route 19. He then

London Central had an elderly fleet working in central and south-east London. A Leyland Titan arrives at London Bridge from Peckham on the P3. The route was tendered in 1993 and lost to London & Country, who used single-deckers. (Colin Fradd)

153 The interview was held in Central London, on a day when there were no red buses running due to a strike. He vividly recalls wondering what he could be letting himself in for!

attended his first LBL meeting as Managing Director of London Northern and had to look Keith Ludeman in the eye, having just taken route 19 off him!

Norman was at London Northern from May 1993 until October 1994 when it was bought by MTL. When he arrived there had been a gap in management as Colin Clubb had left earlier. He inherited the team of Directors and other managers. Morale was good; staff saw the arrival of a new MD as a sign of better prospects for a company which seemed to have suffered more than others up to that time in the tendering process. Loss of the 24 and other routes had seen the closure of Muswell Hill, and Norman had asked his interviewers about whether the company did in fact have a future. "It was not a dynamic company, and had been very unsuccessful in keeping its work. When the block grant routes were allocated to companies in 1993, London Northern seemed to lose all its shared routes to the other participants – it was as if no one was really fighting for it. People did not seem to be told anything – only bad news."

Norman had never expected to work in London Buses when he started his career. He recalls his 20 months at London Northern as enjoyable though challenging, working with good people at all levels who really wanted the company to succeed. He had to pick the company up – there had clearly been leadership issues before with inactivity when faced with deregulation and a Managing Director who was approaching retirement. "The staff were willing and supportive, but numbers were still bloated and unfortunately some had to go. There was a willingness, and a 'can-do' philosophy that I had not expected. When I arrived in May 1993 I was joining MDs in other LBL companies who had already had more than five years to turn their companies around.

"We had to achieve economies and closed Finchley and Chalk Farm garages, but everybody was remarkably supportive and I would have had every confidence in going forward with the team that was there. Holloway was massively large to manage after the closure of Muswell Hill, Finchley and Chalk Farm. Its management was divided into two parts, minibuses operating from the open-air part next to the railway, while the other routes, crew and opo, worked from upstairs in the historic part."

Norman regrets that Muswell Hill had been closed – in 1990, London Northern had five garages; tendering losses were more apparent in inner London, and the combination of Muswell Hill, Potters Bar and Finchley would have been more appropriate for the company's spread of operations as they had become in 1993. Holloway's 24-hour operations did not sit well in that residential area. He understood that the role of the subsidiary Managing Directors was to mind the company for London Buses. His task was to make sure the company was profitable going forward. "I had to let the Commercial and Engineering Directors go: City financiers were eyeing the opportunity presented by privatisation and were simply not prepared to take people with shorter working lives left, as they were unlikely to be willing to put their life savings and more into the company."

Norman got involved in performance on the road, and was driving on his first weekend at London Northern. "It was late turn on the 135/139 because staffing at Chalk Farm was particularly bad at the time. Then when the 13's turn came for tender I was anxious to learn how Finchley made their flagship route work and spent some weekend duties on the front or the back of the Routemasters. I made some heads roll when I discovered how badly the service was running one day when there was disruption in the middle of the route. There was an Inspector at North Finchley who had the crews on the pavement and the buses parked up on the stand, but he did not have the nous to swap over the running numbers and get the buses moving!"

BTS

The 13 was the second crew route to be tendered and was taken over by BTS from 4 December 1993. Dave Alexander remembers, "It was 1993 when we won the first contract for the 13. That was a big issue because it required conductors. We later ran it as OPO on Sundays, which was slowly leading to the demise of the conductors. At the beginning, I was Operations Manager. As we grew I became the Operations Director and as we took on more and more work I became the Managing Director. We sold the business to Blazefield in 1994 and I stayed in London until 1999. I put BTS and the London Sovereign businesses together and ran it as a London unit for Blazefield. That was when we moved out of Borehamwood and took on half of the depot at Edgware, shared with Metroline, adding to our small depot in Harrow.

"The Routemasters were leased from London Transport but we maintained them – we did everything, we just didn't buy them. We had separate drivers and conductors who worked as crews, they were rostered to work as pairs. They were good days, and I look back on them now and remember many things, mostly the challenges – you think back to what you learned and what you overcame. We never had trade unions – we had an employee representative group, and it was clear that as the workforce got bigger, this private company approach to representation wasn't really working. The staff thought I was bonkers because I went to what was then the T&GWU and said to them, 'I need you to come and set up a branch.' So they came in at our invitation, and that was good because trade unions are great if you engage with them. If you're open, and if you have a relationship which is very much two-way, they become very much part of the solution as opposed to part of the problem."

LT and LBL in 1993
London Transport celebrated its Diamond Jubilee on 1 July 1993 in a very low-key manner without any special events. LBL had now gone through some dramatic changes. Its main activities had been devolved to the subsidiary companies to sharpen up accountability and create companies comparable to those in the private sector, in readiness for privatisation. Those companies now had several years of experience behind them.

Each company had its own board, with a Managing Director, Commercial, Finance and Engineering Directors, and chaired by a member of the LBL Board. Each had a home territory, most of them aligned with Borough boundaries, with between 350 and 600 buses, several bus garages and responsibility for defined routes. There was co-ordination in central London, and some other functions such as vehicle purchasing were also retained at the centre. The subsidiaries were encouraged to develop an independence, within a framework of LBL-wide policies and standards. But losses through tendering had resulted in significant shifts of work from one subsidiary to another, and to the closure of one company, leaving ten companies together with Westlink and London Coaches.

These organisation changes and the thrust of competitive tendering had sharpened management performance, leading to substantial cost reductions from around 4.1p per mile in 1984/5 to under 3p per mile in 1991/2, at 1992/3 prices. Performance had improved to become the best for many years, averaging around 96% of schedule operated compared to under 92% in 1986/7. These improvements had enabled companies to win about half the routes tendered by LT. At first, independent companies,

BTS took over route 13 in December 1993, using Routemasters leased from LT and panted in a more orange-red than London Buses. RML 2443 at Oxford Circus turns into Regent Street in June 1994. (Colin Fradd)

155 LBL's main activities had been devolved to the subsidiary companies to sharpen up accountability and create companies comparable to those in the private sector.

concentrating on one or two routes, were able to achieve considerably better performance than LBL's overall performance, but that gap had now been closed.

LBL continued to provide over half the total network, including many of the most difficult and expensive to operate routes, through the block grant network. The companies had displayed considerable innovation in reshaping their networks, the most visible evidence being the rapid move to midibuses in all parts of London, the majority on block grant routes. About 20% of LBL's network was by then midibus bringing cost reductions, higher frequencies, better penetration into residential areas and significant increases in passengers and revenue. Many changes had been made to improve reliability, both in the suburbs and on the Routemaster services in central London.

The formation of companies was accompanied by devolution of accountability: LBL centrally only retained the functions necessary for overall policy direction, financial management and co-ordinated use of resources – premises and buses were owned by LBL and leased to the companies. Devolution of wage negotiations, trade union consultation, and staff recruitment and training had led to major savings and, it was thought, improved industrial relations, though the TU might not have agreed!

Tendering had continued with 5% new mileage added each year. Routes were now selected to produce packages of varying sizes to allow both big and small operators the chance to compete. Individual routes were selected on the basis of poor quality of service and high cost of operation.

About 40% of services were now tendered and LBL subsidiaries were running just over 60% of them, so including block grant work LBL was running 85% of all London's bus service. LBL's performance was now matching that of independent operators, and its costs were becoming similar.

The better independent companies were performing very well. Peter Larking of Metrobus remembers Nick Newton saying to him: "It's good working with us, isn't it!" "Well," he replied, "there is actually a lot of hard work going on on the ground!"

156 LBL's performance was now matching that of independent operators, and its costs were becoming similar.

Opposite A major win for London and Country was route 188, which they took over in November 1993 using 15 former London Buses Leyland Titans, one of which is crossing Waterloo Bridge in June 1994. (Colin Fradd)

In November 1993, LT photographed buses from all the independent operators on North Weald airdrome in order to show the range of companies, vehicles and liveries then involved in London bus tendering, in addition to the London Buses companies which were about to be privatised. Buses from 20 companies were included, from the left: Docklands Minibus, Sovereign, Javelin Coaches, R E Thorpe & Sons, Crystals, Thamesway, Luton & District, R&I, London Buslines, County Bus, London & Country, Kentish Bus, Capital Citybus, London Coaches, BTS, Metrobus, Armchair, Grey-Green, Atlas Bus, London Suburban. (Ian Bell, courtesy TfL)

157 In late 1993, 40% of London's bus services were tendered and 20 independent companies were running around 40% of these.

7 DEREGULATION – London is different

The London Buses subsidiaries wanted deregulation to happen. Tendering for services was gradually cutting away at them, and each company was suffering death by a thousand cuts. They wanted to be masters of their own destiny and argued that they would be better off with full deregulation, as had happened outside London in 1986.

There were different views within LT. David Bayliss, the Director of Planning, felt that the LBL companies wanted deregulation because they felt they knew better about running buses in London than 'those wretched planners in the centre of LT', and because, with deregulation, they could exploit their privileged position with garages and make a lot of money out of it. The crucial issue was whether bus services should be planned as part of a co-ordinated network, or be developed by individual bus operators responding to the market.

The politicians continued to insist that deregulation was on the way, but were increasingly nervous beneath the surface. They were aware of the results in the rest of the country, and whilst they might be willing to put up with chaos for a time in, for example, Sheffield, they didn't want it in London on their own doorstep. There was also concern that London Buses was not yet in a good enough shape for deregulation.

The debate continued for 10 years. Nicholas Ridley had proposed it from his appointment as Secretary of State in 1983, and it would be 1993 before the situation became clear. But each succeeding Secretary of State and Transport Minister faithfully declared his determination to proceed. In 1988, Michael Portillo MP became Minister of State for Transport and said, "As a London MP I want to see my constituents

Block grant red bus services still formed around half the London bus operation in 1993. A sea of buses on Victoria Embankment demonstrates the problems regularly faced in central London. A demonstration in Whitehall one Saturday in April 1987 led to all bus routes being diverted. Keith Wood, the photographer, remembers a wall of buses that were not going anywhere! The original New Scotland Yard of 1890 is on the left. In 1967 the Metropolitan Police had moved to another New Scotland Yard in Broadway, SW1, opposite LT's headquarters at 55. (Keith Wood).

158 The politicians continued to insist that deregulation was on the way, but were increasingly nervous beneath the surface.

reaping the benefits of deregulation as soon as possible. There are no ifs and buts about deregulation in London. It will happen." The 1985 Act had envisaged deregulation once LBL had had time to adapt to a competitive environment. It was generally assumed that it would be privatised simultaneously with, or shortly after, London deregulation over a timescale of about three to four years. Clearly this was not happening, initially because it was realised that further legislation was needed to repeal parts of the 1984 LRT Act which conflicted with it.

John Telford Beasley continued to be an enthusiastic cheerleader. Speaking at a transport symposium in Newcastle he said that, "All my business experience shows that competition means that people are constantly striving to give their customers an improved service. Improvements do not necessarily mean cheaper services – it could mean a higher standard at a higher price. What the public really want is value for money, or a certain quality at a certain price." He greeted potential rivals: "Welcome. Come on in. Come and compete – but don't think LBL will be any sort of a pushover." LBL was fully geared up for deregulation to the extent of introducing commercial services. Minibus schemes such as the change of routes 28 and 31 to smaller buses was evidence that the subsidiary companies were moving forwards and preparing for deregulation.

The results of bus deregulation outside London in October 1986 became an issue in the June 1987 General Election. Opposition parties argued that the government's belief that all the bus industry's problems had been caused by too much regulation was naive. Their concerns that deregulation would result in the loss of early morning, evening and Sunday services had been justified. A report to the Department of Transport by the London Regional Passengers Committee (LRPC) in 1988 argued that deregulation in London would be "a total disaster" if it were to be on the same basis as elsewhere in Great Britain.

Peter Sephton, Managing Director of South Yorkshire Transport, was very clear. "In my experience, deregulation of buses in London cannot work. It is true that competition brings change, innovation, more buses, the very occasional new routes and competitive fares. However what people really want is conformability, predictability and reliability.

Competition in the bus industry adds an element of uncertainty for the consumer that will not be tolerated indefinitely". He added that "Deregulation will also produce stress for passengers and London Buses must be prepared to take the blame for the changes made to deal with competition. The sun will shine from the exhaust pipe of every incoming operator but changes made by LBL will be heralded as draconian, unnecessary, profit-seeking, inconsiderate and so on."

John Telford Beasley responded that South Yorkshire "had a shock to their system, but we have three years in which to prepare". But Peter Sephton's observations gained weight by Department of Transport statistics showing a 7% drop in bus passengers outside London since deregulation, whilst in London there was a rise of 1%.

Press reports confirmed the political concern over deregulation, and the need for time to assess its effects. *Bus Business* said that "… there could be a real danger of deregulation upsetting the knife edge balance of ensuring day to day mobility for millions of people spread across a wider social spectrum than in any other part of the country."

Government delay
Early in 1988, the government suggested to LT that there might not be time during the next Parliamentary session to deregulate London's bus services, but that it was still their firm intention to do so during the 1990s, and LBL's restructuring should continue without delay.

At the same time, the Government sought to transfer LT's costs from the taxpayer to the passenger, wherever possible. But in February 1989 they were forced to make a 'U-turn' and concede additional funding. This was for major safety improvements on the Underground following the Fennell report into the King's Cross fire; to finance improvements on

Roundabout's fleet was now all red. Mercedes MC2 passes through Orpington in May 1991. (David Cole)

"Welcome. Come on in. Come and compete – but don't think LBL will be any sort of a pushover."

the Underground and to Docklands; and to finance the reorganisation of London Buses into smaller companies. The government achieved this by a 50% increase in the levy on Borough Councils, conflicting with its policy of removing ratepayer support for LT. But they were still committed to removing this subsidy by 1990 when their new poll tax was to be introduced as the new form of local taxation. London Boroughs would receive additional grant to cover the levy without increasing rates, but they pointed out the inconsistency between the Department of the Environment, who were trying to keep rates low, and the Department of Transport who were now levying a higher rate precept.

In 1989, three years after the Roundabout operation started, Bryan Constable approached John Telford Beasley suggesting that he would like to buy Roundabout. Bryan thought the initiative would be welcomed in the run-up to the privatisation of LBL, and would help to give the process a start. JTB called him in and said, "Roundabout will never be sold off separately because it would be a key element in Selkent's total value. Forget any ideas you might have for siphoning it off for yourself or your mates!" The attraction of Roundabout was clear – it was a very good operation. But to LBL it would need to be sold at the right time as part of the sales process.

Consultation Paper

In March 1991 the Government released a consultation paper called A Bus Strategy for London with its proposals for deregulation and privatisation.

It acknowledged the important role that buses in London play and stressed that the Government believed that they did have a promising future, but that that future depended on buses' ability to win and retain passengers in competition with other transport options. In particular, operators needed the freedom to tailor bus services more closely to passengers' requirements. A ten-point plan was set out to achieve the Government's objectives:

1. deregulation of the London bus market as soon as possible in the next Session of Parliament;
2. safeguarding the future of concessionary travel in London and encouraging the provision of pre-paid ticket types;
3. an on-going tendering programme after deregulation, ensuring that bus services are provided on uneconomic but socially necessary routes;
4. privatisation of LBL subsidiaries;
5. improvement of traffic conditions;
6. making bus priority measures more widespread and effective;
7. encouraging LT to ensure that LBL enters a deregulated market with a satisfactory bus fleet;
8. encouraging provision of proper waiting facilities;

Needing a short-term vehicle to cover refurbishment of existing vehicles, Roundabout made use of Bristol LH BL85, which was surplus in the LBL fleet, between December 1993 and May 1994. It was popular with some drivers and was used on all Roundabout routes, here on the R1.

"Roundabout will never be sold off separately because it would be a key element in Selkent's total value. Forget any ideas you might have for siphoning it off for yourself or your mates!"

9. encouraging promotion of bus services and ensuring provision of reliable and comprehensive passenger information; and
10. research into the ways in which different approaches to bus operation impact on congestion.

It was proposed to apply a similar deregulated regime in London to that in the rest of the country. Operators would register services they intended to run on a commercial basis. A central agency would assess whether additional services were needed on social or community grounds, and these would be subsidised and bought in by competitive tendering.

The strategy discussed the possibility of selling the bus garages separately from the bus companies, upgrading the bus fleet to be competitive with other operators, and improvements to bus priority measures in London.

Two concerns acknowledged in the paper were the future of concessionary fares for elderly and disabled people, and for the co-ordinated Travelcard scheme. The paper proposed safeguards for concessionary travel to ensure that if the scheme were to hit difficulties, a London-wide scheme would continue to function. It was less clear about the future of the Travelcard, because participation of companies in a joint ticketing arrangement under deregulation would have to be voluntary and on a basis which allowed each participating operator to recover a fair share of the revenue at a high enough level to make it worth participating.

While the basic powers needed to deregulate in London already existed in the 1985 Transport Act, further legislation was needed for two reasons: firstly, to put London's concessionary fares scheme on a secure footing, and secondly, to amend LT's statutory duties to complement rather than conflict with deregulation. Legislation was envisaged as soon as possible in a new Parliament, and an approximate timetable was set out by which the existing arrangements and regimes, including existing LT contracts and road services licences, would be gradually wound down and operators invited to register their commercial intentions under deregulation. All these processes would take up to two years, meaning that April 1993 was the earliest possible date for deregulation. That would be followed in the third year by the privatisation of LBL subsidiaries. Whilst privatisation could start a year later, that would give the LBL subsidiaries little chance to establish a commercial 'track record' under deregulation. It also depended on many factors, including the outcome of the 1992 General Election.

A role was seen for a residual bus authority in London, whose duties would include:

- registering services (this could be done by the Traffic Commissioner, as outside London);
- identifying services which are socially necessary, but which have not been registered by bus operators;
- awarding contracts by competitive tender for the operation of such services;
- ensuring the provision and maintenance of bus stops, stations and stands;
- ensuring dissemination of information about bus services in London;
- facilitating use of bus passes or through ticketing arrangements;
- facilitating and, if necessary, implementing a London-wide concessionary fares scheme.

The paper identified a number of possibilities for providing this central co-ordinating authority. One was London Transport, but while it had the expertise, there could be a conflict of interest as it would still be running the Underground, which would be competing with bus services after bus deregulation.

There was varying reaction to the Consultation Paper. Roger Freeman, Minister of State for Public Transport (1990–1995), confirmed his backing for deregulation despite admitting that it had failed to halt the decline in bus usage outside London. He blamed the drop in bus passengers outside London on economic circumstances rather than deregulation.

He stated in June that, "Tendering has led to improved bus services throughout London. But tendering is still planning led and is no substitute for market forces. Deregulation will force local operators to tailor their services to meet the needs of passengers, while the taxpayer will continue to subsidise social services". He added that "Buses have a vital role to play – I want to see more buses running in London. London is a very congested metropolitan area and there is absolutely no alternative to the bus."

John Telford Beasley wrote that, "Deregulation and privatisation will let commercial concerns get on with operating buses themselves – and will ensure that the passengers rightly determine the services which are provided." Harry Blundred of Transit Holdings was naturally in favour, saying that, "If deregulation happens in the way proposed and the Travelcard is open to all operators as in other major conurbations, London will see a great resurgence in bus service provision, resulting in a large increase of passengers and leading to a major contribution in the reduction of congestion."

Grey-Green's General Manager, John Pycroft, was less enthusiastic, stressing concern at the timing of the sale of the LBL companies a year after deregulation. "I for one am not happy at the prospect of competing against state-owned companies in a deregulated London. Although the LBL companies are not supposed to make a loss in the run-up to privatisation, they are still being given an ideal opportunity to see off any competition while still under state ownership." He considered that deregulation would be "an unmitigated disaster". Len Wright of London Buslines was critical of the plans to upgrade the LBL fleets before sale. "Any aided upgrading of the fleet could be seen as a way of fattening them up for privatisation. I'm sure there isn't a private operator around London which wouldn't welcome the opportunity to have its fleet upgraded with government help."

The Chairman of the London Regional Passengers Committee, Dr Eric Midwinter, described it as 'a curate's egg!' "There is much in this Paper that passengers will welcome. The tragedy is that the government has found it necessary to include an irrelevant and potentially damaging scheme for deregulation when so much else of what it proposes will be beneficial." John Prescott, Labour's shadow transport minister, restated the Labour policy that the London tendering system should be applied to the whole country.

LT's Corporate view was that everything on London's buses was now moving in the right direction. The bus network had been significantly reshaped after having been frozen in stone for many decades. There were more passengers, performance had changed through tendering that held people to account. Measurements, accounting, and financial discipline was now there. What more would you gain by deregulation? Barry Le Jeune was LT's Corporate Public Relations Officer and worked to spread this message amongst London Boroughs, London MPs and the Department of Transport. They also approached bus companies, not all of whom agreed. In an article in the *London Bus Magazine* for Summer 1991, he wrote:

"The Consultation Paper said little about the arguments for deregulation or its results in the rest of the country. It briefly stated the political view that the system in London was planning-led and that central planning was not an acceptable substitute for the free play of market forces. The Government was anxious to open up bus operation to further competition, which it claimed would bring a more flexible response to passenger demand for new, more frequent and more accessible services.

"While the Paper quoted the increase in bus mileage following deregulation elsewhere, and the reduced cost of providing socially necessary services that were not provided commercially, it did not recognise that much of the increase was due to the introduction of high frequency minibus services, and that a statistic based on seat miles rather than vehicle miles might produce rather different results. Also, much of the increased service was brought about by new operators doing battle with established ones on trunk routes rather than by opening up new facilities. The 'acid test' should be whether the number of passengers had increased under deregulation outside London. It had not.

"The Department of Transport's own published statistics showed that while the amount of service, measured in bus miles, had increased less in London (+3.3%) than elsewhere (+16.4%), passengers in London had grown by 5.5% compared with falls of 7.1% nationally and 16.2% in the Metropolitan areas. Fares increases had clearly contributed to this. Fares in London were similar to those in Great Britain generally, suggesting that tendering in London had secured reductions in bus operating costs comparable to those achieved by deregulation in the rest of the country. But fares in the Metropolitan areas had risen much more markedly as commercial pressures uplifted the previous subsidised PTE fares. In addition, the confusion and instability caused by deregulation would also have contributed to the loss of passengers in the Metropolitan Counties.

"It was difficult to know what would happen if deregulation was applied to London. Independent contractors to LT would have enough information about their passengers to decide whether to register the tendered services they were running, but it was not known how much direct competition would be generated between the various operators.

"Whilst deregulation should bring commercial innovation, route developments over the past few years, particularly the spread of midibus services into suburban residential areas, had filled many of the obvious gaps in the network. There might be more express bus services competing with, or complementing, the rail network, unless traffic congestion made this too difficult. A major concern would be the number of buses using congested streets in central London. Whilst choice is superficially in the passengers' interest, it does not help if it creates the level of congestion apparent in Glasgow in the early days of deregulation there. And if buses in London were to play a role too in reducing the pressure on London's rail networks, was that not more likely to be achieved under a co-ordinated planning regime rather than by market forces?

"Deregulated competition had led to frequently changing routes and timetables, leaving passengers confused. One operator might be running a route on a commercial basis during the daytime, but another may operate the same route under contract at the quieter times. Joint ticketing may not be available between one operator and another on a common section of route, and there may not be a comprehensive source of up-to-date timetable information. These uncertainties undoubtedly go a long way to explaining the reasons for the drop in bus patronage outside London despite the service increases.

"What was the alternative for London? Clearly, extending the system of route tendering to all services, whether commercial or non-commercial, could provide the best of both worlds. It would achieve the benefits of competition for contracts, particularly the downward pressure on costs which should be reflected in fares levels, but without the wasteful disbenefits of 'naked' competition on the streets."

Barry Le Jeune concluded the article by quoting the following words from Lord Ashfield, the Chairman of the Underground Group in 1923. "London cannot exist upon one form of transport alone. Its prosperity depends upon the provision of many kinds of transport all co-operating together in the closest harmony to provide facilities for travel of the highest efficiency and at the lowest fares.

"Competition is a dangerous weapon. It may seem to offer immediate gains, but they are at the expense of future losses. This is the universal experience. Competition causes congestion in the more remunerative routes, destroys reliable services on the less remunerative routes, and curtails the unremunerative routes. Competition weakens the undertakings so that the fresh capital required for progress cannot be obtained on reasonable terms, and therefore becomes a greater burden upon the passengers.

"Competition ends in obsolete vehicles being retained in service when they should have reached the scrap-heap, and this means a poor, slow service instead of a fine, fast one. It is a question for Londoners which they will have."

London Bus Executive, DLR and London Coaches
In July 1991 the Government announced plans to create a London Bus Executive to administer services after deregulation. This would bring to an end to LT's 58-year involvement in the running of London's buses, and London's co-ordinated public transport system. This was one of several options included in 'A Bus Strategy for London'. Malcolm Rifkind, the Transport Secretary, suggested that LT would be distracted from its major challenges in running the Underground and DLR, that the new Executive would ensure equal terms of competition between bus operators, and also give an authority with no transport interest except buses. LT would therefore be responsible for the Underground, DLR, the Disabled Passengers Unit including Dial-a-Ride, and the Travelcard. It would mean that, for the first time in 60 years, London would not have a single organisation with overall responsibility for its transport services.

LT News headlined this as a 'Government Bus Bombshell'. The Chairman, Wilfrid Newton, stated in *LT News* that he was both surprised and disappointed at the decision. He said, "We do not believe it to be in the best interests of passengers to discard the many years of experience and knowledge which LT has accumulated and to start again. Her Majesty's government is choosing the most costly and least efficient solution." He gave his staff an assurance that he would continue pressing the government with LT's view that it should retain its current role and responsibilities.

In November, Malcolm Rifkind announced that ownership and control of the Docklands Light Railway (DLR) would be transferred from LT to the London Docklands Development Corporation (LDDC) with effect from 1 January 1992. Together with bus deregulation and the creation of the London Bus Executive, this further knocked LT's hopes of retaining its position as London's transport co-ordinator. Wilfrid Newton said the decision was "one with which LT disagrees, but must nevertheless accept and implement". He could not see how the change would benefit travellers in Docklands.

Looking back at this decision, David Bayliss who was then LT's Director of Planning, stressed the Government's continuing concern at the expense and poor quality of the Underground and its monolithic monopoly. "The government wanted to get the DLR away from what they saw as the bureaucratic, gold-plated world of London Underground, where there were not enough business people involved, and so they gave it to the LDDC. Civil servants were not so troubled by London Buses, and were largely content as route tendering progressed and the subsidy came down. The less money London's buses needed, the less interest they took. It was £350 million a year before tendering, which was a real concern, but after tendering it came down below £100 million per year and they were happy to have it off their backs."

On 2 August 1991 it was announced that London Coaches would be privatised. Some of their Routemasters began to appear with London Coaches fleetnames as, in due course, they would be unable to use the London Transport name.

The 1992 Election
The campaign for the General Election on 9 April 1992 made politicians more cautious about presenting their policies. The Public Transport Minister, Roger Freeman, admitted that the government might have to rethink its total commitment to deregulation in London. He told the LRPC that special rules may be needed in central London after deregulation. He pledged that he would not introduce a free for all, and that deregulation would bring about a controlled market with rules covering access to bus stations,

"Competition causes congestion in the more remunerative routes, destroys reliable services on the less remunerative routes, and curtails the unremunerative routes."

stops and streets. This was a significant change of tone, and he went further by saying that, "If I can be convinced we are taking a step backwards rather than forwards with deregulation, then I will think again ".

However, there was a widespread expectation of a Labour victory or a hung Parliament, so that many people were beginning to think about network franchising of bus services. In the event, this proved irrelevant as the Conservatives were returned, and everyone involved with buses in London looked instead to the implementation of "A Bus Strategy for London".

The new Transport Secretary was John MacGregor, and a new position was created of Minister for Transport in London, to which Steven Norris was appointed. He had been Conservative MP for Oxford East from 1983 to 1987, where he observed the introduction of Harry Blundred's Thames Transit minibuses. He re-entered Parliament as MP for Epping Forest at a by-election in 1988 and – as described in Chapter 2 – was PPS to Nicholas Ridley, then at Trade and Industry.

Steven Norris was interested in public transport and pleased to be appointed. "I was given the job of determining how we would deal with privatisation and deregulation in London. The Prime Minister, John Major, had been very conscious of the lack of strategic overview in London of services like transport, caused by Margaret Thatcher's abolition of the GLC. I was very supportive of the abolition of the GLC, but I'd always been clear that, whilst the GLC may have been the wrong entity, the concept of a strategic authority for London was so powerful that it had to happen.

"That of course is why, after I left Parliament, I persuaded my party to support the Greater London Authority Act, which initially they didn't want to do, and then subsequently stood for Mayor a couple of times. So what John Major did in part to deal with the criticism that there was no strategic authority for London, was to give me a specific remit as Minister for Transport in London. And it was an extraordinary career changing moment for me, because it gave me this wonderful opportunity to look across all modes and, of course, specifically in London in the days of LRT, to look at this issue of privatisation and deregulation."

Moving to privatisation
Deregulation was clearly being reconsidered and given a lower priority. It was not mentioned in the Queens' Speech and Steven Norris said there was not enough time in the current session of Parliament. Government announcements continued to stress that it was the plan, and how good it would be for London, but actual moves to make it happen were not there. The argument and debate continued, and pressure grew from a number of sources to avoid deregulation in London.

This was not necessarily to the liking of the Directors of the London Buses subsidiary companies, who had been recruited to take their companies into deregulation, and who wanted freedom from London Transport in order to compete openly in the marketplace.

Declan O'Farrell was MD of Metroline and is very clear. "I came in 1986 with the promise of privatisation of the buses in about 1988/89. They had to get rid of the GLC, then they had to break up London Buses, then they had to create companies and then they could get on with the sale of it. But John Major became Prime Minister and it became increasingly obvious that nobody in London, none of the London MPs, whether Tory or Labour, wanted bus deregulation because of the publicity of what had happened in the rest of the country.

"So by the early '90s, there was absolutely nothing coming out of the government as to moving forward. Then we had a meeting of the London Buses Board and all the Managing Directors to discuss deregulation and privatisation, because we had come to the conclusion that, if deregulation was off the table, why should privatisation be?

"It actually made more sense, if you are going to deregulate, to privatise first. You would know what you were privatising, whereas after deregulation it was too fluid. Peter Hendy was, I think, quite instrumental in convincing the other Directors that it was worth talking this through, and we convinced Clive Hodson that it was worth speaking to Steven Norris. There was a group of four of the ten MDs who had several meetings with Steven Norris and his officials, and they managed to convince them that it was doable. So then if there is a free-for-all following deregulation, public assets are not involved – it is all private sector. It made a lot of political sense."

At Leaside, Steve Clayton found it a very challenging period. "It was very difficult maintaining morale. I had 10 years not knowing whether we were going to be sold or not! We had a number of meetings with Steven Norris. He was a good minister; he understood the business, he understood the brief and he got on well with people. At the same time he was tough and did not give people what they wanted." They still did not know whether they would be privatised in a deregulated or a regulated environment.

Clive Hodson recalls that the general consensus was, 'We want to be privatised because we are haemorrhaging,' which was quite true – the private sector was coming in with different wage scales, and they were delivering the performance. Clive went to the

"It became increasingly obvious that nobody in London, none of the London MPs, whether Tory or Labour, wanted bus deregulation because of the publicity of what had happened in the rest of the country."

Board of LT and proposed that the bus companies be privatised. "That was endorsed and the Chairman Wilfrid Newton took it to Steven Norris. I think actually that we were the pro-active people; it wasn't the government saying to us we think you ought to privatise the subsidiaries, it was LT Managers, the MDs.

"It is very important to remember that the whole concept was set up with deregulation in mind. Deregulation was on the cards and what we intended to do was sell the companies ahead of deregulation. Deregulation was set out in the initial prospectus. Anyway, the Board then approved the proposal, the government agreed it and it was set in motion."

Norman Cohen recalls the debate about which should come first, privatisation or deregulation. "The government was keen on deregulation, but the more they thought about it the more scared they became. So they decided that privatisation would come first, under the tendering and contract system, so that's what we set about doing. Part of the argument was that, with deregulation before privatisation, LT/LBL could be accused either of wasting public funds by allowing free competition between publicly owned subsidiaries, or alternatively being accused of collusion and acting against the public interest by restricting competition between companies. Any route duplication between LBL subsidiaries would waste limited public resources."

The first of the LBL subsidiary companies to be privatised was London Coaches, a non-core business which could go quickly. Guide Friday, the sightseeing tour company, was selected as preferred bidder in early 1992 but this fell through and LBL halted negotiations until after the General Election in May. When John Major was un-expectedly returned to power, LT moved quickly and it was announced that there would be a management buy-out. Most of the coaches were leased from Hughes DAF, and a sale and lease back deal was agreed for the Routemaster sightseeing buses. Only five vehicles were then owned by the new company. 'London Transport' was removed from the vehicles, and the sightseeing tour was renamed 'The Original London Sightseeing Tour'. Pat Waterman was Managing Director of London Coaches and recalls that, "LT had a difficult job – it was on, and then off, and then on again. But it pioneered the process. London Coaches entered an exciting period of trying things out, developing new ideas, particularly in the sightseeing business. The coaching business was interesting, but not as successful as sightseeing tours." The Pullman Group was formed in 1994 with London Coaches as its subsidiary. In 1992 the company, now in the private sector, was encouraged to bid for LT tenders. The 52, between Victoria and Willesden, was a large route with 22 buses, which had been operated by Metroline and London General from the two ends. London Coaches took over in December 1993, running a 24-hour service with elderly Leyland Titans from their Wandsworth base some distance from the southern end. They soon found that running tendered routes with old buses did not work, and that sightseeing and tendered services did not go well together. Pat Waterman recalls that "Robbing a driver off a sightseeing bus that's making money, for a tendered route, was not good business." They passed the 52 to Atlas Bus in August 1994, but Atlas soon failed and Metroline took over again in 1995. Here, a Titan of London Coaches loads at Hyde Park Corner in July 1994. (Colin Fradd)

165 "London Coaches entered an exciting period of trying things out, developing new ideas particularly in the sightseeing business."

In a paper to the CIT Metropolitan Section in January 1993, Norman reported that LBL and LT now suggested that circumstances had altered sufficiently to make early privatisation of the LBL subsidiaries a viable and sensible option. This would:

- Give a level playing field, so that LBL and existing independents would compete on equal terms. Their approach to bidding would be commercial and not – as for LBL at the time – subject to public sector accounting rules. There would be no suspicions of favouritism for companies owned by LT, no unfair use – real or imagined – of public money to fight competition, no more perceived advantage to LBL in having premises and vehicles; and equal access to raising capital.
- It would also clarify LT's role, confined to regulating the total network and fares, and to managing contracts with the operators, all now privately owned.
- It would avoid a conflict of interest after deregulation, because LT would not have subsidiaries bidding for routes.
- The former-London Buses companies would continue to drive for greater efficiency and could diversify into other activities and operate outside London.

Deregulation would then bring:

- Market-led provision of bus services,
- Competition, which would lead to greater efficiency through lower costs,
- Fares should reduce through competition,
- The result should be increased bus usage, and
- Lower subsidy from the public purse.

The possibility of lower bus usage, as happened in the UK Metropolitan areas, would be tackled by measures to retain bus priorities and tackle traffic congestion, by seeking ways to improve co-ordinated information to passengers in the deregulated environment, and by retaining some form of multi-operator Travelcard – perhaps using smartcard technology.

In 1992, the Department of Transport appointed consultants Price Waterhouse to consider proposals for the privatisation of London Buses in advance of deregulation. In December, it was announced that privatisation of the LBL companies would go ahead 12 months later.

Bus Engineering Ltd (BEL), the privatised company which had been formed from the Chiswick and Aldenham engineering works, ceased trading in January 1993.

Block Grant buyout

A major issue for the LBL companies was the pay and conditions which still applied to the block grant network. Meetings of all the Managing Directors were held to plan action on this, and it led to tough negotiations with the trade union. Keith Ludeman recalls the sessions at the Inn on the Lake hotel in Godalming. "There was a hanging basket outside the window with a duck sitting in it, looking in! It was there throughout the meeting. When I got back to London General, Pat Mahon wanted to know what was going on. I told him to ask the duck – he heard everything!"

David Humphrey takes up the story. "London Buses made an attempt in 1986 to change its scheduling and wages agreement for drivers and conductors, called the 'New Operating Agreement'. It represented a significant improvement in the efficiency and overall cost of operating buses, but it was from a very low base that was poorly regarded in the rest of the industry. With the advent of competitive tendering in London, other operators could bid for routes with a driver cost advantage of around 20%. The low cost units set up in London had successfully retained some of the business, but once the new companies had been established, about 90% of the operation in London was still not competitively operated, and was still funded under the block grant from government.

"London United's desire to convert much of its operation to high-frequency midibus operation presented it with both a challenge and an opportunity. We would be needing a large number of midibus drivers, and though staff turnover at the time was high, we needed to move more quickly than by converting routes when enough of the old staff left and new ones could be recruited on the new midibus terms and conditions. We felt that one way out would be to offer some form of 'up front' compensation to drivers, say two years' difference in average weekly rostered earnings, to help people adjust to lower incomes. It is important to mention that the work content changed from about 36½ hours per week, paid with a 38 hour minimum, to about 39½ hours on average, so was still quite reasonable.

"The trade union had no intention of even discussing the proposal, but people had wind of it and in any case it was obvious that major changes were on their way. Two drivers in Fulwell garage in particular did not want to see themselves and their colleagues disadvantaged by default, nor let an opportunity pass, so they came, separately, and on several occasions, to see me. The first was simply concerned about his job security and being able to provide for his family, while the second was perhaps being a bit more mercenary, but they were both straightforward guys with straightforward worries. It was particularly pleasing that two 'ordinary' drivers felt able to come into my office for a chat, not something that

"Two drivers did not want to see themselves and their colleagues disadvantaged by default, nor let an opportunity pass, so they came, separately, and on several occasions, to see me."

readily happens in large organisations. In effect, they did the negotiating, and our offer ended up at £10,000 for any driver who would volunteer to switch to the lower rates and worse conditions. It was over-subscribed.

"We managed to find the funding from within our own budget, so no permission from LBL Centre was necessary – the LBL directors knew, of course, as each company had an LBL director as its Chairman – we were not operating as a loose cannon. But the running cost reduction meant that the following year's budget would be underspent, so we had more money with which to fund subsequent buyouts. The course was set. We made sure that subsequent offers were not quite as generous as the first – a year's difference in wages was about £1,500 – but set about establishing competitive industry-standard agreements. The wage rates and scheduling constraints themselves were by agreement with the trade union – not only did we apply the process to midi-bus conversions, but also when 'big-bus' routes were put out to tender.

"By late 1992 we had no 'New Operating Agreement' or 'block grant' operation at Stamford Brook garage or Wood Lane outstation. Some 64 drivers at Hounslow, and just 12 at Fulwell, were on block grant conditions, with Shepherd's Bush garage the only one still fully block grant operated, with conductors as well as drivers. Had we had more time, I always reckoned that another two years would have seen us with so few people left on block grant conditions that it would not have mattered, as the higher costs would have been such a small proportion of the whole. Block grant could have then been left to wither on the vine, with perhaps a final buyout at the very end.

"But bigger change was afoot, affecting all companies. The need to accelerate the LBL subsidiaries' competitiveness was increasingly pressing. At a meeting with the LBL directors, Bryan Constable of Selkent announced that he had had informal meetings with a senior full time officer of the trade union. It was suggested that a buyout of terms and conditions across all companies might be feasible. LBL sought and obtained the necessary funding from government, and all companies announced simultaneously that the whole of LBL's operation remaining on block grant would be taken out of it. All remaining staff would be offered the option of receiving a two-year compensation payment (on the same principle as London United's) to transfer to whatever new conditions each company had by then established. This time, however, there was compulsion involved. Any staff who did not accept the offer were also refusing to accept the offer of a revised contract of employment – they would in fact be out of a job. Each company therefore had to write to each employee concerned, giving them notice of termination of their existing contract of employment and offering them a new contract, the acceptance of which would trigger the compensation payment.

"What a letter to have to write. What a letter to receive. Each MD had the task of drafting the letter. I saw Keith Ludeman's draft for London General – it was to the point, and described the compensation as 'generous'. I later saw Peter Hendy's for CentreWest – this was quite lengthy, and was couched in apologetic terms which were quite sincere. Mine was not good. It was later rightly criticised by some of my management team as being 'brutal'. I had taken the expedient of copying sections of other people's letters, rather than taking the time to draft my own.

"The first few months of 1993 were extremely fraught. The LBL directors at one point seriously considered abandoning the project and handing the funding back to the Department of Transport before the year end, as the project seemed so endangered. In the end, the majority of staff across London accepted. I think there were only 15 "refusenicks" across the whole of London, all of whom subsequently took their companies to Industrial Tribunal for unfair dismissal. It was very much the nadir of staff relations at London United. There was no formal industrial action, but many staff, especially at Shepherd's Bush, simply didn't turn up for work, such was the anger. We typically had cancellations running at about 30% for several weeks. Visiting the garage was horrible, the atmosphere was thick with antagonism. Nobody smiled and greetings, if any, were very curt. There was not a trace of the normal banter that used to prevail.

"We were also, coincidentally, still running seminars for staff, partly customer care, partly staff motivation, partly staff briefing. At the end of each day's seminar, one of the company directors would attend for an 'open session' at which staff could raise any subject they liked. Hardly surprisingly, the block grant buyout created a major item. The sessions were extremely uncomfortable and tense, but we could not have abandoned them – that would have been quite cowardly, and would have been perceived as such. One particularly difficult driver at Shepherd's Bush managed to rattle me in one session, and in another a Fulwell driver simply walked out, but all the other sessions that I attended were at least conducted with basic courtesy, most staff simply wanting to know why it had had to happen, and some wondering why there had been no recognition of long service in the compensation package – the trade union had rejected such a proposal, as it happens.

"A subsequent wage round saw a ballot reject the company's offer, and partial industrial action followed. There was an angry mood about, and no

"Each company therefore had to write to each employee, giving them notice of termination of their existing contract of employment and offering them a new contract, the acceptance of which would trigger the compensation payment."

small amount of determination to regain some of the lost wages, with probably an element of revenge mixed in. Feelings were pretty high, especially at Shepherd's Bush. It got quite nasty when some crews worked and drove out past the picket line, with the TU committee taking names. One 94 appeared to be heading out without a conductor, but she was cowering on the back seat of the top deck. The atmosphere in the canteen was explosive. Hounslow and Fulwell were more civilised, with some strike-breaking Hounslow drivers organising themselves to provide the most even service they could (who needs service controllers?). At one point there was only one bus operating route H37, driven by the Commercial Director, Martin Whitley.

"Gradually, very gradually, things returned to near normal. Many staff left as soon as they could get a new job, taking their compensation with them. Within a year I was touring the garages attempting to explain privatisation and the benefits of employee share ownership."

Peter Hendy has equally strong memories of these events, and personally signing letters to all of his drivers. His staff voted in favour of the changes and didn't go on strike – this was primarily because the minibus drivers were not affected and were such a large proportion of the drivers that they voted against a strike and won the vote.

Staff throughout the LBL companies received the letters. The effect varied between companies as they set their own pay rates, but cuts of £30-£60 per week were typical, with longer working hours and possible pension changes, with a one-off payment in compensation. Union meetings in garages led to a loss of service and industrial action. Strikes took place on three days in March and April 1993. CentreWest, East London and Westlink worked normally, as did Potters Bar (London Northern) and Wood Lane (London United). LBL claimed 48% of all its services operated but the trade union complained at the way some managements had left little time for negotiation.

Comparable negotiations took place in garage engineering. John Trayner remembers the politically charged atmosphere, the general change from public to private sector, the atmosphere after the miners' strike and widespread competitive tendering. He looks back now at negotiating a 2-3 hours longer working week with a £30 pay cut at a militant garage. "There was obviously confrontation and they said it wasn't going to happen – but it did. Quite a few realised that the world was changing and you either had to be part of it or drown!"

Net Cost Contracts for Block Grant routes
A key condition for early privatisation was to put the remaining Block Grant routes onto a contract basis. At the time, roughly half of the network was tendered and half was still run by the LBL companies under the block grant arrangement. Of the half tendered, half was run by LBL companies and half, around a quarter of the network, was run by outside companies. To sell the LBL companies, the routes that had not been tendered needed to be quickly put onto contracts so that the companies could be sold with an inventory including a number of gross cost contract routes, and a number of negotiated contracts for the routes which had not yet been tendered.

To do this competitively would take at least three years, and so it was decided to negotiate contracts with the existing LBL operators and to competitively tender any routes where the negotiation failed, or where existing service performance was unsatisfactory. These contracts were negotiated and supervised by LBL centrally, rather than by the TBD. In the long term, they would be replaced by deregulation.

David Sayburn, in charge of the Central Traffic Division (CTD), ran the process. "The companies were invited to bid for the block grant routes that they operated, but they were warned that the 10% of routes that were the worst value in their bids would be put out to competitive tender. Each company only bid for its own routes, without competing bids. If any routes looked expensive, we would say to them that 'We are minded to tender these, and would you like to reconsider your price.' 10% of all the routes were indeed put out to tender at the end of this process."

The approach was therefore to replace the block-grant system by route-specific contracts by 1 April 1993; to continue the existing TBD route tendering programme; to offer the LBL companies for sale in late 1993 and to complete the sales during 1994. Deregulation was then expected to be implemented by mid-1995. A London Bus Executive, separate from LT, would be set up to secure socially necessary services and to manage bus stations and stops after deregulation

The negotiated route contracts for the block grant routes achieved cost levels midway between the block grant levels and those achieved under competitive tendering, giving average reductions of around 10%, a major achievement for such a large block of business in a single year.

As a result, Nick Newton and the TBD were managing the tendered routes and David Sayburn at the CTD was managing the negotiated contracts for all the non-tendered routes. Gradually, more and more of the negotiated routes would become tendered. Quality of service and average waiting times were monitored through spot surveys and mileage run, and David Sayburn would call in operators if quality of service was falling short. In Norman Cohen's view,

"One Routemaster on the 94 appeared to be heading out of the garage without a conductor, but she was cowering on the back seat of the top deck."

the bus system was then running very well. "We had overall co-ordination, the routes were being properly monitored, our wholly owned bus companies were free to compete. They were also driving down costs, and they were also trying to create a bit of extra profit through coaching and other activities."

TBD tenders were on Gross Cost Contracts (GCCs) in which the operator was paid a fixed sum for successful operation of the contract with all revenue going to LT. The negotiated contracts for the block grant routes were Net Cost Contracts (NCCs) where the operator kept the on-bus revenue and a share of the off-bus revenue from Travelcards and other passes. Mike Heath, who managed the privatisation process, says that, "The ethos of the time was free market competition, so NCCs were seen as a precursor to deregulation."

But Clive Hodson found it bizarre. "Steve Norris was the one that pushed for this whole concept of net cost contracts. He would suggest things like, 'Supposing we've privatised and it's raining and the company thinks it can pick up more traffic by putting on a few extra buses.' You wouldn't do that, so I think the whole concept of net cost was a bit of dogma." David Bayliss, as Planning Director, had always been concerned about NCCs. He took the view that "Gross cost contracts were more appropriate, because the opportunities to abuse the system with net cost contracts outweighed the opportunities of stimulating competition and improving performance. John Rigby's work showed that small operators didn't understand the market well. The concern about NCCs was that the London Buses companies would abuse their position and steal the revenue of the small operators. With net cost contracts, the temptation would be to run late and pick up the other operator's passengers on the same section of road." The LBL companies did like NCCs, because they understood the revenue allocation system and knew how to make it work for them.

DMS 2109 was one of four Bexleybus DMSs pressed into service at Merton for a few weeks in early 1990. They kept their Bexleybus livery except for the front, which was repainted LBL red with grey skirt. This bus, seen at Tooting on the 44, had had a varied life in LBL with long periods in store. It was later loaned to the Fire Research Establishment, and was then converted to open-top for the Big Bus Company who used it in London and Philadelphia before selling it for further sightseeing work in the USA. (John Miller)

"We had overall coordination, the routes were being properly monitored, our wholly owned bus companies were free to compete."

House of Commons Transport Committee

The House of Commons Transport Committee considered deregulation of London's buses in the spring of 1993. Dr Alan Watkins, LT Deputy Chairman, told the Committee that LT had backed deregulation for the last nine years but had concerns about certain issues, including the future of the Travelcard, passenger information and the stability of services after deregulation. Whilst bus service tendering had produced dramatic cost reductions and improvements in the quality of service, he believed that even more could be achieved from privatisation and deregulation. The Committee agreed that the benefits of the Travelcard should be retained and suggested that the government should legislate to require operator participation in the scheme.

However, LT's evidence document to the Committee (*Privatisation and Deregulation of Buses in London*, by London Transport for the Transport Committee, April 1993) promoted tendering rather than deregulation. It showed that the London bus service was performing better than for many years, whilst the costs were being cut. Bus route tendering now covered half the network and further savings would result from the route contracts then being set up for the remainder of the network as a preliminary to the privatisation of the LBL subsidiaries. The document states, "The reductions in costs in London bear comparison with any achievements elsewhere and the increases in service volumes and deployment of midibuses are greater than in many of the deregulated areas. At 1992/3 prices, revenue grant from the taxpayer has fallen from £350m pa in 1982 to around £100m in 1992."

Bus usage and revenue in London had been broadly maintained, whilst both had fallen significantly outside London since deregulation. For London, the complexity and scale of the network made the Travelcard particularly valuable and popular, the risk of London passengers switching to cars would be damaging, causing further congestion, and the large numbers of visitors from outside London and overseas needed consideration.

The evidence suggested that privatisation of the bus companies followed by a move to 100% tendering, which could be accomplished by 1998, would retain the planning framework, the bus network as a whole would broadly break even, and service planning would be co-ordinated by LT with the private operators. Existing fares policies and structures would continue together with initiatives in areas such as traffic management, electronic ticketing and improved passenger information.

Deregulation, however, would be a radical change. Individual operators would provide services and set fares which, it suggested, would be likely to be higher than envisaged by LT. Benefits could arise from bringing operators closer to the market place with commercial pressure to reduce costs, but against this would be the difficulties that had come with deregulation elsewhere in the country and the particular risks in London.

"Whereas under the 100% route tendering option, it might be that no subsidy for bus operations is required after 1998, a permanent grant of £50m to £80m per annum seems likely to be needed under deregulation, to pay for those social bus services secured by the Bus Authority."

The report concluded that, at April 1993, LT bus tendering had achieved:

- A strong competitive market for the supply of bus services. 136 routes, about half the contract total, were being run by 19 independent operators. Of those, nine had entered the market for the first time as a result of the route tendering system.
- Tendered services had achieved significant cost savings and performance improvements, putting sustained pressure on LBL's non-tendered services.
- Cost savings through tendering averaging 15% net of administrative costs had been achieved. For LT overall, costs per operated mile had fallen by 20% in real terms since 1986/7, and
- Service quality had improved.

The Transport Committee's report in July 1993 warned that deregulation in London could prove to be a disaster. They pointed to the significant fall in passengers outside London even though bus mileage had increased. The Committee, led by the former Conservative Transport Minister Paul Channon, considered that deregulation would be a "leap in the dark" because of London's unique features. They considered it unwise to justify deregulation in London on the basis of experience elsewhere in the country, and were sceptical of whether the advantages claimed by Ministers would actually be achieved in London. They asked for an urgent study of the relative merits of net cost tendering, franchising and full deregulation as a means of providing bus services in London.

LT News headlined this report on 29 July 1993 with the heading "MPs demand rethink on transport". In June, a BBC Radio 4 programme about deregulation mentioned that, in Greater Manchester, there were approximately 2,000 bus route changes each year.

Leon Daniels, MD of Capital Citybus, generally agreed with the report saying that it highlighted the weaker parts of the government's proposals. Harry Blundred, of Transit Holdings, was critical complaining that the wrong people were called to give evidence, adding that, "The doctrinaire views of

---

"Under the 100% route tendering option, it might be that no subsidy for bus operations is required after 1998, but a permanent grant of £50m to £80m per annum seems likely to be needed under deregulation, to pay for social bus services."

the T&GWU are irrelevant to the needs of the consumer. London has to be better under deregulation". The LRPC welcomed the report as its views on retaining the present tendering system were in line with their own thinking.

In the autumn of 1993 there was still an expectation of a Bill to introduce deregulation in London in the new session of Parliament beginning in November. However, a number of senior Conservative MPs, led by Sir Rhodes Boyson, voiced doubts about the wisdom of proceeding. They were concerned at the effects on the London Borough elections in May 1994, and suggested that the government should be looking to consolidate in the Queen's speech, not to go for more controversial legislation. Acknowledging that the effects of deregulation were likely to be unpopular, he said that the Conservatives in London were going to have enough difficulty holding onto seats, but if they went ahead with deregulation it would be a disaster. "We need to calm down," he said. "At the moment we are running in all directions and falling off every cliff edge."

The Chairman of LT was knighted in the 1993 New Year Honours, becoming Sir Wilfrid Newton.

No deregulation, London is different
LBL now had the go-ahead to privatise the subsidiary companies, and Clive Hodson was appointed Director of Bus Privatisation. "We set up a team with Mike Heath as Project Manager, Ian Barlex working with him: we had the Solicitors on board, and appointed BZW as our advisers. KPMG cleared the accounts and then the government appointed Price Waterhouse. There was a tremendous amount of work to be done, as well as running the business.

"We had a very good team all round, but the key thing with it all was deregulation. One day I went over for a meeting with Steve Norris and his civil servants. Handley Stevens was one of the senior civil servants, and Tony Poulter from Price Waterhouse was also there. Steve suddenly said to Handley, 'If I was asked about deregulation and I gave this answer, you know the problems with traffic congestion and so on ....' Steve was rehearsing the whole business of Parliamentary questions about deregulation, and really he was saying, 'Perhaps we won't do deregulation, we will just privatise and have a regulated network.' I was stunned, because none of us had been given any warning about this. I saw Tony Poulter afterwards and said, 'You never told us. Nobody has told us this! You know that we're starting this process. Our outline document, 'London Buses – the road to privatisation', was written in light of deregulation.' 'Oh well,' he said, 'you know now!'"

The Queen's Speech in November 1993 made no mention of London bus deregulation, and the government announced that it would not take place before the next general election. Privatisation of the bus companies would go ahead as planned, and LT would continue to be responsible for bus services, and all routes would be tendered in due course. However, the system of tendering would be revised so that operators would retain all the revenue and receive a minimum level of subsidy from LT for running the service.

Peter Hendy remembers being called to a meeting with Sir Wilfrid Newton and others of the Main Board in November 1993 and being told that there would not now be deregulation. They thought that the managers would be pleased but they were all devastated – firstly, because they had all done so much work, and secondly because it was no longer clear what they would be buying for their money. Peter had just finished a plan for deregulation, and he tipped the whole thing into the shredder! "We were sick when it was abandoned. We were concerned about our survival, and we had prepared for it with lots of little buses, a good proportion of our business."

David Humphrey was also at the meeting. "We Managing Directors collectively usually only met the London Buses executive directors, not the LT Main Board, so we knew something important must be afoot. The meeting was held in the main boardroom of 55 Broadway, around a massive polished oval table, with a painting of Lord Ashfield staring sternly down, as if making sure that the organisation was under prudent and responsible stewardship.

"Sir Wilfrid was delighted to announce that the government had abandoned its plans to deregulate the London bus market, and this was a moment to celebrate. He stressed that the privatisation of the bus companies was still firmly government policy, and that the privatisation process would now be expedited with all due dispatch. This now stabilised market would, he was sure, represent a much sounder business proposition for the MDs and their teams, and he hoped that some would be successful in their aspirations to buy their own companies. We all then decamped en masse to the nearest wine bar in Strutton Ground to make what we could of this sudden volte-face. We had all spent the previous five years structuring our companies for a privatised existence in a deregulated market.

"After a while, we went our separate ways. My next task was to travel to Eastbourne to join the start of a conference I had arranged for the London United management team and all its trade union representatives. Privatisation, deregulation, management and employee share ownership, and the future direction of the company were all on the agenda.

"On arrival at the T&GWU conference centre, I walked straight into a delegation of union reps demanding immediate response to their concerns

---

"I was stunned, because none of us had been given any warning. I said, 'You never told us. Nobody has told us this!' 'Oh well,' he said, 'you know now!'"

Steve Norris addresses the London United management and Trade Union Conference on privatisation in Eastbourne. David Humphrey, on the right, has learned the day before that deregulation will not go ahead in London, followed by detailed TU negotiations into the early hours! (David Humphrey)

about adequate legal representation for the interests of the employees in the proposed purchase of the company, and who would pay for it. Participation in the conference would not take place, they declared, until a resolution was found. After the earlier news, I really did not want another brain-stretching exercise. A fairly tense and lengthy side meeting then took place between the directors and the senior representatives. We worked out a way forward, the funding and appointment of their legal advisers being tentatively established, with legal constraints, fiduciary duties to the current owners, and undercurrents of sectional self-interest all having to be considered. All was happiness again, and we joined the rest of the assembled company in the bar, where I then let them know what I had been told that afternoon. The conversation swirled around, and bedtime was in the early hours of the following day.

"Early next morning I was not at my best, but had to get things started and then introduce a guest speaker, Steve Norris, who had kindly agreed to allocate a big chunk of his diary to come to Eastbourne and expand his thoughts on the forthcoming privatisation process. He was his usual upbeat self and kept his audience engaged. And after the conference it was back to the office and, as Peter Hendy had intimated, starting the preparation of a new Business Plan."

Making the decision
Steve Norris recalls, "I was not the only person who was very worried as to whether we wanted those effects of deregulation in London, where the complexity of services was even greater than it was in Sheffield or Glasgow. That experience persuaded not just me but a great many people in London, who supported the general idea of getting the state out of it but felt that the state shouldn't get out of it completely. What was interesting was that the purists, the absolute purists in my party, thought I had gone soft. But I was quite clear, it's not a question of being soft or hard, it's a question of doing what works.

"There were obvious choices in terms of the order in which this exercise was conducted – deregulate and then privatise, or privatise and then deregulate. And what was very interesting to me is that the option which officials were originally intent on persuading me of, was to deregulate first and then privatise. I think this is a classic example of officials genuinely wanting to follow what they felt is the government's overall view, but I was very very clear from the outset and had very strong views about this, having spent all my previous life in business before going into Parliament, that this really did misread the market. I mean the market both in terms of bus passengers and potential buyers of bus businesses, because it seemed to me that whilst deregulation and then privatisation worked outside London – where if I'd bought a business in Hartlepool I would decide where I would run services and where I would not run services unless they were supported by the local authority or anybody else – inside London the complexity of the network, the density of services and the frankly terrifying prospect of major bus wars in central London was just very unappealing indeed, and I saw no merit whatsoever in just jumping to

"The experience of deregulation elsewhere persuaded not just me but a great many people in London, who supported the general idea of getting the state out of it, but felt that the state shouldn't get out of it completely."

deregulation in London. If I have a reputation, it's a reputation for not being a party hack, in terms of 'My party right or wrong.' My point is, my party right, yes, but if my party is wrong, then no! And in this particular case, I got the argument about deregulation perfectly because it was obviously working outside London, but it wasn't going to work in London immediately.

"The second issue was that I was quite convinced that if we privatised the existing routes, and effectively therefore the existing bus divisions that operated inside London, what we would deliver was, maybe, not the potential to go out and spread your wings across the whole of London, but a *very nice* consistent revenue stream to potential buyers which they would find extremely attractive. And that was incidentally the genesis of my very gentle but firm argument with Wilfrid Newton. I had a huge respect for Wilfrid, a genuine respect, but on this I was convinced I was right, that we would actually do far better as taxpayers to reverse the order that was being pressed on me and privatise first."

The Government announcement had been that deregulation would not take place before the next general election. Did he in fact mean that it would never happen? "It's very funny," said Steve. "The cynics say, 'Until after the next election', and I probably would have said that, knowing me. But I suspect I had my tongue in my cheek. This is what politicians always say when they want to defer something they don't like. And so I'm sure I did say, 'At least until after the general election.' But actually the truth was, I just didn't feel it was right for London at the time.

"The steer that Norman Fowler, then Party Chairman, had had from the Tory constituency associations in London was that whilst they were relaxed about privatisation, they were worried about what they had been told would be a deregulated free for all in London. I argued strongly that the original plan was bad business, and we should reverse the order of play. Some of the young ideologues in the Treasury actually suggested that this would depress proceeds because the great deregulated market opportunities would not be available in London.

"I knew perfectly well that the opposite would be true. Only those who have never worked in business imagine that businesses like competition. On the contrary, what businesses like are cosy monopolies that generate vast amounts of cash. I knew that although one or two potential bidders might be disappointed not to have the advantage of a completely free market, many more would be encouraged by the relative stability that the regulated market after sale would produce, and in the event, I was right."

"Only those who have never worked in business imagine that businesses like competition. On the contrary, what businesses like are cosy monopolies that generate vast amounts of cash."

8 THE END OF PUBLIC OWNERSHIP — 1994

"Wilfrid Newton was convinced that privatising the bus companies would be a disaster," Steve Norris remembers. "He did not see them as profitable and did not know who would buy a business that was not doing particularly well.

"I was clear that any private operator would immediately see where the opportunities were, and that having a nice guaranteed revenue stream for at least a number of years was a terrific incentive. Wilfrid warned me, 'I don't think you're going to get anything for them, Steve. They're going to end up costing us money,' and I said, 'No, not a chance, Wilfrid, we're going to do extremely well out of this. I'll bet we get £100m!' This was the Treasury estimate of what we would raise.

"I told him that not only would we make £100m, we would actually more than double it and I solemnly bet him a crate of champagne that I was right. Wilfrid, clearly thinking that I had lost my marbles, accepted."

Privatising without deregulation allowed the private sector to bid for definable entities with routes, and bidding for routes was the means of ensuring that there was real competition in the market. This was not a public share offer, because it was simply privatising a number of relatively small companies into the open market – very different from, for example, the electricity industry.

Mike Heath was LBL's project manager for the sales process. They studied previous privatisations, in particular the National Bus Company which was the subject of a report by the National Audit Office. Their formal objectives were:
1. to involve management and staff;
2. to sustain public transport with proper businesses and the network; and
3. to maximise the proceeds of the sale, subject to objectives 1 and 2.

The businesses were treated as assets. The vendors did their own due diligence on the buses and the

A photocall was held at Hyde Park Corner with a bus from each of the LBL fleets. There were then around 4,000 buses in the combined fleets, and the vehicles present showed what a variety of vehicles were now operated, compared to the rigid standardisation of the 1950s. (Ian Barlex)

---

174 "I told him that not only would we make £100m, we would actually more than double it and I solemnly bet him a crate of champagne that I was right."

The LBL brochure issued in 1993 to publicise the privatisation process and invite potential purchasers to pre-register their interest. The 16-page document gave summary information about each of the ten companies and the expected programme of sales which it was expected would be completed by autumn 1994 – with deregulation expected in 1995.

London Buses – the road to privatisation

An introduction to London Buses and the privatisation process

garages, and there was a description of each company in a data room, giving details of the contracts operated, the vehicle fleet, its age profile, and summary details of the staff.

When the NBC companies were privatised, some purchasers had immediately sold off the garages and bus stations at a handsome profit. So claw back clauses were included in the London contracts to prevent buyers from quickly selling the garages, as they were on sites that would be far more valuable in other uses. This was to preserve the public transport infrastructure as well as avoiding buyers making a quick profit at public expense. The amount clawed back progressively declined so that selling a garage after 10 years would bring no penalty.

Each of the companies had the tendered routes they had won, negotiated net cost contract routes that had not been tendered, and routes in their area which had been won by other companies. In order to maximise the proceeds of the sale, they did not want any of the companies to look vulnerable, for example if all of their routes were coming up for tender very soon. So a new tendering programme was created from scratch to spread the risk evenly between the companies, so that bidders knew when they would have to retender their routes and replace buses. There was much discussion over the length of contracts which until then had been for three years. After consideration of seven years, a decision was reached on five-year contracts, though after a number of changes they are now five years and can be extended by a further two years provided the pre-determined performance standards are met.

The new programme therefore set dates for every London bus route to be retendered between January 1995 and March 2001, organised so that an equal proportion of the mileage of each company would be tendered each year. The programme also had to be manageable by LT, include the big routes at appropriate intervals, and be fair to everybody. It also had to take account of work already in the hands of other operators and so resulted in the life of some existing contracts being extended. As a result, the independent operators were treated in the same way as the LBL companies. So no company was vulnerable to too much mileage being retendered in any one year, and in this way they were creating an economy for the companies and for the bus manufacturers who would need an even spread of orders for new vehicles. The first route to be tendered under the new programme was the smallest of all, route 511 running on three days a week between Romford and Grange Hill.

During 1994, LT agreed with the Department of Transport on a phased progression to net cost contracts for all other routes. For these to be converted, data had to be collected on their existing revenue on their gross cost basis, so that when re-tendered they could be net cost. Contracts to be implemented before the end of March 1997 would continue to be awarded on a gross cost basis, after which all would be net cost. The Airbus services were not put out to tender as they were already commercial services and potential competitors could start competing without constraint.

Purchasers also needed to be given details of fares, the policy for fares increases, the economic forecast for Net Cost Contracts and details of the service planning procedure. There was considerable detail on service planning and on the Off-Bus Revenue Agreement, which allocated revenue from Travelcards and Passes between services and operators.

Staff pensions were also a key issue. There was a need to protect the interests of London Transport staff transferred to the new companies, whilst also

175 The new programme set dates for every London bus route to be retendered between 1995 and 2001, organised so that an equal proportion of the mileage of each company would be tendered each year.

protecting their jobs by leaving the companies competitive and not, it was felt, over-burdened with an expensive pension scheme. LT provided final salary pensions and the purchasers were required to provide a pension scheme which was "broadly comparable" to this. Some of the successful bidders met this requirement by setting up an appropriate scheme for staff transferred from LBL, but they did not then offer it to new entrants who instead could contribute to a different scheme.

Of the government departments involved, the Department of Transport took the lead with the Treasury looking over their shoulders. The Office of Fair Trading took a close interest in the sale and required that no one purchaser should be permitted to buy more than three of the companies, and no more than two of them could be contiguous. OFT liked the proposal for net cost contracts because this could be seen as competition on the road.

Mike Heath recalls that the Treasury were more interested in macroeconomic issues, like the net cost contracts, tendering and the length of contracts. But interestingly, the Treasury wanted all the buses to remain red!

Red buses and smartcards

The colour of London's buses has been a regular source of controversy. It was considered at the beginning of tendering and the question came up again now. The *Evening Standard* returned to the story from time to time. Typical was a full page in August 1991 headlined 'Hands off London's famous red buses' which announced a campaign by the London Tourist Board to avoid 'chaos and confusion on the streets' which would result from 'convoys of garishly painted buses which could mean the end for London's fleet of red double-deckers'!

Steve Norris knew the importance of the issue. "Any kind of privatisation is quite controversial. When we suggested privatising the London buses, the

The Harrow Smartcard trial started on 5 February 1994 on all routes in the Harrow area, which were operated by Metroline, London United, Sovereign, Luton & District and BTS. The smartcard was seen as a means of retaining the benefits of Travelcard into the future whether there was to be tendering or deregulation. It could provide for multiple operators and a range of ticket types, whilst making checking the passes simpler for the driver and collecting improved data on ticket use. Passengers who participated in the trial were given a Smart Photocard in place of their existing photocard for use on the Harrow buses, but retained their magnetic ticket for use on the Underground and on buses elsewhere. Harrow was selected as a large but relatively self-contained area in which to conduct the experiment alongside the existing ticketing system. 200 buses and 2,000 passengers were involved, making it the largest test of contactless smartcards on public transport in the world at that time. Together with parallel work on the Underground, it eventually led to the Oyster card.

Below Luton & District displays the Smart Card Bus logo in this 1995 view in Wealdstone. (Capital Transport)

Right Larry's contribution to the Harrow publicity, showing how to obtain a Smart Photocard for use on Harrow's buses.

question I always got asked was, 'Will the buses be red?' I remember being rung at 2 o'clock in the morning by a Japanese live radio station who said, "Ah, Mr Norris, Minister for Transport, you are going to privatise London's buses. Will the buses be red?' 'Yes,' I said, 'Don't worry, they'll be red.' 'Good,' he said, 'because we like red.'

"I went to see John MacGregor and I said, 'Now look, John, I want us to say in the legislation that the buses must be red. The operators can put their logo on, and have say 20% of the vehicle so they could have their banner, but the rest has got to be red.' And John said, 'But Steve, I thought you were a Conservative. We believe in free markets. Why shouldn't people paint their bus sky blue pink if that's what they want? You can't be serious, Steve.' I said 'I'm deadly serious, John, if we keep them red, 90% of the problems will fall away.' He said, 'Are you sure?' I said, 'Trust me!' And thank God he did, because he knew that I knew what I was talking about. And he said, 'Well, if you say so, against my better judgement.' And I said, 'Because if you keep them red, which costs nobody anything, it will get rid of all the politics of the privatisation, all the public reaction.'

"And strangely, it did. When the *Evening Standard* reported that we would keep them red ('London's buses will stay red, says Norris!') it was enormously reassuring for some reason. It was like, 'Well, maybe a different person owns this bus, but it's my bus. It's a bus I recognise. It's not something coming along that's white, I don't want white with odd stripes, I want my red bus.' It is iconic, a bit like the GPO postbox, or telephone box or the black taxi, people just feel comfortable with it. So I said, 'Yes, I know, I'm a terrible socialist, but only in this respect, John, because if you let me do this we'll make £100 million!'

"The companies who were bidding all got it straight away. They knew exactly what they were doing and none of them ever pushed the limit. Nowadays, they are all red buses and you can see the company logos if you look. It's different if you are in a competitive situation, where you need your buses to look different because you are offering a different service. In London, it makes no difference."

So the government made clear that buyers of former LBL subsidiary bus companies would be required to keep the red livery for services in central London, though this would not affect existing operators of tendered services such as Grey-Green and Kentish Bus.

Trade Unions
The Trade Unions knew that privatisation would happen and worked to protect their members' interests, and in some cases to try and ensure that they benefited, or at least were compensated for the major changes in their conditions that came with it. Pat Mahon recalls, "It was a bit of a rough ride. The Union didn't want to have anything to do with privatisation, and some colleagues wouldn't get involved. I said, 'It's going to happen, so it's either going to be some kind of a shared scheme or these boys are going to take it all. So, if there's something in it for the drivers, we should get involved."

Steve Norris had direct contact with the Trade Union at conferences held by the London Buses companies. "In general, the trade unions had a perfectly understandable and natural opposition to change, because they believed that privatisation would lead to job losses. They were probably right, because over-manning is a consistent feature of public services. However, the Union could see which way the wind was blowing, and they worked to ameliorate the situation rather than trying to challenge it through strike action. And so we didn't have resistance from staff in the way that you might otherwise have expected. I think that was partly because the Managing Directors of the bus companies went to their own staff to try to reassure them, and some of them were saying, 'We will cut you in on the proceeds.'"

Steve comments that industrial action was more at the earlier stages with the beginning of tendering, when garages were being closed down or turned into low-cost operations, and over the change in the block grant pay and conditions. "By this stage, there was very little industrial disruption, and that's largely I think a tribute to the common-sense attitude that the

"If you keep them red, which costs nobody anything, it will get rid of all the politics of the privatisation, all the public reaction."

Trade Union achieved. I'm not suggesting for a minute that the trade unions approved of what we were doing, I don't think they did, because they are there to try and protect and preserve their members' jobs, and they saw privatisation as a threat to that. I think it's not unreasonable for them think that. But what they did not do was cause any significant difficulty."

But the Union continued to fight its corner. Pat Mahon remembers that, "Clive Hodson, not many people liked him. You can probably look back now and see that he was a reasonably honest kind of broker, doing a very difficult job preparing it for privatisation. Because we gave him a terrible time."

Moir Lockhead of the GRT Bus Group had come to London to talk to the management buyout teams and staff representatives about what he had done in Aberdeen. This took place in the KPMG offices in Farringdon Road, and Pat Mahon recounts, "We had a bit of a spat with Clive. We turned up with TV cameras to doorstep him on his way out." Clive Hodson remembers it well. "When we left the KPMG offices, a television crew was there and they wanted me. They were doing a programme about bosses' pay and workers' pay nationally – it wasn't just about London Buses – and Pat Mahon had set them up. So when I came out we saw them at the front door with a camera and a bloke with a microphone and I said to KPMG, 'Have you got a rear exit? And when we got there, they'd gone round that side.

"So we went out through the front door and this bloke has his microphone in my face, 'Mr Hodson can you tell us what you're paid, what your pay rise has been,' and so on. And there was a man with a camera and someone else with a boom, and I just walked." Mike Heath adds, "Clive, to his credit, decided to walk straight through them. The TV reporter was asking him, "Why are you selling these people down the road?" This was stopped by a cab driver going past, who wound down his window and shouted out, "Why don't you f*** off and leave him alone!" Pat replied, "I'll f***ing leave him alone alright!" But the intervention gave Clive, Mike and the others the opportunity to walk straight through!

"But at a funeral a few years later," says Pat, "Clive stuck a finger in my back saying, 'I've got you now, you bastard!' and I turned round and I said 'Are you still alive?' I think that's the beauty of it – after all those years the people that you had the tough times with are decent people. They were just doing the opposite job to what you were doing. "I said to him, 'I've dined out on that story, and he said so have I.'" Clive recalls Pat Mahon's view of privatisation. "The last time I met him, he said to me that he hadn't been in favour of privatisation, but if that's the way it was going to go, then they would see what they could get out of it."

The Team

Mike Heath was the Project Manager for the privatisation. He was previously Operations Systems Manager and had a track record in selling off parts of the business such as the ticketing and computer operations. There were three main groups involved: LT itself, the Department of Transport and the legal and financial advisers to each of the teams. The LT Steering Group consisted of the Chairman Sir Wilfrid Newton, Clive Hodson, David Bayliss (because of TBD's involvement), LT's Solicitor and Company Secretary, and two other LT Board Members who had supervisory responsibility. The DoT team included the Permanent Secretary, Sir Alan Bailey, who was the senior civil servant involved. Steve Norris was the Minister all the way through the process.

LT wanted clean quick sales, and therefore did many aspects of the due diligence process beforehand, in order to save time. Ian Barlex and Brian Everett worked with Mike Heath as lead negotiators, each closely involved with five of the companies. Mike drove the process onwards. Norman Cohen remarks that, "Mike Heath was the man behind the scenes. He worked extremely closely with Clive throughout the whole process. He was the closest I have ever come to a Machiavellian, a real live Machiavellian!"

The original documents on the sale were based on the understanding that deregulation would come shortly after privatisation. Then the plan changed from deregulation to tendering with net cost contracts, but LT still met the timetable. Clive Hodson recalls, "We had to work hard to get all the criteria changed; it was quite a task but it was still delivered. We had to work very closely with people in the planning department, fares and ticketing and so on to arrange it all, and with the solicitors to devise a formula for allocating bus passes and Travelcards, based on passenger miles. This all worked, but it was a very complicated formula. The net cost contracts were, I think, a bit 'pie in the sky'. It seemed a good idea but I don't think it was practical, given the whole integrated network of buses, Underground, DLR, National Rail and now the Overground.

Westlink

Westlink, the second company to be sold, was bought by its management on 19 January 1994. This was a full practice run for the sales of the larger companies and attracted considerable interest.

Jeff Chamberlain, Westlink MD, had put together a management bid but was soon told that the preferred bidder was the Go-Ahead Group. Jeff did not wish to work for somebody else and said, "I'm not working for them. I've built this up and I'll take redundancy." He planned to sell his house and move to Cornwall,

"After all those years, the people that you had the tough times with are decent people. They were just doing the opposite job to what you were doing."

expecting to lead a simple lifestyle. The due diligence process took a considerable time, and then Jeff had a phone call from Martin Ballinger of Go-Ahead. They met in a London hotel one Saturday to discuss what Jeff would want in order to stay at Westlink. They did not want to buy it without him, and they wanted to know what pitfalls there might be before signing the contract. Receiving a good offer, Jeff agreed to stay. But he gave a warning about Westlink being the first subsidiary to be privatised, and that the Trade Union might make an issue of staff pensions in order to set a precedent for the other LBL companies. It would be easier for them to fight this battle in Westlink than in one of the larger companies.

On the Sunday Jeff had another phone call from Martin Ballinger saying they were withdrawing. Jeff thinks his concern about the TU and pensions had put them off, but it was announced that the government's rethink on deregulation in London had discouraged them. On the Monday morning Jeff had a call from Mike Heath inviting him to improve his bid to become preferred bidder. Jeff replied, "Be careful Mike, I might reduce it!" Mike said, "You already know, don't you!"

Jeff then went through the process as preferred bidder. He did not want venture capital and with his financial adviser put together a deal including Hughes DAF, who advanced the money for the purchase in return for ownership of the buses which

When Westlink won the 131 from London Country South West in 1990, Gary Filbey chose Titans rather than Metrobuses. Titans were not well known in west London but he knew that they did not suffer body rot, unlike Metrobuses, and "If you maintained them properly they would run for you." But it took time to get over the considerable mechanical problems with the buses that that were transferred to him. Freshly-painted Westlink Titan 960 is looking smart at Kingston in October 1990, waiting to depart to Wimbledon. (Barry Le Jeune)

would be leased back on a five-year contract. Jeff had a majority interest in the new company, his other directors and managers each having significant holdings, and the financial adviser receiving shares rather than a fee. The buses would come from London Buses as part of the purchase. Jeff says that, "Most of the buses were crappy old Titans and Nationals – there were no decent buses."

The meeting to finalise the deal lasted late into the night while all the points of detail were settled. Eventually the papers were signed and Jeff and his team had now bought the company for £2 million with no venture capital. In a public statement, he said the newly privatised company would be consolidating their quality. They would keep the red with white and green stripe livery, and they would look for tenders outside London in the immediate future as few tenders would be offered there until the other LBL companies had been sold.

> He warned that Westlink was the first subsidiary to be privatised, and that the Trade Union might make an issue of staff pensions in order to set a precedent for the other LBL companies.

Jeff says that two things then happened fairly quickly, within days of each other. Firstly, London Buses announced a new tender programme as part of the privatisation in which all the contract renewal dates were changed, in some cases long before their previous renewal date. So Westlink's contracts were being curtailed and Jeff was left with five-year contracts on the leased buses but shorter contracts for the routes. New tenders for those routes could lead to new contract prices, and possibly a need for new buses – and Westlink might not win the contract.

Secondly, his financial adviser was also working on the flotation of West Midlands Travel (WMT) and knew that they were interested in the London market. They might buy Westlink as a way of getting into London without waiting for the privatisation of the other companies. So a door opened, and as a result Westlink was sold to WMT who retained Jeff as a consultant for a year.

This sale took place on 11 April 1994, for a small premium over the original price. In a public statement, Westlink said they were concerned that some of the largest groups would come into London on privatisation and they wanted a strong partner, so the largest employee-owned company seemed ideal. WMT was said to have paid between £2m and £2.5m for 90% of the company, the existing management retaining the balance.

The sale of Westlink remained controversial, partly because of the quick sale to WMT, and also because other bidders were unhappy with the process. Julian Peddle complained that he was not given the opportunity to compete. He was not put off by the U-turn on deregulation, and said he preferred a regulated London to a deregulated one, where Westlink could be wiped out. "We were interested in Westlink because it was not too big, it was a real-world company, and I knew the area well. It was working on the Surrey border, with opportunities outside London. But it was clear that London Transport was thinking up the sales process as they went along, which was fair enough – NBC had also changed the process as they went along and turned what had been shambolic into what became a very slick process."

But Julian says he could not get the information he needed. "I was given information about the fleet, depots, buses and so on, but I was not allowed the information that I really wanted like the route revenues, costings, staff information and so on. When I asked for these the answer was always, 'No!' I had bought around 30 companies over the years so I knew what I was looking for."

Steve Norris poses in front of the buses at the Hyde Park Corner launch of the sale of the companies. (Ian Barlex)

Westlink's contracts were being curtailed and he was left with five-year contracts on the leased buses but shorter contracts for the routes.

So he put in a pessimistic bid, and did not get it! He had got used to poor information with the NBC sales when local managers wanted to buy the company themselves. "They would try to put you off by telling you that the roof was falling in. In another case, I was warned that the depot had been built in the 1930s partly on BR land – a strip of about 6" width right along the back wall of the depot, which was all right at the moment but might not be once the company was sold." After this debacle with Westlink he decided he was wasting his time, and all the rest of the London Buses privatisations were too big for him.

The sales process
The experience with Westlink led to lessons being learned for the sales of the other companies. It was planned to sell the ten remaining subsidiaries during the course of the year. The need for stability and certainty during the sales process resulted in a decision that there would be only a small amount of route tendering in 1994/95. Passengers would not generally be aware of the organisational changes taking place, with bus routes, frequencies and fares largely unchanged in the short term. Eventually, however, all routes would be competitively tendered.

The Sales Memorandum was issued and a photo call was held at the Wellington Arch, Hyde Park Corner, on 24 March 1994 where ten buses, one from each of the companies, were lined up with Steve Norris and Clive Hodson. The timetable was not now dependent on deregulation legislation passing through Parliament, and the sales were to be completed by the end of the year.

The sale was advertised in the press and potential bidders were required to respond declaring their interest, paying a fee to be prequalified and to receive the Information Memorandum. This set out as much detail of the companies as possible, with a matrix for each company of the age and length of service of their staff and their bus fleet – there was to be no chance of bidders having inadequate or misleading information. They would then give an indicative bid, on the basis of the information in the Memorandum.

A shortlist was then created of the most likely bidders for each company. This was purposely done at an early stage, and these companies only were then given access to the Data Room so that they could firm up their bids. For this, a corridor at LBL's 172 Buckingham Palace Road headquarters was taken over with a separate room for each company being sold. This was all kept under security with passwords and appointments for companies to come and visit each data room for which they had been shortlisted. In each room, there was a table, chairs and a filing cabinet with all of the documents.

The management teams of the LBL companies were each required to produce a business plan which was only seen by Mike Heath and Clive Hodson. All were expected to put in management bids for their companies and, Mike Heath recalls, "We needed to be sure that they had proper plans going forward and that we would not be selling the companies to a bunch of clowns." This was justified by the fact that a 5% preference on the price was being given to management buyout teams and they had to demonstrate that they could run the companies effectively. "Most of them were very enthusiastic about their possibilities, and when we added up the business that the companies thought that they would get between them, this came to one-and-a-half times the bus market in London! The most realistic was Leaside, who seriously assessed what they thought they would win and lose, and were the only one who contemplated losing anything at all!"

A particular concern was Plumstead garage, which was built on the site of the old Woolwich Arsenal, and where the ground was polluted with arsenic, gun metals and so on. Another concern, at another garage south of the river, was that the fuel bill was excessive for the vehicle types and mileage. They came to the conclusion that someone must be stealing fuel from the garage, and Ian Barlex spent a night on the roof waiting to see if anybody came, but no one was observed. The next morning they noticed that foliage was dying in the back gardens of neighbouring properties, and this was traced to a leaking fuel pipe.

London Transport Buses
LT took over ownership of the 10 LBL subsidiary companies from 1 April 1994 and a new organisation, London Transport Buses (LTB), took effect to manage the bus system and the contracting process, taking over the role of the Tendered Bus Division. All bus-related activities, including planning, contracting and marketing of bus services, management of off-bus facilities and bus priority, were brought into this single division. LT retained responsibility centrally for strategic and corporate planning matters across all modes of transport.

Clive Hodson was appointed Managing Director of LTB. The role of the new organisation was to procure safe, reliable, attractive and efficient bus services for its customers throughout London. Its chief objectives were to provide a high-quality comprehensive bus network, to maximise passenger benefits and usage, to support multi-modal travel facilities and to improve infrastructure and information services.

In awarding contracts, quality would be an important factor as well as price. In future, they would be let for a five-year period and from 1997/8 onwards all would be on a net cost basis. These contracts would be offered using the benefit of LT's

"Most of the companies were very enthusiastic about their possibilities, and when we added up the business that they thought that they would get between them, it came to one-and-a-half times the bus market in London!"

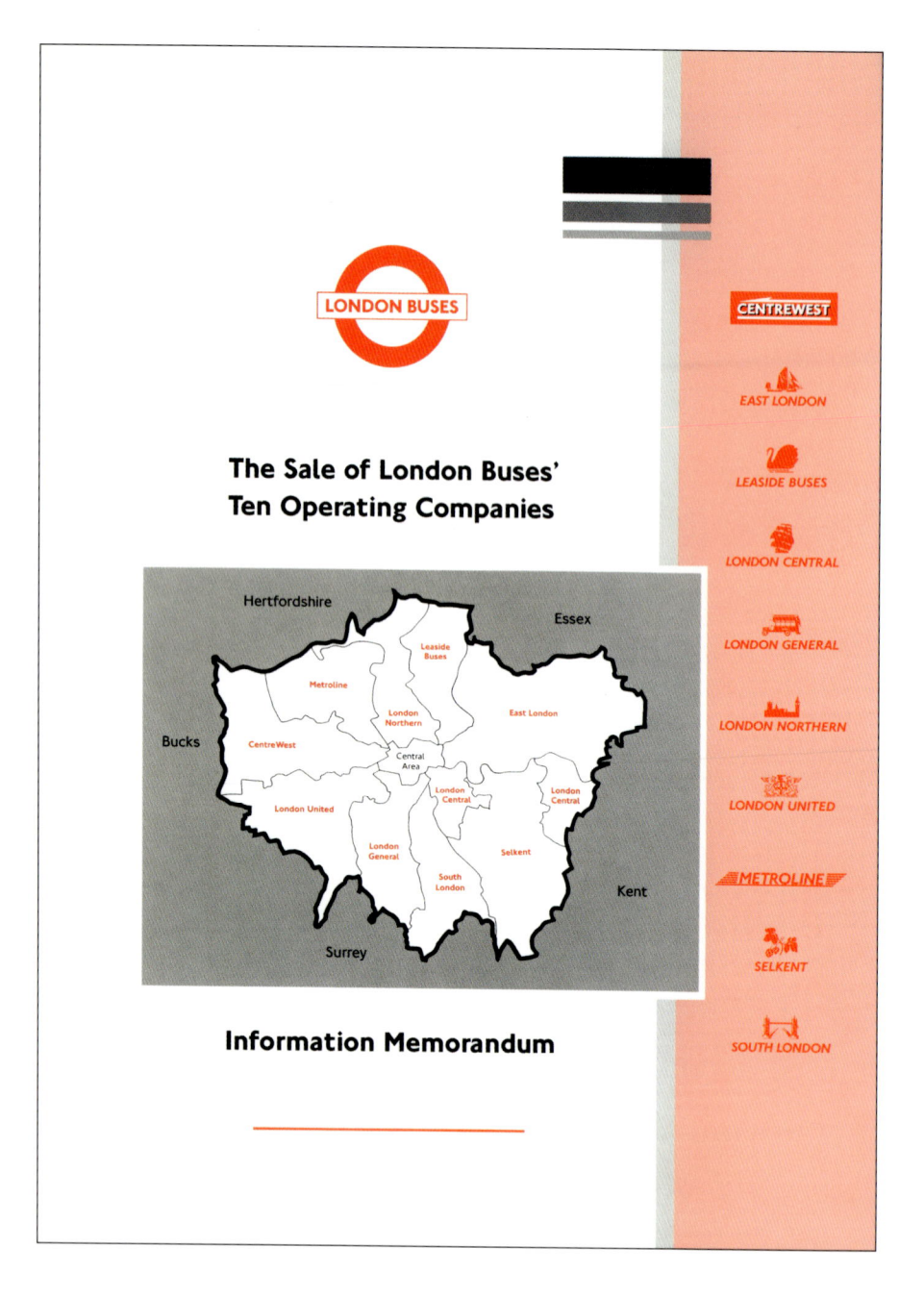

data on bus travel, and operators would be able to renegotiate contracts if factors outside their control significantly affected income.

After privatisation of the bus companies, a new review procedure would commence giving particular attention to operators' views on service innovations. The Red Routes traffic programme was being developed with a further 200 miles identified to give improved priorities to buses in conjunction with the central Government's Traffic Director.

A London Bus Passengers' Charter was published setting out LTB's commitment to its passengers. This included performance targets for service operation and commitments to passengers. It also told passengers how to let LTB know if things were wrong. Notices were placed inside buses to inform passengers of their new rights, with a dedicated telephone line, and the intention was that the charter would help bus operators to improve their performance by focusing on the needs of their passengers. But unlike similar rail charters, there were no refunds promised in the event of poor service.

Nick Newton, who had created and run the Tendered Bus Unit, was seconded to OPRAF to work on the franchising of rail services.

Service performance figures for March 1994 showed significant improvement with 99.3% of scheduled mileage operated, greatly exceeding the

182 A London Bus Passenger's Charter was published setting out LTB's commitment to its passengers.

LEASIDE BUSES

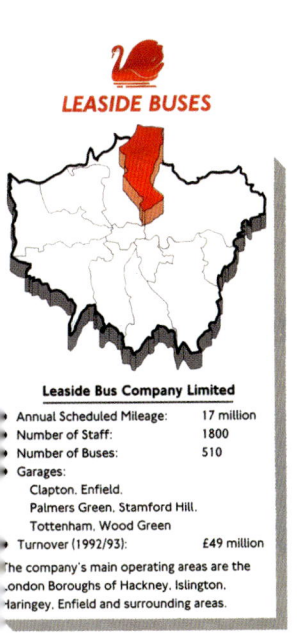

Leaside Bus Company Limited
- Annual Scheduled Mileage: 17 million
- Number of Staff: 1800
- Number of Buses: 510
- Garages:
  Clapton, Enfield,
  Palmers Green, Stamford Hill,
  Tottenham, Wood Green
- Turnover (1992/93): £49 million

The company's main operating areas are the London Boroughs of Hackney, Islington, Haringey, Enfield and surrounding areas.

LONDON GENERAL

London General Transport Services Limited
- Annual Scheduled Mileage: 20 million
- Number of Staff: 2150
- Number of Buses: 600
- Garages:
  Battersea Midibus Base, Merton,
  Putney, Stockwell, Sutton,
  Waterloo Operating Base
- Turnover (1992/93): £60 million

The main operating areas are in the London Boroughs of Merton, Wandsworth and Sutton.

LONDON UNITED

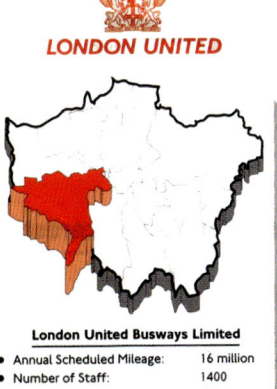

London United Busways Limited
- Annual Scheduled Mileage: 16 million
- Number of Staff: 1400
- Number of Buses: 430
- Garages and Operating Bases:
  Fulwell, Hounslow,
  Shepherd's Bush, Stamford Brook,
  Wood Lane Midibus Base
- Turnover (1992/93): £43 million

The main operating areas cover the London Boroughs of Richmond-upon-Thames, Hounslow, Hammersmith and Fulham and surrounding areas.

SELKENT

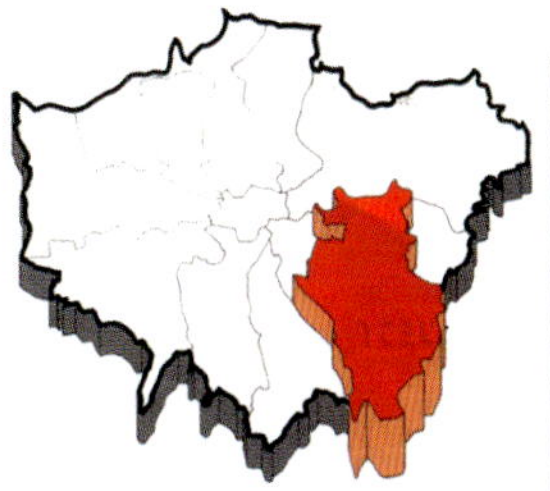

South East London and Kent Bus Company Limited
- Annual Scheduled Mileage: 16 million
- Number of Staff: 1400
- Number of Buses: 390
- Garages:
  Bromley, Catford, Orpington
  Midibus Base, Plumstead
- Turnover (1992/93): £38 million

The areas served include a large part of the outer southeast London suburbs including Bromley, Orpington, Eltham and Woolwich.

LONDON CENTRAL

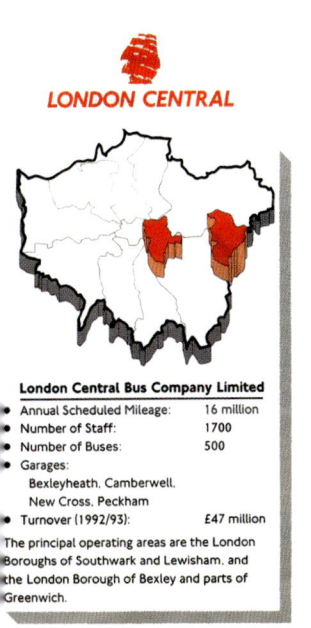

London Central Bus Company Limited
- Annual Scheduled Mileage: 16 million
- Number of Staff: 1700
- Number of Buses: 500
- Garages:
  Bexleyheath, Camberwell,
  New Cross, Peckham
- Turnover (1992/93): £47 million

The principal operating areas are the London Boroughs of Southwark and Lewisham, and the London Borough of Bexley and parts of Greenwich.

LONDON NORTHERN

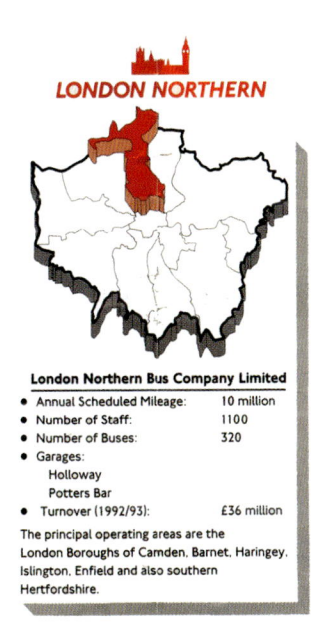

London Northern Bus Company Limited
- Annual Scheduled Mileage: 10 million
- Number of Staff: 1100
- Number of Buses: 320
- Garages:
  Holloway
  Potters Bar
- Turnover (1992/93): £36 million

The principal operating areas are the London Boroughs of Camden, Barnet, Haringey, Islington, Enfield and also southern Hertfordshire.

METROLINE

Metroline Travel Limited
- Annual Scheduled Mileage: 11 million
- Number of Staff: 1150
- Number of Buses: 370
- Garages and Operating Bases:
  Cricklewood, Edgware Base,
  Harrow Weald, North Wembley
  Midibus Base, Willesden
- Turnover (1992/93): £33 million

The principal operating areas are the London Boroughs of Harrow and Brent, part of Barnet and surrounding areas.

SOUTH LONDON

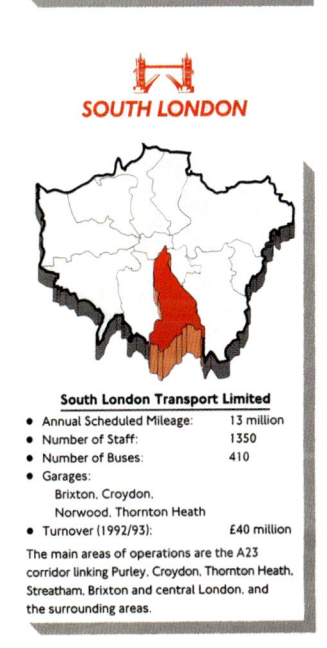

South London Transport Limited
- Annual Scheduled Mileage: 13 million
- Number of Staff: 1350
- Number of Buses: 410
- Garages:
  Brixton, Croydon,
  Norwood, Thornton Heath
- Turnover (1992/93): £40 million

The main areas of operations are the A23 corridor linking Purley, Croydon, Thornton Heath, Streatham, Brixton and central London, and the surrounding areas.

---

government target of 98.5%. This compared with 86% of scheduled mileage operated on LT bus services in 1982. The 1993/4 Annual Report showed an operating profit for the first time since LRT was formed in 1984. A £5m operating surplus was achieved compared with a loss of £77m in 1992/3. Tendered bus operations provided 49% of the network, operated by 10 LBL subsidiaries and 22 other operators. Passenger numbers had fallen slightly to 1,112 million journeys. The Department of Transport's performance targets for operated mileage were achieved or bettered.

Sir Wilfrid Newton remained in his post beyond his planned retirement date of 12 March 1994. His replacement Peter Ford, who was previously chairman of P&O European Ferries, then took over from 15 September and remained until 1998. In July, Brian Mawhinney replaced John MacGregor as Secretary of State for Transport. MacGregor had been in post for a little over two years, and Mawhinney remained for 12 months.

The Information Memorandum supplied to prequalified bidders was a ring-binder of 500 pages with full details of each of the companies.

183 Service performance figures for March 1994 showed significant improvement with 99.3% of scheduled mileage operated. This compared with 86% in 1982.

The sales of the companies

The deadline for receipt of bids for the companies was 12 May 1994. There was substantial interest from across the bus industry, including overseas. "All of the LBL company management teams did bid as some of their costs were paid by LT," says Mike Heath, "and all were shortlisted because of the criteria and the 5% price preference being given to management employee teams. Were they all credible bids? Generally yes, though one spent most of his bid stuffing his neighbour, and two were pretty hopeless."

All the bids were evaluated and a confidential shortlist of potential purchasers for each company was drawn up. Mike continues, "The deals went through quickly – they were properly structured at the outset. We were careful to properly describe what it was we were selling. The objective was to get value for the companies, but we did not want the purchasers coming back and complaining. So the sale agreement looked at the transaction from the purchaser's point of view and we conceded in advance everything necessary to be reasonable, in order to avoid being negotiated down later."

Most of the preferred bidders were known by early September. The sales team had a clear strategy to get a Management Buy Out agreed early to help set the expectations of companies on what they would have to pay. The first to be announced were the management buyout at CentreWest, and then the Stagecoach purchase of East London and Selkent.

Clive Hodson recalls, "We sold one more or less every fortnight. We couldn't sell them all in one go, and so had to base it on who was nearest to getting something agreed, who was going to be ready." Mike Heath adds, "The commercial strategy was to tell the likely winner that they were the preferred bidder, and then suggest that they now offer us more and we would give them an exclusive four weeks to close the deal. These companies were tough negotiators but they wanted the certainty, which is what we gave them." This strategy achieved sales for some of the companies at prices higher than were necessary to beat the next bid.

CentreWest

CentreWest was the first to be sold. The sale was announced at Hyde Park Corner on 2 September 1994. The management team paid £25.6m for 524 buses, 1,470 staff and £40m annual turnover, with garages at Alperton, Acton and Westbourne Park.

Clive Hodson and Peter Hendy in the centre, with the LBL sales team on the left and the CentreWest team on the right, at Hyde Park Corner on 2 September 1994.

"We sold one more or less every fortnight. We couldn't sell them all in one go, and so had to base it on who was going to be ready."

Peter Hendy had consciously developed his company, heading off the TBD by making service changes before they did, and by restructuring CentreWest with minibuses replacing big buses while he was a part of LT so that they would pay for the changes. Some of the other companies thought that they should do as little as possible and then rip out cost when they had bought the company. Peter took the opposite view – he did as much as possible while in public ownership and got LT to pay for it. He got rid of expensive drivers at Hanwell – he couldn't have afforded it and he wasn't going to buy staff that he didn't want. But the Hanwell site was extremely valuable as a supermarket, and LT got the benefit from selling it. He got rid of the premises "and a load of troublesome drivers. We were not permitted to buy big buses at the time but we could get lots of little ones, so you had more patronage, more income and reduced costs." Others thought that minibuses were not suitable, or that they were a good idea which they would do after buying the company. He moved faster than the TBD could to move things.

So when Peter Hendy looked for backers he had a track record. His prospectus said he had entirely changed the business in the last four years. They had a record of innovation to show the bankers. They had been successful in tenders, with minibus alternatives, but had had less tenders than other companies. Peter recalls, "We evaluated the company and did a prospectus. We had several offers of capital and chose one that left us in charge with a voting majority." He had £16.1m from NatWest and £8m from Montague Private Equity (part of HSBC). Venture capital companies wanted 30% return within three to five years.

CentreWest went for a Management and Employee Buy-Out (MEBO) led by the four directors and the seven general managers, known as "The Magnificent Seven". Some shares went to the equity providers and some to the employees. David Brown was one of the General Managers and thought this a very good investment. He wanted a share of it, suggesting 1% of the total. But Peter Hendy told him, "You don't want to risk your house on this," to which David replied, "Yes I do!" However, he had to settle for less. He remembers the meetings with lawyers late into the evening to sign the huge documents which no one had the chance to read properly!

Peter Hendy adds, "We wanted to include the staff, but the trade union didn't know what they were doing – they were against privatisation and were coming up with ideas of workers' control. Some staff wanted workers' control, some wanted workers' shares. The Trade Union members and lay officials were all over the place. Some opposed management purchase

LBL logos were quickly removed from CentreWest's fleet following sale of the company. Routemasters at Westbourne Park were given Gold Arrow fleetnames, and RML 2405 is seen in Oxford Street in February 1996. (Roger Torode)

185 "The trade union were against privatisation and were coming up with ideas of workers' control. Some staff wanted workers' control, some wanted workers' shares."

because they didn't like the managers and they wanted them to be punished. They had no view on the other potential buyers that they didn't know, they just objected to those they did know."

He was well aware that he would not get the company cheaply and worked out what he should offer, the 5% management preference making it more likely that he would succeed. He suggests that some of the other MDs felt that the 5% preference allowed them to bid more cheaply, and so they were outbid and lost their company.

Their first indicative bid for CentreWest was £22.5m. Peter delivered the final bid of £25.6m himself by hand, consciously increased from £25.5 million in case someone else bid that same round figure.

CentreWest issued free shares to their staff, who were given certificates entitling them to about 12% of the company's share capital. Their shares were held in trust, and the longer serving staff got more. Peter Hendy's statement at the time was that, "The future of our company depends on the hard work, effort and commitment of our staff. It is therefore right that they should be able to participate in CentreWest's success as shareholders as well as employees." He recalls that, "Everyone made a load of money, but in the end seven or eight union members would not take any."

CentreWest also bid for London Northern and London Central. They were shortlisted for the London Northern purchase and met the management – "An interesting experience!" says Peter. The London Northern trade union objected to CentreWest and tried to interfere to get the company sold to its management, who were not successful as described below. Peter Hendy thought his colleague MDs had not properly assessed the value of their companies. Some were bidding based on the prices of the NBC sales, but the London companies were very good at generating cash and you had to raise venture capital.

East London and Selkent
On 6 September East London and Selkent were sold to Stagecoach for £42.2m, £28.9m for East London and £13.3m for Selkent. Stagecoach had been the UK's largest bus group and with this purchase, it became so again. Its fleet increased by 30% and turnover by 50%.

Roger Bowker was Managing Director of East London. They had put together a strong bid for their company with full employee participation. They were a good team who worked well together. They took advice on the value of the company and Roger was very confident of the price that they were bidding with the 5% discount. It was to be a Management and Employee buyout (MEBO) and they had had meetings with the drivers and their wives, renting a local hotel on three occasions to meet them all with presentations from the Directors. As a result, they had pledges totalling £2 million from the staff. The unions were also co-operative.

During the presentations to staff they were warning them that, "If you don't back us and it goes wrong, you might be eaten up by Stagecoach!" Paul Lynch recalls that, "The talk in the canteen was, if the management buyout didn't succeed, 'As long as it's anybody but Stagecoach.' Nobody knew anything about Stagecoach, but because of their reputation, nobody wanted to be bought by them." The East London managers had had to show the other bidders around the company, though Roger Bowker did not meet Brian Souter until later.

The management bid was for £28 million, the maximum they could arrange with the bankers, and a high sum compared to other companies.

Selling Selkent for a good price was a particular challenge to Mike Heath. "Selkent was the problem. The management team bid was low – they had decided that it wasn't worth very much."

Mike Clayton, Selkent's Finance Director, was leading the buyout team. "Selkent was definitely a viable company in a very competitive situation. The volume was constrained by all the competition. It wasn't going to be the most valuable of the companies for sale. There was more competition for the local bus routes than anyone else had." Mike remembers there was a problem getting financial backers. This seemed to be different compared to other companies, but Selkent had an older management team, and not all the team were participating. Bryan Constable was approaching retirement and stood back from the privatisation. So the management bid was low and outside purchasers were more interested in the other companies. With 10 companies on offer, Selkent was no-one's first choice.

Norman Cohen was Chair of Selkent. "I think that large sections of Selkent were not particularly profitable, but that is surprising because you would have thought that it is good bus territory." When Bexleybus was won by London Central, it had chopped a large chunk out of Selkent. Bryan Constable says he had achieved the lowest unit costs in the ten LBL companies. He had to have the lowest, to cope with the competition – as the TU said, it was the "rush to the bottom". He considered Selkent to be a difficult area where there was strong competition and costs had to be kept low. "The Selkent area has no Underground. The area was seen as a happy hunting ground for making loads of money for bus operators as there was no tube. But people ruined themselves coming into the area and expecting it to be easy – Boro'line, Durham Travel, and others."

Mike Heath continues, "Brian Souter wanted to buy two companies and these two were close enough for management benefits to be achieved, but not for them to be a cause for competition concern because the river Thames ran between them. So I persuaded Brian Souter of the synergy with East London because both operated Leyland Titan buses."

There was tremendous disappointment in East London when the bid failed and the company was sold to Stagecoach, and there was concern about the reputation of Stagecoach. Barry Arnold recalls that, "Roger Bowker was very angry with Clive Hodson and threatened to seek a Judicial Review, but Clive was anxious to get rid of Selkent and the only other offer of £9 million for Selkent was too low. Brian Souter bid £42.2 million for both companies. This was represented as £28.9m for East London and £13.3 million for Selkent. We were not able or willing to offer more than £28m, and if we had said £29 million the Stagecoach offer would just have been represented as £30 million and £12 million." They therefore did not feel they could win this point.

"We had the Trade Union onside, and we might not have sold out to one of the major groups as quickly as the other companies did. It would have been employee owned, based on what James Freeman did at Provincial. The employees together would have owned as much as the Board. Everybody would have had the chance to be involved. The Steering Committee included the four Directors and a group of four garage trade union people." Each of the directors would have needed to put in around £50,000, and Barry was ready to remortgage his house.

Paul Lynch says that Roger Bowker was very mild mannered, and the angriest that Paul ever saw him was when he got the news that the MEBO had failed. There were rumours that the East London bid had been better than Stagecoach, but the Stagecoach bid for East London and Selkent together was better than the two management bids – so they had been let down by 'those failures' at Selkent. He remembers attending the photocall at Hyde Park Corner with the East London and Stagecoach Directors. Roger had stomped across to Clive Hodson and showed his anger at what was supposed to be a celebration!

Clive Hodson travelled back from the photocall with them. "We went back in a taxi to Broadway and I never sat with four glummer blokes. I mean it was a great team, and Roger said, 'Look, can you assure me Clive that we did fail to meet the 5%'. I said, 'Roger, I could not tell you otherwise, that you did not meet the criteria, and that's why Stagecoach got it."

Mike Clayton was not surprised when Selkent was sold elsewhere. "A lot of people half expected this. A number of companies would obviously go to their management, but LT would not sell all of them to their management, and you also knew some of the key players were wanting to get into London. Stagecoach was doubling in size every 18 months at that time. It grew quickly in the three years I was there and it changed, becoming quite corporate."

Bryan Constable immediately felt the effect of the Stagecoach takeover. On holiday in the Scilly Isles, he received legal documents in the post which he was required to sign with a legal witness and return immediately. He was not to return to Selkent or any of its premises or events. When he phoned a colleague, he was told that they were emptying his office of all personal possessions, which would be returned to him. He would not be allowed in the building. But others are not surprised at Stagecoach immediately deciding who would stay and who would go and taking decisive action.

Stagecoach announced the purchase in a letter to shareholders on 9 September, noting that operating margins at East London had been modest whilst those at Selkent had been only marginal. The Board believed that these acquisitions presented Stagecoach with significant opportunities to improve performance, and that they gave the Group a substantial presence in the Greater London area. In his history of the company, 'Stagecoach', Christian Wolmar suggests that Brian Souter would have wanted to bid for the whole of London Buses, but was not allowed to under the rules which restricted any company to buying a maximum of two of the 10 subsidiaries. But, "In a canny move, (Souter) bid for one of the best companies, East London, in combination with a real dud, Selkent, which had long been a poor performer for LT."

Roger Bowker felt let down by the sales process, but acknowledges that "Mike Heath and Ian Barlex were doing a job in a difficult position and they had to be scrupulously fair to all bidders. They couldn't have been more fair to the management teams but they had to be above everything."

Jean Harris was General Manager at Bow and Stratford and remembers the disappointment; they really didn't expect it. They had worked hard to get the business in shape and to involve the staff. They had had advice from various successful privatised companies including Moir Lockhead at GRT Bus Group and some had hoped that, if they did not achieve a MEBO, GRT – which became Firstgroup – would buy it. Stagecoach had a reputation at the time of being ruthless which Jean didn't feel comfortable with. At the same time, London Buses was recruiting for a new post of Communications Manager which Jean applied for and was successful. She was however pleased to see East London prosper under Stagecoach's ownership.

Barry Arnold recalls, "We were disappointed to

187 Brian Souter would have wanted to bid for the whole of London Buses, but was not allowed to under the rules which restricted any company to buying a maximum of two of the 10 subsidiaries.

East London and Selkent buses received Stagecoach fleetnames which, on Routemasters, were in gold. Stagecoach East London RML2272 heads toward Marble Arch pursued by a Metroline bus on the 6. The young man on the platform shows how passengers liked to travel on open-platform buses in the days when they were permitted to. (Keith Wood)

lose the bid, and there was trepidation about the reputation of Stagecoach. We expected blood-letting when the company took over. But Brian Souter was not daft, and he could see that this London operation was different. He had a lot of faith in Roger Bowker, and the company's results were good. He did not want to stir things up, not initially anyway." Barry found Stagecoach good to deal with – if everything was ok they did not interfere. This was a breath of fresh air compared to London Buses. While LT claimed it had strong buying power, LT's central purchasing did not get good deals. Under Stagecoach, East London got huge savings on fuel, tyres, paint and buses.

Roger Bowker was bitterly disappointed at the time but he admits that he was very wrong on Stagecoach. "The first time I met Brian Souter, he was superb – an incredible person." Martin Stoggell, the East London Finance Director, was also immediately impressed. They had had to produce lots of huge pages of reports to London Buses every four weeks. What Brian Souter wanted was two sheets of paper every four weeks. They had had a good relationship with London Buses and its Directors who had supported them, but Brian Souter brought a different dimension. He made very quick decisions and within a short time it became very enjoyable. They quickly felt that if they were to be owned by anyone then it was tremendous that they were owned by Stagecoach.

"When Stagecoach arrived, the smartest move they made was that they sorted out the pension issue for the staff very quickly and gave them a very good package. This made the staff very confident. Stagecoach were always very courteous. Everything they did they did properly and all us four Directors were very impressed. It was clear that they had done their due diligence, that they trusted the management team and wanted them to stay on. It was a joy – they had clearly done their homework on us." Brian Cox, an Executive Director of Stagecoach, came in as chairman. He was very supportive and decisions were made very quickly.

Paul Lynch, who had moved to East London when London Forest closed, remembers that Stagecoach had a scheme which gave free shares to staff twice a year, a proportion of the profits, distributed to staff at all levels. The staff would also receive a dividend on those shares, which until staff built up a decent number of them could, of course, be quite small, and they would all receive a cheque for this amount. The longer term staff were used to this and, with the build-up of their shares, could receive a useful amount each time as a dividend.

The regular distribution of shares and dividend followed very closely after East London was taken over by Stagecoach, and before anyone was told about the scheme. As a result, within a few days of the takeover all the East London staff suddenly received a cheque for a minute amount, around 27p, as dividend for a small number of shares for a very short period. It was in fact a good scheme, but it had not yet been explained to the staff. "The reaction, obviously," says Paul, was, "Are they taking the mickey?" He remembers being in Barry Arnold's office the next day when Barry opened his envelope, and he could read the shock in Barry's face when he saw the cheque. Paul had already received his, and he teased Barry, "You were on the verge of being a multi-millionaire, and instead, you're holding a cheque for 27p!" This is the only occasion Paul can remember Barry Arnold swearing!

Leaside
On 29 September, Leaside was sold to the Cowie Group. This was the highest valued company at £29.5m.

Preparing a management bid for Leaside was a long and tortuous process. Steve Clayton and his team came to a bid of £26.5 million, which was what they thought it was worth and what they could raise. He was not willing to worsen staff pay and conditions more than they had already been. Some advisers had told him he would have to do this in order to win the company, but Steve was clear, "I'm not doing that. If I have to do that, then I won't do it."

As part of the sale process they had to show potential bidders around their company, but only Cowie came, so he knew who else was in the bidding.

"We fought a good fight and we've lost. If you don't want me or any of my senior team, just say so now and we'll get out of your hair."

John Trayner recalls, "The four Directors wanted the three Garage General Managers involved in the management buy-out team, so we came in also and were called the Magnificent Seven! I don't know how magnificent it was – in fairness it was Steve Clayton and Robert Newson who put the bid together and dealt with the advisers. They left us to run the business with Mark Yexley and Ted Milburn. We ran a lot of communications exercises with the staff and trade union about what it would mean, and what part they would play in it."

Steve and Robert put the Business Plan together and had advice from a City firm of merchant bankers. They were given advice on a contingency fee basis – if they were successful in buying the company, then the advisers would take a fee, but if not they would pay nothing and the Directors were not liable. They had a good Business Plan and the financial backing to buy the company.

But Leaside was sold to the Cowie group, based in Sunderland where it had been founded in 1938. Cowie already owned Grey-Green which they had purchased in 1980. Though the two companies were physically close to each other, they continued to be managed as separate entities.

"So we didn't win. Cowie beat us," said Steve Clayton. He learned soon afterwards from Gordon Hodgson, the Chief Executive of Cowie, that they were determined to buy Leaside specifically – it was a good company and it was on their patch with Grey-Green in the same area. Whatever Leaside had bid, Cowie would have outbid them – Cowie would have simply added another million pounds. "If I'd known that, I'd have saved myself a lot of heartache", said Steve. He was, he admitted in hindsight, too quick to get off the starting blocks. Several people had complimented him on his business plan – it was a good and honest plan.

Mark Yexley recalls the day they were sold, "We all trooped down to Freshfields to sign the documents with Cowie, and then went to Hyde Park Corner for pictures. It was typical that the Leaside bus, one of our newest, was a J plated Olympian from Stamford Hill, whereas Cowie brought a brand-new bus off route 24. This immediately showed the difference between the public and private sectors."

Two days later, the company lawyer, Chris Applegarth, and John Pycroft, the Grey-Green MD, came down to see them. Steve said to them, "Look, we fought a good fight and we've lost. If you don't want me or any of my senior team, just say so now and we'll take what we're entitled to and we'll get out of your hair." This led, two days later, to Steve having a pot of tea in London with the Chief Executive who made it clear that, "We bought this company because it is a good company and we want to keep the management team in place." Steve was very relieved and went back to tell his team. As a result, they gave their heart and soul to it, and it became far more profitable than many of the companies.

Were Leaside given the chance to match Cowie's bid? Yes, but they realised that Cowie had set its heart on getting Leaside. "When we wised up to the reality that whatever we bid, Cowie would top it by £1m, we ran out of gas," says Mark Yexley. "This was a bit of a backhanded compliment, of course, but it was a shame that we would miss out. If our motivation had been to get rich quick, it would have been tragic – but we just wanted to carry on running Leaside. We believed in it, and it had an emotional tag. When Cowie bought us, it was not the end of the world. It became clear that they had huge respect for us as a management team and would leave us to carry on doing what we would have been doing if it had been a management buyout. Also, they were backing it with serious money, for example buying South London.

"With tendering, the Cowie Group in London had moved from coaches to buses and then, of course, they won route 24, on which they made an absolute fortune. They were suffering difficulties with their car dealerships as the manufacturers wanted to dictate how they sold the cars, how they presented their outlets and so on, while LT was throwing money at them. So they decided to get more into buses, with privatisation."

Robert Newson had heard on the grapevine that Cowie were extremely keen to get Leaside. He understood that this was because Grey-Green had done so well from London Transport tenders. The early contracts had included an annual RPI +1% inflation uplift, put in by LT because, in the long term, wages go up more than inflation. But in the private sector, suppliers are expected to reduce prices from year to year through productivity improvements. So these contracts were a golden goose – Grey-Green didn't put wages up more than inflation, their costs were under control, and they were doing rather well on them. But being located in the middle of Leaside's territory they were worried that after deregulation and privatisation they would be squeezed out by Leaside, who could have competed them off the road. So they determined to buy Leaside, which they knew was well run and had a lot of potential. After a time, the Grey-Green depot at Stamford Hill closed and was absorbed into Leaside, and then the site was sold.

So the Leaside team no longer had to put up the money themselves, nor worry about mortgaging their homes! "We no longer had London Buses Head Office on our case every week, and it was fairly hands-off management from Gordon Hodgson – they were happy to let us get on with things," says Robert Newson.

"We had wised up to the reality that whatever we bid, Cowie would top it by £1m. This was a bit of a backhanded compliment, of course."

Metroline

On 7 October Metroline was sold for £20m to a management and employee team led by Declan O'Farrell, the Managing Director.

"In early 1994, we were doing three jobs – we were running the company, we were selling the company, and we were buying the company," explains Declan.

"Firstly, we had to carry on running the operations. London Buses continued having Board meetings right up to the start of the bid process, they wanted the usual monthly reports telling them what we were doing with public money, making sure that we were delivering our mileage and that we were within budget.

"Secondly, we had to give a huge amount of assistance to selling the company with our London Transport hats on, to provide documentation and supporting information that ended up in the data room. Everything either had to be validated, or you had to make a statement about it being an opinion. We had to supply most of the information, and then we had to be interrogated by the lawyers to establish verification before those documents could go into the Data Room. So that was our second job, right up to the start of the actual bidding.

"And of course the third task was to buy the company. That was a separate discipline and a major pressure on us and I'm sure on all the other management teams too. From late 1992 we were instructed to ensure that we observed very strict demarcation lines between working for our employer and working for ourselves. Anything we did towards the bid should not impact on the day job and must be done outside normal working hours. For a Managing Director like me running a 24/7 operation, it's difficult to know when the normal hours finish – there is no such thing. So it was difficult, but we all understood the principles involved. Once the first bids were going in we were allowed to spend daylight hours on them – they accepted that it would be impossible for a management team to be part of a bid process and also completely divorce that from running the operations, it was only one set of people. They then also allowed us a certain amount of funding to purchase advice and support to prepare our bid.

"We decided that we would split the executive team, so Gordon (Tennant) and Mike (Smith), the Commercial and Engineering Directors, would run the company while John (Golledge), the Finance Director, and myself would turn most of our attention to the bid process. And that's how we ran for several months, more or less up until when we got the company.

"Then came the day when we had to put the first bids in. Ours went in at £9–10m to buy the company. We knew they were expecting around £100m for all the companies, we knew what percentage we were of the market, so that would meet their expectations. The process was Bid, Shortlist, Preferred Bidder, Sale. And then, shock, horror, when LT announced who was on the shortlists, one company didn't have a shortlist; one company was recommended for sale immediately. CentreWest, next door, had put in a bid of more than £20m! It was a huge number and they were accepted as preferred bidder. The thinking behind it was that if they got a really good price for the first one, that would set the marker for everybody else, but that marker was about twice as much as other companies were expecting. Then all of a sudden, Hendy was bidding over £20m! But it quickly set a marker and of course they went on to do the deal.

"So we were asked to reconsider our price, and we had a meeting with Mike Heath, Ian Barlex and their team, and they suggested that maybe our initial bid was a bit on the light side, and without giving us numbers they were trying to steer us to up it. So we went back with a revised bid, and then we were asked to come back and make a final best price. But by that stage, we knew who the shortlisted people were for Metroline – they were British Bus, MTL, and us.

"We had also put in a bid for London Northern, but were not shortlisted. LT didn't think it was right for us to get the company next door – that wasn't going to be allowed. I think other companies also expressed interest in London Northern.

"Before the final bids we had to set up meetings with the shortlisted bidders, with our sales hats on. There were two rounds of meetings. In the first, their teams came in and interviewed the Directors, and we were able to ask them questions about their plans and all the rest of it. They knew that we would be bidding as well. And then they had a meeting with the trade unions and, of course, in order to play fair, we had to have a meeting with our own trade unions. So the two outside bidders were presented to the trade unions, and we had to present to our trade unions – we didn't have to present to ourselves!

"The Chief Executive of British Bus came, and he brought along the Managing Director of one of the former London Country subsidiaries from south London. There were two of them and they interviewed us, and asked questions about what we wanted to do and what we didn't want to do, and we asked them what their intentions were. I suppose it became pretty clear, talking to them, that when you stopped looking at their mouths and looked at their eyes, that John Golledge and I didn't have a future with British Bus.

Opposite Metroline's notice to staff.

"In early 1994, we were doing three jobs – we were running the company, we were selling the company, and we were buying the company."

To all Metroline employees

PRIVATISATION – *The way forward*

Today, Steven Norris, the Minister for Transport in London will publicly launch the privatisation process for London Buses Ltd.

Metroline is one of the ten London Buses subsidiaries to be offered for sale and will take its place in a line up of buses in Central London.

Metroline Directors are proposing a Management/Employee bid for the company which we hope will give every member of staff the opportunity to have a stake in the future of the business.

We believe that with the continued efforts of all employees, Metroline will survive and succeed in the private sector and continue to deliver a high quality service to its customers.

A steering committee comprising representatives of Metroline management and employees has already been formed to consider the bid process and the interests of the staff.

We intend to advise you on a regular basis of developments in the process.

Declan O'Farrell
Managing Director

John Golledge
Finance Director

Mike Smith
Engineering Director

Gordon Tennant
Commercial Director

24 March 1994

"When MTL came in there were about fourteen of them. There was their Chairman, a very nice soft-spoken man, and the MD Dominic Brady, and then they had members of their trade union and others because they ran their operation as a co-operative and what they really wanted was for us to join the cooperative and the touchy-feely Socialist Liverpool way of life, which of course actually sounded very nice. They were a really pleasant group of people, but when they left we thought, how could you work for a setup like that, because the management were clearly not in control – all the big decisions were being made by the staff. You just couldn't see them coming down into the London environment – how were they ever going to take a tough decision. So, we thought that it sounded great but it's just a recipe for disaster.

"So then we made our presentation to our own unions, and of the three bidders we came third! They thought that our presentation was pitiful, our answers to their questions were feeble, and all in all they were majorly disappointed by their management. Of the three, we were rubbish. London Transport warned us that, 'You really missed a great trick there to get your trade unions on side.' The trade union were angry and very disappointed with us, but in the funny sort of upside-down world that we live in, that disappointment actually told us that they were quite supportive of us. They were telling us, 'You should have done a lot better. You could have screwed this up.'

"Then we put the best and final bids in. We bid about £20m and the process carried on. The bid document was pages long, and included confirmation that we had the insurance and the pension fund in place, and that we had the financial backing – it was not just a number. That whole process was probably one of the greatest intellectual, mental, and emotional challenges I think I have ever had, and I think the MDs carried more than the rest of the team, but certainly John Golledge, my Finance Director, carried a huge load.

"A week or two after we had been named preferred bidder, British Bus made a direct approach to Steven Norris. They didn't win any of the companies and complained that they thought there had been a bit of unfairness – I don't know what the reason was. They were prepared to up their bid to match ours, plus a bit more. The issue came back to Clive Hodson with the question, 'Are there grounds here to review your decision?' I have often wondered whether this put them under a significant amount of pressure to change their mind. If British Bus is going to offer slightly more money, it's public money, why shouldn't they accept it? I have subsequently found out that their view was, 'No. We have had the process, we have followed it scrupulously, there is nothing in the process that can be questioned and this is the outcome. The management team is preferred bidder. We are going to stand by our decision.' I have always been grateful to them for that, because they could have buckled, but they didn't. They followed their duties scrupulously.

"In the preparation to make a bid, we needed to assemble a professional bid team. So we advertised, interviewed and then appointed a Financial Adviser, Ernst and Young, who would provide the financial advice, do the financial modelling, effectively provide the assurance to the bankers and venture capitalists, if relevant, and help us with the process generally. They would confirm that the numbers stacked up and sort out the tax issues, the share schemes and trusts, and individual directors' financing. So they were quite heavily involved. We also had to appoint our legal advisers, so again we advertised, we interviewed and we appointed a city firm. So as we started the bid process, we had these two sets of advisers.

"The whole process was a bit like a free for all, as 10 companies were all trying to do the same thing, we were all interviewing the same professional advisers. The professional advisers were also interviewing us in order to work out which teams stood the best chance of being successful. Apart from the small allowance underwritten by government, the vast bulk of their time and cost would be at risk – that is, they would only receive their full fee if the bid was eventually successful.

"Now, I'm generalising a bit, but I can say that those two advisers were definitely on our side. We had to negotiate contracts with them, but basically once those deals were signed we had them on our side and committed to help us succeed.

"Everyone else we dealt with had their own different priorities. We had Pat Mahon and the trade unions negotiating for an employee public company. Their view was, we want Metroline to succeed, but we want it to be an employee share company. And if they couldn't have that, then all they wanted was the majority shareholding! There were of course three sets of TU negotiations – operating, engineering and salaried staff. For pensions, they all came together in a combined committee led by a full time official. We were negotiating with them about terms and conditions – we weren't proposing any great changes apart from pensions, and those negotiations went on right up until just before we signed the deal with LT.

"To finance our bid we needed to appoint bankers, but as the bid prices increased we needed to change providers. We originally had high street bankers supporting us for our initial £10m bid, but when the price went up to £20m, the maximum they were prepared to lend us against all our assets was around £12m. So we didn't have a banker and our bid had hit the buffers! We had a huge gap, but Ernst and Young managed to bring in Societe Generale who were opening up a new portfolio of transport investments and were willing to meet our requirement of around £16m. Their information demands were just enormous, and we would never have done the deal with them had it not been for John Golledge, our Finance Director, who almost single-handedly dealt with them and their lawyers. He had to, effectively, negotiate every single document with them, in total more than eighty of them! So Societe Generale were good eggs in that they came up with the money, but they were very hard work because they kept on demanding more and more – warranties, sureties, trigger points, and different fees for different tasks – it just went on and on, and right up to the week that we actually signed the deal we were *documents* away from having a deal with them. A couple of all night sessions and special bank committee meetings eventually cleared all hurdles by the Wednesday of completion week. We had our debt provider in place.

"But we still needed to raise more finance because the bank funding was a few million pounds short of the agreed purchase price. The shortfall was made up by a venture capital house called Granville Private Equity and they became shareholders in Metroline. They were on our side to the extent that they wanted the deal to work for us and also for their investors. But they were also very demanding in the sense that, right up until the night before we completed the deal, we were still negotiating the final details of their investor agreement.

"And then a terrible 'wobbler' came up a couple of weeks before completion, as the companies were being sold and shortly after the engineering problems at South London came to light, so tensions were high. LT carried out a scan of Metroline's finances which showed up an additional bank account holding a large sum of money. Such accounts had been outlawed some years before after an unrelated fraud case, but Metroline had an approved Escrow account with a substantial sum in it awaiting the outcome of a disputed industrial tribunal. Once the facts were established relative peace resumed. But the good news was my head, having been in the noose, was now out of the noose! The whole thing was teetering at that stage and Clive was talking about sacking us all! So, were nerves on edge? I would say!"

"So we were still being held to account for anything that was happening in the business. We were still having to answer question after question and going into meetings on this and that matter, and getting all the documentation right.

"It all came to a head at the end of September when we came to the last week and still had a lot of issues to solve. London Transport told us on the Wednesday evening that they were ready, but the last five days were full of negotiations with our own investors and bankers.

"For some time John Golledge and I had been going up to London most weeks, but in that last week I went at 7 o'clock on Monday morning and I got back home at 2 o'clock the following Saturday morning, and in that time I notched up, I think, 14 hours sleep. John Golledge notched up about 10 or 11 hours – he had two through-the-night experiences, and I had one.

"The reason he had less sleep than I did was that he was going through these 80 or more documents with the venture capitalists. The key one was the Investor Agreement, which is quite a thick document because it is based on every investment that ever went wrong in the history of man, every possibility being covered by some paragraph or other. He went through the night more or less on Monday, while I went off and had a couple of hours sleep.

"But there was still the outstanding issue of gaining staff/trade union support for the deal and that was one of the outstanding conditions from our private equity partner who wanted to be assured that the business would not be disrupted by industrial action after the deal was done. The TU were still pressing for a majority controlling interest and they wanted the directors to have nothing at all, other than what they were entitled to as employees. I think they had conceded that maybe the venture capital company might want some shares! The venture capital company was of the view that the trade union could not have a majority and they would walk away from any deal like that. They wanted the management to have the majority and they didn't mind if the staff had a 10% stake – they thought that was a good deal. So we had to convince them that giving the staff 25% was actually a very good idea, because it was a way of offering them a stake in the future of the organisation, and actually it made a lot of sense.

"Granville's bottom line was that they were prepared to go along with this as long as there wasn't a blocking percentage, and as long as management retained overall control. So Pat Mahon and one or two of his team came and met with Granville, their managing director and two business advisers and us, and they went eyeball to eyeball to try and get an agreement we could all accept. We had no idea how it would play out. Our job was to get them in the same room and to allow each side to put their positions. We thought it best that we just stay quiet and maybe help out with any points of clarification. Basically Granville said that they thought that it was a good deal, they thought that what the management were offering was extraordinarily generous, and not necessary, but they understood and agreed with the

---

193 "The trade union were still pressing for a majority controlling interest and they wanted the directors to have nothing at all, other than what they were entitled to as employees."

management motivation for it, and the union ought to be pleased. But if they didn't accept it, that was the end, there was no bid going in. Pat Mahon stayed respectful and made their case but we sensed that they knew that the management were not in a position to make any further concessions and if the TU said 'No way', the whole thing would collapse. Pat called for an adjournment to talk to his colleagues, and when he came back he very quietly said, 'If that is the way it will be, that's the way it will be.'

"So that last week, we were negotiating with our debt provider, we were continuing to negotiate with our venture capital provider, we had the trade union still to reach agreement with, and London Transport who we were continuing to negotiate with, and there were lots of details that needed to be resolved – and we were still running the business.

"By Wednesday, we had the staff side and the bank side sorted, and we thought we had come to the end of the negotiations with London Transport, who had all their documents complete. We were sure about all the legalities, and the tax, because we had been spending nights going through all the documents, not least because a lot of the bus fleet had been bought on grant, and grant funding gave the buses a different value.

"And then Granville withdrew their team and brought in two new guys that we didn't know. One of them was a 'heavyweight', and his job was to renegotiate the deal from the beginning. So we went back into negotiations with them and that went on all the way through Thursday night and Friday morning. Granville wanted the best deal for their investors and they wanted to test our resolve to 'walk away' if the terms became too onerous to sign up to – the breaking point – a place where most serious negotiations get to before both sides agree. They proceeded to question all the key elements of the deal, suggesting along the way that they had to get authorisation from their Board to sanction the investment and that the terms weren't attractive enough for them to recommend the deal, let alone believe that the Board would give their approval. As they went through it, and they pressed for more, I was tempted maybe to give them something, but John Golledge was very very angry, because he felt that this was a gross betrayal of the purchase. Anyway, I can't remember making any substantial changes to the deal but the whole process took us through a third all night session.

"So on Friday morning, sometime around 10 o'clock, we phoned up London Transport and said, 'We are ready,' and they said, 'Come along.' They

The celebration at Harrow bus station, with the Staff and Management Buy-Out team, which included the four Directors with Engineering and Operating staff and supervisor representatives. (Courtesy Gordon Tennant)

> "So that last week, we were negotiating with our debt provider, we were continuing to negotiate with our venture capital provider, we had the trade union still to reach agreement with, and London Transport who we were continuing to negotiate with – and we were still running the business."

were using Freshfields solicitors, in huge offices just off Fleet Street, and as we walked in we met the MTL crowd walking out. We both said to each other, 'What are you doing here?' but they wouldn't tell us and we wouldn't tell them.

"We went to a vast room way up in the building with an enormous table in the middle which must have been 8 or 9 feet wide and at least 25 feet long. And when we rolled in, all the directors had to be there to sign, the venture capitalists and the bankers were there, and there must have been a dozen of us. We took up quite a small area of this huge table. All along the back were all the London Transport lawyers and their advisers and all the Freshfields people. There must have been 40 or more people in there. We sat and had a bit of small talk and so on, and the partner from Freshfields then said, 'Right, we're here to do the business, and this is what we have to do.' There was an awful lot of signing to be done, and the Directors had got to do most of it. So then, for the next couple of hours, we just signed over 100 documents. And every now and then, others had to do it as well.

"But as we got into the documents, something happened which led to a perceived difference between ourselves and our venture capital partner, and so the signing stopped and we were invited to go into a separate room to sort out our differences. We spent time in there negotiating and finally agreed what it was that we had agreed, and we went back in and carried on with the signing. An astonishingly stressful experience.

"By about 2 o'clock in the afternoon we finished, having started at about 10 in the morning, but all the documents had to be witnessed by all the representatives of all the banks, and based on the banks' lawyers being satisfied that all the documents were signed and in the right order, and the same with the venture capitalists. They were then able to instruct their people to move the funds. Everybody had to wait while the funds were moved, so we sat around chatting for 20 minutes or half an hour. Eventually the partner came back into the room and she stood at the end of the table and she said, "Ladies and Gentlemen, we are complete." And then it was handshakes all round, and everybody was friends again, we were all back in the same industry working together for a great future and all the rest of it. Whereas up until that point we were still daggers drawn! So then we made our way back to our lawyers' offices on Friday afternoon.

"We got the message back to Harrow that the deal was done and so there were great celebrations there – they had an early day and all went down the local pub. When we arrived at Harrow there was nobody in the office, so we went and joined them and had a good old drink up. I phoned my missus and said, 'The deal is done, great, I'm not coming home, I'm going down the pub.' I hadn't seen her since Monday morning, but I wanted to be with the staff celebrating – it's got to be done! So she said, 'Well, we'll join you,' and she got some of the kids and a couple of her brothers, and just as the staff celebration was winding down, my family turned up and we decided we had better go and have a nice meal, and we got home at about 2 o'clock in the morning.

"I don't remember much about going to bed, and I had not had a good night's sleep for days, but I went to bed at 2 o'clock and at 7 o'clock I was wide awake and I had this awful feeling in the pit of my stomach. I was talking to myself, as you do, and I said, 'You've done it now! What have you done? What have you let yourself in for? You've now got to deliver on all the things you have said you will do!' I woke up and I couldn't get back to sleep.

"You can survive on 14 hours in the week, and John managed on even less. So come the Monday morning, I sat the Directors down in my office in Harrow, and I told them what I had thought on Saturday morning and they were all feeling much the same. And I said, 'Right, well the good news is that we don't have to report to London Transport any more. We've got a stakeholder, and we have an employee trust to report to. So from today, we have to very quickly change all the stuff we are doing. So all the 'Twice a Week' reports, and all the management reports, all the rest of it that had been going up to London Transport, we junked. We instituted what we called the Monday morning meeting, and basically we ran the company from that. We all got together every Monday morning, decided what we were going to do, went away and did it, and met again the following Monday. Of course we all saw each other regularly during the week, and then once a month we had the management accounts, and we had the Board meeting with representatives from the venture capitalists. And the amount of oversight diminished by 90% – they were trusting us to get on with it, and we got on with it!"

The Metroline team were elated, a wonderful experience. Gordon Tennant had to remortgage the house to raise his share of the purchase price, which was scary, but he had worked with Declan and John for a long time; he trusted their judgement completely as they understood the finances well. He had absolute trust in their judgement. Of course, he woke up a couple of days later thinking "S**t! – this had better work!"

A key factor was to have the involvement and support of the workforce; Pat Mahon drove a hard bargain but the advantage was that with him you knew where you stood. When he said they would do a deal you knew it would be done and honoured. This

"Eventually the partner came back into the room. She stood at the end of the table and said, 'Ladies and Gentlemen, we are complete.'"

Metroline's notice to passengers. (Courtesy Declan O'Farrell)

METROLINE

THIS BUS UNDER NEW OWNERSHIP!
No change for our passengers

Metroline, North West London's leading bus company, is now in private ownership.

On the 5th October 1994, Metroline's employees - drivers, conductors, engineers, clerical staff, supervisors and managers - became joint owners of the company.

> **We would like to take the opportunity to reassure all our passengers that the privatisation of Metroline will not affect you in any way.**

Metroline will continue to operate all of its routes throughout North West London. The bus fares and timetables will not change. These and the management of bus stops, shelters and stations will remain the responsibility of London Transport Buses.

Metroline is committed to the new Bus Passenger's Charter and to meeting the targets set by the Government's Department of Transport.

We believe that ownership by the current management and workforce means a continuity of service and a continued emphasis on improving the quality of service to you.

Metroline plays a vital role in the community. Our aim remains to provide a reliable, safe and comfortable journey to everyone who uses our buses.

METROLINE *locally owned, locally run.*

---

was necessary for it to be a joint enterprise – without it, it would not have flown. Metroline had set up a privatisation steering group with staff representatives involved in order to fully engage them in the major challenges that lay ahead including changes to terms and conditions and establishing a new pension scheme. Metroline took them into their confidence and the meeting with the financial backers gave comfort the plans were realistic and deliverable.

There were many other details to sort out. London Transport was self-insured, so all the newly private companies had to organise insurance. They set up an organisation called Routemaster Reinsurance and every subsidiary had a share in it. It didn't last long because the big groups had their our own schemes and gave 12 months notice, so Metroline had to find an alternative.

The other major issue was pensions. They could not stay in the London Transport Pension Fund, and the requirement was to offer staff a pension broadly

"London Transport itself was self-insured, so all the newly private companies had to organise insurance."

equivalent to the London Transport scheme. The big groups offered their own schemes, whereas the buyout teams had to create their own, which meant that they needed pensions advisers as well. The trade union insisted that it should be the same as the London Transport scheme, but this could not be afforded. Declan adds, "It wasn't the basic pension that was the big issue, it was the provision for taking early pensions, early retirement on grounds of ill-health, and various other benefits. There was no way we could entertain that. So what we did was offer an equivalent pension with harsher other benefits – they were good but not like the London Transport ones. The basic pension was much the same. We opened it on the day that privatisation took effect and we closed it on the same day, so anyone who transferred on privatisation got the broadly equivalent pension. Anyone who joined later went onto a defined contribution scheme. I think the other companies did much the same thing."

London Central
On 18 October London Central was bought by the Go-Ahead Group for £24.5m. The London Central management team remained in place under Douglas Adie. The sale included Camberwell, New Cross and Bexleyheath garages, while Peckham was leased.

London Central had put together a Management Employee Buy Out (MEBO) bid with staff involvement. Douglas Adie recalls that, "Pat Mahon represented the operating staff. He was very pragmatic and wanted to get a good deal for his troops. We had good financial advice but we did not bid high enough." Robin Reynolds recalls the frustration. "We put our bid in, but were told that another bidder was 10% ahead of us. We increased our bid but they were still just ahead. And it happened again! And then Go-Ahead bought the company." Douglas Adie said at the time that the staff were "a bit shattered" at losing to Go-Ahead, but the situation settled and the management team was asked to stay in place. "Go-Ahead was very de-centralised, and London General fitted in well."

London Northern
On 26 October, London Northern was sold for £20.5m to MTL Trust Holdings of Liverpool, including about 320 buses, 1,000 staff and turnover of £27.5m, with garages at Holloway and Potters Bar.

London Central also quickly removed logos from its buses. SP5 was an Optare Spectra, one of 25 delivered in late 1992 and early 1993. (Keith Wood)

"We put our bid in, but were told that another bidder was 10% ahead of us. We increased our bid but they were still just ahead. And it happened again! And then Go-Ahead bought the company."

Norman Kemp had led the management buyout team – all the managers were involved and would have invested in the company. Norman had had five years less than the other MDs to prepare for privatisation, and the race was on. "In London Northern, the troops had not been wound up enough and they thought the company was destined to fail."

Norman knew this would be his biggest challenge to date. He put together a management and employee bid and they had their advisers organised. "It would not have worked if the Trade Union had not been involved – given that it was an LT company, it was right for the staff to be included. You needed the involvement of the ground level troops who contributed most to the company's success. The personnel manager kept the trade union on side – they hadn't had a lot of involvement in MEBOs – others were not as inclusive as we were".

Norman recalls, "Holloway staff were very supportive of our privatisation plans. They could see the benefits as they would get a share in the business. Potters Bar had been less enthusiastic: it was working as a separate unit under different conditions. So it was as if we had two or three separate companies: Potters Bar, Holloway 1 and Holloway 2. It was appropriate that Potters Bar should be left alone to do what it had been doing well for five years – the two garages did not mix, but they didn't need to. We held staff meetings and put together a strong bid, but the only busmen in London who didn't benefit at some stage from all these changes were those at London Northern. They had no financial recognition or reward at any stage."

London Northern also made a bid for Selkent, and CentreWest bid for London Northern. It was an interesting situation, and there were a lot of people hovering. CentreWest were shortlisted for the London Northern purchase and met the management. Peter Hendy recalls that the London Northern trade union objected to CentreWest and tried to interfere to get the company sold to its management, leading to a bitter wrangle. "MTL were unctuously nice to the TU and then changed when they came in."

Mike Heath recalls that the MTL bid was a good one. They came down to London but didn't have lawyers representing them. They asked Mike Heath for a recommendation, so he asked his lawyers to find another company who were good but who they could beat!

Norman Kemp heard that MTL were the preferred bidder in July, three months before the sale date. Preferred bidders were allowed some access to their target in the run up to purchase and at London Northern there were significant tensions as a result, as the company's own management-employee buy-out had been pipped at the post but was still in the background in case the preferred sale failed. Norman felt at the time that MTL had little or no understanding of the regulatory and contractual framework in London, had no feel for the capital's economic and social geography, underestimated the strong 'family' atmosphere which still existed at both Holloway and Potters Bar – and above all did not have their plans worked out. "MTL's relative lack of success with the company would suggest that my impressions then were not far off the mark!"

Mike Heath kept Norman dangling. More than once, when MTL nearly walked out, he was asked if he could improve his bid. He thinks that it "went to the wire" in that they only got the money together at the last minute. MTL paid more than Norman was willing to pay and he left immediately: the day after the sale he was summoned to a hotel in Euston with his Finance Director and told that he no longer had a job. This was not a surprise – he looks back on his London experience as very enriching. He was replaced as MD by MTL's Dominic Brady. Andy Griffiths who remained for a time thinks that MTL later realised that they had paid too much for the company.

London General
On 2 November, London General was sold to a management and employee team under MD Keith Ludeman for just over £28m, including 630 buses, 2,150 staff and a turnover of £52m.

Keith Ludeman had built up London General into a bigger company by the time of privatisation. However, he had £52m turnover and just under £2m

Clive Hodson hands over London General to Keith Ludeman on 2 November 1994. (London Transport Museum)

"Holloway staff were very supportive of our privatisation plans. Potters Bar had been less enthusiastic."

profit. When he went to the City institutions they told him that that he would not be able to raise the money he needed with only £2 million profit on that turnover – he needed £9 million. When he said that two thirds of his costs were staff costs and he had already hit them hard, he was told he would have to do it again. So he started the long process of further changes to staff terms and conditions. He had sessions with the T&GWU at Eastbourne, with the garage representatives, and they talked through the problem.

The Conservatives had just been re-elected for a fourth term under John Major. Keith warned the unions that privatisation was coming and they needed to achieve a solution together or be sold to someone else. "It's either us or Stagecoach, and you know what they're like." They went through a few hoops, with the trade union winding them up saying, "We'd be better off working for them, not you." Eventually they came round, and they negotiated a package for all the operating and engineering staff, changing the way the company worked.

Keith did not make service proposals at that time because there was no need due to the gross cost contracts which covered 70% of the operation. But Clive Hodson had told them that if the block grant drivers continued to be paid what they were being paid, the work might end up with other people. Keith therefore made an agreement with the Union for new conditions, which achieved the buy out of the block grant conditions.

It was an arduous process with a long series of negotiations, but some lighter moments. For one of the trade union sessions, Keith got down to Eastbourne a bit late. He arrived at the reception and saw there was a message for Pat Mahon marked "From Moir Lockhead". At the time, FirstGroup was his chief competition, and being nosy he took a look at it. The note was confirming arrangements for a meeting.

Pat Mahon laughs. "Oh, there were some great times during all this. Ludeman said one day he's not coming down to Eastbourne, and I said, 'If he's not coming down, I'm going home.' So he said, 'All right then, I'll come down.' Then I went to the secretary at the reception and got her to write a phone message, as if from Moir Lockhead to me, saying 'Pat, thanks for coming up to see me,' and arranging the next conversation, from Moir Lockhead. I had her type it out, and she scribbled my name on the envelope and just left the note on the counter, but didn't seal it. I got her to put it in an envelope and when Ludeman came in to check in she just said, 'Can you give this to Mr Mahon.'

"When he comes in, he gets the note, and starts walking slowly towards the dining room. He had a look at it, and he told Martin Elms who said, 'You've got to be fair to Pat, he's got to keep his eggs in separate baskets, and if we don't succeed he has to be ready to deal with the others. Just relax and see how it goes.' Keith found Pat Mahon and said, "We need to talk!" He took him to the pub and went through everything with him, after which Pat said, "There's no need for this!" – it was all a big wind up and Mahon had caught him, hook, line and sinker!

Ludeman and Mahon had a very sparky relationship. "There was something likeable about him," says Pat Mahon, "and I think every manager was scared of him, but they all liked him. You know he had his office painted red, and he had a red seat! A journalist who came to see him said, 'It's the same colour as the buses,' and he replied, 'It's so you can't see the blood on the walls.'

"Ludeman turned out to be the most straightforward and honest of the new managers. Strange, as everyone thought he was the biggest bastard around, and he turned out to be very sincere in wanting to have a management-employee buyout. Of course, the directors were going to make more out of it than anybody else – you understand that from the very beginning.

"He said to me that there would be a key point where the people involved would be on the same take-home pay, though they would be working a little harder for it, but then they were going to have a share in the company. They had the big change in wages and conditions, the New Operating Agreement, which took six weeks. They had everything on the table, and we gave up a week's holidays. Now holidays are the thing that you can get back fairly quickly because another time I would say, 'There'll be no further expense for you this year, but a day's holiday next year probably ties it up.' Things like that are easy to get back.

"We installed games machines in the canteens and had a box and people dropped money in it; it was like a savings box, we saved money and then we bought more shares in the company for the staff and distributed the allocation of the profits, so there were plenty of shares for people to go around.

"Now that became a success, but then you have to be able to repay the capitalists. People in the city don't very often lose money, they want to be able to put a telescope up your rear end to see what your insides are like. They were about making money out of their capital. It was very clear that that was what they were doing. They had it strapped round us. They weren't going to lose any money any way. One investor wanted to see the signed deal on the pay and conditions agreement that would take effect after privatisation before they were prepared to put money in. So along came another session of 'looking each other in the eye', and 'can we trust each other?' Martin Elms and I signed the deal, to take effect the

The London United Busways management and employees, on the launch of the company in December 1988. Metrobus 1069 was painted in an adaptation of the London United Tramways livery. (David Humphrey)

day after privatisation. It went into a safe and we agreed that we would together put a match to it if the deal failed. It started off the new company with cuts in wages, and was not to be seen if London Buses remained in control or if the management-employee buyout wasn't successful. If that happened, we would burn it ourselves. Nobody saw it except the investors."

Part of London General's deal with the trade union for the new terms and conditions was that they would offer as much as possible in share ownership to the staff. They facilitated loans through the Co-op bank so any bus driver could borrow enough to buy 10,000 shares. General Managers had to purchase 20,000 shares and Directors had to be made to sweat! The trade union pushed hard for shared ownership. Pat Mahon again: "Well, it was a bit of a rough ride. The union didn't want to have anything to do with privatisation, and some colleagues wouldn't do that. I said, 'It's going to happen, so it's either going to be some kind of a shared scheme or these boys are going to take it, winner takes all.' So if there's something in it for the drivers …!

"People used to say to me, do you think it's a good idea to put money into this company? I'd say, 'I can't buy shares, but if I could do I would re-mortgage my house because if I was backing anybody it would be his company. He's no fool and he's not going to lose out on this.'"

Keith Ludeman was most concerned that Brian Souter might try to buy his company. He went to great trouble to arrange to see him and eventually they met in Souter's suite at his hotel in London, with Souter in his dressing gown. Keith said he wanted to know whether Brian was interested in London Buses, and if so to keep away from London General. "It'll be no good to you," he said and explained the TU situation. "I can't stop you bidding but I'll make life difficult for you if you do." Brian said, "You need to know I'm not really interested in London General." Keith was so passionate about it. "You have to have complete single-mindedness. I slept, dreamt and ate it for two years. It was very stressful, a life-changing experience."

In the end it was only FirstGroup and the Management Team on the short list for London General. They had to show FirstGroup around the company. Keith had his staff do this, making sure they were shown all the rubbish! "FirstGroup did not win any of the London companies because they were not prepared to pay enough, and then they subsequently paid far more than they might have done for CentreWest."

Keith had approached a number of City institutions and was able to arrange the finance. Montagu Private Equity had apparently decided that they would fund three of the LBL companies and the deal was done on 2 November 1994.

London United

On 5 November, London United was sold to an employee and management buy-out team for £25.5m.

David Humphrey writes: "Once the sale of London's bus companies was formally launched, we had considerable work to do. The sale process would be an auction and each company would go to the highest bidder. So we were up against the rapidly forming big groups, and smaller groups that aspired to be big groups. The price was going to be high. This was against a background of municipal bus companies having recently been sold to employee teams in a closed sale process. We would need to raise outside finance, including external equity funding, to compete with aggressive bidders, yet there was high employee and trade union expectation that everyone would have something like equal shares which would be almost free.

"After much debate we settled on a mixture of significant equity holdings for the directors, a lesser amount for a group of senior managers, and a blend of equity and preference shares for everyone else, including 4% of the equity distributed free to all except the senior teams. When a senior full-time Union Officer attended a meeting to formalise the arrangements he asked me, 'What's the basis of the 4%?' obviously gearing up to ask for more. Before I could answer, one of the main members of the employee team piped up, 'They offered us 2% and we negotiated them up to 4%'!

"Meanwhile the rest of the world was considering bidding for the companies. London Buses set up a secure Data Room for shortlisted bidders. The management teams had to provide much of the content: details of the fleet, the buildings, the workforce, union agreements, the financial performance and more were all placed there. London Buses employed a 'minder' to maintain the security and confidentiality of this Data Room. It was a necessary but very boring job, and it was amusing to see him being far more attentive to writing letters to his girlfriend in New Zealand than his gatekeeping duties!

"There was also a huge effort made by London Buses to have all bidders made anonymous. Each bidder was given an alpha-numeric code, as were the companies, and that is all anyone was allowed to know. When the first external bidding team came to interview the London United Directors, they were settled into our boardroom, and when I opened the door the first person I saw was someone I had known from my days in Merseyside. 'Ah, hello Alan' I exclaimed, 'nice to see you again, now I know who Alpha 4 is!' – much to the discomfort of the London Buses sales team who were mediating the meeting."

One afternoon, Martin Whitley was waiting for a very important fax. "The people in the Centre were paranoid about management buyouts. Someone in their office had to open all the mail to make sure that nothing untoward was happening. All the management buyout stuff had to go via a separate fax machine, which was secretly installed in David Humphrey's office in a tiny room over the staircase which was no bigger than a cupboard. No one even knew that the fax machine was there, not even the Premises Manager, who should have known.

"We had put our bid in, and were waiting to be told by fax that afternoon whether we were the preferred bidder or not. The other Directors had gone out, leaving me there pacing up and down, hovering by the door to the cupboard, waiting for the fax to come in. Then, in David's outer office, I heard the Premises Manager wanting to hold a meeting in David's room, so I went into the cupboard and closed the door. They could not know that I was there, that a fax machine was there, or that such an important message was due to arrive. However, if I was discovered, I couldn't think of any reason to explain why I was in the cupboard, and I was trying not to sneeze! Fortunately, they all went away after a not too long meeting, and then the fax machine spurted into life with the news that we wanted."

Steve Fennell was an Inspector at Hounslow when privatisation was taking place and they were all following events on the 'bush telegraph'. They all heaved a sigh of relief when Stagecoach got East London because, "We thought that meant that Stagecoach would not get us. Anne Gloag had been seen looking around Hounslow garage. Of course, Stagecoach is ok now and is more customer focused, but initially we didn't want to work for them." London United was a management buyout, which was the best they could have hoped for. They heard the news in the afternoon and everyone was happy on the shop floor, giving a collective sigh of relief. So privatisation was not the horror story that everyone felt it was going to be.

David Humphrey continues, "Having successfully secured an attractive finance package and strong legal advice, London United was sold to its management and employee team shortly after 1am on 5 November 1994, giving us a further reason for setting off fireworks on that date for evermore. The following morning, I went back to my office in Fulwell garage to pick up my car to drive home. I decided to have breakfast in the canteen. We had arranged for large notices to be posted overnight once the deal was done, and I thought that a few people might stop to make some remark. I was a bit deflated when not one person said anything other than 'Good morning, guv' or some other passing greeting.

Martin Whitley adds, "It was always the intention to have staff shares in an MEBO. This was agreed in the first 20 minutes of conversation I had with David Humphrey when we first met. It was David's intention, and I immediately said, 'You're doing right, I agree with you fully, that's what we should do.' Some diehard lefties burned their share certificates, and it was amusing seeing them come back three years later for duplicates, and getting them. You could see how long their principles were lasting."

The privatisation was very nerve wracking, and there were sleepless nights. Martin didn't put his house at risk because it had been obvious for so long that privatisation was going to happen. So he was saving furiously for six or seven years to make his contribution. He says it is important to note that he would not have stayed had anyone else bought the company, and he left when it was sold on a few years later. "The management buyout was a heady experience. You also met some of the most nasty individuals in the city that you can imagine, and they impose requirements on you."

South London
This left South London, where the management team put a bid together, but found it difficult to get buy-in from the staff. The trade union was antagonistic to the proposals and were not co-operating. In some places, the staff took a hard line trying to prevent it from happening, whilst in others they could see the benefits of staff involvement and co-operated. The lower wage rates paid on tendered services gave the

"I went into the cupboard and closed the door. They could not know that I was there. However, if I was discovered, I couldn't think of any reason to explain why I was in the cupboard, and I was trying not to sneeze!"

impression that wages would be lower under privatisation, which discouraged them. However, South London put together an MEBO, the bid went in and they were the preferred bidder.

But at the beginning of November, South London was called to a hearing of the South East and Metropolitan Traffic Commissioners and criticised over its maintenance standards. There had been a large number of vehicle prohibitions following inspections. Engineering management and the major garages were paired up, for example Norwood and Brixton, because they were trying to be competitive in a very tight market.

Mike Heath now had only South London left to sell. "South London had the management team as the preferred bidder, at the head of a number of not very inspiring bids. But they were called before a Traffic Commissioner's hearing. This was serious and it was clear that, had they not been part of London Buses, they would have had stop notices served."

The public hearing was at Eastbourne. Ian Barlex went to observe it, and immediately afterwards reported back to Clive Hodson on what had happened. This was the longest mobile phone call he ever had. No buses were taken off the road but their reputation was on the line. The Operator's Licence was curtailed to expire on 30 April 1995 and spot checks were expected.

The Managing Director and Engineering Director left the company immediately and LBL's Principal Engineer, Simon Brown, became MD under Norman Cohen's Chairmanship. Mike Heath adds, "The sale of the company was halted and the management bid was debarred, because they would otherwise have been profiting from their own incompetence. This demonstrated that even with the best laid plans for privatisation, something can always go wrong.

Clive Hodson went to South London to carry out the management changes. "I remember meeting the office staff on the next working day, the Monday, and saying, 'I am sorry but I am changing the Directors and Simon Brown will be taking over as interim MD.' And the staff said, 'Does that mean, Mr Hodson, you won't be selling the company,' and I said, 'We're still selling the company.' And we did – we exchanged contracts in December and completed in about the second week in January."

Mike Heath looked for possible bidders, given the changed circumstances of the company. "FirstGroup considered it, but treated it as a cheap purchase. We did not consider it to be a cheap sale, however, as the problems could be overcome and I spoke to Gordon Hodgson of Cowie, suggesting that this would be a good opportunity at a realistic price. South London had control of the Brixton Road and the Croydon area."

Gordon Hodgson was told, "You've got the best engineering team in London at Leaside, why not bid for South London and we will look favourably at your offer." He consulted Steve Clayton, who was now in his company following the purchase of Leaside, and a meeting was set up with Ian Barlex and LT's merchant bank BZW, Gordon Hodgson and Steve Clayton. Steve recalls, "South London was given only six months on their O-Licence to sort out their engineering problems. This was a major crisis, managing the appalling engineering standards that had led to the Traffic Commissioners revoking the licence of 400 buses.

"BZW were trying to ease up the price. Gordon Hodgson gave his price and said that was as far as he would go, and 'If we walk out of this room, then the deal is off.' Ian Barlex, a good guy, was trying to talk up the position, but I saw through his salemanship and told him, 'Look Ian, I'm on *this* side of the table now.' We walked out, not buying it. However, next day BZW telephoned and said, 'For another half million, it's yours.'" South London was sold to the Cowie group on 10 January 1995 for £17.1m. Cowie was now the largest group in London with 900 scheduled buses.

So Steve Clayton and his Leaside team took over the running of South London. Steve recalls, "This was hell on earth for six months. There were horror stories in the engineering – it was in a terrible state." Steve is clear that it was bad management on the engineering side, with economies being made by cutting back on engineering. "John Withey was a decent man but he was not well served by some of his people. We spent hundreds of thousands of pounds

"A triumph!" announced Steve Norris celebrating completion of the sales with Clive Hodson and Mike Heath.

replacing parts that should have been replaced years ago, and we gradually got it better."

Mark Yexley remembers that in the run-up to privatisation, when they were still owned by LBL, South London had started to get into trouble on the engineering front and Leaside was instructed to transfer 40 Metrobuses to South London and receive 40 Titans in exchange. "We made damn sure that every newish engine and gearbox was stripped out of those Metrobuses and retained in Leaside, being replaced by older ones before they went south. Then, of course, we took over South London and got them all back again!"

Steve Clayton went with Ted Milburn, the Engineering Director, and their company lawyer to the subsequent hearing of the Traffic Commissioner at Eastbourne. The Commissioner said he didn't want to speak to the Engineering Director, who breathed a huge sigh of relief; he wanted to speak to the Managing Director. He had heard from the Vehicle Inspectorate, who had said a lot of good things, and he asked Steve a series of questions and then adjourned. After a long wait the Commissioner came back and summed up. He talked at length and it was not clear what decision he was coming to. He then concluded by saying, "As Wellington once said, there is no such thing as good and bad regiments. There are only good and bad commanders. I have complete confidence in renewing the O-Licence for five years. I will ask the Vehicle Inspectorate to monitor things and keep me informed."

Steve phoned his Chief Executive, who was at home on holiday. It was a 60-second phone conversation and the response was, "Good, well done, I expected nothing less." Three days later, he was asked, "When are you going to start making a profit?"

Review of the sales
The sales brought to an end over 60 years of bus operations by London Transport. The companies in total were sold for £233 million against an original estimate by BZW of £100 million. BZW had, however, negotiated a success fee and were now claiming commission against the difference. This led to considerable debate because their original estimate had proved to be wholly inaccurate!

The National Audit Office examined the sale (The Sale of London Transport's Bus Operating Companies, National Audit Office, 6 December 1995) and concluded that the sale objectives were achieved. The sales were completed on target and no purchaser had achieved more than a 25 per cent share of the London bus market – this is still not exceeded in 2014. Employee participation had been successfully promoted, four of the ten companies being purchased by management and employee teams. At £233 million, gross proceeds were substantially higher than expected. A high level of interest had been generated by LT's marketing campaign and a bidding process was successfully devised which took advantage of this, generating substantial bidding competition and obtaining final prices which were in total £30 million higher than the eventual purchasers' initial indicative bids. London Transport and the Department of Transport took account of best practice from previous sales and the recommendations of the Committee of Public Accounts. Overall, the sale had been managed effectively.

Several other bus operators had shown interest in purchasing the companies. British Bus were not successful but already had subsidiaries working tendered services, and bought both Luton and District and Kentish Bus during 1994. Their Chairman Dawson Williams said, "We are disappointed but not unduly concerned. British Bus will be vigorous in its attempts to win tenders as they become available." He said that they were the largest contractor to LT and would be aggressively tendering in the future. GRT Bus Group, the forerunner of FirstGroup, did bid but was not successful.

Badgerline and Capital Citybus did not bid for any of the companies, both taking the view that – if they wanted to be involved in London – they could bid for any routes they wanted when they were retendered. Blazefield had grown to around 700 vehicles, 100 of which were in London, but most of the London companies being sold were bigger than this and Blazefield did not bid for them.

The participants in the sale process look back at this as a successful project which was well executed. All speak well of the experience when they look back twenty years later. Clive Hodson and Steve Norris speak highly of each other and of Sir Wilfrid Newton. The project team led by Mike Heath clearly worked well and achieved its objectives. The liaison between LT and government was slick. Clive Hodson remarks that they had decisions very quickly. "Steve Norris had a very good civil servant called Martin Capstick who worked with Mike Heath and myself. We would take Martin through the papers and explain the bids and our recommendations to him for each company. He used to comment on it, take it to Steve Norris and next day, agreement! No messing around for weeks on end, you got an instant decision which I thought was marvellous. Everybody was put out of their misery and got on with the job."

The total sale price of £233m meant that Steve Norris won the crate of champagne from Wilfrid Newton. "And he paid up – as you would expect Wilfrid to do!" said Steve, who happily remembers enjoying the champagne over the following months.

9 BRAVE NEW WORLD 1994-1999

The morning after the night before. When the Metroline directors met on the Monday morning, they each admitted that they had woken with a jolt thinking, "What on earth have I done?" As Directors of the newly independent company, they had to go in on the Monday and lead their troops into the brave new world.

Metroline had an immediate stroke of luck with a major rail job replacing the Piccadilly Line into Heathrow Airport. Other management buy-out companies were not so lucky when the venture capitalists came in next morning and dictated the way the company would be run. East London and Leaside found themselves highly regarded by their new owners and in many ways life was easier than under London Buses control, while South London had to be straightened out. Perhaps London Northern came off worst, with the existing Directors departing jobless after a brief conversation in a local hotel.

From 11 January 1995, all of London's buses were privately owned and working under contract to London Transport Buses (LTB). LBL roundels were removed from all buses and new "London Transport Service" stickers were applied. Stagecoach and MTL London Northern adopted all-red liveries whilst London United experimented with yellow roofs. Metroline tried out different coloured skirts. CentreWest made no change to its livery – they saw no point in wasting the money. LTB set a new policy requiring the use of yellow lettering on black destination blinds, replacing the traditional white on black, to improve visibility to the partially sighted.

LTB forged relationships with the new owners, while the large groups wanted greater autonomy. Both Stagecoach and First pressed the point but were told that London was a regulated market and they were working to contracts. Clive Hodson recalls visiting FirstBus with the LT Chairman, Peter Ford. "Moir Lockhead was quite aggressive and it was a stormy meeting – Peter said afterwards, 'I had to put my tin hat on!'"

Metroline adopted a new logo and a dark blue band along the lower side of their buses, which worked well on the Routemasters. RML 2547 is at Aldwych in May 1997. (Roger Torode)

204 Metroline had an immediate stroke of luck with a major rail job replacing the Piccadilly Line into Heathrow Airport.

Metroline

Before privatisation, Metroline had set up a commercial contract service that used a small reserve fleet of buses for driver training and school contracts in the week, and for rail replacement work at weekends. This prospered in privatisation. On 21 October 1994, two weeks after they bought the company, there was a tunnel collapse at Heathrow and the Piccadilly Line stopped. Every available bus in the area was used to provide a replacement service and Metroline were heavily involved. Then the railway said everything was all right and stood the buses down. Most operators went home, but Metroline's contracts manager decided to wait and see. It soon became clear that the buses were still needed, and more were asked for. As a result, with their buses still in place Metroline got the contract and ran the operation from then on, earning emergency rates for several months.

Declan O'Farrell remembers it with pleasure. "So in the very early days, the venture capitalists were coming and saying, 'How's it going?' and we were able to say, 'we're way ahead of plan!' And we always were. From that point onwards, we got ahead of our yearly and three yearly projections and we stayed there. "Granville Private Equity were as hard as anyone, but their philosophy was, if they believed in the team and they believed in the plan, and the management were delivering the plan, their role was to be supportive and to talk longer term. Whereas I know in some of the other companies, the day after their deal was signed they had a meeting with the venture capitalists who came in and basically read them the riot act and told them how they were going to run the company. They had a very rude awakening. It was the venture capitalists behind the early selling on of the other companies because they wanted their money – they wanted a quick return and that was it.

As a result of its early success, Metroline's backers supported their expansion. They took over Atlas Bus and Coach from the Pullman Group later in 1994, and Brent's Coaches in October 1995, transferring the Metroline coaches to Brent's in Watford. Buying Atlas brought route 52 back to Metroline, together with the 26 elderly Titans of London Coaches, their staff and their base. This was a significant turning point for Metroline, and came with route 107 which Atlas had won in 1989 and were running with new Leyland Olympians. The takeover caused problems because some Atlas staff had been sacked by Metroline due to their poor work performance – and now they reappeared in the company.

Gordon Tennant thinks that the overall outcome of this phase was a good result, because they had one less competitor, gained a new operating base at Atlas Road, Harlesden, and they got the strategically important 52 route back again. This all fitted in with Declan's vision, giving space to expand when they suffered losses; they cut out the overheads and when they had the opportunity they built it up again in the way they wanted.

Metroline then floated on the London Stock Exchange in July 1997. "The venture capitalists are itching to get out within five years and there is a need to get them out by about year three or four," says Declan. "The longer they stay in, the more they can force the pace to sell the company. By five years they are insisting it should be sold, because this is their business." Metroline floated the company at £1.79 per share and bought out the venture capitalists. "They were very very happy, because they made their money. Then in 1998, we went for a Rights Issue and on the back of that we were able to purchase London Northern and Scottish Citylink."

Metroline acquired MTL London Northern on 17 August 1998 for £41.9 million. Metroline's operation in London virtually doubled, and within days evidence of the previous owners was removed: 456 vehicles were acquired along with garages at Holloway, North Acton and Potters Bar. A number of the major bus groups were also reported to have been interested. London Northern then became known as "Metroline London Northern Ltd", and it adopted the Metroline livery and fleet name. The full reasons for the sale were not immediately obvious. "Perhaps MTL found that running in London was harder than they had expected. MTL had already bought London Suburban Buses in 1995, which was not the best operation at the time." It was a major challenge to integrate the

Metroline's other buses had a stylish blue skirt, designed by Best Impressions and providing contrast with the red, white stripe and the flash of orange in the new logo. Metroline experimented with maroon and green before settling on this deep blue. M1192 is at Golders Green. (Colin Stannard)

205 "The venture capitalists are itching to get out within five years"

two companies but Metroline gradually achieved this over subsequent years. London Suburban Bus had been a newcomer to London bus operations in 1994, operating from a base on the Lea Valley Trading Estate. Their parent company, Liverbus, was based in Liverpool.

Metroline also acquired Citylink Holdings from the National Express group for £10.3 million on 24 August 1998. National Express were bidding for ScotRail and were required to sell Citylink to meet competition law. The operation was largely franchised but included one token coach and 25% of West Coast Motors. Scottish Citylink brought confrontation with Stagecoach. Declan recalls, "They told me in the nicest possible way that they were going to set up a direct competitor network and wipe us out."

Metroline's shares peaked at £3.60. Declan continues, "Then things started to get difficult, not because we were in recession – we were in boom, but all the investors we had in the company got fed up with boring old transport stock and put their money into dot.com where they thought they could treble their money overnight." A City contact had kept in touch with Declan and asked if he would be interested in selling to an overseas buyer. Declan met one of their board directors and a senior executive. "They had a look around and saw our company and were quite happy, and their philosophy was that they wanted to invest. So I went back to talk to my colleagues, and that's what we did."

In March 2000, Metroline was sold for £74 million to Singapore-based transport group DelGro, the parent company of Singapore Bus Services which operated 2,400 buses there and in Shanghai. In London, DelGro owned Computer Cab and Data Cab with 3,200 cabs. It also had taxi interests in Singapore and China. It was a strategic investor who wanted the Metroline management to stay in place. Declan adds, "They would provide investment at a time when we couldn't generate enough funds for more expansion. We couldn't guarantee what would happen on the tendering front and we couldn't get much more savings out of the businesses, so where were we going to go?"

"Selling to a strategic investor meant we were always going to get a better price than selling out to Stagecoach. We tweaked them up to £2.40, but they couldn't go above that, so it was walk away time or do a deal. The trade buyers from the UK were always going to want an exceedingly good deal on the basis that we were being forced to sell, whereas we got £2.40 from the Singaporeans. I don't think Brian Souter was offering us more than around £1.70." Metroline had 12% of the London bus business at the time, which was too big for some UK groups to buy because of the share of business they already held.

Gordon Tennant adds, "The staff did well from the sale – around £36,000 to the longest serving member of staff, based on a fixed sum plus extra for each year of service. The staff had played a big part in the performance of the company – they did things that, a few years before, would not have been possible in areas of improved flexibility and industrial relations. The staff were not a walkover, but they were able to separate day-to-day business issues from the longer term good of the company. Pat Mahon kept them fixed on the big picture."

Gordon chose to leave Metroline in May 2001. He did not want to work for new owners in what had been partly his own company, and did not want to be the guy in the company from the previous ownership who was always telling the new owners, "We've tried that and it didn't work!" And he had now bid for route 140 four times! Declan O'Farrell stayed for a time looking for opportunities to expand in London, the UK and throughout Europe. But DelGro were focusing on Singapore and China and soon announced a major merger with the Comfort Corporation, who had the biggest taxi network in Singapore. They also expanded into railways in Singapore and in taxis and bus networks in China. So Declan left in 2004, remaining involved as a non-executive Director for a further year.

London United

Shortly before London United was privatised, David Humphrey recalls a small matter being blown up into a big issue by the trade union. His secretary had said, "Don't worry David, it will be completely different when we're private." "I had my doubts at the time," says David, "but she was right. The atmosphere and the culture did indeed change. Trade union discussions were as robust as ever, but were much more confined to real issues. As one representative told me, 'We just used to use Health and Safety as a stick to beat management with.'"

Once London United became private they found out that all the central LT functions were unnecessary. For example, central purchasing might achieve bulk discounts, but would add a similar amount to the charge to cover their costs. The Car Department would only permit medium specification cars, but you could add lots of extras to them.

David Humphrey continues, "After privatisation, we had to buy our own buses. Martin Lewis did what bus company engineers do, just invited bids from vehicle manufacturers and chose one in consultation with his fellow directors. The requirement for new buses was primarily driven by bus route tender awards, the vehicle specification being largely set by LT.

"Airbus was different, being a completely commer-

"All the investors got fed up with boring old transport stock and put their money into dot.com where they thought they could treble their money overnight."

cial operation. Under LT, it had become impossible to obtain permission to buy new buses for Airbus since all capital expenditure was part of the block grant and had to be limited to such services. Part of London United's Business Plan included the renewal of the fleet, so Martin Whitley, the Commercial Director worked up a passenger specification, and off we went.

"One detail needing considerable thought was the price to be set for the equity shares. It was decided to set the price at 1p, so that even a small investment would produce ownership of a good number of shares. To facilitate an internal market in the shares through an Employee Benefit Trust, as well as give effect to the condition that only current employees could hold shares, the company was valued every six months, followed by a short period of trading. At the first valuation, the shares went up to seven pence each. At the second, the price jumped again to 14 pence. A not very savvy employee was then heard to comment, 'Ah, the shares are worth something now, I think I'll buy some'! Generally, the valuations created great interest, and many employees were encouraged by seeing the value of their employer rise – except for those few at Shepherd's Bush who ceremonially burnt their free shares in protest against the horrors of capitalism!

"Once privatised, we thought we might be able to develop into a group of bus companies by buying other newly independent companies around Britain. Sadly, 1994 had proved to be one of considerable consolidation in the industry. By the time we were on our own just about everything else buyable had already been bought! However, we got wind that

Above London United adopted a traditional and attractive colour scheme by Ray Stenning of Best Impressions, who developed a style with an air of quality to give more synergy with London United's operating area in south-west London. The livery reflected London United Tramways, with a reworked crest. The fleetname emphasised United rather than London, as most of the companies had London in their name. (Keith Wood)

Left London United upgraded its Airbus services in 1995 with new Volvo Olympians, fitted with air-conditioned, coach seated Alexander 'Royale' bodies. (David Humphrey)

207 "A not very savvy employee was then heard to comment, 'Ah, the shares are worth something now, I think I'll buy some'!"

Westlink, right on our doorstep, might be up for sale by its new owners, West Midlands Travel, who had not long previously bought it from Jeff Chamberlain. Westlink had been a London Buses subsidiary, but Jeff had managed to keep it separate from London United, unlike all the other quasi-independent tendered bus units such as Bexleybus, Sutton Bus, and Harrow Buses, which had all became integral parts of the LBL Units in 1988.

"To us, purchasing Westlink merely represented a correction to a previous aberration. As negotiations progressed, the rumours spread. The matter became complicated by the parallel merger of West Midlands Travel with National Express, with whom the final deal was eventually done. I was bound by confidentiality undertakings not to either confirm or deny the rumours. 'Oh, come on boss, we know you're going to buy it, just let us know the truth,' was an oft-repeated greeting. It turned out that one of the drivers at Fulwell Garage was the nephew of one of the employee worker directors at West Midlands Travel, and had been told all about it. So much for confidentiality!

"Finally, in September 1995, the deal was done and I could let everyone know. One driver said, 'Does that mean we can wave at their drivers now?' Then came the job of melding London United and Westlink, which had developed its own individual characteristics and culture. It took not a little time, and many little Westlink quirks were uncovered."

The Westlink name was retained and the vehicles came under the control of London United's Fulwell Garage Manager. WMT said that it had originally purchased Westlink prior to the sale of the London bus subsidiaries in order to gain a foothold in the London area, but it was then considered too small and unlikely to be able to generate the economies of scale necessary. WMT still had its County Bus operations in the Harlow area.

London United was itself a takeover target. David Humphrey continues, "Early the first Monday of privatised existence, I received a phone call from the Chief Executive of one of the emerging large groups inviting me to lunch. We had a pleasant meal, he congratulated me on successfully buying the company, admired the deal we had done, and made it clear that when we felt we wanted to sell, we were not to omit him from our considerations. The pressures to sell started immediately.

"Similarly, the directors were invited to dinner by the three private equity providers. In a private dining room on the north bank of the Thames we were repeatedly reminded of the need to plan for the 'exit', a word used in almost every sentence uttered by the lead investment director.

"The external equity providers were in fact quite supportive during the time they were with us. They didn't interfere at all and backed our various capital investment proposals with very little demur. But a clause within the Shareholders' Agreement gave them the right after three and a half years to require all shareholders to sell. Attempting to remain independent after that time would have placed an increasing burden on the business to continue to generate an increasing rate of growth of shareholders' returns, without which a forced sale would have been imposed.

"It would be much better to sell at a time and in conditions of our choosing. After an attempt by one of the groups quietly to purchase the company failed (they dropped their price by a large margin at the last minute), the board decided to hold a private auction. Our financial advisers ran this very well. We had firm bids from about six different and disparate organisations which were whittled down to a shortlist, and then to a preferred bidder, at each stage with firmer prices based on the disclosure of increasingly detailed financial and other information about the company. During the course of this process, I met at an industry conference the two main guys of one of the bidding teams that had been eliminated at the first stage. 'So, you thought our bid was crap', said one of them as we took time out for a cup of coffee!

"Eventually, the best price came from Transdev, of whom none of us had heard before. We found out that it was one of the then three main public transport operating groups in provincial France. As we discovered who they were and where they operated, it became clear that this would be a good firm to have as a parent company. It had been the leading exponent of the renaissance of tramways in France, starting with Nantes in 1985. Having taken an interest in European public transport operation for some time, I realised that the noticeably good quality operations that had previously impressed me were Transdev-operated, a very good omen.

"The London United management team made a presentation to the Transdev bidding team, who were led by Philippe Segretain, Transdev's irrepressible President. The presentation was made in a secret location in a hotel near Heathrow – how we loved the intrigue! After the presentation, lunch was organised. We had a pre-lunch drink, and Philippe asked us if we would like to join him and his team in a beer. 'Ah, no,' we rather apologetically replied, and explained that all the operators in London had adopted a 'no alcohol' policy. The French were impressed at the virtuous nature of their potential new subsidiary, and had their beers whilst we had our glasses of fizzy water.

"We sat down to lunch, and Philippe sat directly opposite me. 'Will you have some wine with us?' asked Philippe. My brain quickly went through the thoughts of how important wine with a meal is to the French, hadn't he been listening, we mustn't insult him, but we have to refuse. 'Er, no, Philippe, if you recall, we have a 'no alcohol' policy, we can't take any wine I am afraid,' said I. Feigning shock, glancing from side to side at his colleagues he exclaimed, 'But wine is not alcohol!' He was being very clever, making a play on the French convention of referring to beer, wine and "alcool" ('spirits' in English) as separate types of drink, and simultaneously playing up to the British stereotype view of wine in French culture. Immediately, one of our garage General Managers, Derek Lott, said, 'Here, Guv, can we have the French definition of alcohol in our policy?'!

"And so London United became a subsidiary of Transdev on 12 August 1997. It proved to be a long lasting relationship, only fairly recently broken as a part of the merger of Transdev with another French group Veolia, a by-product of which was the passing of ownership of London United to RATP. So having been sold by London Transport in 1994, London United is now owned by LT's Parisian equivalent!"

David joined Transdev's international committee as London United was their first operation outside France. They subsequently went on to bid for Nottingham trams and for the Porto Metro. Martin Whitley left within three months of Transdev taking over. "I had nothing against them, but working for someone else was not what I wanted, so I handed over gracefully and left."

David Humphrey with Philippe Segretain, President of Transdev, on the sale of the company. (David Humphrey)

London United's recruitment of French drivers caused a stir. Patrick Blower's cartoon in the Evening Standard was based on Renault car adverts at the time, which featured Nicole and her Papa driving different Renault models. (Courtesy Leon Daniels)

"Feigning shock, glancing from side to side at his colleagues he exclaimed, 'But wine is not alcohol!'"

London United had difficulty attracting drivers and suffered particularly through competition from Heathrow Airport. At one point a third of new recruits were leaving within a year. They had considerable media coverage in June 1999 in both the national press, TV and radio, when it was announced that they would employ French drivers. There were sarcastic comments about boules tournaments and canteens without wine, though London United already had French drivers and the story was based on a significant increase in their numbers. Ten had been taken on over a year before, eight of whom remained. In early June, another 45 were in training and 50 more were on their way. The drivers had been given English language training and were to be used on both crew and OPO work at Shepherd's Bush, Hounslow and Fulwell.

Cowie, Leaside and South London
Leaside immediately noticed the difference of private ownership. They had lost the time-consuming London Buses bureaucracy. Mark Yexley remembers, "In LBL, when we wanted to replace a stores lorry whose lease had run out, we needed to produce a nine page dossier justifying the purchase. Once we were in the Cowie group, Gordon Hodgson said, 'Do we want to do it or don't we?' to which the answer was 'Yes'. 'Then do it,' he said!"

South London was a huge challenge, needing considerable finance and effort to turn it around. It was quickly decided to close the South London headquarters and run the company from Wood Green. The Leaside directors became directors of South London also, and they were working against the clock in the run-up to the second Traffic Commissioner's enquiry. Prior to the Hearing, the VOSA inspectors came to do a fleet check. Unfortunately, the first four buses failed, but the next 36 were all right and the Operators Licence was renewed for five years. Finance, schedules and payrolls all went to Leaside, and South London then just had the garages and some local knowledge in their headquarters. Mark Yexley suggests that Leaside and South London was a good combination because they joined each other without being adjoining. "It was a nice shape to work with. After we had worked our way through the engi-

The Leaside livery on privatisation was red with a black skirt and a thick white band. New buses arrived for tender awards in 1995 in a livery of mostly red relieved by two yellow flashes. These included 13 DAF double deckers with Northern Counties bodies which came from stock held by the Cowie Group member Hughes DAF. They were painted into the new Cowie corporate livery at Palmers Green garage. This one is in the City of London on the Sunday variation of the route to Liverpool Street bus station. (Keith Wood)

210 "Leaside and South London was a good combination because they joined each other without being adjoining."

neering issues the combined company came together well and South London rapidly acquired a reputation for doing an amazing amount with very few managers."

Having competed for many years with Grey-Green, it was strange to now be together in the same company. In the past, they had refused to give Grey-Green the keys to the Inspector's Box at Wood Green, or allow them to use the canteen there. In February 1996, Cowie bought County Bus of Harlow from West Midlands Travel, ending WMT's involvement in London following the earlier sale of Westlink to London United. This included the LeaValley, ThameSide, TownLink, Green Line and Sampson's Coaches operations along with the staff, six operating bases and 239 vehicles. It was placed under the management of Leaside. Sampson's coaches was merged with Leaside Travel in order to bring all private hire work under one management. County Bus & Coach had been formed out of London Country North East in January 1989. It had been sold to WMT in October 1994, and in April 1995 West Midlands Travel merged with the National Express Group.

In June 1996 Cowie bought the entire British Bus Group for £282 million. British Bus had around 12% of the UK bus market with a strong market share in the south-east including London and Country (which had rebranded as London*links* from 1 January 1995), Kentish Bus, and Luton and District. Cowie already owned Leaside, Grey-Green, South London and County Bus. This transformed Cowie into the third largest bus group in the UK, and it now included most of the old London Country Bus Services area. British Bus had been bigger than Cowie in terms of its bus operations.

Steve Clayton was involved in the team that put the British Bus deal together. When it was close to conclusion it was to be announced on the Stock Exchange. "I told Gordon Hodgson that they should brief London Transport Buses confidentially, because LBL would not like to hear it second hand. I offered to speak to Clive Hodson, but Gordon was determined that it should be announced first on the Stock Exchange. Unfortunately the news was leaked to the Daily Telegraph the day before and Clive Hodson read it in the paper on the train on his way in to work. He was greatly displeased to hear it through the press, rather than from the operators themselves."

Clive Hodson remembers the occasion. "I came up to town one day and, reading the Telegraph, it said

Leaside's Leyland Olympian L330, in the new Cowie livery, leads a line-up in the Narrow Way, Hackney, outside Clapton garage, a street that has now been pedestrianised. The bus is one of 40 delivered in 1992 when limited purchases of new single-deckers were permitted in LBL. Leaside successfully argued that all their routes were big bus and without new vehicles their fleet would simply get older. These Alexander-bodied buses were specifically to update the 253. (Keith Wood)

"Having competed for many years with Grey-Green, it was strange to now be together in the same company."

Cowie group had bought out another company, and we didn't know about it. So I spoke to the Managing Director at Cowie, and I said, 'Excuse me, you didn't tell us, and you are obliged to tell us. It is in the contract clauses; if you want to take somebody over you have to tell us.' He said he couldn't because of confidentiality and the stock market. I had a bit of an argument with him and from then on we said, if you are going to take over one of the smaller outfits in London you have got to tell us, and we have to give it approval."

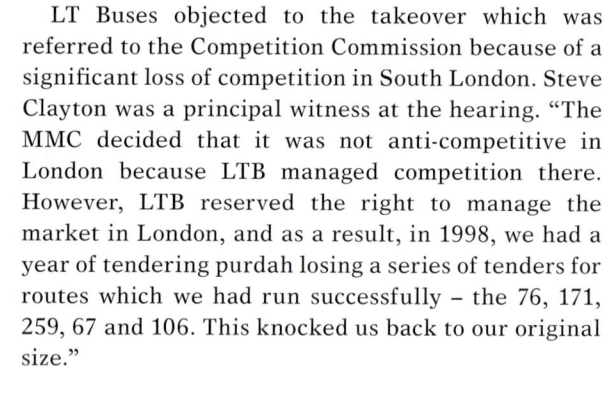

LT Buses objected to the takeover which was referred to the Competition Commission because of a significant loss of competition in South London. Steve Clayton was a principal witness at the hearing. "The MMC decided that it was not anti-competitive in London because LTB managed competition there. However, LTB reserved the right to manage the market in London, and as a result, in 1998, we had a year of tendering purdah losing a series of tenders for routes which we had run successfully – the 76, 171, 259, 67 and 106. This knocked us back to our original size."

Above As Cowie became Arriva and reorganised its operations, buses on Route 24 – which had made such an impact in Grey-Green livery – once again became red from May 1998, with 'Arriva serving London fleetnames.' No. 126 passes through Parliament Square on its way to Pimlico. (Keith Wood)

Left A 'suburban' version of the Arriva livery with less red, is seen on a Dennis Dart in Enfield. (Colin Stannard)

Right CentreWest won most of the Orpington network when it was retendered in 1995 and set up a new operation named 'Orpington Buses'. In 1996, route 336 was also won and added to the operation and a Mercedes minibus is shown on the way to Bromley North Station in 1996. (Colin Stannard)

212 "The Monopolies and Mergers Commission decided that it was not anti-competitive in London because LTB managed competition there."

Amalgamating British Bus meant bringing several different operations together, with very different pay and conditions. They took over route 19 of Kentish Bus with its RMLs and the Battersea site, which they closed in 2002; they also closed Walworth garage. Staff shortages became a major problem in the late 1990s and needed an improvement in pay and conditions. Due to severe staff shortages in east London route 367 was transferred to Blue Triangle. By 2000 they had an 80% staff turnover at the Edmonton Lea Valley site, the rates of pay were so far adrift. In August 1997 the Cowie group bought the buses and routes of West's coaches which were absorbed into County Bus. West's retained their small coach operation and the depot.

In October 1997 the group renamed itself 'Arriva' and introduced a new corporate logo featuring 'wheels within wheels' which began to appear on their London buses. The new logo was quickly applied to buses from Leaside and Grey-Green, so that it was immediately apparent on buses running into the City of London. Buses in London would be red whilst elsewhere they would be in a new turquoise and cream livery. Routemasters on route 38 received a new logo with yellow outline numbers arranged to form a heart shape in the centre. Arriva also acquired the Original London Sightseeing Tour from London Coaches in December 1997.

In April 1998 the Arriva bus companies took on new corporate identities with Leaside, Grey-Green and South London fleetnames all disappearing. They were replaced by names including Arriva London South Ltd which was shown as "Arriva serving London" on the buses. The livery was red with the Arriva "cow horns". Grey-Green closed down its coaching operation during 1998. The Essex commuter work was sold to Essex operators who continued to market them together with the name "Essex Express".

Steve Clayton was appointed to the main board of Arriva in February 1998 to manage the group's UK bus operations. Mark Yexley then became managing director of Arriva London. Arriva's 1997 Annual Report showed it to now be one of the UK's largest bus operators and the largest supplier of bus services in London. They also expanded into Denmark and the Netherlands.

London Coaches

During 1997 London Coaches acquired the sightseeing operations of Blue Triangle and also took over the London commuter services of Kentish Bus and Maidstone & District to and from the Medway towns. These were operated by London Coaches (Kent) and marketed as the North Kent Express, requiring around eighty coaches for the fourteen routes. As mentioned above, the Original London Sightseeing Tour was sold to Arriva in December 1997.

CentreWest

CentreWest caused a stir by winning five of the Orpington routes when these were retendered in 1995. Peter Hendy and Bob Muir had set up Roundabout in 1986, before the creation of the LBL units. All the Roundabout routes went to other operators: CentreWest, Crystals and London*links*. CentreWest ran the routes as Orpington Buses and

213 CentreWest caused a stir by winning five of the Orpington routes when these were retendered in 1995.

used a combination of Dennis Darts and Mercedes midibuses, whilst 12 Volvo double-deckers were provided for route 61. The R2 and R7 routes passed to Crystals Coaches.

As MD of Selkent, Bryan Constable had set up Roundabout and run it through three three-year contracts before it went to CentreWest. Bryan was now advising Metrobus and had prepared their bid. He was disappointed when CentreWest won the routes but acknowledged that that was now the way things worked. Stagecoach Selkent were not amused, however. Roger Bowker visited Peter Hendy saying, "Don't do that again or you might get a bloody nose!" In general, Peter suggests that there was much less competition after privatisation than you would have expected. "Everyone realised you had to defend your position."

Above CentreWest upgraded the 607 Express in 1996 with 15 new Volvo Olympians and by improving the frequency. The new buses had Northern Counties bodies with improved seating, tinted glass and Euro-2 engines. V53 heads along the Uxbridge Road in 1997. (Colin Stannard)

Below left CentreWest received 120 new Dennis Darts in 1997 for the Ealing Buses network and other services. DM220 is on Gold Arrow service 31 at Earl's Court. The FirstBus livery began to appear in April 1997, removing the grey skirt and adding a yellow band below the windows, producing a clean, up-to-date image. (Keith Wood)

Below The double-deck version of the FirstBus livery had the yellow band above the lower deck windows, again tidying-up the appearance. (Colin Stannard)

214 In general, there was much less competition after privatisation than you would have expected. "Everyone realised you had to defend your position."

Released from Clive Hodson's financial controls in LBL, Peter Hendy had to keep his new financiers happy. He later told Clive, "I thought you were a bugger, but these venture capitalists are even worse! They want their two penn'orth, they are only in it for the short term, they want to sell out as quickly as they can."

In March 1996 CentreWest bought the Berks Bucks Bus Company which traded as Beeline and included London Buslines, the Len Wright company which had been the first independent operator of an LT tendered route in 1985. David Brown became Managing Director. CentreWest and Peter Hendy were offered Selkent by Stagecoach, but the venture capitalists would not finance the deal, preferring rather to take their profits. At that point, Peter realised that the company had to be sold.

In March 1997, CentreWest was sold to FirstBus for £52 million, including the Berks Bucks Bus Company and CentreWest's 20% stake in Tramtrack Croydon Ltd. This gave FirstBus a significant presence in London for the first time – they already owned Eastern National and Thamesway which operated LT tendered services in north-east London. Peter Hendy assumed responsibility for the London and South Eastern Division of FirstBus which, he said at the time, shared the philosophy of service quality, and all staff would benefit from being part of a larger group. CentreWest staff with more than five years service at September 1994 would have made £6,000 each from the sale without having made a cash contribution.

London Northern

At London Northern the management team viewed the arrival of MTL with trepidation. MTL was the company formed for the management buyout of Liverpool PTE buses. The new MD was Dominic Brady. Andy Griffiths knew that his marketing job was no longer justified and he left within four weeks.

In April 1995, MTL took over the London and Merseyside operations of Gemsam Holdings, including London Suburban Bus Services who were running the 4 and the 271. Whilst LSB initially continued as a separate unit, it was absorbed into MTL-London Northern in November. MTL also bought the complete operations of R&I Tours on 24 October, including the fleet of 64 vehicles based at premises in North Acton and Park Royal. R&I had been looking for a buyer and had also had discussions with Armchair. MTL-London Northern were then bought by Metroline on 17 August 1998.

MTL London Northern took the simple approach and painted their buses all-red. M879 approaches the end of its journey at London Bridge. (Keith Wood)

215 "I thought you were a bugger, but these venture capitalists are even worse! They want their two penn'orth, they are only in it for the short term, they want to sell out as quickly as they can."

London General and London Central

For London General, the first year of the company was the most difficult. There were widespread changes to staff Terms and Conditions to provide the returns the company needed to satisfy its investors, who were represented on the Board. However, performance did improve and the investors relaxed.

The changed conditions led to considerable bad feeling amongst staff. 50% of the drivers left in the first year and the company was 140 drivers short. This was unmanageable and Keith Ludeman knew they could have gone under, but he phoned everybody he knew for staff, and gave up some of his contracts. Two routes went to Len Wright and one to Epsom Coaches. LTB understood what was happening and that he was taking appropriate action. Keith came to an arrangement with Brian Fisher at Plymouth Citybus, who had an entirely different employment situation with a waiting list of drivers. They arranged that Brian would recruit drivers in Plymouth and get them the PCV licence. Keith would find accommodation for them in London, give them route learning 'and throw an A-Z at them'. This worked well – he got 200 drivers and became the Rachman of south London! But he was nervous at Christmas because the drivers might go home and not come back – but they did come back and some of them are still there 18 years later.

Dave Weller was involved in the recruitment and training. They went all over the country to Plymouth, Bristol, Bradford, Manchester, Newcastle and Belfast. At one stage, they had 50 houses they were renting out. In one of these, one of the drivers sold the three-piece suite! Another new recruit was collected at Victoria Coach Station by car. By the time they had got to Colliers Wood and explained the duties, he had insisted that he never worked 40 hours a week and was only going to work 38. They put him back on the train to Victoria Coach Station and sent him home – that was the briefest new recruit they had. Drivers were given three months free rent in the accommodation, and three free coach tickets to go home when they wanted to. Providing accommodation caused problems if staff were sacked or left, as they had to get them out of the accommodation as well.

Long serving staff experienced significant changes to their conditions. Roy Lambe is a driver at Stockwell, and was previously at Victoria. Privatisation had an immediate effect on his hours because he had been working 35 hours a week on nights with an unsocial hours bonus. "Suddenly, it became 45 hours a week

London General took advice from Best Impressions and tidied up their livery with an orange and a white stripe. Ray Stenning found the company's name old fashioned and accentuated London rather than General in the new logo. (Keith Wood)

216 They arranged that Plymouth recruit drivers and get them the PCV licence. London General would find accommodation for them, give them route learning 'and throw an A-Z at them'.

and a 40p per hour pay cut, a big difference. Management told us, 'This is what we can afford, that's what it will be, that's what we are giving you.'" The only compensation was when Victoria closed and everybody put in for redundancy, but he had only done 12 years at that time and wanted to stay, so he didn't apply for redundancy. "A lot of people went, and then they found that they needed some of them back again. So all of those who got redundancy got the chance of coming back without losing their redundancy pay." Roy had not wanted redundancy, he just wanted to continue with his job which he enjoys. "It is physically demanding and mentally tiring because you have to concentrate all the time, and the hours are now long. And in 2014 we're having to learn to work with conductors again," he said, referring to the Customer Assistants on the New Routemaster.

However, Keith Ludeman was pleased that the staff attitude did change positively in the company. "Pat Mahon and the garage reps were on side at this time – what was right for London General was right for them." So they had achieved an ideology for the company that was separate from London Buses. All the stress, the Eastbourne sessions and so on had built up a loyalty to the business.

London General was sold to Go-Ahead for £46 million in May 1996. It had been bought for £28m. Keith recalls, "It gave an eightfold return on investment; the share price of £3.10 had gone up to £28. This changed people's lives and paid off their mortgages." He went back to London General and was treated as a hero. Keith describes himself as "a Marmite character, loved by some and hated by the others who had to put up with the different conditions." Why did London General sell so quickly? Keith explains, "We had a lot of routes coming up for tender which would need new buses, and we couldn't raise that amount of money, so we sold the company to Go-Ahead and were very happy with them taking over."

Martin Ballinger was then the Chief Executive of Go-Ahead group. They had bought London Central in the first round of privatisation, so then had London Central, London General and later bought Metrobus. Go-Ahead increased its share of the London market to around 18%. LT Buses were not concerned by the effect on competition because the joint market share was below 20% and assurances were given that the two companies would be kept distinct.

Roy Lambe didn't take the original shares offered because he was too dumbfounded by the whole process. "I know I cut my nose off to spite my face,

Success with tenders in Sutton led to 42 new double-deckers, 44 low-floor Dennis Dart single-deckers and 10 low-floor Marshall Minibuses for London General in 1996, with five more minibuses for route C3. The Marshall minibus looked attractive and was the only low-floor 8.5m minibus available at the time, but it was not successful, whilst route 413 was given up by London General in November 1997 due to their difficult staff shortage. ML9 is in Morden town centre. (Keith Wood)

217 "Management told us, 'This is what we can afford, that's what it will be, that's what we are giving you.'"

but my view was, you've sold us down the river and now you're trying to give us 20 pieces of gold. Others snapped the shares up, and good luck to them." He has taken part in the share save scheme which saves money from his wages each week, because that is a good way of saving – you don't have to buy the shares. But his wife insisted that he should get some shares and then started looking at the share price all the time and insisted that he should keep them. So he bought some and kept them just to satisfy her.

London Central had settled into the Go-Ahead organisation. Douglas Adie recalls that, "London Buses was very structured, but Go-Ahead was very decentralised. Their office consisted of three Directors and the Pension Fund. Their view was that the key managers knew what they were doing – better than they did on local issues. It was very liberating."

When London General joined the Group, Douglas Adie moved to join the Go-Ahead Board. Keith Ludeman became Managing Director of both companies and a 'reverse take over' took place in which London Central was amalgamated into London General. The London Central head office was closed down but it was kept as a separate company because the terms and conditions were different. London Central had a very mixed set of terms and conditions, some for individual routes, and over time the London General conditions took over those of London Central. Keith Ludeman went on to become Chief Executive of the Go-Ahead Group.

Dave Weller felt that the drivers' situation got better when Go-Ahead took over. Conditions improved at SuttonBus and changed to those of London General. The duties became better, they had no pay rises for a couple of years but their anniversary date went back to the original one, as with other people in London General. There were SuttonBus, Central London Midibuses, new entrant rates, and Bexleybus. They got a £500 lump sum just before Christmas but no pay rise. So everyone in London General was now on the same terms and conditions, except that new staff came in at lower rates. "It was very different in London Central," says Dave. "They had 27 different pay rates at Camberwell alone. The D1 drivers were earning £3.75 an hour. When they merged with London General, paying £5 an hour, large groups of drivers came over saying they wanted to transfer because of the rubbish pay that they were getting. Someone said, 'If you want to see a grown man cry, come and see the people at Camberwell when they get their first payslip!' They were paid such rubbish wages."

But staff shortage became widespread throughout London and was causing serious unreliability in the later 1990s. In 1997 London General reached

London Central continued to receive Volvo Olympians with Northern Counties bodies including NV92 in 1998, which has crossed Westminster Bridge and is turning into Parliament Square. Best Impressions adapted the London General livery and logo, here emphasising Central. (Keith Wood)

agreement with the Trades Unions on a pay deal which, introduced in 1998, gave an increase to pay and allowances and a reduction in the rostered working week. Keith Ludeman was reported saying that, "We will no longer be prepared to win contracts at any price. This will lead to a loss of some work, even from some garages that perform well. The company will in the short term reduce in size, but this will enable us to contract to a healthier base from which we can grow again in the future."

East London & Selkent
Roger Bowker was delighted when he got to know Stagecoach. "Brian Souter visits his managers on the ground, he knows the network, and he has an unbelievable memory." For Roger, it is all about operations and the commercial business. He loves passengers and growth, and he was making the organisation lean and effective. He had been doing things the Stagecoach way without knowing it. "The great thing about East London was the quality of staff at all levels, and the quality of the management team that supported me, and then the quality of Stagecoach. I am passionate about the quality of the buses and the service that is provided. It didn't cost any more, and I insisted on it being perfect. I am sure that this is seen and understood by passengers. I insisted that a bus didn't go out dirty, and I kept my word on this. The staff knew the standards and were committed to it."

Barry Arnold had been in LT throughout his career. "It was good getting out from under LT – all those returns having to be provided on a tight deadline, compared to the simplified monthly returns with an explanation provided to Stagecoach." Barry was surprised how little interference there was compared to what his former colleagues faced with First and Arriva. There was far more letting them get on with it, but it was important not to give Stagecoach any surprises. East London did very well out of Quality Incentive Contracts. They would work out which routes to concentrate resources on and then put a lot into service quality to get the rewards.

East London's Stratford base started as a minibus base for Route 100 but grew to be one of the biggest depots – they kept buying additional pieces of land to add to it. The new West Ham garage replaced it when their two low-cost depots, at Stratford and Waterden Road, were compulsorily purchased for the Olympic site. But in the end, the new West Ham garage, built by TfL, was large and expensive, like another Ash Grove!

Selkent was a problem and Stagecoach tried to sell it in the summer of 1996. As mentioned earlier, CentreWest was negotiating to buy it – Peter Hendy had agreed the price with Brian Souter, but could not

London Central won route D1 from Stagecoach East London in 1994 and commenced operation in May 1995 using Northern Counties bodied Volvo Olympians, one of which is seen at Harbour Exchange Square. (Keith Wood)

219 "We will no longer be prepared to win contracts at any price."

get the capital from his backers. Then Souter decided not to sell and arranged for East London to take it over instead. So from 1 October 1996, Stagecoach East London and Stagecoach Selkent came closer together under the management of the existing East London board, Roger Bowker becoming Chairman and managing director of both companies. Barry Arnold recalls, "Stagecoach then decided to have East London manage Selkent. If we failed, they would be no worse off. The Selkent trade unions saw East London as knowing what we were doing, and they got good vibes from the East London trade unions. There was good rapport so East London gradually got the situation under control with TU co-operation, sickness down and simplified pay rates."

Jon Batchelor was sent from East London to tidy up Catford. "They had 30 spare drivers a day, the performance was good but at a high cost. If a driver wanted to work his rest day, he was given a day's work and brought in as a standby. Selkent was very different to East London – the performance had been good but at a cost. Stagecoach put up with this but when they looked hard at the figures they realised that it was too expensive."

Barry Arnold adds "Brian Souter found he could not do anything to the operation in London and washed his hands of it. He wrote letters to Clive Hodson about proposed changes but his hands were tied. They had thought they would change fares and service levels, for example on Sundays and in the evenings, but they were not able to. They had thought that engineering costs were high, but had not taken into account that it was a 24-hour seven-day operation and so the mileage was higher than anywhere else. The Stagecoach engineering director had leased Olympians at standard industry mileages, but Volvo had not realised the very high mileages being run in London. Stagecoach decided to let the London operation run itself as it was a good company." In fact, Barry was surprised by the restrictive practices that he came across in the other Stagecoach companies – conditions in London had already changed significantly as a result of tendering so that it was running well.

Now part of the Stagecoach Group, East London could borrow buses from other group members when needed. This Volvo B6 on route 294 at Romford Station was one of several loaned by Ribble in spring 1995 as part of a series of moves to provide buses to replace the East London Line of the Underground while the historic Brunel tunnel was repaired. (Keith Wood)

Stagecoach preferred longer lower buses and pressed LT to accept them, together with a front, rather than central, staircase to allow more downstairs seats and a more spacious environment. These changes were agreed by LT and VN43 of 1996 is seen leaving Ilford for Oxford Circus. (Keith Wood)

220 "Brian Souter found he could not do anything to the operation in London and washed his hands of it."

Docklands Transit

In 1996 Docklands won route 106. Their commercial work, including tender bids, was done at Oxford at that time. Simon Thomas of LT Buses evaluated the bids for the 106 and, although the Docklands offer was attractive financially, and Docklands had a good track record on its other contracts, he was concerned that insufficient vehicles had been included in the tender. It was therefore agreed that additional buses would be added if subsequently required and, after experience, peak vehicles were indeed provided within the contract price.

The Docklands operation grew from five drivers in 1989 to 150 at the peak. Frank Cheroomi says that, "I believed in looking after people, and they got good pay, which was less than the LT basic but with bonuses. I called drivers by their first name and I was always ready to speak to people and to know about them in a friendly way." He and his managers also drove buses and so there was a different relationship with the staff. His operation went well – he lent drivers to East Thames – and in all the categories of lost mileage (mechanical, staff and traffic) he had virtually no lost a mileage due to staff causes and was always in the top five TfL operators. "Drivers never left unless they were sacked, due to the atmosphere and friendly nature of Docklands."

Frank did not ban trade unions but none of his drivers wanted to join. He did have a drivers' representative which worked well. He knew from a contact at East London that Barry Arnold had told his drivers he could not give them the pay rise he wanted to because Docklands had undercut him on tender bids. He only tendered for routes that he knew, and TfL told him that his prices were good. He bid unsuccessfully for several routes and was annoyed not to get them. They were unwilling to give him bigger contracts though he already had three routes which he was running successfully and was lending drivers to East Thames, London Buses' own operation. But LT was cautious following earlier problems with the 106.

In July 1997, Stagecoach purchased the Transit Holdings group including Docklands Transit in east London and Thames Transit in Oxford. Frank Cheroomi knew that Harry Blundred had links with Brian Souter so was not surprised when Stagecoach bought the company, which was amalgamated into the East London operation. Stagecoach therefore acquired the 106, which they had unsuccessfully bid for, and which now went to their Stratford depot, with routes 287, 366 and 368 going to Barking. Docklands had just bought new two-door Dennis Darts for the 106.

Barry Arnold arranged for Frank Cheroomi to keep the Reuters contracts and the depot to work on his own. Frank recalls, "When Harry Blundred sold all his operations to Stagecoach, all my drivers who had originally come from Barking garage in 1993 with redundancy packages went back to Barking garage in 1997, and they were all laughing. I didn't want to go to Stagecoach – I did not like the company, and set up on my own. Barry Arnold persuaded Roger Bowker to let me have vehicles, which they released to run the contract."

Docklands Transit took over the 106 in April 1996 using 16 Dennis Darts including Plaxton-bodied 424.
(Colin Stannard)

221 The Docklands operation grew from five drivers in 1989 to 150 at the peak.

By 2000, Frank was tendering for TfL routes under the name Docklands Buses and in 2006 he sold out to Go-Ahead. Four companies were interested because they wanted to move into east London, and only Docklands Buses and Blue Triangle were available to buy. Frank is still running the Reuters contract because Go-Ahead only bought Docklands Buses and left him with the coaches. He now has four coaches on the Isle of Dogs working the Reuters contract, and one of the drivers has been with him ever since 1989.

Capital Citybus
Leon Daniels left Capital Citybus briefly in 1994/5 because the Chinese were looking to sell the company and the management team wanted to buy it. Leon drove the purchase from outside while Brendan Glyde, the Finance Director, stayed within the company. Norman Kemp then spent six months there in early 1995, between Leon departing and returning as buyer. This was in the fallow period just after privatisation, when the tendering programme had been revised and was slowly building up again. "Capital Citybus had, in just a few short years, seen rapid growth with new opportunities every few months. This frantic pace had slowed to a trickle and there was impatience in the company, and especially with the owners, wanting the sort of growth seen in earlier years. In the end, I was really just minding the shop – there was not a lot new happening." The sale to the management team led by Leon Daniels took place in December 1995, and included the operations from both Northumberland Park and Dagenham.

Capital Citybus was one of the few independently owned bus companies still remaining in the London area. Leon describes the co-operation between bus operators, who helped each other when needed, despite the competition. "The advantage of the London tendering system is that the real 'head to head' competition ends when the bids are lodged. Thereafter, good professional co-operation can exist for the benefit of the passengers. Roger Bowker and I used to swap vehicles and staff sometimes when it was necessary. So you might have a blue and silver bus in Walthamstow driven by East London staff!"

Steve Norris was appointed as non-executive Chairman of Capital Citybus in 1997. He was then MP for Epping Forest but had already announced his intention to step down at the next election. He had previously developed his own car dealership network. Steve recalls, "Leon approached me and said would you take this on. He and Brendan Glyde had done a deal to buy the company from TT Tsui in Hong Kong. I'm probably more business-focused than the average Member of Parliament – I'm interested in making things work, so as far as I was concerned this was a natural step to go back into business.

"It was a very enjoyable business and gave me a lot of insight. I thought the system was working perfectly well – we won some tenders and we lost some tenders. When we lost we lost because other people bid more competitively, because they were closer, because they could reduce cost and so on. We oversaw some useful innovations; I think we really improved relationships between our staff and the company, for example."

Docklands Transit was the first operator of the 368, which commenced in 1993 between Chadwell Heath and Barking Station. The company and route passed to Stagecoach in 1997 and has since been run by Blue Triangle, First and Go-Ahead Blue Triangle. A Docklands Transit Dart is in the Broadway, Barking in 1997 before the handover to East London. (Colin Stannard)

222 "The advantage of the London tendering system is that the real 'head to head' competition ends when the bids are lodged. Thereafter, good professional cooperation can exist for the benefit of the passengers."

In 1994, Capital Citybus purchased five articulated single deckers from British Airways. These were Leyland DAB buses with bodywork by Roe, using Leyland National components, and had been used on airport transfer work at Heathrow and Gatwick. Citybus removed the right-hand doors and LT agreed their use on school service 550, which passed underneath a low railway bridge. Citybus also planned to bid with them for Red Arrow routes when they came up for tender, but caused embarrassment when one was shown at the North Weald bus rally in June 1994 with Red Arrow blinds, before the tenders had been announced. The Red Arrow routes were retendered in 1995 and retained by London General using refurbished Leyland National Greenways. (Keith Wood)

Sale of Capital Citybus to its management led to a new logo without the Chinese script. Dennis 424 is seen at Ilford bus stand in summer 1997. (Keith Wood)

Sale of Capital Citybus to FirstGroup brought adoption of First's red London livery. The rear vehicle here shows the '80% red' Citybus livery with yellow lower panels, whilst Volvo VFL26 shows the later First livery. (Colin Fradd)

In July 1998 Capital Citybus was sold to FirstGroup for £24.1 million and became First Capital. Its central London red livery was adopted throughout the fleet and the new FirstGroup 'f' logo began appearing on buses. Leon Daniels adds, "When we came to sell the company on, there were lots of people bidding for it. We went out to the market, the sale being driven by the venture capitalists. First Group offered the best substantive deal. Metroline also made a very attractive offer." The existing management team stayed in place and came under the London and South East Bus Division of FirstGroup headed by Peter Hendy. The company had achieved a 5% share of the London bus market in just over 10 years and wanted the purchase by FirstGroup to allow expansion. The purchase gave FirstGroup a national market share of 21%, followed by Stagecoach with 16% and Arriva close behind at 15%. There was an immediate exchange of routes with Thamesway. Control of the First Thamesway depot at Ponders End was transferred to First Capital, with the same vehicles and staff being used. Thamesway was to open a new depot at Harold Wood.

Metrobus
In 1995 Metrobus gained the ISO 9001 award in recognition of the high level of efficiency it had achieved throughout its activities over a sustained period. The award was presented by LT Chairman Peter Ford and Metrobus added the wording 'Setting out to set standards' to their fleetname.

Metrobus also took on Bryan Constable as Development Manager following the Stagecoach takeover of Selkent. Bryan produced the Metrobus bid for the retendering of the Orpington network in 1995, based on his knowledge from Selkent and Roundabout of the routes and the operating costs of the minibuses. Metrobus was confident of their bid because of their good reputation on LT routes. Peter Larking thought their bid was 'in the bag', so they were particularly disappointed when the routes were won by CentreWest.

Metrobus also lost route 61 to CentreWest: they had run it well for two contract terms, as recognised by the ISO award, and felt that their high standards of operation should have been recognised. He was surprised that CentreWest won the 61 because he was certain that his costs would be lower than theirs. Peter Hendy was happy to demonstrate that he could run it successfully.

In response, Metrobus registered a commercial service numbered 610 over the same routeing as the 61 between Bromley North Station and Orpington in competition with the CentreWest tendered operation. Peter Larking recalls, "Our plan was to ruffle some feathers. It was easy to get a London Commercial Service Licence from the Traffic Commissioner." His proposed commercial route would make use of buses that would be redundant after he lost the service. In December there was more cash on buses and, though he would not receive pass revenue, there was probably going to be enough cash to pay the direct costs in the short term. "However," says Peter, "ruffle feathers it did, as LT had never had to deal with competition against one of their routes. It coincided with a meeting between LT and Kentish Bus who were struggling to operate some of their routes. The upshot of this was that LT brokered a deal where Metrobus took over routes 161 and 138 from Kentish Bus in early December 1995, followed by the 181 and 284 in January 1996. This ensured the surplus buses were not available for the 610, which was never operated, and Metrobus acquired additional buses to cover the increased work."

Metrobus is a good example of an operator who grew within the tendering system and earned respect from the public and from the transport industry. But Peter Larking was growing concerned at the scale of Metrobus's commitment to London tendering, with around 120 buses, and they preferred to have routes which were 'their own' rather than contracted to TfL. "You could easily lose all of your contracts within a few years if things didn't go your way. So we decided to look outside London." In 1997 Metrobus bought East Surrey of South Godstone, a share of Leisurelink in Newhaven, and took over a service between East Grinstead and Haywards Heath from Lewes Coaches. In a successful year they added LT services 64 and 233 to their operation. In September 1999 they sold out to Go-Ahead, which continued to operate Metrobus

"Our plan was to ruffle some feathers. LT had never had to deal with competition against one of their routes."

as a separate entity alongside London Central and London General. The whole company, based at Orpington, Lewes and Godstone, was included in the deal at £15.5 million. The directors Peter Larking and Gary Wood remained in day-to-day control of the business. Go-Ahead was then the second largest group in London, behind Arriva, with 18% of the LT bus market.

Armchair
Armchair were awarded two single deck routes in 1996, the 117 from 31 August and the 190 from 7 December. Huw Barrington jokes that, as always with buses, you wait for ages and then two come together! These had peak vehicle requirements of five and six single-deck buses, eleven in total. As the tendering programme developed, they were looking for routes close to their depot. The E bus network then came up and they were able to win the E2 and E8 from CentreWest, running from Brentford to Ealing and Greenford.

Huw was very happy with net cost contracts – if you had growing routes they really enhanced the revenue. But he realised that for every route that got a bonus, there would be another one that lost out. The 65, E2 and E8 all ran between Ealing and Brentford by three different routes – they could not all be growing at the same time.

Armchair was a quality operation, but new vehicles cost a lot of money and they needed to know that they would have work for a full life, not just for a three-year contract. Armchair retained every route except the 65, which went to London United. The other routes were enhanced with greater frequencies, but their profitability went down.

Huw was with Armchair for 12 years from 1990 to 2002, but they could not expand further. By this time the peak vehicle requirement was around 90 buses, they had over 200 staff and had moved depot, renting a larger space at a BRS depot in Brentford, just in time for the Ealing area expansion. They were able to sell the previous property and this site enabled them to bring back the maintenance in-house, rather than contracting it out, which was completed over a period of time.

A picture from 1997 shows Metrobus Dennis Trident 426, which was by then one of the last remaining London buses not running in red livery. (Colin Fradd)

225 "Net cost contracts really enhanced the revenue. But for every route that got a bonus, there would be another one that lost out."

New buses and low floors
In late 1996, new bus orders were increasing to the levels of the 1980s following the continuing policy of LT Buses to award most contracts on the basis of new buses. The former London Buses companies had around 400 vehicles on order or being delivered, while many other operators were also investing heavily, particularly Capital Citybus, Cowie County Bus, and London and Country. The Metrobus fleet of 100 vehicles was achieving an average age of around three years. Vehicles tended to be ordered for specific routes, rather than for general fleet replacement, and single-deckers were arriving in greater numbers than double-deckers.

A new Disability Discrimination Bill was under discussion which was to require that all new buses should be wheelchair accessible. Manufacturers were developing low-floor, fully accessible buses, and new double-decker designs followed later. Low floor single-deck buses had been entering service around outer London since 1994, and they now reached central London with the conversion of Routemaster route 139 to Dennis Darts from March 1998. The benefits of low floor buses were greater than originally expected, because in addition to providing wheelchair access the easy entrance helped those travelling with young children and buggies, and passengers carrying heavy shopping or luggage. Many operators found that revenue increases quickly covered the additional capital cost of the buses and that new types of passenger were being attracted to buses.

The first low floor double-deckers in London entered service on route 242 in November 1998 when Arriva London North placed DAF vehicles with Alexander bodywork into service. These formed part of an order for 130 similar buses placed by Arriva for London services.

Government proposals published in 1998 to implement the 1995 Disability Discrimination Act required all single-deck buses in service to be fully accessible by 2015 and double-deckers by 2017. These dates were set to take account of the normal replacement programme of modern buses. There was no requirement for disabled access to the upper deck of double deckers.

London's buses in 1997
In 1997, Ken Glazier wrote in the *London Bus Magazine* reflecting on the changes in London's bus operations over the previous 25 years. He suggested that in 1997 political control was still present but must have been at its loosest ever. 1972 was the third year of direct political control of London Transport by the Greater London Council, whilst 1997 was the third year of private ownership of the London bus fleet, though London Transport itself was still a publicly-owned corporation and political control was exercised through the appointment of the Chairman and members of the Board. However, the direct intervention in day-to-day matters which was marked in 1972 had gone. The government did take a close interest in the fares and charges, but the tight formal controls which previously existed had been dismantled.

The move to tendering required central planning of routes for tender so that it ceased to be appropriate for local managers in the competing bus operating companies to participate. Planning was now by experts with heavy use of computer analysis, rather than by direct local knowledge of need. Consultation with London Boroughs and other stakeholders was still required but this now came at the end of the planning process, rather than providing input at the beginning. The consultation process had become more complex and now contributed to the slow process of change.

In 1972 London Transport was, as always, trying to solve the three problems of staff shortage, traffic congestion and balancing its books. However, in 1997 service planners could leave the problems of staffing and cost control to their contractors. This led to substantial improvements to service in the evenings and on Sundays, including the reintroduction of some services which had not operated for many years. The 'midibus revolution' had also allowed buses into areas which had not seen them before. The major reduction in costs that permitted this was due to the reductions in drivers' pay and the increase in their working hours. The economy in 1997 made lower wages possible.

In 1972, in the early years of control by the GLC, there was growing public support in favour of public transport, and in 1997 this seemed to be coming again with support from the new government to encourage people to use buses.

Staff shortages
Driver recruitment became a major problem for all the London bus operators in the later 1990s. This resulted in service cuts and, in some cases, a failure to meet performance standards. Government statistics showed that, between 1985/6 and 1996/7, bus drivers' wages had fallen by 4% in real terms compared to an increase of 20% for the workforce overall. Working hours at 48.6 per week were unchanged but were longer than the national average of 40.3 hours.

The jobs market had become more competitive and the need to put in low-priced tenders to win LTB contracts, with prices locked in for up to five years, caused pressure on wages. LTB had been increasing the frequency on many routes, as well as extending

"In 1972 London Transport was, as always, trying to solve the three problems of staff shortage, traffic congestion and balancing its books. However, in 1997 service planners could leave the problems of staffing and cost control to their contractors."

the operating day into the evenings and adding Sunday services. Whilst this was to be welcomed, it put additional pressure on the recruitment of staff.

Complaints and investigations
In September 1998, the House of Commons Transport Select Committee demanded an inquiry into an alleged cartel on LT bus services. They pointed out that six operators then controlled 93% of London's routes, which was correct, though it was a wider spread of ownership than in other UK cities, while the balance of London's operation was by 13 other smaller operators.

There were also operators who complained about the awarding of tenders. Some suggested that a cartel was being managed by LT, and others that LT was too zealous in its efforts to attract new operators. This comment became more prominent following LT's apparent toleration of poor performance by some operators, such as on route 60. Route awards were made to achieve 'best value' but LT had never published details of the tenders received, and this secrecy encouraged some to think that awards were not necessarily being made fairly. LTB's Procurement Director Brian Everett said that information about bids would now be made public, including the number of tenders received, the amounts of the highest and lowest bids, and the reason that the successful bidder was selected. LT were also seeking Government approval to offer longer contract periods as a way of getting more investment in routes and vehicles.

New operators did continue to be attracted to LT contracts. Newcomers in 1999 were Hackney Community Transport (HCT), London Traveller, Mitcham Belle and Wings Buses.

Route 60
In early 1998, route 60 was awarded to Capital Logistics, replacing Arriva London South. The contract was awarded to them on the basis of the high quality operation proposed, together with a bid that offered good value for money. The company had also stated a desire to expand with the support of its parent company, National Parking Corporation. Route 60 was amended at both ends to run between Streatham Common and Old Coulsdon, becoming a significant trunk service.

Capital Logistics had been formed in August 1997 following the merger of Whyte's Airport Services and Capital Coaches. It operated a variety of coach and contract services around Heathrow Airport, together with some LT services. However, in April 1998 National Parking Corporation was taken over by Cendant Corporation, who undertook a critical review of all aspects of NPC's business. This resulted in local bus operation no longer being considered a core part of the group's operation. The contract for route 60 was due to start on 29 August together with other changes in the area. Capital Logistics had ordered 16 DAF buses, but production of these new low floor double deckers was delayed, and the buses were not ready until 1999. Immediately prior to the proposed start date Capital Logistics advised LT that they could not start the contract on time, as the new vehicles were not available. They also did not find a suitable operating base near the route, nor did they recruit sufficient drivers. It was suggested at the time that they would have liked to give up the contract. Capital Logistics were required by LT to meet their contractual obligations, and made arrangements for Stagecoach Selkent and Blue Triangle to operate the service on a temporary basis as subcontractors, initially with a reduced frequency. The full frequency was restored in October 1998.

Capital Logistics were then approached by Driver Express of Horsham, who wished to take over the contract as a way of entering the London bus operating market. This was planned for 23 January 1999, when Stagecoach Selkent's temporary operation had to cease due to their other commitments. Driver Express anticipated using the new buses that Capital Logistics had ordered, and negotiations reached an advanced stage. However, the transfer did not take place and a group of companies and vehicles continued to operate the service to an emergency timetable through December and January.

When Stagecoach Selkent had to withdraw in mid-January, to take over their new contracts in Bexleyheath, an emergency service was operated by a range of elderly buses and coaches drafted in from far and wide with seven operators becoming involved in its operation. The local newspaper ran a front-page piece "Bus firm with no buses brings out the old bangers" and spoke of passengers, "waiting for an age for buses to arrive and then, when they do, face the ignominy of transport buffs lining up to take their photographs". The enthusiast group LOTS acknowledged that the comments about photographers was certainly true. Local councillors commented that, "If this wasn't so serious it would be laughable". LT acknowledged, "Route 60 is unprecedented in the number of problems we've had. It's a sorry situation".

The service had become fairly regular by early February and Capital Logistics was able to operate from March 1999, using the 16 new DAF double-deckers. Capital Logistics also operated route U3 and the former Green Line route 726 gained from London Coaches. It was sold to Tellings Golden Miller in June 1999. TGM Transport and Capital Logistics were then grouped with other companies outside London into the "Status Bus and Coach Group" under its Chairman Julian Peddle and were awarded LTB route 344.

The variety of vehicles used on route 60 included the following

DMS 2333 of 1978 had four owners between leaving LT in 1991 and joining Nostalgiabus in 1996. (Colin Stannard)

Nostalgiabus also provided B102SED, a former Warrington Corporation Leyland Olympian with East Lancs body, while First Capital provided Metrobus 262. (Colin Stannard)

Nostalgiabus also provided RM1571 with a hand-painted number plate. A Leyland National was supplied by Classic Coaches. (Colin Stannard)

Capital Logistics' new DAF double-deckers arrived in early 1999 and one is seen at Croydon South End in April with its Capital Connections logos. (John Miller)

Route 60 was passed back to Arriva London South in April 2000. Simon Thomas remarks that, "Route 60 was a sorry tale of what can happen when things go wrong, but it hasn't happened since."

Harris Bus

John Wilson was General Manager of Harris Coaches for some years and had experience of tendering with Essex County Council before they decided to bid for London contracts. He set up Harris Buses as a separate operation from October 1986, formed as a separate company so that Harris Coaches would not be affected if there were problems. John was the only person in the company with bus operating experience.

He had bid for tendered routes in Grays and Brentwood and developed some commercial services. He then bid for LT tenders but did not get them – he found out later that while he had put in sensible prices, he had been undercut – he was not willing to win the work at any price. He then left the company, which began to win tenders in 1997 by putting in lower bids. These included services south of the River Thames, a considerable distance from their existing operating area.

The first win was for school route 661, followed by the 108 which was very high profile at the time as it served the Millennium Dome. Routes 128, 129 and 150 in east London commenced in July 1997, and the 132 and 180 were awarded for implementation early in 1998.

Simon Thomas recalls evaluating the bids for the 128, 129 and 150. They were attractive prices, but this was considerable additional work for the company to take on. Simon and Mike Weston were concerned at the possibility of overstretching Harris and recommended awarding them one of the routes only. However, this was overruled and it was decided to give Harris all three routes. But the bids were too low and Harris could not deliver – they were overstretched, and this led to their downfall.

Simon adds, "On all contracts, operators make greater profits in the early years and need a cycle of new profitable contracts in the later years to balance the older contracts. Whilst a Contract Price Adjustment (CPA) is paid, based on standard price indexes, if fuel, labour and maintenance costs increase to a greater extent, the contractor might well find it more difficult. The contracts are therefore generally profitable at first but less profitable as time goes on. Further, Harris may have been costing bus maintenance on coach experience, which would have been too little for intensive bus work."

Towards the end of 1999 it became clear that Harris Bus was experiencing problems and the owners were seeking to sell the bus side of the company. Increasing losses from higher wages and fuel tax were made worse by deductions for lost mileage. LT negotiated with other operators who might have taken the operation over but this led to nothing, as those other operators would not run the service at the Harris prices. Administrators took over the running of the company but reliability became

Harris Bus arrived as newcomers to tendering with a good image using modern vehicles and a livery by Best Impressions. Their first route was the 108, which was operated by new Optare Excels branded 'Lewisham Link'. One is seen at Stratford Bus Station after its journey through the Blackwall Tunnel from Lewisham and Greenwich. (Keith Wood)

worse as drivers left to work for other operators. Notices appeared on bus stops in the Ilford area during January 2000 warning that there would be reduced services.

LT Buses then caused surprise by announcing that it would take over the day-to-day management of the company directly. It revived the name 'London Buses Ltd' and advertised for drivers and supervisors, but subsequently used the trading name 'East Thames Buses', running services from the Harris Bus site at Belvedere and from the former Ash Grove garage in Hackney, which was still owned by LT but had been empty. This was intended to be a temporary arrangement until the re-tendering of all the Harris routes. As a result LTB, the regulatory authority, was now operating buses in its own right through a subsidiary called LBL which reinstated the name which had not operated buses since privatisation of the last subsidiary in 1995. Later in the year it was announced that LBL would continue to operate the routes until the end of the current contracts, and the buses were painted red.

Whilst Harris Bus came from the Harris of Grays coach company, which had a good reputation, there was no arrangement for the debts of Harris Bus to fall on the coach company. LT contracts included the provision that a company who dropped tenders should pay the additional cost of retendering, but Harris Bus went into receivership and there was no 'grandfather agreement' that put responsibility with Harris of Grays. Following this experience, papers were quickly sent out to contractors requiring them to identify who would cover re-tendering costs if they failed.

The failure of Harris Bus was unfortunate. They had presented a good impression with good buses, livery, and enthusiasm but they had got their costings seriously wrong. LTB said that they were taking the work in-house partly to provide a 'public sector comparator', as it was increasingly felt that there was a lack of competition between the big bus groups. But East Thames Buses was a costly operation throughout its life.

Net cost and gross cost contracts

In preparation for privatisation, the block grant routes had been put onto negotiated contracts on a net cost basis in which the operator kept the on-bus revenue and a proportion of the off-bus revenue allocated on the basis of surveys. This was intended to motivate and directly reward operators to produce a good service to passengers, and the plan was to convert all contracts to net cost contracts (NCCs) when they became due for renewal.

NCCs proved cumbersome to work and opinions varied on their effect. Steve Norris, who as Minister had required their introduction when deregulation was dropped, argues that gross cost contracts discourage operators from carrying passengers – they are rewarded for running the bus to schedule, and this is easier done if you have fewer passengers getting in the way! With net cost contracts, an operator who thinks he can grow the market for that route will put in a lower bid.

Twenty-two Volvo Olympians with East Lancs Pyoneer bodies were bought for routes 128, 129 and 150 and branded 'Ilford Link'. Both single-door and two-door examples were bought. A single-door version is seen at Gants Hill. (John Miller)

231 LTB said that they were taking the work in-house partly to provide a 'public sector comparator', as it was increasingly felt that there was a lack of competition between the big bus groups.

On the other hand David Bayliss, then LT Director of Planning, argued that passengers do not distinguish between operators and that net cost contracts simply encouraged operators to run late, so that they picked up their own passengers and those who would have caught the next bus. David added that if potential changes to services are identified, "The route structure could be revisited from time to time, but because of the interlinked nature of the London market, NCCs are not the best solution. The argument against gross cost contracts (GCCs) is that they stifle innovation by the operator. But the more interesting argument is, does it stifle productive competition?" He suggests that the competition would be intended to generate profits rather than innovation. If an operator wanted to propose something better in a tender bid – a better service pattern or buses – it was always considered. "The difficulty was, you could only go so far before the losing bidder cried foul and said that the contract had been awarded on a different basis. Whilst there might be little change in routes during the life of the contracts, this is not a bad thing as you need a fair amount of stability in the service." As an example, he quotes Len Wright being given an extended contract in order to justify new vehicles and guarantees of high performance.

The former LBL operators were very happy with NCCs. At Leaside, Mark Yexley thought them motivating, and wishes they could have continued because they encouraged operators to market the routes and to be innovative. There had been recession in the early '90s, but later on there was growth which led to a real increase in income. The major problem was that the formula was so crude and difficult to work with. If the route varied, then a revenue adjustment had to be made to the net cost contract but it was difficult to accurately forecast what the effect would be. If the change was greater than a benchmark, it became material. You needed to know the financial aspects, and their Finance Director Robert Newson really understood this and successfully argued the cases that were worth pursuing. When Robert Newson left Leaside he acted as Revenue Consultant to the Net Cost Operators, with all of the tendered London bus operators jointly paying for him. He was a party to the negotiations with LT over any changes to the contracts, for example due to the fares increasing or in the structure of fares through Travelcard changes. This continued until all the net cost contracts were bought out by LT in around 2000. CentreWest was the last operator with them, and then his role vanished.

Mark Yexley describes Arriva's activities to increase cash revenue on the NCC routes. An example was the night bus routes where they produced spoofs of the old grey London Transport advertisements telling people how to get on and off the bus. These joke cartoons were put on beer mats and coasters and distributed in areas where there were plenty of students to pinch them. It worked well and contributed to a great build-up in the night bus routes. By 2015 they had 37 buses on the N29 on Friday and Saturday nights, an outstanding growth. Another example was the heart symbol on Route 38, and McDonald's vouchers which were distributed for cash passengers on Route 68A. They also introduced the first low floor single deck buses on the 144, allowing baby buggies to be rolled on and off. With hindsight quite how these initiatives compared with other influences on increasing bus usage is debatable. London's economy and population both rose in the latter part of the decade and there was always a belief in LT that their initiatives were the bigger drivers of growth. This prompted the move away from NCCs to Quality Incentive Contracts (QICs).

Those who understood the complex system were able to benefit from it. Peter Hendy recalls that net cost contracts were so complicated that hardly anyone understood them – they were unintelligible to people outside the market and gave him a distinct advantage. But Robin Orbell at Thamesway, whose tendered routes were working on a gross cost basis, wanted nothing to do with net cost contracts as he considered that the operator would take all the risk but not have control of any of the levers to put the operation right when necessary. He was pleased that they were not extended to other routes and that they ended after a short time.

NCCs made it difficult to change the network, because an incumbent operator might claim that this would affect the takings on which they had based their bid for the contract. But cash revenue was

Leaside's marketing of route 38 included the large new logo with a heart in its centre. (David Cole)

Net cost contracts were so complicated that hardly anyone understood them – they were unintelligible to people outside the market and gave him a distinct advantage.

New operators in the late 1990s included: Travel West Midlands, who took over route C1 from 13 June 1998. Their Optare Excel is at Earls Court when new. It was later transferred to the West Midlands. (Keith Wood)

Blue Triangle won the new route 474, from Canning Town to East Beckton, which commenced on 1 May 1999. (Colin Stannard)

233 In the financial year 1997/98 the previous operating loss on London's buses was transformed to a small surplus.

declining, and the allocation of off-bus revenue was complex and time consuming, particularly if there was disagreement. If an operator miscalculated and got their bid wrong, they would have to find other ways of reducing their costs.

Travelcard revenue had to be split between TfL and ATOC for the national railways, then between the Underground and buses. With NCCs, it then had to be split again, between the bus routes and operators – a horrendous task. The time taken to calculate all this was unsettling to operators. Barry Arnold recalls, "You were waiting to see what the off-bus revenue was at the end of the financial period and this could be the difference between profit and loss for the company. However you had little real control over the revenue, which was more affected by the weather and other events. The surveys were a bit hit and miss. After a time, TfL realised that there were too many variables, and it was an expensive system to run with the cost of the surveyors and the cost of converting their results into money. There was the feeling that companies were benefiting from revenue increases that were due to TfL, for example paying for publicity and marketing campaigns leading to improved loadings which benefited the companies."

Clive Hodson, as Managing Director of LT Buses, was concerned about the increasing cost of the NCCs. "I was very unhappy about it and we started to do some contracts on a sharing basis where we had 50% and the operator had 50% – and eventually I set up a trial of Quality Incentive Contracts to see if they would work. And they took off! Let's be clear about net cost contracts – they were not delivering the goods as far as getting good value for LT, so that's when we introduced quality indicators, average waiting times and certain criteria for low frequency routes, and if the companies came up with the goods they were rewarded, and if they didn't they were penalised."

So QICs were introduced and switched the emphasis for operators from growing passenger numbers to concentrating on improving reliability. Mark Yexley adds, "The QICs have led to an amazing improvement in quality, once some money had been put into them. It took until 2006 to complete the transfer from Net Cost Contracts to Quality Incentive Contracts. Dave Alexander agrees, "With the Quality Incentive Contracts, the QICs, you started to get all the qualitative as opposed to just the quantitative aspects incorporated into the whole contract management process. Which was good, because that meant you really then had to engage the drivers in a different way, it wasn't just about ringing the bell and getting the buses out. You had to get the right buses out in the right way, to the right quality. It was a real challenge."

A further development was Quality Partnerships with the London Boroughs. The first was with the London Borough of Islington for new measures along route 43. LT Buses had announced a major programme of improvements to the route, while Islington Council would rebuild kerbs at bus stops to help passengers to board the new low-floor buses, and place more resources into keeping bus routes clear of parked cars. Quality partnerships were also agreed with the London Boroughs of Bromley and Richmond, and in 1999 the first experimental new 'Super Routes' project was announced for route 32, between Edgware Station and Kilburn Park, which was to have stricter enforcement of new bus lanes and parking rules. This produced a significant reduction in bus travel times.

Revenue neutral
In the financial year 1997/98 the previous operating loss on London's buses was transformed to a small surplus. This was credited to the success of the tendering programme together with increased demand. A surplus of 0.01 pence per bus kilometre was reported, compared to a 3.3 pence subsidy the previous year. Bus kilometres had increased by 3%, partly through conversion to midibus operation, and passenger journeys increased by 3.5%. But the subsidy returned to 3.4p in the following year. Clive Hodson remembers, "We did one year make a small profit of about £25,000, quite marginal really, so the only grant we got was for capital which again was quite small, so the grant came down a considerable amount in total. But then wages were starting to move in London and the loss started to go up again. You couldn't go against the tide of the general economy and wages, but we did get it down."

A report *Buses in London: A comparison with the rest of Great Britain* (LT Planning, January 1998) showed that, between 1985/6 and 1996/7, bus operating costs per mile in London had reduced by 45%, similar to the 46% throughout Great Britain, whilst costs per passenger journey had declined by 32% in London compared to 8% throughout Great Britain and 0% in the English Metropolitan counties. Bus usage had declined by 23% throughout Great Britain and by 40% in the Metropolitan areas, whilst there was an 8% increase in London. Subsidies had declined by 78% in London compared with 60% in the Metropolitan Ares and 52% in Great Britain overall. Bringing these figures together, London had the lowest rate of financial support per passenger journey at under 5p per journey, while all other areas of the country had between 10p and 15p per journey.

Many felt that costs had been cut too harshly to achieve this result. Peter Hendy suggests that though the subsidy was briefly zero, "You couldn't survive and it was a poor quality service, with lost mileage

---

"Ken Livingstone was pragmatic. He wanted a bigger, better bus service more than he wanted public ownership and he got it. And he employed someone he called a capitalist to achieve that – me!"

due to staff shortages once again." Norman Cohen recalls that, "The idea of actually running any extra routes went completely out of the window. There were all these extra services that the service planners had identified – they were just regarded as dreams in those days." Gordon Tennant agrees that while the bus operation was virtually self-sufficient for a brief time, it was completely unsustainable as the wages were not keeping pace with London wage rates; for example, Metroline had 42% staff turnover in one year.

However, the zero subsidy that year was an important achievement on which later expansion could be based.

New Labour Government and the Mayor
The Labour Party won the May 1997 General Election with Tony Blair as Prime Minister. It was committed to setting up a new strategic authority for London and a Mayor, both to be directly elected. These would take responsibility for London-wide issues such as planning, policing and transport, including London Transport, the Metropolitan Police and the London Fire Brigade. The proposals were put to a referendum in May 1998 that supported them and the new Greater London Authority was set up in 2000.

The bus service continued to be disrupted by traffic congestion and increasing staff shortages. LT Buses' financial position worsened due to increased tender prices resulting from the need for operators to increase staff wages and reduce shortages. It was, however, suggested that the formation of large groups had reduced the scope for competitive bids. LT Buses encouraged more operators to tender, and offered some contracts on a gross cost basis, or for seven years instead of five. The LT Chairman, Peter Ford, was sacked by John Prescott, Secretary of State for the Environment, Transport and the Regions in 1998.

The Government's Transport White Paper was followed by a 'daughter paper' on bus policy in 1999. There would be no return to regulated services outside London, and the emphasis was on developing quality partnerships with local authorities in which bus operators would invest in new fully accessible buses and improved frequencies, while councils would provide more bus lanes and other priority schemes.

Transport *for* London was created in 2000 responsible to the Mayor of London and the London Assembly. Major changes took place in the Board, the structure and the management of the organisation which would once again become more of a local government organisation. Ken Livingstone was elected Mayor and introduced Congestion Charging to tackle London's traffic problems head on, together with a major build up in the London bus operation.

Clive Hodson chose to retire rather than face a change of direction and a new upheaval. He was used to working with ministers and Civil Servants and TfL would, once again, become a local government organisation. "I said I would like to retire, so I had a one year contract from April 2000. I had several meetings with Ken and Dave Wetzel, and what they wanted me to do was completely stop the tendering process. But we were required under the LRT Act to tender the routes and we could only extend contracts under certain conditions, but not stop the process. Clearly we weren't going to work together so we parted ways and I left in March 2001. I had done 41 years so I couldn't complain – I've had a bloody good innings actually!"

In fact Ken Livingstone continued with tendering, and Peter Hendy returned as Managing Director Surface Transport and, from 2006, Commissioner of Transport. "Ken was pragmatic. He wanted a bigger, better bus service more than he wanted public ownership and he got it. And he employed someone he called a capitalist to achieve that – me!"

And finally
The first LRT Business Plan in 1985 concluded with a description of a future journey to work, ten years later in 1995. In the course of her journey, Sue gets on her local bus and greets Jane the driver. Then we are told, "Jane used to be a taxi driver, until her taxi co-op tendered for the franchise to run the feeder bus service to the nearby Tube station." It was clearly expected when tendering commenced that small operators would become involved and provide fresh input to London's bus services, but in practice the consolidation of the bus companies into larger groups meant that this never happened.

The smaller companies have fallen by the wayside and the larger companies combined into ever bigger groups. When Metroline was sold to Delgro in March 2000, it was the last individual company left from the privatisation of London Buses. All the former LBL subsidiaries were now owned by large transport groups, a process which had taken about five years. Many of those who ran the London Buses companies had very successful careers, retiring with their profits or becoming senior executives of the companies that bought them, or in many cases both.

Steve Norris remembers addressing the annual dinner of the Confederation of Passenger Transport and saying, "It's an enormous pleasure to be here. Looking around the audience, I've made half of you millionaires and the other half redundant!" "And actually," he adds now, "there was more than a grain of truth in it."

10 LOOKING BACK: A VIEW FROM 2015

Buses are important to London. They benefit the whole community and the London economy. They take people to work, kids to school, customers to the shops, and everybody out and about for their entertainment. As London grows, only buses can be adjusted quickly to changes in demand. Railways take many years to build, while cars cause congestion and pollute the atmosphere. Every bus in service is estimated to replace 30 cars – dependence on cars in place of buses would bring London to a halt, and it would not be able to function. Over half the buses in the UK, and over half the passenger journeys made on buses, are in London. Carrying 2.4 billion passengers a year, there are almost twice as many bus journeys in London as on the Underground.

Buses are worth more to London than the fares people are able and willing to pay to use them. Even those who do not use them benefit from the service they provide. Someone who travels to Harrods in a chauffeur driven car benefits from the buses that took the shop staff and many of the other customers there, and which keep the roads clearer of other cars. The city banker in his tower benefits from the buses which keep the city working, and his staff and customers mobile.

Buses do 'pay their way' when all the benefits they bring are taken into account, so public funding is justified as long as it achieves defined objectives. The complexity of London, its geography, its 24-hour activities, and its comprehensive public transport system make dependence on individual fares for individual bus rides insufficient. For the bus system to

LT took the lead in developing fully-accessible buses with a government-sponsored project to introduce 68 low-floor single-deckers to five routes in five different LBL companies. The first was London United's 120, and one of the Wright-bodied Dennis Lance SLF single-deckers introduced in June 1995 is seen at Southall. (Mike Harris)

236 "London's citizens, workforce and visitors deserve a decent public transport system, at an affordable price, and which comes at frequent intervals."

perform at its best, it is appropriate for public funds to be used to provide a better quality and more frequent service. London's citizens, workforce and visitors deserve a decent public transport system, at an affordable price, and which comes at frequent intervals. They deserve to travel in pleasant conditions, and the staff similarly deserve to be properly rewarded for their work.

Tendering, not deregulation
Privatisation sold the operation of London's buses into the private sector. It did not privatise or deregulate the planning, organisation, funding, marketing and infrastructure of London's bus services, which remain publicly owned and accountable through London politicians. The operation of the services is similarly accountable, being run by private operators to standards set and monitored by Transport for London. This was a highly significant decision by a Government committed to the market but which realised the particular situation of London where deregulation could not work effectively. The decision was led by Steve Norris who explains, "You have to be able to order traffic generally on predictable route patterns. When you're doing something like refiguring the Tottenham Court Road junction, you have to be able to say, 'Don't go here, do go there, you're not allowed in that area,' and so unfettered deregulation in London would still be the disaster that it was briefly in cities outside London."

London is different from other UK cities, a densely populated city of over eight million people which is continuing to grow rapidly, with narrow streets and limited road space. Steve Clayton saw this throughout his career which took in London and deregulated operations elsewhere. "The only way buses can operate successfully in London is if there is good management of the road network and excellent operational management of the bus services. If politicians have the resolve to do this then it is ok – otherwise services will be unreliable. London is very different from the rest of the country. All the pressures – operational, financial and political – are far stronger than elsewhere."

Norman Cohen was relieved when deregulation did not come. "I never thought it was a good idea, and certainly not for London. I'm still not convinced that it's a good idea for the metropolitan areas – I think there's a lot of waste even now in places like Manchester and Liverpool where the very large operators compete with each other, each running third-full buses at best. And the whole idea of a coordinated integrated network is subsidiary to that."

Steve Norris saw that operators would be attracted by the greater certainty that London tendering brought them. Tony Kennan, who came to operate in London after experience in the north of England, agrees that the system in London is probably better for operators. "We got a guaranteed cash flow, we knew what our margin of error was; we were quite happy with the cash flow which was different than in the deregulated environment, and deregulation in London was never really politically acceptable."

Tendering by a central authority also brings common standards throughout the network, and an organisation with the buying power to lead the industry. Andrew Braddock points out that "London has had a fully-accessible bus system since late 2005, long before the legal requirement of 2016 (for single-deckers) and 2017 (for double-deckers). This has been achieved by requiring accessible buses in new contracts, which accelerated the development of suitable vehicles. London has a properly-funded public authority buying its requirements from a competitive private sector on performance contracts and monitoring their quality against those contracts." London has similarly led the development of hybrid buses in the UK.

Competition in London
In London, there is competition for the contract to run each route – competition *for the road* rather than competition *on the road*. Constraints on road capacity mean that deregulation may never have worked in London, yet the plans went on for many years. Robert Newson, who joined LT in September 1981 as a Finance Trainee, and rose to become Finance Director of Leaside, has looked at the theory behind this:

"The principle of the market economy is that competition and free trade make everyone better off, because market competition aligns the self-interest of those seeking to make money with the satisfaction of their customers' desires by supplying those customers with goods and services. However, there are situations where a free market does not work properly, and where governments should intervene to promote competition.

"The London bus market is different from other consumer markets. Bus services quickly came up against the capacity of the road network, and this started to become a problem in the early 1920s. To regulate the situation the London Traffic Act 1924 gave the authorities the power to restrict the numbers of buses working on particular routes or streets. The effect of this was to divide up the market between the incumbent operators at the time, and prevent competition by new entrants on particular roads, so this was not an ideal solution. Those who proposed deregulation for London's buses in the 1980s had to be reminded of these lessons of the 1920s. Given the lack of spare capacity on many roads at many times of the day, it is clear that deregulation would have led to serious traffic problems and almost certainly to gridlock.

"If on-the-road competition is rejected, then it is necessary to find a way for bus operators to compete for the available road capacity. A franchise system, where operators keep the traffic revenue, risks granting local monopolies that operators could exploit if they retain control over fares and service levels; but if the authorities have control of fares and service levels, then operators cannot respond to changing demand, and may find they are locked-in to an un-profitable franchise.

"These objections led to the solution that we now have, of contracting-out the operation of bus routes while the authority retains the revenue. It has stood the test of time for many years, during which perceptions of bus travel have greatly improved and passenger numbers have soared to the 1950s levels. TfL has to be alert to the possibility of collusion between its contractors, and there needs to be political oversight of TfL to avoid the complacency and inflation of costs that can occur in any public-sector body.

"Having decided that we need a transport authority, it does have benefits, in particular the integration of services and ticketing that would be much less likely, and might be illegal, in a deregulated market."

Most urban public transport around the world is organised by a transport authority, and in a dense, complex city like London, the route network must fulfil the needs of all people in all areas. It must fit in with the geography, the communities and the forward plans of the city and the localities it serves, and it is too important for this to be left to the individual decisions of a wide range of bus operators, each pursuing their own separate interests. It is best left in the control of the transport authority. David Bayliss adds that, "It is not that many bus operators are unable to design high-quality and cost effective networks – but rather that they are rarely in a position to do so. The constraints imposed by the presence or threat of commercial competition means that their freedom to design 'optimal' networks is limited. The debate should not be about the competence of operators and authorities – but about the ability to design and implement cost effective service networks, and fares and ticketing arrangements, that reflect demand, need, cost and the level of subsidy."

Route planning needs to be fresh, responsive and consultative and five-year tenders can mitigate against this. On the other hand, a wide range of new services have been introduced in London since 2000, while roads, communities and journey patterns do not change so frequently. Passengers need some stability as they build their lives and activities around the network of services – it should not be changed too frequently.

Change was needed

Every organisation needs a shake-up from time to time. In the 1970s London Buses had become a high cost and low quality operation. The causes were well known but the response was inadequate. As the service declined, greater subsidies were needed but they were increasingly used to prop up inefficiency and poor standards. There were certainly able staff who recognised the problems and worked to tackle them and modernise the organisation, but the nature of LT made this difficult. The militaristic organisation was for many years left to its own devices by government, and produced a bureaucracy that was increasingly remote and unused to challenge. Robert Newson adds, "London Transport in the 1970s and 1980s is a prime example of a publicly-owned monopoly in which management effort was devoted to securing continuing subsidies rather than tackling high costs. Over-manning could be seen in all departments of the bus division, but perhaps the worst examples – because of the sheer numbers of employees – were at the supervisory level of garage operating and engineering staff and roadside inspectors.

"It is sometimes said that management conceded inefficient working practices to give themselves a quiet life – but to a great extent they had no alternative, because the monopoly nature of the organisation gave the employees and their unions far more power than they would have in a competitive industry. Ultimately there was no sanction that the business could lose market share to a competitor, and employees' jobs were not at risk even if they went on strike."

Change was needed and the huge scale of what was

In 2000, London Central provided two special services to the Millennium Dome using gas-powered DAF SB220 single-deckers with East Lans Myllennium bodies. MD9 is seen at the Dome on Greenwich Peninsular on route M1. (David Cole)

"It is not that many bus operators are unable to design high-quality and cost effective networks – but rather that they are rarely in a position to do so."

done has been described in the preceding chapters. These changes gave the impetus to get rid of attitudes, practices, procedures and, in some cases, people who were in the way of change. Once the changes had been made, it became possible to do things that people had always wanted to do but had not been able to against the inertia of the status quo.

Tendering – a good system that worked
Today, London's bus system is once again working to a high standard and is again admired around the world. John Rigby, one of the team who designed the original tendering scheme, acknowledges "A free marketeer would see the whole project as the state interfering through its transport planners in a market that could function perfectly well without bureaucratic intervention. But based on what LT set out to do, and judged by the longevity of the system, it can be concluded that this was a highly successful strategy in the short, medium and long terms.

"In the short term the system delivered significant cost reductions, improved service quality and introduced new market entrants. It retained a co-ordinated service, with good frequencies at unsocial hours and tickets that are valid on all operators' services and by different modes of travel – all features of travel that British people are enthusiastic about when they travel on public transport in the rest of Europe.

"For the medium term, LT demonstrated its commitment to both the roll-out of the tendering programme and cost cutting, with the result that revenue support to LT halved between 1984/5 and 1987/8 and was, briefly, not needed in 1997/8. Perhaps the success of tendering is best reflected by the fact that deregulation did not take place in London.

"The long term perspective is also instructive. It took ten years to tender the whole of the London bus network but the core principles of the 1984 tendering system were retained throughout. Indeed, a bus company which tendered in 1984 and which had not submitted another tender until 2015 would recognise a very similar approach to the first tranche tenders, despite the passage of three decades. The biggest variation is in contract length, which is now five years with a possible extension to seven, and the introduction of Quality Incentive Contracts.

"So which has produced the 'better' results – full privatisation and deregulation outside London, or privatisation of bus ownership retaining regulation inside London? A review by John Preston of Oxford University in 2004 produced some telling figures for the two decades 1981/2 to 2001/2:
- Passenger journeys outside London fell by 37%, while inside London they rose by 33%;
- Vehicle kms outside London rose by 21%, while inside London they rose by 35%;
- Subsidy outside London fell by 37%, while inside London it rose by 8%.

"Preston's conclusion, based on this data, is that 'on the road competition can lead to too much service at too high fares with too low a quality of service'. He goes on to say that competition for the market, as in London, 'can in theory provide the optimal mix of service quantity, quality and fares at an efficient cost'. He expresses concerns that planners may provide 'too much service at too high fares' but goes on to conclude that quality contracts with route or small area based tenders, of three to five years duration with quality and revenue incentives, provides the optimum solution.

David Bayliss also stresses that London's bus performance is superior to the other metropolitan areas. While there has been a very large increase in subsidy levels in London, bus journeys in London are subsidised at substantially lower levels than elsewhere. With average loadings 85% higher than in the Metropolitan Counties, London's buses are clearly more productive."

Those involved in operations, such as Leon Daniels, speak highly of the tendering system. Leon is clear, "The system initiated in the 1980s by LT to liberalise a publicly owned bus service, and introduce the private sector into a government owned business, has withstood the test of time and a range of circumstances. They moved the block grant routes to zero subsidy, moved to gross cost contracts, then net cost contracts, and then added the subsidy back, and now moved to a situation where the contracts are run by a handful of big companies, mostly foreign-owned, all with no change to the tendering model. It is quite clear that this was a very elegant solution. Is it the right solution? The system in 2015 is very similar to what was initiated in 1984. We have gone through economic recession, privatisation, the coalition government, and it remains the same. Weren't they clever!"

Nick Newton sees the success of London bus tendering as being due to simplicity. There was just one sentence in the LRT Act which left them to develop the system – it did not prescribe how it should be done. They started small, to see how it went, and developed it in the light of experience. "Tendering has brought lower costs, greater reliability and higher standards. It works because the politicians left it to the experts to design the system. It has grown and developed from experience." Nick is proud of the safety and accessibility developments they introduced which led the industry, and manufacturers came to include these requirements in their basic specifications. He suggests that the problem with rail privatisation was that the politicians influenced the way it was done. "It was the last dogma-driven priva-

"The system initiated in the 1980s by LT to liberalise a publicly owned bus service, and introduce the private sector into a government owned business, has withstood the test of time and a range of circumstances."

tisation by the Major Government, embodying the Thatcherite view of not subsidising the railway." A number of those involved stress that a lot of the success of tendering is down to Nick Newton himself – his management style and his ability to push things to the limit and not to be hamstrung by the bureaucrats. He built an effective and successful operation, though at the time they did not think that tendering would last long because of deregulation.

Peter Hendy sees tendering as one of the few Government actions towards London Transport that actually worked! So many others have not, such as the Public Private Partnerships on the Underground. He did not like tendering at the time because the emphasis was on cost and not quality, whatever anyone might say otherwise, and the result was a dreadful service provided for a time by some of the operators. For those tendering from within LBL, the public sector accounting went round in circles – sometimes he could bid marginally and sometimes he could not. The system is not perfect now but does produce a decent result, probably the best that can be achieved in the circumstances. There is still enough competition to keep prices down.

David Bayliss thinks the present system has shown itself to be fit for purpose. "It works – it's the best way of doing things." As long as the contract and the market situation are sufficient to retain healthy competition then the requirement that the routes and fares are centrally controlled is good. He has not seen anything superior, and operators are clearly happy to be in the market making money out of it.

Dai Powell runs Hackney Community Transport who commenced tendered operations in 1999. He notes that the London system works on a number of levels: financially, the quality of service and the cost of the network for the number of miles operated. He is astonished that around 99% of mileage is being achieved – in the 1980s it was around 85%. This is achieved by the incentives and the penalties if you don't do it. TfL works better than most of the PTEs, as there is a large level of brand awareness, a network, brand compatibility – it works for the customer.

Julian Peddle is an entrepreneur who has been involved in London tendering. He thinks the London arrangement of tendering and the route system is excellent. "I don't think you can better it – they couldn't do a better job with it." He adds that, "Tender prices are gradually going down as time goes on. This can be very difficult for operators as there is a gradual falloff of profits on a contract, just as the vehicles get older and the maintenance costs increase. If they lose one or two contracts, they quickly get to the point where they are not covering their overheads." He praises the Oyster card as "a huge success and a brilliant system phenomenally well done."

But some operators have ended their involvement. Peter Larking would not want to be involved in the current system with five or seven-year contracts and being told what to do. It doesn't appeal to his entrepreneurial sense as an operator. He thinks planners sometimes have their head in the clouds and no local knowledge – they are nice people who are committed and can always justify what they are doing, but they are too far from the local operation. Also, margins are down to around 5% if you are performing well and he isn't interested in that sort of operation. "We didn't get into the business to run a contract for five years, we did it to run well and expand the patronage."

Leon Daniels enjoyed the early years of tendering. "Like all procurements, in the first year it is fantastic. I was glad I was in the game in the eighties when the prices were good. The tendering authority was immature, and your bid had only to be slightly cheaper than London Buses, who could not get their costs down. Now prices are screwed to the bone." He is surprised by the low prices being offered for contracts, sometimes at cost, and bidders are gambling over the QIC bonuses. Peter Hendy points out that operators are now prepared to operate with higher volumes, significantly higher than in the past, and to take a lower margin in the relatively risk-free environment. So TfL is able to expand its operations because tender prices are coming in lower than budgeted. It is striking that the nationalised European entities can get capital cheaper than anybody in this country, so their prices are excellent.

Drivers' conditions
In the early years of tendering, it was the London Buses drivers who suffered major changes to their pay and conditions of service, and the loss of the facilities they enjoyed at work such as canteens and games rooms. The scheduling conditions and limitations on the work of platform staff were inefficient and had to be changed, but wages reduced and working hours increased. This led to high turnover of staff and severe shortages. When elected in 2000, Ken Livingstone paid a £30 weekly bonus which helped ease the situation. This has subsequently been incorporated into wage rates, which now have to keep in line with market rates to ensure there are sufficient staff. In the past, bus drivers and tube drivers received similar pay, but tube drivers – who have not gone through comparable changes – now receive far more than bus drivers.

After some years as a driver and then trade union officer, Pat Mahon joined the management of London General. "For the drivers, the average rostered earnings are now not far off £600, which is not bad, with sick pay and holidays back on a par. We are tougher on attendance, performance and accidents.

"Drivers have now got air conditioning in the cabs, but then you might think we always had it if you didn't have enough newspaper to stop the wind coming up around the foot pedals."

But is it better for the drivers? They've got air conditioning in the cabs, but then you might think we always had it if you didn't have enough newspaper to stop the wind coming up around the pedals. And then you didn't have any power assisted steering, and you couldn't adjust the steering wheel, you didn't have heaters and climate control, bus lanes, and traffic lights giving you the right of way. I say to them, if you were around in my time on the 14s on a one-minute headway through the West End, you had to cut in and cut out and you couldn't hit anything! I think it is an easier job now. Someone arrived at Merton and said how nice it is! I tell new staff, 'We keep you happy as long as you keep us happy!' I think the job is better, but there is more pressure now. There are eight cctv cameras on the bus – the driver is being watched the whole time."

David Brown acknowledges, "There is far more supervision and control of the drivers now; the controllers know the drivers, where they are and what they are doing. They can talk to them on a regular basis, tell them they are going too fast or too slow, if they've gone off line of route, or if they are scratching someone (following another bus without overtaking, so that the bus in front does all the work). They know everything about what is going on and are more in control. Some of the longer term drivers dislike this, but if you wind the clock back 20 years or more, no one knew where the drivers were, no one knew what was going on, and the drivers often ran the network for their own benefit."

Roy Lambe started in 1981 as a driver on the 11s at Riverside. "It has changed dramatically. What you did in the past, if there was a bus in front, you helped them out, a hop system and you shared the load. Now, you stick to the headway. There is a time card but the idea is to maintain your headway from the one in front. We are run electronically now and are told what we can and can't do.

"The biggest blow was the splitting up of LT. LT was family, there were days out, there were sports activities from the LT Sports Club, there were golf and snooker competitions. Until then, we were in line with the Tube, the same pay and conditions, and the same sorts of hours. Now, if you want to better your pay and conditions, the answer is, 'Up yours, mate, we've got plenty of people willing to work.'

"When Ken Livingstone became Mayor, it was nice for a while getting the weekly bonus, being told that they recognised the important role of drivers, but in time, of course, it was taken off in various bits and pieces and amalgamated. Management tell me that I am on a high earning rota. But I say, 'Am I getting more per hour? I'm getting the same per hour, so I call it a longer hours rota, not a high earning rota!' But I love this job, and I like route 11 so I'll stay on it. I'm 61 now and I've got four years to go. Different people every day, and you develop regular passengers over time, a joke with some, and with some they say good morning to you when they recognise you because you say good morning to them. Some drivers complain that route 11 drivers think they are an elite. We don't think we are an elite, we know we are the elite!"

Was privatisation necessary to achieve the changes?
Was it necessary to privatise London's buses? Peter Hendy believes that as good a service could have been achieved without privatisation if there had been good management in the 1960s, '70s and '80s with the determination to succeed. Tendering was the political solution of the Thatcher government who would not have waited or wanted to let good public sector management succeed.

Norman Cohen adds, "The organisation went through a huge period of uncertainty, of disruption, of a drive towards improvement. Most of the improvements were good, driving down costs with an emphasis on quality of service, on management responsibility, and all of that has been good. But I don't think you needed privatisation or deregulation to achieve that. We *were* achieving that and we were running some pretty good bus services when we had the wholly owned subsidiary companies who were competing with each other. But the privatisations did perhaps free the companies so that purchasing is easier, because they are not subject to public sector capital restrictions. But this dogmatic emphasis on competition, regardless, is crazy. It doesn't recognise what bus operation and bus markets are about – the network and linkages between them, and the idea of multimodal travel."

Martin Whitley comments similarly. "I doubt if it was really necessary to spend nearly 10 years of perpetual upheaval. This was not just the creation of 11 bus companies out of the bus Districts, but detailed shuffling and weeding of supervisory and management responsibilities right down to garage and local area level. This process permitted the deader wood to retire with some honour and gave the brighter shoots the scope to make themselves a name, but at the expense of a huge diversion of higher management time in re-arranging the deck chairs when there were bigger fish to fry." Martin personally did well from privatisation, but he would have been quite happy had it not happened, and for Cardinal District to have gone on until his retirement.

However, Barry Le Jeune thinks that there would always have been a suspicion about a tendering process run by LT if London Buses was still the major operator and owned by LT. However many and effective 'Chinese walls' there might be, it would not appear to be a fair system. There would always be a

The end of London Buses Limited was marked by an event in November 1994.

comments that the social enterprise sector has values which are close to the public sector. They are running it commercially. They have motivation and they are measuring success in a way that isn't just financial – they talk about a double bottom line, with financial and service measures. "If it is public transport, it is therefore a service to the public. It cannot only be about profit maximisation, there has to be a social objective as well. It is easy to make double-digit returns on very busy routes, but hard to make them in isolated housing estates and rural areas. How do you get true public transport without a network? There needs to be a more holistic approach to it."

Are the benefits due to tendering and privatisation?
By 2000, the new ownership and tendering process had been put in place and the subsidy had been dramatically reduced. Though this had earlier led to a loss of quality in the service provided, it gave a solid base on which the later improvements could be built. The new TfL organisation developed the bus service and now has 15 years experience, with a major build up of the quantity and quality of the service offered. The current success of London's buses is due to a combination of events: tendering and privatisation, together with Congestion Charging and other traffic and parking constraints, the funding and commitment from both Mayors since 2000, the increasing population of London and the benefits of i-Bus, Oyster and other technology.

Steve Norris confirms that the system is now far better. "Of course it would be true that had we left the system as it was, I'm sure that investment of the kind that we've seen in recent years would have improved the quality of service. If you can reduce the average age of the fleet in the way that TfL has managed to do, then I suspect that whether it had been contracted or had all been wholly owned you'd have seen improvement.

"If you have people of the quality of Peter Hendy, David Brown and Leon Daniels running the bus service, I don't believe that there would have been no improvement. So it's perhaps unfair to suggest that the situation is much better now and imply that it is the changes that I introduced that made the difference. But I think that the changes even before the creation of TfL did deliver better service, and have continued to do so. What I thought was interesting was how much innovation came from people who had spent their lives as public servants in the bus industry. I think that there is a born entrepreneur inside many of us, and when you give people the opportunity to do things the way they know they should have been done

suspicion, even if it was not justified. As operating tendered buses became a significantly bigger part of their business for other operators like Grey-Green, this would become more important and privatisation meant that they would be reassured that the red London buses would finally be equivalent to them, outside the LT family.

Dave Wetzel prefers the red buses to be in some form of common ownership, either municipal, or co-operative, or government owned. Even with competition, he would like there to be a standard wage in the contract so that the companies were not competing on drivers' wages. "The cost of diesel and the cost of the buses does not vary, so the staff are the biggest variable in what you pay and the number of staff that you employ. The conditions of the staff should not be what companies bid with."

Dai Powell of Hackney Community Transport

"Peter Hendy should be credited for being blunt enough to say to the politicians, 'If you want to do this, let's do it properly, and this costs money.'"

all along, it's amazing what good business people you can make out of all those who went on to make their fortunes out of the bus companies." While this may be the case, it is unfortunate that they were prevented from doing it before under the previous regime, while Bryan Constable makes the point that the very vigorous competition in the late 1980s led to the downfall of a number of very competent senior managers throughout the industry.

Peter Newman agrees about leadership in London. "One good thing is that with Peter Hendy and Leon Daniels, you have genuine busmen running TfL, rather than politicians. They can temper the politicians from extreme decisions." Gordon Tennant stresses that "Peter Hendy should be credited for being blunt enough to say to the politicians, 'If you want to do this, let's do it properly, and this costs money.' The improvements in driver pay since 2000 were essential – but it is difficult to separate the effects of privatisation from all the other things that have happened since then – the growth of London, the increase in the network, the Oyster card, the congestion charge – all these are important factors which contributed to change."

Peter Hendy adds, "Would there be more passengers anyway even if the service had not improved – would it have happened anyway? The real challenge was to recruit people at all levels who wanted to do the job properly."

Jon Batchelor suggests that, "Whatever your politics, Ken Livingstone did a good job – he was not scared to put his money where his mouth is. Nor is Boris Johnson. Ken Livingstone got congestion charging going. If you want to run a reliable service, you have to over-bus. You do not want the buses to be full – a BMW driver won't get out of his car into a full bus." They now have accountability – when he started, there was no commitment to solving the problems. "When I talk to drivers, we run a much better service than we did years ago. We have now got accountability, we run a good bus service." Pat Mahon adds, "I think between privatisation and Ken Livingstone, buses were a success story. Because Ken put his money where his mouth was in reduced fares and increasing services, and he gave the drivers more."

Other UK cities
Most of these issues apply in the other UK metropolitan areas. Dave Alexander started his bus career in London. He compares London to other UK cities. "I run buses now in Leeds, Manchester and Sheffield. I see similarities between those big cities and London. There is more priority in London. I think the highway management, infrastructure, all the bus priority, are far more evident in London than in any of the other big cities. That's not to say there isn't any, but I wish there was as much outside London in some of the bigger cities. In that respect, London does very well, creating as good an environment for the bus as they can. And I'm sure if you speak to operators in London they'll say they that not enough is being done, but there is no comparison with outside."

"My introduction into buses was in the regulated London world, the structure and the discipline of London. Running those contracts was a really good grounding for me. If you apply those principles of disciplined operations outside London, all you then need to do is top it off with the commercial, entrepreneurial, retailer's view of the world and mix the two. They are not mutually exclusive, it's great if you blend the two and get this discipline in a commercial world."

Some of the UK metropolitan areas see the situation in London and would like to replicate it with a more regulated environment using Bus Quality Contracts and Bus Improvement Areas – there have been attempts at more co-ordinated operations, but none have been successful because the Competition Commission says it infringes competition rules. David Quarmby also supports this view, adding that, "We are the only country in the Western world that has fully deregulated local buses. I think it is a disaster."

But the services in other British cities *are* deregulated and the network is 'owned' by the operators, unlike London where these changes were introduced by LT to itself and its own subsidiaries. David Brown, now CEO of Go-Ahead group, started his career in London but is now responsible for operations throughout the country. He responds, "The thing to remember about London is that bus route contract tendering has taken place over a long period of time. When it started in 1988 we were doing it largely to ourselves as public bodies. There were no private companies losing out – private companies came in and won tenders and changed the cost dynamics of running buses in London but it was also public bodies winning or losing from other public bodies. Whereas the current plans in the north-east by Nexus will potentially completely take away my business, which is a very different situation. We have paid for some of our business, as have others, from the Government, either via NBC or directly from the local authority. We have still got goodwill on the books. Nexus are basically proposing to requisition our business without compensation.

"The other thing is that with tendering everyone looks to London and says 'We just want a London situation.' So when people look for new forms of regulation, what they are really saying is that they want what London has got. London has had 40% growth, which is fantastic, but if we go back to the mid-1990s, it wasn't so great. Yes, it didn't have any significant subsidy by the late nineties, but it also was not good quality either. And it wasn't until money was pumped into the system that it improved.

"So there are two crucial things here. One is the governance of London. Outside London there is a variety of different organisations controlling transport. You've got the PTEs, Local Authorities, ITAs etc. The big transformation, in my opinion, was the introduction of a London Mayoralty which had control over transport – a strong Mayor with the ability to control the transport financial levers with a longer term financial plan makes a substantial difference.

"Secondly there is the huge population growth in London. About a million extra people were attracted to London between 2002 and 2012, and they all need transport. A large population growth drives growth on buses, whilst the economy drives the growth on the Underground. And then you add the fact that most of that population growth took place out of central London, where two-thirds of the bus operations take place. And then you superimpose on top of that the fact that perhaps 40% of the expansion of the bus network was, either off-peak or at weekends, and that coincided with a big growth in the economy and social activity at those times.

"Put all that together, and add in Congestion Charging in 2003, Red Routes, bus lane fines, the high cost of parking, lower car ownership; all of those things joined together means you can have fantastic growth in public transport. It is not just about a regulated bus environment. There is a regulated environment in Northern Ireland, for instance, but with declining growth, lower population rises and increasing car ownership, you have a decline in bus patronage of 15%. So regulation does work in London but you've got other factors and other issues that have helped it. That is not to demean the fact that an integrated network is a good thing for passengers, and Oyster is good, but you can have both of those outside London without taking control of the bus network."

Consolidation and foreign ownership
Ownership of the bus operating companies has gradually consolidated into larger groups. It is not the range of small companies originally envisaged, and the independent sector is barely represented. So Jane's taxi co-op, described in the 1985 Business Plan and mentioned at the end of Chapter 9, does not run the bus service to the station, and it is difficult for newcomers to enter the market. In those London bus companies bought by their management, with staff involvement, the onward sale of the companies was driven by the venture capitalists who had invested in the company but wanted a quick return. None survived for long as an independent concern.

Was this envisaged by Margaret Thatcher and Nicholas Ridley when they started the privatisation ball rolling? As with other utility privatisations, the free market ideal of a mass of small companies providing public services has not been achieved – instead, a market dominated by a small number of very large companies has replaced a publicly owned, publicly accountable undertaking. However, competition remains strong and TfL always has three bids for each tender.

Peter Hendy is clear that he needs operators with the size and resources to do this huge job professionally. It is too risky for small companies to lose their contract, and he is not interested in one-man-bands! "Running buses in London is a serious business – we need competition between people who know what they are doing. It isn't difficult for the right quality new entrants to enter the market – we'd be pleased if they did, but they don't really exist.

"There have been no new entrants trying to start a business from scratch. They would inevitably make a loss at the beginning and it is easier to buy a business than to start one up, so that is what they do. Tendering works well and there is no requirement to change it. The Mayor has political control over fares, TfL give the private operators money and they provide a reliable service. TfL pays well for a professional service, and the contractor takes the risk on five years' labour and the other costs."

The experience with small operators was not a happy one. Norman Cohen recalls, "Privatisation and tendering brought more and more of the competition from small operators, and some of those small operators were pretty terrible in terms of their standards. As has happened everywhere else in the country, most of the little operators have been swallowed up by the big companies, and the big companies have themselves got bigger and been bought out. The small London Buses units that had been set up found it more and more difficult to be viable. The large groups that came into London and bought companies found the best way for them to continue was to buy more companies. So they did, and London General took over London Central, and Metroline bought London Northern."

Dai Powell acknowledges that the biggest companies now dominate. He suggests that it is unfortunate that we have lost so many small operators. "From a management point of view, it is easier to work with fewer companies, but I'd have thought you'd want at least one small operator in all areas of London, as a market moderator and because it is slightly market disruptive. The small operator wouldn't have a huge share, but it makes the system honest."

TfL does manage the market, and prevents contractors from getting too big, which would lead to *them* managing the market. Mike Weston, TfL's Director of Buses, knows from the Office of Fair Trading that they would take an interest if any operator had more than 25% of the London bus market. TfL have this guideline in mind, but no operator has come to that level, though there are areas of London where an operator exceeds it. Keith Ludeman notes that nothing is ever said overtly about keeping operators to a certain size, but he suggests that's a good plan. "When your contracts get up to a certain size, they begin to fall away again. It is a pretty robust system which has been copied elsewhere. Anyone can come in, but they fail if they don't understand the bus market."

Peter Newman sees that operations are much improved now. It is a far cheaper and better service, but he considers it a job for the Big Boys. "Why do we not want to be involved now? Because it is 'not us'. We are fiercely independent and we protect our brand, have our own colour scheme, and 97% of our operation is commercial. We have no tendered work for any local authority or agency. TfL is now for the big boys and it wouldn't work to be a small operator for them. What is necessary is to meet their criteria – it's needing things that are not what a small operator would do."

A further development is that London's bus services are now operated by large national and multi-national companies or by subsidiaries of state owned European undertakings. Steve Norris's view is that, "The British have always been very relaxed about foreign investment and in my view quite rightly, because that foreign investment does two things. Firstly, we learn from it. In the motor industry, it taught us how to make motor cars again, a discipline that we had lost. I was directly involved in that and saw how Honda and Toyota and Nissan, and the Germans like BMW, came in and showed us how to make reliable cars in a way which we had clearly forgotten.

"The second thing about private capital is that it may come from abroad but it's global funds. I'm very relaxed about the fact that some of these operations are privately owned. They'll only get the job if they compete effectively, and if they do, and if they're picking up a subsidy from the Dutch government to run Abellio, then all I can say is, thank you very much. If you looked at the shareholder base of FirstGroup and Stagecoach I'd bet you'd find that a large percentage of those companies are foreign owned."

Conclusions

This book has described the dramatic changes that took place in London's bus operations over twenty years from the late 1970s to the end of the 1990s. The changes in that period turned a poorly performing bus operation into a cost-effective, competitive and well planned service. For a brief period it covered its operating costs, but at the expense of both quantity and quality of service. However, this provided a solid base on which the improvements from 2000 onwards could be built.

Buses are essential to London, and tendering has shown itself to be the best way of providing the service. There is competition for the contract to run the service, not competition on London's congested road network. Services are planned and co-ordinated to meet the needs of London and its many communities, and achieve a balance between continuity and responsiveness to change. Those who organise the system are responsible to Londoners through their elected representatives.

Deregulation would not work in London, but tendering has shown itself to produce similar or better benefits while providing a co-ordinated network and ticketing. Together with the Underground, railways and other services it provides a full public transport service to London.

There is a continuing need to be responsive to new and changing travel patterns, to ensure that TfL does not become complacent, and that it is not dictated to by political whim. There is also a need to ensure that bus staff are properly rewarded for what is a demanding and safety critical job. The benefits of the bus system reach far beyond the passengers on the bus, and justify continuing public funds to ensure a full service, meeting the needs of Londoners.

From 2000, the situation changed radically with a London Mayor committed to building on what had been achieved by developing and improving the bus service, constraining the use of the private car in central London through Congestion Charging, and using the funds raised to further improve the bus service. The operation has grown to its largest and most successful ever, with over 7,600 buses at work in the peaks, 6.5 million passenger journeys each weekday, and customer satisfaction at 86%. But this is a story for another book!

245 The changes turned a poorly performing bus operation into a cost-effective, competitive and well planned service.

Appendix 1. **Time Line of key events for London's buses 1970 – 2000**

1 January 1970	Control of London Transport passes to the GLC under the Transport (London) Act 1969, becoming the London Transport Executive (LTE). The Country Buses and Green Line coaches pass to the new National Bus Company (NBC).
5 May 1977	The Conservative Party takes control of the GLC with Horace Cutler as leader.
April 1978	Ralph Bennett is appointed Chairman, replacing Kenneth Robinson. David Quarmby is appointed Managing Director Buses.
3 May 1979	Conservative Government elected with Margaret Thatcher as Prime Minister.
1 October 1979	LT Buses is reorganised into eight Bus Districts.
6 October 1980	Long-distance coach services, excursions and tours deregulated (1980 Transport Act).
24 July 1980	PA Consultants report on LT management is published. Ralph Bennett departs and Sir Peter Masefield becomes temporary Chair of LT.
7 May 1981	Labour wins GLC election. Ken Livingstone becomes leader.
11 September 1981	London Borough of Bromley challenges the GLC Fares Fair proposals.
4 October 1981	Fares Fair scheme introduced.
17 December 1981	Fares Fair scheme ruled unlawful by Law Lords.
September 1982	Dr Keith Bright arrives as LT Chairman for 5 years
17 December 1982	AMOS minibus proposals – LT announces a public hearing.
22 May 1983	Travelcard and 25% fares reduction introduced.
9 June 1983	Conservative Government re-elected. Tom King becomes Secretary of State for Transport.
mid 1983	Monopolies and Mergers Commission reports that Chiswick and Aldenham are unable to be competitive.
July 1983	Government White Paper proposes transferring LT from GLC to Secretary of State for Transport. LT to become a small holding company with separate Bus and Underground subsidiaries. Private sector to be involved in the provision of services.
16 October 1983	Nicholas Ridley becomes Secretary of State for Transport.
2 January 1984	Eight Bus Districts reduced to six.
29 June 1984	London Regional Transport takes effect.
July 1984	AMOS minibus scheme turned down by Secretary of State.
October 1984	Dr David Quarmby departs LT to join Sainsbury's. John Telford Beasley arrives as Managing Director Buses.
November 1984	First tranche of tendered routes published.
1 April 1985	LBL, LUL, BEL take effect as separate subsidiaries.
11 April 1985	First tender results announced for 12 routes.
July 1985	New Orpington network announced.
13 July 1985	First tendered routes start operation.
December 1985	Results of 2nd tranche of route tenders.
Feb, March 1986	Results of 3rd tranche of routes, including cross-boundary and out-county services.
Feb-June 1986	2nd tranche routes start in Feb-June 86.
April 1986	4th Tranche results announced for Orpington network.
24 May 1986	3rd tranche of route tenders commence during May and June. Loughton garage closes.
21 June 1986	Potters Bar new tendered operation commences.
9 August 1986	Westlink commences operation.
16 August 1986	Orpington network commences.
25 October 1986	Central London Midibus routes C1, C20 and C21 commence.
26 October 1986	Deregulation of bus services implemented in England, Scotland and Wales.
15 November 1986	Aldenham Works closes, with work transferred to Chiswick.
November 1986	Chiswick Bus Training Centre closes.
December 1986	Kingston network announced and put out to tender.
13 June 1987	Paul Channon becomes Secretary of State for Transport.
27 June 1987	Kingston scheme implemented.
August 1987	Central Traffic Division of LBL created, and Bus Districts reduced from 6 to 5 Regions.
14 November 1987	Harrow scheme implemented.
1 February 1988	Sale of Bus Engineering Ltd (BEL) to Frontsource, using part of the Chiswick site. Effra Road ticket machine works closed and work transferred to Chiswick.
16 January 1988	Bexley scheme introduced, Bexleybus and Boro'line London commence operations.
5 November 1988	Grey-Green take over operation of route 24, the first central London route to be tendered.
7 November 1988	11 new bus Units introduced.

9 November 1988	Sir Neil Shields becomes interim Chairman of LT following the report into the Kings Cross fire. John Telford Beasley, Chairman and Managing Director of London Buses Ltd, is also appointed Chief Executive of LRT.
1989	The 18 original tendered routes are retendered - 6 remain with their original operators. Chiswick Works site is demolished for redevelopment.
March 1989	Wilfrid Newton becomes Chairman 1989-1994.
4 March 1989	Gold Arrow service introduced on route 28, followed by route 31 on 15 April.
30 March 1989	Launch of Docklands Transit.
1 April 1989	LBL Units established as limited companies, wholly-owned subsidiaries of LBL, with their own Operator's Licences.
16 November 1990	Docklands Transit ceases operation.
28 November 1990	John Major becomes Prime Minister, replacing Margaret Thatcher. Malcolm Rifkind becomes Secretary of State for Transport.
March 1991	Government publishes consultation paper on 'Bus Strategy for London'.
June 1991	Green Line services cease operation, excepting airport services.
22 July 1991	A London Bus Executive is proposed to administer bus services after deregulation.
2 August 1991	Announcement that London Coaches was to be privatised.
23 November 1991	London Forest Travel closes following a strike and consequent tender losses.
9 April 1992	John Major re-elected in General Election. John MacGregor becomes Secretary of State for Transport. Steven Norris becomes Minister for Transport in London.
19 May 1992	Announcement that London Coaches was to be sold to its management.
29 January 1993	Bus Engineering Ltd (BEL) ceases trading.
24 April 1993	Kentish Bus commences operation of route 19, the first crew route to be tendered.
November 1993	Deregulation in London is 'postponed', at least until after the next election.
4 December 1993	BTS take over operation of crew-operated route 13.
19 January 1994	Westlink is sold to its management, then sold on to West Midlands Travel in April.
24 March 1994	The Sales Memorandum for the Sale of London Buses' Ten Operating Companies is issued, with a photocall at Hyde Park Corner.
1 April 1994	London Transport Buses (LTB) takes effect as the new organisation managing London's buses.
2 September 1994	CentreWest is sold to its management.
30 November 1994	Eight more companies are sold by the end of November.
10 January 1995	South London is the last company to be privatised.
December 1995	Capital Citybus is sold to its management by CMT Group (Hong Kong).
2 December 1995	CentreWest takes over services in Orpington from Roundabout and Metrobus.
May or June 1996	London General is sold to the Go-Ahead Group.
June 1996	Cowie buys British Bus.
March 1997	CentreWest is sold to FirstBus.
1 May 1997	Labour Government elected, Tony Blair becomes Prime Minister and John Prescott becomes Secretary of State for Environment, Transport and the Regions.
July 1997	Metroline floats on the London Stock Exchange.
August 1997	Government Green Paper published with proposals for Greater London Authority and directly-elected Mayor.
12 August 1997	London United sold to Transdev.
March 1998	Government proposals to set up Greater London Authority (GLA) with a Mayor. Transport *for* London will replace London Regional Transport and be responsible to the Mayor of London.
May 1998	Referendum approves Government plans for London Mayor.
8 July 1998	Capital Citybus sold to First, becoming First Capital.
17 August 1998	Metroline acquires MTL London Northern.
June 1999	Metrobus sold to Go-Ahead Group.
15 December 1999	LTB takes over the services of Harris Bus.
March 2000	East Thames Buses starts operations to take over Harris routes.
March 2000	Metroline, the last management-owned company, is sold to Delgro (Singapore).
4 May 2000	Ken Livingstone elected Mayor of London, with Greater London Authority taking effect from July.
3 July 2000	Transport *for* London (T*f*L) replaces London Regional Transport. London Transport Buses (LTB) became London Bus Services Ltd (LBSL).

Appendix 2. The sale of the London Buses subsidiaries

		Number of bids	Date of sale	Buyer	Sale price £m	Turnover £m pa (estimates for year to 31/3/1994)	Profit pa (estimated for the year to 31/3/1994)	Annual scheduled mileage at 4/12/1993	Number of employees at 4/12/1993	Number of buses at 4/12/1993	Garages	Market share
1	CentreWest	8	2/9/94	MEBO	25.6	39	3.2	16 m	1,500	510	5	8.1
2	East London	11	6/9/94	Stagecoach	28.9	49	2.3	21 m	1,950	590	6	10.1
	Selkent	9			13.3	33	0.7	16 m	1,400	390	4	6.7
4	Leaside	11	29/9/94	Cowie	29.5	43	1.0	17 m	1,800	510	6	8.1
5	Metroline	11	7/10/94	MEBO	20.0	28	1.6	11 m	1,150	370	5	5.6
6	London Central	10	18/10/94	Go Ahead	24.5	40	3.3	16 m	1,700	500	4	7.9
7	London Northern	13	26/10/94	MTL	20.55	28	1.4	10 m	1,100	320	2	5.1
8	London General	9	2/11/94	MEBO	28.05	50	1.6	20 m	2,150	600	6	9.3
9	London United	10	5/11/94	MEBO	25.5	37	2.5	16 m	1,450	430	5	7.0
10	South London	10	10/1/95	Cowie	17.1	33	2.1	13 m	1,350	410	4	6.3
	Total	102			233.0	380	19.7	156 m	15,550	4,630	47	74.2

Notes

In addition, London Coaches was sold to its management in May 1992 with 109 buses and coaches for £750,000, and Stanwell Buses (Westlink) was sold to its management on 19 January 1994 with 102 buses for £2m.

MEBO – Management and employee buy-out.

Only Cowie operated tendered routes in London prior to the sale, having a market share of 2.6%. Their market share after the sale was 17%. 22 operators ran the remaining route mileage. No buyer gained control of more than 25% of scheduled mileage in the privatisation.

Sources

London Buses, Information Memorandum for the Sale of London Buses' Ten Operating Companies, March 1994.

National Audit Office report HC29, 14/12/1995: The Sale of London Transport's Bus Operating Companies.

Appendix 3. Operators with LT contracts April 1992 (diagram) and Private Operators in April 1994 (List)

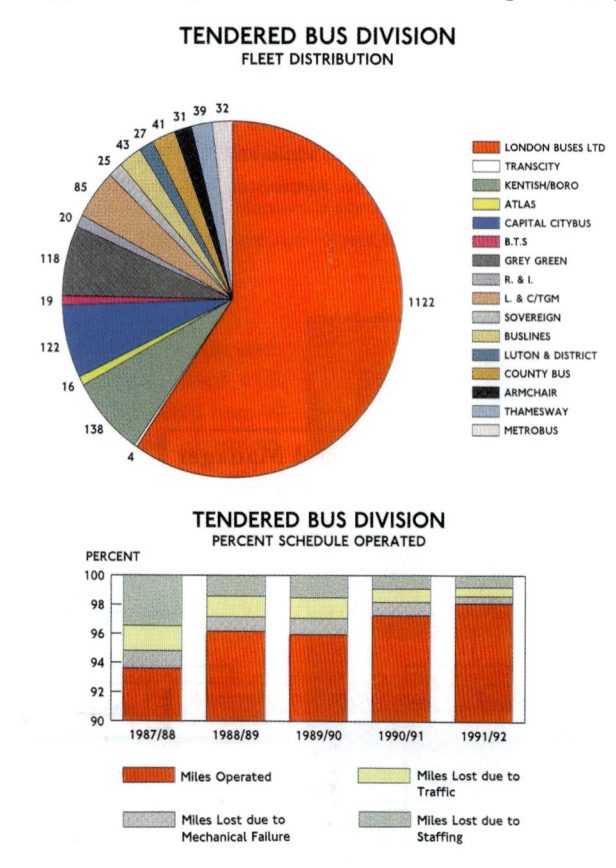

Company	London Locations	Number of LT routes	Number of buses on LT work
Kentish Bus (Proudmutual)	6	34	181
Capital Citybus	2	26	155
London & Country (British Bus)	5	19	133
Grey-Green (Cowie)	2	21	95
Westlink (West Midlands Travel)	2	8	71
Thamesway (Badgerline)	2	11	60
London Suburban Bus	1	3	43
London Buslines (Q-Drive)	1	8	43
County Bus	3	9	42
BTS Coaches	1	2	34
Armchair Passenger Transport	1	2	32
London Coaches	2	2	28
Metrobus	1	6	28
Luton & District	1	3	26
Sovereign Bus	2	5	26
R & I Buses	1	6	20
Atlas Bus	1	2	16
Docklands Transit	1	3	13
Capital Coaches	1	1	3
Javelin Coaches	1	1	3
Crystals	1	1	2
F E Thorpe	1	1	2
Total: 22 operators	39	174	1,056

Bibliography

LT documents

London Transport and Transport for London Annual Reports, Reviews, Business Plans, internal reports and staff newspapers.

London Buses Strategic Review, May 1982 and March 1984.

LRT's Approach to Bus Service Tendering, LRT Group Planning Office Report R261, February 1985.

Bus Service Tendering, an LRT Case Study, Conference Paper by Nick Newton and John Rigby, November 1985.

LRT Bus Service Tendering: The Activities and Intentions of Independent Bus and Coach Operators, Martin Higginson, University of London, September 1986.

London Buses' Local Subsidiary Companies' Design Manual, August 1989.

'At the Crossroads.' Paper presented by Norman Cohen, Operations and Marketing Director, London Buses Ltd, to the Bus and Coach Council Scotland Annual Conference 1992.

'Should privatisation precede deregulation – what are the options?' Paper presented to the Chartered Institute of Transport, Metropolitan Section, on 18 January 1993 by Norman Cohen, Operations and Marketing Director, London Buses Ltd.

Privatisation and Deregulation of Buses in London, evidence by London Transport to the House of Commons Transport Committee, April 1993.

London Buses – the road to privatisation. An introduction to London Buses and the privatisation process, published by London Buses, 1993.

London Buses, Information Memorandum for the Sale of London Buses' Ten Operating Companies, March 1994.

London's Buses: A Decade of Change, London Transport 1995.

Report on a Review of Route Tendering and Area Franchising, LT Buses, December 1996.

Buses in London: A comparison with the rest of Great Britain, London Transport Planning, January 1998.

London Transport Buses, Oral Evidence to the House of Commons Transport Sub Committee 5 May 1999.

Internal LT reports on bus operations, tendering, privatisation etc.

Internal reports and Business Plans of CentreWest, London Forest and Metroline.

Government

Transport Acts of 1978, 1980 and 1985, HMSO.

Buses White Paper, HMSO July 1984.

House of Commons Transport Committee, Transport in London, HMSO 127-11 1982.

Problems with Franchising, Department of Transport Economics Directorate, March 1985.

London Bus Deregulation, Implications for the London Boroughs, London Boroughs Transportation Group, June 1988.

LRT Bus Tendering, Report to Department of Transport by KPMG, May 1990.

A Bus Strategy for London, Consultation Paper, Department of Transport, March 1991.

National Audit Office, report HC29, December 1995: The Sale of London Transport's Bus Operating Companies.

Transport White Paper 1998 and daughter paper 1999.

Books, reports and journals

London Transport and the Politicians, Paul E Garbutt, Ian Allan 1985.

My Style of Government, memoires of Nicholas Ridley, Hutchinson, 1991.

Whither the Clapham Omnibus? The Future for Buses in London, Chartered Institute of Transport, October 1994.

Metrobus, Andrew Boag, Capital Transport, 1994.

London Bus Tendering, by David Kennedy, Stephen Glaister and Tony Travers. London School of Economics March 1995.

Changing Trains, the Autobiography of Steven Norris, Hutchinson, 1996.

London Buses 1985-1995, Tom McLachlan, Venture Publications, 1996.

Stagecoach, Christian Wolmar. Orion Business Books, 1998.

Grey-Green, from Ewer to Arriva, Owen Woodliffe, 2001.

Roundabout, Orpington's Little Buses, Tom Gurney, 2010.

Ramblings from my old Armchair, John W Watts, 2012.

London Omnibus Traction Society (LOTS) journals: London Bus Review, London Bus Magazine and The London Bus, throughout the period covered.

Website

London Bus Routes, by Ian Armstrong.

Index of People

Adie, Douglas, 101, 112, 113, 197, 218
Alexander, Dave, 81, 92, 95, 154, 234, 243
Arnold, Barry, 100, 140, 187, 188, 219, 220, 221, 234
Arrol, Willie, 42, 70, 110
Ballinger, Martin, 179, 217
Barlex, Ian, 171, 178, 181, 187, 190, 202
Barrett, Nigel, 117, 119
Barrington, Huw, 47, 93, 121, 225
Batchelor, Jon, 220, 243
Batty, Peter, 146
Bayliss, David, 8, 9, 34, 52, 158, 163, 169, 178, 232, 238, 239, 240
Beasley, John Telford, 35, 59, 79, 95, 96, 97, 99, 100, 106, 125, 159, 160, 161
Bennett, Ralph, 8, 15, 17, 18, 24
Blacker, Ken, 42, 65, 70, 71, 73
Blundred, Harry, 28, 33, 63, 117, 118, 119, 147, 161, 164, 170, 221
Bowker, Roger, 100, 101, 116, 118, 140, 141, 186, 187, 188, 214, 219, 220, 221, 222
Braddock, Andrew, 237
Brady, Dominic, 192, 198, 215
Brewer, Ron, 16, 50, 87
Bright, Sir Keith, 22, 24, 27, 30, 99
Brown, David, 69, 89, 95, 98, 151, 185, 215, 241, 242, 243
Brown, Simon, 202
Buck, George, 13
Chamberlain, Jeff, 43, 58, 59, 108, 178, 208
Chapman, Leslie, 17
Cheroomi, Frank, 118, 119, 147, 221
Clayton, Mike, 74, 112, 186, 187
Clayton, Steve, 10, 13, 101, 109, 110, 140, 148, 164, 188, 189, 202, 203, 211, 212, 213, 237
Cohen, Norman, 8, 10, 17, 35, 42, 43, 74, 96, 97, 98, 99, 104, 110, 114, 116, 165, 168, 178, 186, 202, 235, 237, 241, 244
Colin Clubb, 101, 110, 111, 153, 154
Constable, Bryan, 14, 16, 22, 23, 42, 61, 62, 74, 76, 98, 100, 101, 112, 116, 160, 167, 186, 187, 214, 224, 242,
Cowie, Andrew, 86
Cox, Brian, 188,
Cutler, Horace, 7, 17, 18, 24
Daniels, Leon, 21, 36, 66, 67, 84, 94, 136, 138, 140, 141, 170, 222, 224, 239, 240, 242
Duff, Peter, 132, 138
Elliott, Graham, 90, 119, 132, 138, 140
Elms, Martin, 104, 199
Everett, Brian, 178, 227
Fennell, Steve, 39, 69, 91, 201
Filbey, Gary, 43, 179
Ford, Peter, 183, 204, 224, 235
Fowler, Norman, 24, 26, 173
Freeman, Roger, 146, 161, 163
Fuller, Ken, 133, 138, 142
Gilbert, Bryan, 43, 47, 100
Glazier, Ken, 8, 226
Golledge, John, 190, 192, 193, 194
Greystock, Charles, 9

Griffiths, Andy, 110, 111, 198, 215
Gunning, Bill, 110
Hanley, Jeremy, 105, 106
Harkness, Ian, 36
Harris, Jean, 59, 97, 187
Heath, Mike, 169, 171, 174, 176, 178, 179, 181, 184, 186, 187, 190, 198, 202, 203, 206, 207
Hendy, Sir Peter, 7, 42, 43, 69, 76, 89, 101, 103, 104, 151, 152, 164, 167, 168, 171, 172, 184, 185, 186, 187, 190, 198, 213, 214, 215, 219, 224, 232, 234, 235, 240, 241, 242, 243, 244
Higginson, Martin, 33, 94
Hodgson, Gordon, 189, 202, 210, 211
Hodson, Clive, 35, 95, 99, 110, 111, 125, 126, 133, 140, 164, 169, 171, 178, 181, 184, 187, 189, 192, 198, 199, 202, 203, 204, 211, 220, 234, 235
Humphrey, David, 100, 101, 105, 106, 145, 166, 171, 172, 200, 201, 206, 208, 209
Hurst, Brian, 62, 83, 84
Jenner, Peter, 84, 85
JTB, see John Telford Beasley
Keeler, Derek, 35, 97, 99, 100, 101
Kemp, Norman, 62, 77, 83, 92, 120, 136, 149, 153, 198, 222
Kennan, Tony, 83, 91, 149, 150, 151, 237
Lambe, Roy, 216, 217, 241
Larking, Peter, 37, 61, 62, 92, 95, 156, 224, 225, 240
Le Jeune, Barry, 10, 56, 162, 163, 241
Lewis, Martin, 206
Livingstone, Ken, 8, 21, 26, 31, 44, 90, 112, 234, 235, 240, 243
Lockhead, Moir, 178, 187, 199, 204
London, Paul, 64
Ludeman, Keith, 99, 100, 101, 104, 105, 129, 131, 154, 166, 167, 198, 199, 200, 216, 217, 218, 219, 245
Lynch, Paul, 116, 132, 133, 136, 137, 138, 140, 186, 187, 188
MacGregor, John, 164, 177, 183
Mahon, Pat, 10, 105, 129, 166, 177, 178, 192, 193, 194, 195, 197, 200, 206, 217, 240, 243
Major, John, 164, 165, 199
Margrave, Phil, 9, 13, 22, 90, 104, 105
Masefield, Sir Peter, 18, 22
McLachlan, Tom, 91
McMahon, Peter, 12, 114, 132
Mecham, Alan, 76
Milburn, Ted, 110, 147, 188, 203
Muir, Bob, 42, 76, 213
Newman, Peter, 13, 14, 38, 42, 47, 66, 67, 75, 94, 121, 141, 242, 245
Newson, Robert, 22, 110, 148, 188, 189, 232, 237, 238
Newton, Nick, 32, 34, 36, 37, 38, 48, 50, 51, 52, 53, 56, 63, 67, 76, 81, 84, 90, 91, 92, 94, 104, 123, 127, 128, 129, 131, 133, 136, 138, 141, 142, 144, 145, 151, 156, 168, 182, 239, 240
Newton, Wilfrid, 123, 125, 163, 165, 171, 173, 174, 173, 183, 203

Norris, Steven, 27, 28, 125, 164, 165, 169, 171, 172, 174, 176, 177, 178, 180, 181, 189, 192, 202, 203, 222, 231, 235, 237, 242, 245
O'Farrell, Declan, 101, 109, 126, 131, 164, 190-197, 205, 206
Orbell, Robin, 37, 39, 52, 65, 122, 232
Parkinson, Cecil, 26, 125
Parsons, Tony, 16, 43, 89
Peddle, Julian, 180, 227, 240
Phillips, Ian, 24, 30
Portillo, Michael, 158
Powell, Dai, 240, 242, 244
Prescott, John, 162, 235
Price, Alan, 62, 77, 120
Pycroft, John, 161, 189
Quarmby, David, 7, 8, 13, 15, 18, 22, 23, 24, 30, 35, 39, 243
Reynolds, Robin, 112, 197
Ridley, Nicholas, 26, 27, 28, 31, 33, 35, 37, 44, 47, 100, 158, 164, 244
Ridley, Tony, 15, 30, 99
Rifkind, Malcolm, 163
Rigby, John, 31-35, 169, 239
Roberts, George, 11, 12, 114, 132, 136, 140
Rymer, John, 63
Sayburn, David, 42, 79, 114, 168
Segretain, Phillippe, 208, 209
Self, Linda, 100
Sephton, Peter, 159
Smith, Marcus, 22, 35, 41-43, 58, 74, 80,112
Smith, Mike, 199
Smith, Richard, 32, 34
Souter, Brian 28, 83, 186, 187, 188, 200, 206, 219, 220, 221
Stenning, Ray, 77, 150, 207, 216
Steward, Michael, 151, 152
Tennant, Gordon, 70, 109, 110, 190, 195, 205, 206, 235, 242
Thatcher, Margaret, 17, 26, 27, 28, 31, 37, 44, 164, 241, 244
Thomas, Simon, 122, 221, 230
Torode, Roger, 87, 114, 131, 133, 138
Trayner, John, 22, 23, 98, 168, 188
Waterman, Pat, 101, 165
Watkins, Dr Alan, 170
Weller, Dave, 87, 216, 218
Weston, Mike, 91, 120, 139, 141, 230, 245
Wetzel, Dave, 18, 19, 21, 43, 108, 239, 242
Whitley, Martin, 10, 17, 43, 59, 98, 108, 168, 201, 207, 209, 241
Wilson, John, 38, 127, 230
Withey, John, 101, 104, 113, 202
Wood, Gary, 62, 225
Wood, John, 34, 39, 48, 57, 89, 95
Wren, Malcolm, 10, 39, 80, 85, 89, 91, 92, 94, 95, 121, 133, 141
Wright, Len, 36, 37, 38, 39, 43, 44, 48, 91, 93, 94, 95, 162, 216, 232
Yexley, Mark, 11, 13, 110, 147, 188, 189, 203, 210, 213, 232, 234
Young, Robin, 112, 113
Young, Tom, 101, 114, 116, 131, 133, 136, 138, 140

General Index

Aldenham Works, 6, 13, 22, 23, 42, 44, 45, 59, 66, 112, 166
AMOS, 24, 25, 27, 31-33, 35, 118
Armchair, 121, 122, 157, 215, 225
Arriva, 96, 212, 213, 219, 224, 225-227, 230, 232
Atlas, 84, 109, 124, 157, 165, 205
Autocheck scheme, 74, 80
Best Impressions, 77, 131, 150, 205, 207, 216, 218, 230
Bexleybus, 14, 74-77, 101, 112, 113, 119, 123, 169, 186, 208, 218
Blazefield, 127, 154, 203
Block grant: *definition* p41, *further references* 66, 71, 79, 112-114, 129, 131, 139, 154, 156, 158, 166-169, 177, 199, 207, 231, 239
Blue Triangle, 213, 222, 227, 233
British Bus, 190, 192, 203, 211, 213
BTS, 80, 81, 82, 92, 109, 124, 127, 145, 154, 155, 157, 176
Bus Engineering Ltd (BEL), 44, 45, 66, 67, 80, 117, 166
Bus Strategy for London, 160, 163, 164
Capital Citybus, 84, 131, 139, 141-144, 157, 170, 203, 222-224, 226
Capital Logistics, 227-229
Capital Transport Campaign, 103
Central London Minibuses (CLM), 63, 64
CentreWest, 96, 101, 103, 129, 151, 152, 167, 168, 184-186, 190, 198, 204, 212-215, 219, 224, 225, 232
Chiswick Works, 6, 13, 18, 22, 23, 34, 44, 45, 47, 66, 106, 112, 166
Cityrama, 44, 47-50, 89, 93, 94, 104, 121, 146
Classic Coaches, 229
County Bus, 86, 131, 136, 138, 157, 208, 211, 213, 226
Cowie Group, 86, 94, 188, 189, 202, 210-213, 226
Crystals, 50, 145, 157, 213, 214
Docklands Minibus, 119, 157
Docklands Transit, 117-119, 147, 221, 222
Driver Express, 227
East London, 84, 100, 101, 114-119, 131, 138, 140, 141, 144, 147, 168, 184, 186-188, 201, 204, 213, 219-222, 230
East Thames, 221, 231
Eastenderbus, 68, 82, 86
Eastern National (ENOC), 10, 37, 38-40, 44, 50-57, 65, 87, 93, 94, 96, 122, 124, 128, 131, 215
Ensignbus, Ensign Citybus, 13, 14, 37, 38, 42, 44, 47, 48, 50, 61, 66, 67, 72, 74-76, 84-86, 92, 93, 97, 117, 124, 136, 138, 141, 150
Epsom Coaches, 216
Fares Fair, 18-23, 27, 31
First Capital, FurstBus, FirstGroup, 28, 122, 187, 199, 200, 202-204, 214, 215, 219, 222, 224, 228, 245
Frontrunner, 67, 84, 85, 117
Frontsource, 67
Greater London Council (GLC), 7-9, 17-19, 22, 24, 26, 27, 30-34, 43-45, 112, 164, 226

Go-Ahead, 144, 178, 179, 197, 217, 218, 222, 224, 225, 243,
Green Line, 9, 24, 128, 211, 227
Grey-Green, 37, 38, 68, 81, 82, 85, 86, 91, 93, 94, 97, 110, 125, 131, 136, 137, 149, 157, 161, 177, 188, 189, 211-213, 242
Gross Cost Contracts, *defined* p37, *further references* 94, 168, 169, 199, 231, 232, 235, 239
Hackney Community Transport (HCT), 227, 240, 242
Harris Bus, 230, 231
Harrow Buses, 71, 73, 91, 101, 109, 123, 208
House of Commons Transport Committee, 170, 227
Javelin Coaches, 149, 157
Kentish Bus, 37, 62, 76, 77, 83, 84, 93, 96, 110, 113-115, 120, 121, 124, 128, 136, 137, 146, 149-151, 153, 157, 177, 203, 211, 213, 224
Kingston Bus, 67, 69, 89, 101, 123
Lambeth Transport Campaign, 92, 145
Leaside, 15, 16, 41, 42, 65, 70, 71, 72, 87, 96, 101, 109, 110, 111, 113, 114, 138, 140, 141, 147, 148, 164, 181, 188, 189, 202-204, 210, 211, 213, 232, 237
Limebourne, 47, 94
Liverbus, 206
London & Country, 89, 113, 124, 125, 146, 153, 157, 211, 226
London Buslines, 36, 38, 39, 67, 94, 121, 124, 136, 137, 152, 157, 162, 215
London Central, 98, 101, 105, 112, 113, 141, 153, 186, 197, 216-219, 225, 244
London Coaches, 45, 46, 101, 128, 155, 157, 163, 165, 205, 213, 227
London Country Bus Services (LCBS), 24, 32, 38, 83, 129, 211
London Country North East (LCNE), 65, 80, 81, 176, 211
London Country North West (LCNW), 63, 64, 124, 127
London Country South East (LCSE), 48, 83
London Country South West (LCSW), 67, 69, 110, 179
London Forest, 101, 114-116, 131-142, 148, 188
London General, 88, 101, 104, 105, 113, 129, 131, 150, 165-167, 197, 198, 200, 216-218, 223, 225, 240, 244
London Independent Bus Operators, 91
London Northern, 72, 101, 110, 111, 147, 149, 153, 154, 168, 186, 190, 197, 198, 204, 205, 215, 244
London Omnibus Traction Society, 144, 227
London Sovereign, *see Sovereign*
London Suburban Bus, 149, 157, 205, 206, 215
London Traveller, 227
London United, 59, 70, 89, 98, 101, 105-108, 123, 135, 145, 146, 166-168, 171, 172, 176, 200, 201, 204, 206-211, 225, 236
London*links*, 211, 213
LRT Act 1984, 26, 31, 159, 235, 239

Luton and District, 127, 128, 157, 176, 203, 211
Metrobus, 33, 37, 50, 51, 56, 61, 62, 66, 75, 93, 124, 145, 156, 157, 214, 217, 224-226
Metroline, 101, 105, 109, 111, 123, 126, 127, 131, 132, 140, 141, 149, 152, 154, 164, 165, 176, 190-197, 204-206, 215, 224, 235, 244
Mitcham Belle, 227
MTL, 149, 154, 190, 192, 195, 197, 198, 204, 205, 215
National Audit Office, 174, 203
National Bus Company (NBC), 6, 7, 27, 32-34, 38, 39, 44, 46, 65, 67, 77, 83, 95-97, 106, 110, 112, 114, 174, 175, 180, 181, 186, 243
Net cost contracts, *defined* p37: *further references* 119, 168-170, 175, 176, 178, 181, 225, 231, 232, 234, 239
New Operating Agreement (NOA), 45, 166, 167, 199
North Mymms Coaches, 50
Nostalgiabus, 228, 229
Off-Bus Revenue Agreement, 169, 175, 231, 234
Office of Fair Trading, 119, 176, 245
Proudmutual, 83, 120, 121, 150
Pullman Group, 165, 205
R&I, 109, 124, 157, 215
Roundabout, 42, 43, 50, 58-60, 76, 91, 97, 101, 112, 123, 124, 159, 160, 213, 214, 224
Sampson's Coaches, 50, 51, 89, 93, 94, 211
Scancoaches, 44
Selkent, 14-16, 22, 42, 43, 61, 74, 98, 101, 112, 113, 123, 124, 126, 146, 160, 167, 184, 186, 187, 198, 214, 215, 219, 220, 224, 227
Smartcard, 139, 166, 176
South London, 96, 101, 104, 105, 113, 114, 146, 189, 190, 193, 201-204, 210-213
Sovereign, 127, 128, 154, 157, 176, 247
Stagecoach, 28, 67, 86, 184, 186-188, 199, 201, 204, 206, 214, 215, 219-222, 224, 227, 245
SuttonBus, 87, 88, 95, 208, 218
T&GWU (Transport & General Workers' Union), 24, 45, 67, 69, 87, 135, 138, 142, 154, 171, 199
Tellings Golden Miller, 227
Thames Transit, 119, 164, 221
Thamesway, 122, 131, 136, 138, 139, 157, 215, 224, 232
Thorpe, 149, 157
Transcity, 113, 151
Transdev, 127, 208, 209
Transport Acts 1980 and 1985, 31-33, 44, 120, 161
West Midlands Travel (WMT), 45, 46, 70, 71, 73, 180, 208, 211
West's Coaches, 50, 51, 213
Westlink, 43, 50, 58, 59, 70, 91, 97, 101, 108, 123, 131, 149, 155, 168, 178, 179, 180, 181, 208, 211
Wings, 227

Biographies of people mentioned in the text

Douglas Adie was appointed Managing Director of London Central on formation of the LBL Units. He had been a Divisional Director with the National Bus Company, and ran the United Transport minibuses in Manchester following deregulation. He continued as MD when the company was bought by the Go-Ahead Group, and subsequently moved to join the Go-Ahead Board.

Dave Alexander joined Borehamwood Travel Services (BTS) in the early 1980s as Operations Manager, subsequently becoming Operations Director and Managing Director. He joined the Blazefield Group when it bought BTS, and is now Regional Managing Director (North) for the UK Bus Division of First.

Barry Arnold OBE was a senior member of the bus planning and service development team of London Buses. He became District Operations Manager of Forest District and Commercial Director of East London Bus and Coach. He remained with East London when it was bought by Stagecoach, becoming MD of Stagecoach London in 1997. He retired in 2006 on the sale of the company to Macquarie Bank and was awarded the OBE for services to the London bus industry.

Willie Arrol was a London Buses engineer. He became Engineering Manager of Leaside District in 1985 and was Engineering Director of London Northern from 1988 to 1993.

Ian Barlex has worked in the bus industry for over 40 years, initially at London Transport and, at the time of bus privatisation in London, as a consultant. He has been a Director of the Omnibus Society since 1995.

Nigel Barrett joined LT as a bus conductor in 1970 and rose to become an operating manager and Garage General Manager in East London. Following privatisation he moved within the Stagecoach Group before returning to London as MD for Stagecoach London at the time of its sale to Macquarie. He subsequently joined First as a Regional Director and has now retired.

Huw Barrington joined Cityrama in 1985 to develop their tendered bus operations. He moved to Armchair in 1990 as Assistant General Manager until 2002 when he joined BTS. He continued in the bus industry and is now Commercial Director of Epsom Coaches.

Jon Batchelor joined LT in 1974 and progressed to become a bus operations supervisor and manager in East London and Selkent. He moved within the Stagecoach Group but left London following the sale to Macquarie. He is now Operations Manager with Abellio London.

Peter Batty was Traffic Manager of South London Transport and was appointed Commercial Development Manager in preparation for deregulation and privatisation. He remained with the company when it was bought by the Cowie Group and is now Commercial Director of Arriva London.

David Bayliss OBE was Chief Transport Planner of the Greater London Council from 1968 to 1984, Director of Planning for LT from 1984 to 1999 and a Director of Halcrow Consulting from 1999 to 2000.

John Telford Beasley CBE joined LT in 1984 as Managing Director of London Buses Ltd. He had previously been with Cadburys and the pharmaceutical industry. He became Chief Executive of LRT in 1988 and retired in March 1992.

Ralph Bennett was a municipal busman who became General Manager at Bolton in 1960 and then of Manchester City Transport in 1965. He joined LT in 1968 as Board Member for Planning and became Deputy Chairman and MD Buses in 1971. He was LT Chairman from 1978 to 1980.

Ken Blacker joined LT in 1951 as a junior clerk in the Traffic Development Office, and progressed mainly in bus operations management but including a spell in charge of the Training School at Chiswick. In 1985 he was appointed District General Manager of Leaside. He retired on the formation of the Units in 1988. He is author of a number of books on London's buses.

Roger Bowker was General Manager of Eastbourne Buses and was recruited in 1988 to be Managing Director of East London. Under Stagecoach ownership he became MD of Stagecoach London and then developed his career further within the Stagecoach Group. in Sweden and the USA before retiring in 2005.

Andrew Braddock has had an extensive career in the UK bus industry including NBC companies and London Transport. From 1991 to 2002 he was responsible for London Transport's Unit for Disabled Passengers. He is now an independent consultant specialising in urban public transport and accessibility issues.

Dominic Brady was MD of Merseyside Transport Ltd (MTL) who ran MTL London Northern from privatisation in 1994 until its sale to Metroline in 1998.

Ron Brewer had a long career in London Transport, initially in planning and then as District General Manager of Forest District from 1979. He retired from LT in 1988 and worked with the London Transport Passengers Committee for some years before retiring.

Sir Keith Bright was appointed LT Chairman for 5 years from September 1982, becoming Chairman of LRT in June 1984. He had previously managed the Huntley and Palmer food empire. He retired in 1988 following publication of the report into the Kings Cross fire.

David Brown joined LT in 1983 as a Graduate Trainee and moved into bus operations in Cardinal District. He became a Garage General Manager in CentreWest and, following privatisation, ran the Berks Bucks Bus Company. He became Operations Director for London General / London Central in 1998 and later Chief Executive of Go-Ahead's London Bus division. He was appointed MD Surface Transport of TfL in 2006, and became CEO of the Go-Ahead Group in 2011.

Jeff Chamberlain joined LT as a bus driver and was promoted to Inspector and Relief Garage Manager. In 1981 he was seconded to act as Adviser to the Transport Committee of the newly elected Labour GLC. On his return to LT he became an Area Traffic Manager in Cardinal District where he set up Westlink as one of the first LBL tendered units. He then bought the operation on privatisation in 1994, selling it on to West Midlands Travel shortly afterwards.

Frank Cheroomi joined Docklands Transit as a minibus driver in 1989 and became manager of the operation. He continued running the contract operations when the minibus operation ceased in 1991, and in the following years won a number of LT contracts. In 1997 the bus operations were sold to Stagecoach, while Frank continued the contract operations on his own account. He again won London bus contracts under TfL, and this operation was sold to the Go-Ahead Group in 2006.

Mike Clayton joined LT in 1977 as a Finance Trainee and moved to Bus Finance where, amongst other duties, he put together the financial aspects of the initial tender bids. He was appointed Finance Director of Selkent in 1988. When the company was sold on privatisation he moved within the Stagecoach Group but subsequently left the industry.

Steve Clayton joined London Transport in 1975 and rose through the bus operations department in a number of line management positions, including a secondment to Mexico City in 1985. In 1989 he was appointed Managing Director of

Leaside Buses which was acquired by the Cowie Group on privatisation. He continued with Cowie, which became Arriva, and was appointed to the Arriva Board in 1998 with responsibility for the group's UK bus operations.

Colin Clubb held a number of engineering positions within NBC including at North Western Road Car and United Counties. He was MD of London Country South West and was appointed to lead London Northern on formation of the LBL companies in 1988. He expected to take the company into privatisation but when this was delayed, he retired in 1993.

Norman Cohen joined LT's Operational Research Department in 1971 and then moved to bus operations to develop radio and computer systems. On formation of the Bus Districts in 1979 he was appointed District General Manager of Abbey. He subsequently became Operations Manager and then Operations Director of London Buses, before moving to LT as Marketing Director until his retirement in 1997.

Bryan Constable was a London Transport engineer and became Engineering Manager of the South Division of London Buses. He was appointed Engineering Manager of Selkent District and went to manage Aldenham works while its future was being reviewed. He then became General Manager of Selkent and set up the Roundabout and Bexleybus operations. He was appointed Managing Director of Selkent in 1989, and retired when the company was sold to Stagecoach. He subsequently assisted Metrobus in their engineering and tender bids.

Sir Horace Cutler was a local government politician, and was Conservative leader of the Greater London Council from 1977 to 1981.

Leon Daniels worked with Prince Marshall and ran the Obsolete Fleet bus operation in London in the early 1980s. He then worked with Peter Newman at Ensignbus developing London sightseeing tours and bidding for LRT tenders. He took the tendered bus operation over when it was separated from Ensign's bus dealership and other activities in 1990, and managed it as Capital Citybus on behalf of the Hong Kong owners during its major expansion with the takeover of services in Walthamstow. Leon then led the management buy-out of the company and its subsequent sale to FirstGroup plc. He became Divisional Director London for First in 2001 and Commercial Director UK in 2005. He was then appointed TfL's MD Surface Transport in 2011.

Peter Duff was an engineer with Busways in Newcastle and was appointed Engineering Director of London Forest Travel in 1990. On the closure of London Forest he became Engineering Director of East London and left in 2001.

Graham Elliott was Revenue Manager of London Buses. He stood in as MD of London Forest on the departure of Tom Young. Up until their privatisation he was a Non-Executive Director of London General and Selkent. He subsequently became Operations and Group Safety Services Director of London Buses until his retirement in 2003.

Martin Elms was a senior member of the bus planning and service development team of London Buses. He became Commercial Director of London General in 1988 and was one of the team who took the company into privatisation, leaving when the company was sold to the Go-Ahead Group.

Brian Everett was Deputy Head of Procurement Director at LBL and as a member of the privatisation team managed sales of specific companies. He went on to become Procurement Director of London Buses

Steve Fennell worked with London Country Bus Services at Reigate from 1974, in Traffic Planning and Public Relations. He joined LT as a bus driver at Norbiton in 1978 and was promoted to Inspector in 1986, working at garages throughout south west London before promotion to a management position at Shepherd's Bush in 1995. He left the bus industry in 2000 and is now a Train Manager with First Great Western. He is author of a number of books on London's buses.

Gary Filbey joined London Transport as an apprentice at Chiswick works. He became District Engineering Assistant at Cardinal District and Chief Engineer of Westlink, joining Jeff Chamberlain to set up the company and take it into privatisation. Following the sale to London United, he moved to Metroline and then re-joined Transport for London in 2000 as Engineering Director of LBL (East Thames Buses and London Dial a Ride) and is now TfL Head of Bus Engineering.

Peter Ford was appointed Chairman of TfL in 1994. He had previously been Chairman of P&O Ferries. However, he was removed by John Prescott in 1998 after the election of the Labour government.

Sir Norman Fowler was a Conservative MP from 1970 to 2001. He was Minister, and then Secretary of State, for Transport from 1979 to 1981. He held a number of other Ministerial posts and was Chairman of the Conservative Party from 1992 to 1994.

Roger Freeman was a Conservative MP and was Minister of State for Public Transport from 1990 to 1995.

Ken Fuller was a bus driver for eleven years and became a full-time officer in the London Bus section of the Transport and General Workers Union.

Bryan Gilbert was LT's Personnel Officer Bus Operations. He then worked with Derek Keeler in 1988 on recruitment of the management teams for the new Units before retiring in 1989.

Ken Glazier was a senior member of the bus planning and service development team of London Buses. He became Operations Manager of Selkent District in 1984 and Commercial Director of the Selkent company in 1988, retiring in 1990. He was author of a number of books on London's bus history.

John Golledge was Finance Director of Metroline and worked with Declan O'Farrell on the management buy-out and subsequent running and onward sale of the company.

Andy Griffiths joined LT as a Bus Operations management trainee in 1978 and worked in a number of bus operating positions, specialising in revenue and ticketing. He was a Garage General Manager in London Northern and, following the sale to MTL, returned to LT and was subsequently asked to set up and run the London River Services operation.

Bill Gunning started his career in schedules at Bristol Omnibus and later worked for United Transport in Africa. He was Traffic Manager of London Country Bus Services, and became MD of London Country South East when LCBS was split into four. The company was renamed Kentish Bus and sold to Proudmutual on privatisation. He then left joined his former LCBS colleague Colin Clubb as Commercial Director of London Northern, a position he held until 1993.

Jean Harris was the first female on the LBL Graduate Operations Management Training Scheme, which she joined in 1984. After working in Cardinal District and at Westlink, she moved to LBL as Operations Planning Manager. She then joined East London as Marketing Manager, becoming Garage General Manager of Bow and Stratford. When Stagecoach bought East London she returned to London Buses headquarters as Communications Manager and then became Head of Advertising & Publicity for London Transport. She left LT in 1986 to start a family.

Mike Heath MBE was LBL's Project Manager for the privatisation of the subsidiary companies. He was previously Operations Systems Manager and Rolling Stock Stores

Manager. He went on to become Tramlink Project Manager and Operations and Services Director of London Buses. He was awarded an MBE in 1996 for services to Public Transport.

Sir Peter Hendy CBE joined LT as a Graduate Trainee in 1975 and rose through the Bus Operations Department, becoming District Operations Manager of Abbey District and then Managing Director of CentreWest in 1989. He led the management buyout of his company and its subsequent sale to FirstGroup, becoming Deputy Director UK Bus of First. In 2001 he was appointed MD Surface Transport of TfL, and became Transport Commissioner in 2006.

Gordon Hodgson was Chief Executive of the Cowie Group which bought Leaside Buses and South London Transport on privatisation.

Clive Hodson CBE joined LT in 1960 and was Assistant Company Secretary of LCBS from 1969 to 1974 when he returned to LT becoming Finance Director of London Buses and Managing Director in 1989. In 1994 he became MD of LT Buses on privatisation of the subsidiaries. He retired in 2001 after the formation of Transport for London.

David Humphrey joined the bus industry in 1968 in Oxford. He joined the National Bus Company Senior management training programme, then progressed through management positions with West Yorkshire Road Car, Ribble, Bristol Omnibus, and Hampshire Bus. He was appointed Managing Director of London United in 1988 and led the company through privatisation and subsequent sale to Transdev, when he joined the International Committee of Transdev. He is now a member of the Quality Contract Board and one of the judges of the UK Bus Awards.

Peter Jenner was Commercial Manager of East Midland Motor Services who ran Frontrunner South East, operating LRT contracts from 1988, until the sale of the company to Stagecoach in 1989.

Derek Keeler was Development Director of London Buses. In 1986 he became Director of Business Restructuring, planning and implementing the new organisation. He retired in 1988.

Norman Kemp, after an early career in local authority transport, moved from Boro'line Maidstone to newly privatised Kentish Bus in 1988 as Commercial Manager. Briefly MD of London Northern from 1993 until privatisation, he was MD of Capital Citybus in 1995 ahead of its sale by its Chinese owners. He remains active in the bus industry in Kent.

Tony Kennan CBE was Commercial Director of Northumberland Motor Services, the NBC company formed in 1986 from the northern part of United Automobile services. On privatisation in 1987, the management team formed the holding company Proudmutual and bought both their own company and Kentish Bus. Proudmutual grew through expansion and acquisitions and was sold to British Bus in 1994.

Roy Lambe joined LT in 1981 as a driver on the 11s at Riverside garage. He subsequently moved to Victoria and then to Stockwell when Victoria closed. He spent many years working on Night buses and now drives New Routemasters on route 11.

Peter Larking and Gary Wood were the Directors of Metrobus of Orpington which they established in 1983. They sold the company to the Go-Ahead group in 1999.

Barry Le Jeune was LT's Public Relations Officer (Corporate) during the first years of bus service tendering, as part of a 37 year career with LT, primarily in Public Relations and Customer Services. He took early retirement in 2000, becoming a Vice President of the Omnibus Society and Chairman of the London Transport Museum Friends.

Martin Lewis was Engineering Director of London United.

Ken Livingstone is a Labour politician who was leader of the GLC from May 1981 and led the battle to implement Fares Fair. The GLC was closed down in 1986. He was later elected Mayor of London from May 2000 to 2008.

Paul London joined LT in 1969 as a Traffic Administration Trainee and rose to become Capital Accountant Buses. In the period leading to privatisation he trained in bus driving and garage operations and then moved into revenue control and management of the bus ticketing system, including development of the conductor's electronic ticket machine and implementation of smartcard-based fare collection. He retired in 2014.

Keith Ludeman had a background in the bus industry in Greater Manchester and Hong Kong. He led the Burnley and Pendle bus operation through deregulation and in 1988 he joined LT as it prepared for privatisation. He was appointed MD of London General and led the management buyout of the company in 1994, and its sale to the Go-Ahead Group in 1996. He became Chief Executive of Go-Ahead in 2006, assuming responsibility for all its bus, rail, aviation and parking businesses. He also established their yellow school bus operations in North America.

Paul Lynch was an Assistant Operating Manager at Ash Grove and became Garage General Manager at Leyton and Clapton in London Forest. On the closure of London Forest he joined East London and subsequently moved within the Stagecoach Group, where he is now MD of Stagecoach East Midlands.

John MacGregor was a Conservative MP and was Secretary of State for Transport from 1992 to 1994 in John Major's Government.

Pat Mahon joined LT as a conductor at Wood Green in 1968 and became a driver on the 19s. He was active in the T&GWU and joined the London Bus Committee, becoming a full-time officer in 1989. During the privatisation process he represented staff in London General, London Central and Metroline. Following privatisation he joined the management team of London General and is now General Manager Operations.

Phil Margrave was a London Buses engineer based originally at Chiswick Works. He was appointed District Engineering Manager at Wandle and Engineering Director at London General. He remained with Go-Ahead becoming Engineering Director for London Central and London General and in 2008 was appointed Group Engineering Director, until his retirement in 2014.

Sir Peter Masefield had a background in the aviation industry. He was a part-time Board Member of LT and became interim Chairman from July 1980 in place of Ralph Bennett. His initial appointment was for 12 months but he remained in post for more than two years until a replacement could be appointed.

Peter McMahon joined LT in 1975 as a graduate engineer and was appointed Engineering Director of London Forest Travel in 1988. In 1990 he moved to London Underground as Fleet Manager for the Piccadilly line and progressed to General Manager of the Bakerloo line. In 2003 he joined Metronet as Director of Planning before starting his own consultancy in 2006.

Ted Milburn was a London Buses engineer who was appointed Engineering Director of Leaside when the subsidiary companies were created. He additionally became Engineering Director of South London Transport when both companies were bought by the Cowie Group on privatisation.

Bob Muir was an LT planner who moved into the bus business before privatisation. He was one of the team who set up Roundabout and Bexleybus. On creation of the subsidiary companies he became Commercial Director of CentreWest. Following privatisation and the later sale of the company to FirstGroup, he became Managing Director in place of Peter Hendy.

Peter Newman formed Ensignbus in 1972 as a bus dealer and operator. He achieved fame when he won the contract to purchase all of LT's DMS double-deckers, starting in 1979. Ensignbus has operated commercial, contract and tendered bus services together with sight-seeing tours in and around London. It now runs commercial services in Essex and regularly provides rail replacement buses for London Underground and National Rail.

Robert Newson joined LT in 1981 as a Finance Graduate Trainee. After qualifying as a Chartered Management Accountant he became District Financial Adviser at Leaside in 1985, and Finance Director for Leaside Bus Company Ltd. on formation of the subsidiary companies. When Leaside and South London were bought by the Cowie Group he became Finance Director of both companies. He left in 1998 to become a self-employed accountant and also worked as a consultant, in particular advising London bus operators on revenue apportionment from their net cost LT contracts.

Nick Newton was an LT Purchasing Manager who transferred to the Planning Department to set up the Tendered Bus Unit in 1984 and managed it until bus privatisation and the creation of LT Buses in 1994. He was then seconded to the Office of Passenger Rail Franchising (OPRAF) to work on rail franchising eventually becoming Chief Executive of the Strategic Rail Authority.

Sir Wilfrid Newton CBE was Chairman of LRT from 1989 to 1994. He had been Chairman of the Hong Kong Mass Transit Railway Corporation since 1983. He was knighted in the 1993 New Years Honours.

Steven Norris was Conservative MP for Oxford East from 1983 to 1987, and for Epping Forest from 1988 to 1997. He held a number of Ministerial posts, notably as PPS to Nicholas Ridley at the Department of Trade and Industry. He was promoted to Parliamentary Under-Secretary of State for Transport and Minister for Transport in London by John Major in 1992. He became non-exec Chairman of Capital Citybus in 1997. He stood for election as Mayor of London in 2000 and 2004.

Declan O'Farrell CBE joined LT in 1986 to become Finance Manager for one of the new bus subsidiaries. He joined Leaside and was then appointed Managing Director of Metroline. He led Metroline through privatisation, as an independent company, and in its eventual sale to Delgro.

Robin Orbell was traffic manager of Eastern National who bid for and operated LRT tendered routes in north and east London. He was one of the four directors who bought the company in a management buy-out in 1986, and who then sold the company on to Badgerline in 1990. He left FirstGroup in 1997 and joined Mark Howarth in creating Western Greyhound, the Cornish bus operator.

Tony Parsons, following a series of engineering managerial posts at garage and divisional level, was District General Manager of the Cardinal District of London Buses from 1979 up to the creation of the operating subsidiaries in 1988. He was instrumental in setting up Westlink, and other tendered operations in south-west London.

Julian Peddle is an entrepreneur in the bus industry. He was co-owner of Stevensons of Uttoxeter between 1983 and 1994. During the late 1990s and early 2000s he ran Status Group, a group of small bus companies spread across England. He was a major shareholder in Tellings-Golden Miller, which operated LT contracted bus routes, and was later sold to Arriva.

Dai Powell OBE is Chief Executive of Hackney Community Transport (HCT) and is a member of the Disabled Persons Transport Advisory Committee (DPTAC).

Alan Price was MD of Maidstone Borough Council Transport in 1983, which in 1986 became Boro'line Maidstone, the 'arm's length' council-owned company and which was sold in 1992.

David Quarmby CBE joined LT in 1970 as Director of Operational Research and rose to become Chief Planning Office and then Board Member for Planning in 1975; he was appointed Managing Director Buses in 1978. He left LRT to join the Board of Sainsbury's in 1984 but retained his interest in public transport; he returned to join the Docklands Light Railway as Board Member and Chairman in 1998, and to join the Boards of Transport for London and of the Strategic Rail Authority in 2000.

Robin Reynolds joined LT at Chiswick Works as an apprentice in 1959 and progressed in the bus engineering department. He worked closely with Marcus Smith on improving engineering standards in bus garages and became Engineering Director of London Central in 1988. After privatisation he initially remained with the company and left two years after the sale to Go-Ahead.

Nicholas Ridley was Conservative MP for Cirencester and Tewkesbury from 1959 to 1992. Among his Ministerial posts he was Secretary of State for Transport from 1983 to 1986 and Secretary of State for the Environment from 1986 to 1989.

Tony Ridley CBE was Chairman and Chief Executive of London Underground Ltd. and a member of the Board of LT from 1980 to 1988.

John Rigby provided a substantial part of Chapter 2 of this book. He joined LT in 1981 and was a member of the Group Planning team who devised the London bus tendering arrangements in 1984/5. In 1987 he became Head of City Development for York City Council, and in 1995 moved to Exeter City Council as Director of Development.

George Roberts joined LT as a bus driver in 1975 and subsequently moved to bus engineering. He was appointed GGM Walthamstow in London Forest. On the closure of London Forest he moved to London Underground where he became Engineering Manager of the Victoria Line.

John Rymer was a London bus driver at Battersea garage who transferred to Central London Minibuses where he became a Controller. He is now MD of First Tram Operations, the contracted operator of Croydon Tramlink.

David Sayburn worked in LT's Country Bus and Coach Department from 1961 to 1970 when he became a local government transport coordinating officer. He returned to LT in 1977 and became Operating Manager of Tower District followed by Leaside and Selkent Districts as a result of reorganisations. In 1987 he was appointed General Manager of the Central Traffic Division and then Group Traffic Manager, where his responsibilities included management of the negotiated block grant routes. He left LT in 1995 following privatisation of the bus companies.

Marcus Smith joined LT as Engineering Director (Buses) in 1979, having been GM of the Passenger Division of Leyland Vehicles. He was General Manager Buses from 1981 and retired in 1987.

Mike Smith had a long career at all levels in the Engineering side of London Transport and London Buses. He was Assistant District Engineering Manager in Leaside District before being appointed Engineering Director of Metroline in 1988 and was one of the team who took the company into privatisation and its subsequent flotation. Mike retired from Metroline in 1999.

Ray Stenning is Design Director of the Best Impressions design studio and a transport publisher.

Michael Steward was Assistant Development Manager at London Buses and joined CentreWest as Service Planning Manager in 1989. He subsequently became Planning Director of Tram Operations, the operator of Croydon Tramlink.

Gordon Tennant joined LT in 1979 as a Graduate Management Trainee and became a bus operations manager in Abbey District. He was appointed Operations Planning Manager in 1984 and General Manager of the Harrow tendered operation in 1987. On formation of the subsidiary companies he was appointed Commercial Director of Metroline and was one of the team that took the company into management/employee ownership on privatisation. He left Metroline in 2001 after its sale to the DelGro Corporation in 2000 and became a transport consultant.

Simon Thomas joined London Transport in 1974, initially in Public Relations where he became Operations Manager of the Travel Information Service. He joined the London Buses tender evaluation team in 1995 and as Contracts Tendering Manager took the lead role in tendering, negotiating and awarding contracts for bus services. In 2015 he was presented with a Lifetime Contribution Award which recognised him as one of the driving forces behind better quality services and the many initiatives and successes seen on the London bus network over the last 20 years. He retired in May 2015.

Roger Torode is the author of this book and further details are given in the Introduction. During a 30-year career with LT and TfL he became Operations Manager and then Garage General Manager at Walthamstow, and on the creation of the subsidiary companies he was appointed Commercial Director of London Forest Travel. Following the closure of London Forest he evaluated the new contactless smartcard technology, which led to the Oyster card.

John Trayner joined LT as an engineering apprentice in 1975 and worked at Chiswick and Aldenham. He progressed into garage management and became Garage General Manager at Stamford Hill in Leaside in preparation for privatisation. He remained with Cowie/Arriva on privatisation. He moved to Go-Ahead in 2002 as Operations Director of London Central/General, becoming Managing Director in 2006.

Pat Waterman was Managing Director of London Coaches and led the management buy-out of the company, and the subsequent sale to Arriva. He left the company in 2000 to join the Big Bus Company where he is CEO.

Dave Weller joined LT as a conductor in 1976 and was a driver at Sutton in 1980. He is now a recruitment manager with London General.

Mike Weston is TfL Director of Buses. He joined LT in 1985, initially in bus network planning and then moved to management of bus contracts and bus infrastructure. He became Head of Bus Operations in 2003 and Operations Director for London Buses in August 2004. In October 2013 he was appointed Director of Buses with overall responsibility for procurement, performance and development of the London bus network. Mike is also Vice Chair of the UITP Bus Committee and Chair of the UK Low Carbon Vehicle Partnership, Bus & Coach Working Group.

Dave Wetzel was a bus conductor at Turnham Green from 1962 and became a driver and then a Garage Inspector at Hounslow in 1965. A Labour Party politician in London, he became Chair of the GLC Transport Committee in May 1981 and was Leader of Hounslow Council from 1987 to 1991. He returned to TfL as Vice chair of TfL from 7/2000 until 2008.

Martin Whitley joined LT in 1966 in Operational Research and became a business analyst. Following a spell heading the Bus Communications Centre, he moved to Cardinal District as District Operations Manager in 1983 and became Commercial Director of London United and one of the management team who led the buyout of the company. He left shortly after the sale of the company to Transdev.

John Wilson worked for London Transport, Eastern National, Grey-Green, Harris Coaches and Sovereign Buses during his career. He was General Manager of Harris Coaches where he set up a bus operation on deregulation in 1986. He then joined Sovereign and set up and ran the minibus operation in Harrow in 1992. He retired in 1994.

John Withey had a background in LT management training and became General Manager of Wandle District of London Buses. In 1988 he was appointed Managing Director of South London Transport but left in 1994 when the company's Operator's licence was curtailed by the Traffic Commissioners.

Gary Wood and Peter Larking were the Directors of Metrobus of Orpington which they established in 1983. They sold the company to the Go-Ahead group in 1999.

John Wood joined LT in 1966 in the bus operations department and then moved to the Commercial Office where he dealt with fares and licensing of bus services. He was seconded to the Tendered Bus Unit when it was first started in 1983 and remained until 1997, responsible for setting up services, liaison with bus operators and monitoring their performance. He retired from London Buses in 1997.

Malcolm Wren joined London Transport's Operational Research Department in 1971 working on bus service reliability, fare collection and related matters. He joined the Tendered Bus Unit when it was formed in 1985 and became Development Manager with responsibilities in planning, operations, marketing, performance monitoring and management of the tendering programme. He left London Transport in 1995 to become a freelance analyst, and was retained consultant to Metrobus from 1996 to 2012 to assist in the preparation of London tenders.

Len Wright worked for East Kent Road Car, Grey-Green and National Travel before starting his own company, Len Wright Travel, specialising in transporting rock bands on tours. In 1985 he was the first private operator to commence an LRT contract with route 81. He won further routes in later tendering rounds, and was the first Chairman of the London Independent Bus Operators section of the Bus & Coach Council. After a number of takeovers and mergers the company was sold to CentreWest in 1996.

Mark Yexley joined LT in 1979 and trained in bus operations management. He became Operating Manager at Tottenham and was appointed Commercial Director of Leaside. He stayed with the company when it was sold to the Cowie Group, becoming MD of the London businesses in 1998 until moving on in 2009 to become Arriva's Operations and Commercial Director, UK Bus.

Robin Young was Commercial Director of London Central. He had been Operating Manager at Victoria and Planning Manager of the Central Traffic Division, where he had organised the Busplan 88 Central-London reshaping plan. He was also a GLC Councillor and a member of Ken Livingstone's administration

Tom Young had a background in the National Bus Company and PTEs. In 1988 he joined LT as it prepared for privatisation and was appointed Managing Director of London Forest Travel. Following the London Forest strike, he returned to bus operation in the West Midlands where he started Midland Choice Travel.